INCREDIBLE
NEW YORK

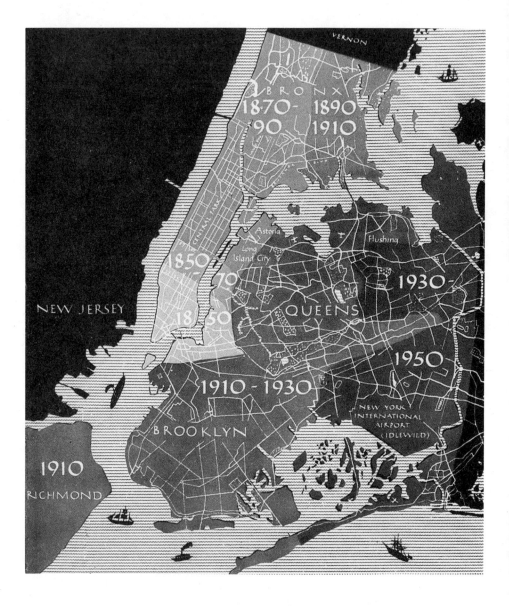

INCREDIBLE NEW YORK

*High Life
and Low Life
from 1850 to 1950*

Lloyd Morris

Syracuse University Press

First Syracuse University Press Edition 1996

96 97 98 99 00 01   6 5 4 3 2 1

Originally published in 1951. Reprinted by arrangement with Random House, Inc.

This edition is published with the assistance of a grant from the John Ben Snow Foundation.

The paper used in this publication meets with the minimum requirements of American National Standard for Information Sciences—Permanence of Paper for Printed Library Materials, ANSI Z39.48-1984. ∞™

Design: Peter Oldenburg

Library of Congress Cataloging-in-Publication Data
Morris, Lloyd R., 1893-1954.
     Incredible New York : high life and low life from 1850 to 1950 /
Lloyd Morris. — 1st Syracuse University Press ed.
       p. cm.
     Originally published: New York : Random House, 1951.
     Includes index.
     ISBN 0-8156-0334-7 (paper : alk. paper)
     1. New York (N.Y.)—History—1865-1898. 2. New York (N.Y.)—
History—1898–1951. 3. New York (N.Y.)—Social life and customs.
I. Title.
F128.47.m865 1996
974.7'104—dc20   95-46297

Acknowledgment

For their courteous and helpful cooperation, I wish to thank the New-York Historical Society; the Museum of the City of New York; the New York Genealogical and Biographical Society; the New York Society Library; the New York Public Library, especially for valued assistance from the Manuscript Division and Theater Collection. I am deeply grateful, for information and suggestions, to Mrs. Frederick G. King, Miss Rita Romilly, Miss Nannine Joseph, Mr. Arthur Todd and Mr. Richard Hubbell.

Some material from this book has appeared in *Park East* and is reprinted by permission of the editors.

L. M.

Contents

List of Illustrations

PART ONE

1850–1870

THE EMPIRE CITY

1

Manhattan Builds Its Legend

As the second half of the nine-
teenth century began, New York became a metropolis. The "Empire City,"
strangers called it. They were awed by the splendor of its hotels and theaters,
its costly, magnificent stores. They were astonished by the incessant torrent of
traffic, the day-long, night-long surge and roar of more than five hundred
thousand people. To many of them, New York seemed a city of crowds and
carnival—breezy, recklessly extravagant, perpetually bent on pleasure. The
bright gaslights of bars and restaurants and hotels threw a glare over Broadway until well toward dawn. The rumble of omnibuses and the clatter of
hackney-coaches was never stilled. New York was a city where men made
such incredible fortunes that a new word, "millionaire," was on everybody's
lips. Two things gave it a quality, a flavor that was unique, and New Yorkers
were proud of both. Nowhere else was the tempo of life as fast. And the only
permanent characteristic of New York was continuous change. From week to
week, almost from day to day, the look of the city was constantly being
transformed.

To give you the feeling of the city, a New Yorker might take you to the
balcony of Barnum's Museum, a large flag-decked building on Broadway and
Ann Street, just south of the City Hall. From there, you could see Broadway
from its beginning at Bowling Green as far north as Astor Place. Along the
wide, straight avenue the white tops of omnibuses, moving swiftly yet densely
packed, looked like a millrace churning into foam. The sidewalks on both
sides of Broadway were thronged, and though it seemed as if these massive
rivers of people must sometime stop flowing, they did not; at certain hours

BROADWAY, 1855, from the New York Hospital to Leonard Street

they merely rose to flood tide. Traffic on the avenue never halted. To cross from the "shilling side" to the "dollar side"—from east to west—sometimes took half an hour, and you attempted it at the peril of your life or limbs. So hazardous was the crossing that John N. Genin, the fashionable hatter whose shop was at the corner of Fulton Street, petitioned the Common Council for permission to build an iron footbridge over Broadway to protect his customers from accident.

Only twenty years earlier Broadway, from City Hall Park northward, was a residential avenue. But now scarcely a private home remained below Bleecker Street. "The mania for converting Broadway into a street of shops is greater than ever," old Philip Hone noted in the spring of 1850. "There is scarcely a block in the whole extent of this fine street of which some part is not in a state of transmutation." Hone, one of New York's wealthiest citizens, was a former mayor, a man of fashion, a celebrated host and diner-out. He had resided on Broadway opposite City Hall Park, but business had driven him north a dozen years earlier. He bought land on the east side of Broadway and Great Jones Street—then near the upper limit of the city—and built himself a fine house. And already his new home was being surrounded by shops and hotels and theaters. "The improvements here are wonderful," James Fenimore Cooper, the novelist, told his wife. "They build chiefly brown free stone, and noble edifices of five and six stories, with a good deal of ornamental pretension." The brownstone era, which was to cover New York with a coating of cold chocolate sauce, had begun.

At midday, downtown restaurants and the dining rooms of the older hotels on lower Broadway were filled to capacity. Only the wealthy could afford Delmonico's, on South William Street, and only the socially elect were admitted by its fastidious proprietors. Gosling's, a popular-priced restaurant on Nassau Street, served one thousand patrons every day. Almost as many thronged the dining rooms of the Astor House, on Broadway at Barclay Street, and its bar, one of the largest in the city, was celebrated for a prodigal "free lunch." This vast hotel, built by John Jacob Astor in the eighteen-thirties, was the wonder of its day, and was still famous throughout the country. The proprietor, Colonel Charles A. Stetson, often told that when he opened it he was glad to accommodate guests with room and full board at three dollars a week. The prices were higher now—much higher—and the Astor House was favored by old-fashioned visitors to the city, and by journalists and politicians.

But its glories were being eclipsed by newer, more pretentious establishments further uptown. The huge white-marble St. Nicholas Hotel on Broadway and Broome Street was erected at a cost of more than one million dollars and could accommodate nearly eight hundred guests. It was elaborately furnished, and boasted the novelty of a central heating plant which piped hot air, through registers, into every room. Before dinner hour the lobby, parlors and reading room of the St. Nicholas resembled a human beehive, and the crowd of loungers often overflowed on Broadway. Just north of the St. Nicholas, at Prince Street, the Metropolitan Hotel was equally costly and luxurious. Occupying a whole block front on Broadway, it was a massive brownstone structure which contained one hundred suites of "family apartments" and could shelter six hundred guests. The Metropolitan was operated by the Leland brothers—the first men to set up a chain of hotels in the United States —and they had imported most of its furnishings and decorations from Europe. They, too, had installed central heating, and had added the further refinement of "sky parlors" high above Broadway where ladies could sit and look down on the fashionable promenade. Once or twice every week, throughout the winter, the St. Nicholas and Metropolitan held evening balls for the pleasure of their guests, at which "polkas of amazing activity and champagne

ST. NICHOLAS HOTEL, 1855, *by F. Heppenheimer*

RULES
OF THIS TAVERN

Four pence a night for Bed

Six pence with Supper

No more than five to sleep
in one bed

No Boots to be worn in bed

Organ Grinders to sleep in
the Wash house

No dogs allowed upstairs

No Beer allowed in the
Kitchen

No Razor Grinders or Tinkers
taken in

of irresistible strength drive dull care away." Both hotels were conducted on the so-called American plan. With care and economy, a family might reside in either at a cost of somewhat more than one hundred dollars a week. Bachelors, if content with the cheapest rooms, paid only fifteen dollars a week for lodging and board.

In 1859, seven years after they opened, these hotels were surpassed by the splendor of the great, gleaming white-marble Fifth Avenue Hotel, facing Madison Square. This was built by Amos R. Eno, a daring capitalist who had determined to give New York the most magnificent hotel in the world. But its location was so far uptown that people derided the project, calling it "Eno's Folly," and prophesying that it could only do business as a summer resort. There was a certain justice in this view. Only a few years earlier, the site had been occupied by Colonel Thompson's popular Madison Cottage, a roadhouse where gentlemen driving out from the city stopped to rest their horses and refresh themselves. But the new Fifth Avenue Hotel was a very different affair. It announced with pride that it offered "more than one hundred suites of apartments, each combining the convenience and luxury of parlor, chamber, dressing and bathing rooms." Private bathrooms were a startling innovation. The Fifth Avenue likewise introduced another widely discussed feature: a "perpendicular railway intersecting each story." Guests and visitors found the elevator a pleasant novelty, for the hotel was a six-story building. Notwithstanding pessimistic predictions, the Fifth Avenue Hotel was successful from the outset. The public rooms on the street floor became the late-afternoon gathering place of Wall Street brokers and gold speculators. And the huge, gilded, brilliantly illuminated parlors on the second floor were soon celebrated as "a field for fashionable flirtation after dinner." The preliminaries to flirtation were easily accomplished at dinner, for in the spacious, ornate second-floor dining room guests were seated at "family tables," each accommodating twenty or thirty people. You could scarcely avoid becoming acquainted quickly. After a pleasant social evening in the parlors, you returned to the dining room for an appetizing "late supper." This fourth meal was unique with the Fifth Avenue, and was included in the daily rate of two and one half dollars. It was one of the attractions devised by Paran Stevens, lessee of the hotel, to lure people away from more centrally located establishments.

Though the luxury of these great hotels gave New York a new cosmopolitan air, many old-fashioned folk deplored their expensive ostentation. Did they not "open an era of upholstery, with a tendency to live in herds, and the absence of a subdued and harmonious tone of life and manners"? After studying their social effect for more than a decade, a pessimistic chronicler felt it necessary to warn visitors to the city. "Hotel life is agreeable and desirable for masculine celibates; but he is unwise who takes his wife and family there for a permanent home. How many women can trace their first infidelity to the necessarily demoralizing influences of public houses—to loneliness, leisure, need of society, interesting companions, abundance of opportunity and potent temptations!" Yet, as New York restlessly pushed northward, the number of these architectural incentives to immorality constantly increased.

During the mid-afternoon Broadway became the fashionable promenade for ladies, for while society was perpetually moving uptown, it was nonetheless constantly and delightedly walking or driving downtown. The chief goal of feminine pilgrimage was the famous department store of A. T. Stewart, a six-story white-marble building which occupied a block on the east side of Broadway between Chambers and Reade Street, with fifteen immense plate-glass show windows on the avenue. Stewart's "marble palace," as New Yorkers called it, was so distinctive that the great merchant never put a sign on it. The store employed two hundred clerks, and its daily sales averaged more than ten thousand dollars. There was always a line of carriages in front of Stewart's. Inside, on display, were silks from Lyons, gloves and dresses from Paris, carpets made in Brussels, Irish linens, French laces, English woolens and cambrics, paisley and cashmere shawls, some of which cost as much as two thousand dollars. Alexander T. Stewart, who had come to New York from Ireland as a poor youth, was one of the city's foremost millionaires, a slight, thin-visaged, sharp-featured man with sandy grayish hair and whiskers, taciturn and disliking all social contacts, but noted for his philanthropies.

Ladies who shopped at Stewart's—the experience was "notoriously fatal to the female nerve" as well as the masculine pocketbook—were likely to refresh themselves afterward at the dazzling new ice-cream saloon of John Taylor on Broadway and Franklin Street. Taylor was the most fashionable caterer in town, and he was considered somewhat daring to open an establishment which served ladies unaccompanied by male escorts. But the light fare

BROADWAY IN WINTER, 1857, looking south from Spring Street, *by H. Sebron*

dispensed there—ices, pastries and dainty sandwiches—was not designed for masculine consumption. Gentlemen, if they felt the need of nourishment other than the copious food provided by the best bars, usually went to an oyster house. There were many of these, and most of them were in basements, but all alike displayed an identical sign: a globe about two feet in diameter, with twelve stripes alternating red and white, raised on a pole.

As the afternoon drew to an end, uptown-bound traffic on Broadway congealed into a solid mass. Nowhere could you see carriages more elegant, or finer horses. But visiting Europeans thought their effect spoiled by the makeshift liveries of the coachmen. When some enterprising imitators of European customs first attempted to introduce liveries in New York, there was great resentment on the part of servants. "The hatband has gained a partial, and the button a general, footing, but the plush has not been able to keep its ground," one observer noted; "so that the servants' costume presents a walking allegory of society—part English form and deference, part French affectation and dandyism, part native independence and outward equality." In the mass of vehicles you noticed a New York oddity: the "bulletin wagon," its sides plastered with advertisements of a theater, a medicine, a shop, or of Barnum's Museum, whose resourceful owner had invented this form of publicity. For some reason, although they could have made speedier progress on other streets, the carmen (later to be called truckmen) favored Broadway. They wore the uniform of their trade, a white-canvas smock, and drove two-wheeled carts with a platform in front, standing with one foot on the platform and the other on a shaft. But the greatest congestion was caused by the huge, gaudily painted omnibuses of three competing companies, popularly known as the "Yellow Birds," the "Red Birds," and the "Original Broadways." These vehicles had seats for thirty people and were invariably packed by as many more who stood. During the mild seasons, they were drawn by two teams of horses. In winter, when snow piled up in the streets, their wheels were removed and they were mounted on runners, and a third team of horses was often required to keep them moving. Throughout the winter a thick layer of straw was laid on the floors of the omnibuses; this, in their overcrowded condition, was considered a sufficient precaution to keep the passengers comfortably warm.

A Brooklyn journalist named Whitman used to come over on the ferry to Manhattan for the pleasure of riding beside the omnibus drivers, who were spinners of vivid yarns; "a strange, natural, quick-eyed and wondrous race." They were men of immense animal qualities, he thought, and great personal pride, in their way, and he liked to declaim, for their pleasure, some stormy passage from *Julius Caesar* or *Richard III,* for you could roar as loudly as you chose in the heavy, dense, uninterrupted street-bass of Broadway. The omnibus drivers were known to him by curious names: Broadway Jack, Dressmaker, Balky Bill, Old Elephant and Young Elephant, Tippy, Big Frank, Yellow Joe, Pop Rice, Patsey Dee—and, thirty years later, he would declare that his jaunts with them "undoubtedly entered into the gestation of *Leaves of Grass.*"

The city was sprawling northward more and more rapidly. Fifth Avenue, from Washington Square to Madison Square, was becoming the new center

THE HOUSE OF MANSIONS, 1858, Fifth Avenue at 42nd Street, *by Anderson*

CRYSTAL PALACE AND LATTING OBSERVATORY, 1853, on the present site of Bryant Park, *by F. F. Palmer*

of fashion and wealth, and there millionaires were erecting, in a solid phalanx, brownstone mansions which, "although stately and spacious, so closely resemble each other as to easily pass for duplicates of the same original." Fifth Avenue had already been cut through north of Twenty-third Street, but was still unpaved and, in 1850, looked like a country road passing between vacant lots and fields. In that year a splendid row of private dwelling houses was erected on Twenty-third Street between Lexington and Fourth Avenues, at a cost of two hundred and fifty thousand dollars, and was to be offered at private sale. Conservative New Yorkers wondered whether there were any citizens sufficiently adventurous to migrate to that social desert. But rumors were current that William Backhouse Astor, now wealthiest of all Americans, and his sons John Jacob III and William, were planning to erect two hundred three- and four-story dwellings between Broadway and Ninth Avenue on the streets from Forty-fourth to Forty-seventh—in what was still open country! In 1859, after the Fifth Avenue Hotel had been opened, Madison Square and the adjacent streets were incorporated in the domain of elegance. That same year, with prophetic social vision, John Jacob Astor III and his younger brother William erected their twin mansions far uptown, on the west side of Fifth Avenue between Thirty-third and Thirty-fourth Streets. These grandiose residences, with their Corinthian columns and pilasters flanking the main entrances, with their double stoops and mansard roofs, their art galleries and banquet halls, were destined to dominate the life of New York society for two generations.

All during the eighteen-fifties, summer and winter, New Yorkers as well as visitors to the city found pleasure in driving out of town to the upper reaches of Manhattan. On warm, sunny days the Croton Reservoir, on the west side of Fifth Avenue between Fortieth and Forty-second Streets, was a favorite destination. Its high walls gave it the look of a vast Egyptian temple, and their top formed a broad promenade from which you had fine views of the city to the south, the Hudson and East Rivers, and the rolling country that stretched northward to the villages of Yorkville, Manhattanville and Harlem. In 1853, New York held a World's Fair for which a replica of London's celebrated Crystal Palace was erected behind the Reservoir, and President Franklin Pierce came from Washington to inaugurate it. Thousands flocked to see the wonders of the Fair, and afterward crossed to the north side of Forty-second Street to visit a curious tower hastily built by an enterprising businessman. This tower was Latting's Observatory and Ice Cream Parlor, and after eating on the ground floor you could be lifted, by an experimental and often balky steam elevator, to the top of the structure for a spectacular view. A few years later, people drove further north on Fifth Avenue to see the site chosen by Archbishop Hughes for the future St. Patrick's Cathedral, and the vast tract of rocky hills and scrubby woods which the city had bought to transform into a public park—already optimistically named Central Park, although still far out of town.

In summer and in winter, New Yorkers who kept fast pacers and trotters exercised them on Third Avenue. The center of this wide boulevard was paved for one mile north of Astor Place, but there were dirt roads left at the sides, and beyond the pavement it was all open road to Harlem Bridge, five miles north. On a winter afternoon, with hard-packed snow underfoot, Third Avenue was a swarm of sleighs of all sorts and sizes, their bells jangling as they sped along. There were gaily painted cutters driven by fur-capped gentlemen, who draped the backs of their seats with bearskin robes that flaunted out behind. Some of these cutters were extremely elaborate—notably one with a body carved in the form of a sea-green shell lined with crimson velvet. There were large, roomy family sleighs, decked out with buffalo, black-bear and gray-lynx robes bound in red ribbon and equipped with sham eyes and ears, in which pretty girls and their parents took the air behind pacers that stepped along at the rate of twelve miles an hour. There were omnibus sleighs, lumbering along behind four or six horses. Out beyond the city Third Avenue climbed and descended many hills. At the bottom of several of these hills there were taverns where, after a stiff brush on the descent, the "fast

COLUMBUS CIRCLE, 1861, *by G. Haywood*

crabs" could "take a horn" and rest their horses. One of the most frequented of these taverns was Wintergreen's in Yorkville, a straggling suburb in the East Eighties. Wintergreen's was famous for its sherry flips, its cobblers, grogs and hot buttered rum.

On the way to Wintergreen's you passed the Irish squatter settlement on Dutch Hill, the high bluff overhanging the East River at Forty-second Street. Shantytown, this was called, a dismal collection of shacks and hovels inhabited by day-laborers, their families and their pigs. There were many squatter communities in upper Manhattan, but none less inviting than Shantytown. Looking eastward at Fiftieth Street, you could see the old Beekman mansion on the crest of Beekman Hill, which Sir William Howe had occupied as his headquarters during the Revolution. At Fifty-seventh Street, on the East River, was the fine country home of David Prevoost. As you drove north, you passed Jones's Woods, a favorite picnic ground in summer. If you turned east at Wintergreen's tavern and drove along the river past Hell Gate, you could see the country estates which, until recently, had been the summer homes of many of New York's wealthiest families—Rhinelanders, Astors, Gracies, Joneses and others. These estates were now seldom occupied, for they were too near the city and their proprietors preferred to spend the hot months at Newport or elsewhere.

As dusk fell, the parade of sleighs turned back to the city. For dinner, in New York, was an important ritual and, if people were not going on to a theater, a well-served repast required two or three hours. Moreover, dinner was a function for which all ladies exacted time to dress. In 1857 William Allen Butler, a New York lawyer with a talent for light verse, published a poem which quickly became a classic throughout the country. It was entitled "Nothing to Wear," and it lamented the fate of Miss Flora M'Flimsey of Madison Square, whose plight would continue to afflict New York ladies throughout a century.

> Nothing to wear! Now as this is a true ditty,
> I do not assert—this, you know, is between us—
> That she's in a state of absolute nudity
> Like Powers' Greek Slave or the Medici Venus;
> But I do mean to say I've heard her declare,
> When, at the same moment, she had on a dress
> Which cost five hundred dollars and not a cent less,
> And jewelry worth ten times more I should guess,
> That she had not a thing in the wide world to wear!

Dining deliberately and well, in the early eighteen-fifties, prosperous New Yorkers still spoke, with awe, of John Jacob Astor. The richest man in America died in 1848, at the age of eighty-five, leaving a fortune that, incredibly, exceeded twenty million dollars. In his last years Astor became a legendary figure, a survivor of the remote past. There were odd tales about the straits to which he was reduced by age and illness. To stir his sluggish blood, his servants were ordered to toss him gently in a blanket; and the only

NEW YORK WATERFRONT IN THE CLIPPER SHIP ERA, a view of South Street during the Gold Rush, *by Dwight Franklin*

food he could digest was milk from the breast of a wet-nurse. When he died, James Gordon Bennett denounced him, in *The Herald,* as "a self-invented money-making machine," and boldly declared that one-half of his immense property belonged, by right, to the people of New York, from whom in one way or another he had managed to squeeze it. Astor left no money to philanthropies. But, as a personal memorial, he set up a fund of four hundred thousand dollars to endow a library. Now, housed in a fine building on Lafayette Place, the Astor Library was one of the sights of the city. Its collection of one hundred thousand volumes was the largest in the country, and in its spacious reading room you might sometimes catch a glimpse of such eminent writers as Washington Irving, Thackeray, Longfellow and Emerson.

Conversation was likely to turn, also, on the gold rush to California. The shipyards that lined the East River from Pike Street on the south to Thirteenth Street on the north could not build enough clippers to embark the crowds of adventurers who hoped to find fortune in San Francisco. People went down to the East River piers to watch the sailings of the "express lines" of clipper ships. As these graceful vessels set off for the long voyage around Cape Horn —ninety-six days was considered record time—their passengers usually struck up Stephen Foster's lilting song, "O, Susanna." Genteel New York had a romantic feeling about the beautiful clippers, about the great merchant princes —the Lows of Brooklyn, for example, and the Grinnells of Manhattan— whose fleets were as familiar to the ports of India, to Java and Sumatra, to Canton and Shanghai as they were to the harbor of New York itself. On the wharves of Brooklyn, under Columbia Heights, you were assailed by the pungent aroma of spices that figured so profitably in this immense Oriental trade. Along South Street and Water Street in Manhattan you saw other merchandise from the Orient being unloaded: tea, coffee, fine silks, Canton china. And, occasionally, you came upon a strange Oriental figure, Chinese or Hindu; or a Lascar. The merchant princes were harrying the Federal Government to force the opening of Japan to commerce. When this was finally accomplished by Commodore Matthew C. Perry, the whole city celebrated his exploit. Commodore Perry was a New Yorker by adoption, father-in-law of the banker August Belmont, and when the Japanese commissioners visited New York on their way to Washington, Belmont arranged a great banquet in their honor at the Metropolitan Hotel, and a special performance of opera at the new Academy of Music on Fourteenth Street. New Yorkers then saw, for the first time, kimono-clad men from the mysterious island empire.

Sometimes, over dinner—a capital clam soup, perhaps, followed by a fore-quarter of lamb with mint sauce; or a turtle soup, and then salmon with peas, and then asparagus, followed by game—you heard aggressive businessmen of the newer school declare that the clipper ships would soon be driven from the seas by steam packets. Regular steamship service between New York and Liverpool had already been inaugurated by the English Cunard Line and the American Collins Line, and there was great rivalry between them to make the swiftest transatlantic crossing. New Yorkers were thrilled when the Collins Line *S. S. Pacific* docked in New York after a record run from Liverpool of ten days and four hours. "What wondrous changes have occurred in our day and generation!" old Philip Hone exclaimed. Like other men of his years, he could remember when it had taken a sloop nine days to sail from New York to Albany, one day less than it now required to reach Europe. And nowadays, by railroad, you could travel to Albany in less than nine hours

Dining out in New York, you were bound to hear about the latest "craze" rampant in the city. Everybody was discussing spiritualism. Clairvoyants and mediums were advertising in the newspapers, offering to put you in touch with the spirits of the departed. Interest in these dubious proceedings had flared up in 1850, when the newspapers sensationally reported the so-called "Rochester Rappings" of two young girls, Margaret and Kate Fox, who claimed supernatural powers. The accounts of their weird manifestations aroused widespread curiosity, and presently the two sisters were brought to New York. Old-fashioned people who condemned the resulting queer, morbid fad blamed a number of distinguished New Yorkers for the part they had played in launching it. James Fenimore Cooper, William Cullen Bryant, Horace Greeley, the historian George Bancroft—these eminent gentlemen, with several journalists, two prominent physicians, a respected clergyman and some others, were the first New Yorkers ever to spend "an evening with the spirits," as one of them described it.

They were invited to attend a demonstration given by the Fox sisters before these two notorious young ladies began holding the public meetings that caused so much commotion in the city. The party was held in the Broadway home of Dr. Rufus W. Griswold, a leading figure in literary circles. He was skeptical about the peculiar accomplishments of the Fox sisters. He doubted that any strange noises would be produced in his sedate upstairs library. And, should any sounds be heard, he was positive that they would not represent communications from the spirit world. Most of Griswold's guests were equally skeptical, and some were convinced that the sisters were brazen impostors. But the assembled lions soon found that meeting the Foxes was a disquieting experience. In Griswold's library the sisters sat on a sofa with a table in front of them. Presently rappings began to be heard from under the floor, then from the table, then from other parts of the room. These sounds increased in loudness and frequency, became clear and distinct. Nobody could deny hearing them. Nobody could trace them to a visible source. The guests formed a compact circle around the table. Several of them interrogated the spirits, either silently or aloud, and were answered—according to a code previously explained by the sisters—with loud rappings.

It was James Fenimore Cooper, however, who brought on the episode that gave everybody a spooky feeling. Addressing the spirits, the famous novelist inquired about an unidentified person whom nobody present could have known. Loud, unhesitating rappings replied that the person was Cooper's sister; that she had been dead for fifty years; that she had met her end in an accident. All this, Cooper acknowledged, was true. His sister had been killed, fifty years earlier, by being thrown from her horse. After this impressive demonstration, the Fox sisters stood in the center of Griswold's library. Loud knockings were heard from the distant door of the room. Two gentlemen, placing their ears against the door, felt the vibrations caused by these rappings. The sisters were then taken downstairs by the host and several other gentlemen to a parlor directly under Griswold's library. Those who remained in the upstairs library heard loud rappings coming from the sofa on which the Fox sisters had been sitting. Still more bewilderingly, they felt Dr. Griswold's decorous sofa quiver and vibrate in a most unseemly fashion. The whole affair was very odd indeed. Even the most skeptical of Griswold's guests found it rather disturbing. They were all men of intelligence, not easily deceived. Was it any wonder, then, that the public demonstrations which the Fox sisters subsequently gave in New York proved to be sensationally successful? Or that attending spiritualistic seances quickly became a fad?

Old-fashioned New Yorkers soon received a far nastier shock from the "strong-minded woman," as she was derisively called. In the autumn of 1853 a Women's Rights Convention, meeting for two days in the Broadway Tabernacle on Worth Street, had the city in an uproar of excitement. It was attended by female delegates from many eastern states, and from western cities like Cleveland and Chicago. Some of these women were already notorious as radical agitators—the venerable Quakeress, Mrs. Lucretia Mott, Miss Susan B. Anthony, Mrs. Elizabeth Cady Stanton, Miss Lucy Stone. Not only did they want the vote, but—as their speeches at the convention made perfectly clear—they demanded full equality with men. Women, they asserted, must no longer be confined to the home. These female firebrands declared that women must be allowed to enter public life, engage in any profession or business they chose, manage their own property, do as they wished with money earned by their own labor. To demonstrate the emancipation which they sought, Miss Lucy Stone defiantly wore the new costume adopted by the more daring suffragists: a short skirt above long, baggy bloomers. This scandalous attire caused an immense sensation. Most of the speeches made at the convention were equally provocative. The Tabernacle often rang with jeers, groans, angry shouting. There were frequent hostile demonstrations. One scene of violent disorder led to a free-for-all fight in the gallery, which was quelled only when Horace Greeley, editor of *The Tribune,* persuaded several policemen to intervene. For two days, all the New York newspapers gave their front pages to this meeting of rebellious women. There was no mistaking the mood of the agitators; they were belligerent, resolute, undaunted by ridicule. Conservative New Yorkers, pondering the changing times, sighed for the good old days when women knew their place and kept it.

ARTIST'S RECEPTION IN 1869. William J. Hayes at His Tenth Street Studio

2

Farewell

to

Simplicity

A new era of splendor had set in. Observing the social scene, elderly New Yorkers were amazed by the magnificence of the mansions being built uptown, the costliness of festivities and fashions. During the winter of 1850 James Fenimore Cooper, who was going about in society, wrote to his wife of a party at which Mrs. William Wetmore had appeared "in a dress that cost, including jewels, thirty thousand dollars." He thought this was doing pretty well for New York, and crustily noted that the city had become "a great arena for the women to show off their fine feathers in." Some years later, another moralist attributed the prevailing "absurd extravagance" to "the influx of vulgar wealth from California." Nothing could have been further from the truth. New York society was not taking its tone from the "Fifth Avenue Noodles," or "avenoodles," as they were called—aliens who had struck it rich in the goldfields, and native upstarts. The cult of elegance was being sponsored by wealth that had acquired a patina as well as a pedigree.

This cult was notably advanced by the decision of young Mrs. William Colford Schermerhorn to give a costume ball early in the winter of 1854. Society had long banned costume balls, with reason. Fourteen years earlier, Henry Brevoort had given one in his new mansion on Fifth Avenue and Ninth Street, and a scandal had resulted. Among Brevoort's guests were Miss Matilda Barclay and Captain Burgwyne, an impetuous young gallant from the South, whose courtship was disapproved by the Barclay family. Nevertheless, Miss Barclay and the Captain were secretly engaged. At four o'clock in the morning, without changing their costumes, they left the ball, contrived to secure a clergyman, and were married before breakfast. This disgraceful

FASHIONS FOR 1850, *by Sarony and Major*. The upper scene depicts the ballroom of the Astor House; the lower scene shows the Astor House and The American
Hotel

elopement had brought costume balls into disrepute, but the Schermerhorns
were so august that nobody dared question the propriety of their giving one.
Resisting the northward migration of fashion, they continued to dwell downtown, in the grim, square ancestral Schermerhorn mansion on the corner
of Lafayette Place and Great Jones Street. From there, Mrs. Schermerhorn
sent out six hundred invitations to her ball, limiting her guest list to the in-
disputable members of New York's élite. It was remarked that she had discarded a traditional form. She did not request the pleasure of your company.
She merely announced that she would be at home, on the stated evening, for
a *bal paré*.

Determined to make her ball the most magnificent *affaire de luxe* ever held
in New York, Mrs. Schermerhorn commanded her guests to appear in French
court costume of the period of Louis XV. Though pleasing to the ladies, this
decree spread panic among the gentlemen. To wear whiskers was an established masculine privilege; many gentlemen had adopted the "imperial"
favored by Emperor Napoleon III; gilded youth had lately taken to a new
decoration, the mustache. At the court of Louis XV, however, all facial foliage
had been interdicted. Did acceptance of Mrs. Schermerhorn's invitation re-

quire a shearing? A deputation of eminent gentlemen took this delicate matter up with the hostess. At first she insisted that her masculine guests remove their cherished growths. But some opposition developed, and a compromise was finally worked out by which they would be permitted to retain either their beards, or their mustaches, but not both. At this juncture, social tension was relieved by a scholarly member of the élite who undertook some research in history. At the court of Louis XV, he announced, the king's musketeers had been permitted to wear as much hair on their faces as might be necessary to give them a look of military ferocity. A great many gentlemen saved their pride, as well as their whiskers, by attending the ball in the costume of musketeers.

For this ball the old Schermerhorn mansion was refurnished and decorated in authentic period style. All the servants were attired in the uniforms and wigs of Versailles. The costumes of the ladies were of unprecedented beauty and costliness, and New York had never before seen so extravagant a display of jewels. In satin breeches and silk hose, the gentlemen for the first time in their lives became jealous of one another's calves. One sanguinary instance of envy occurred. A young man, contemplating the superb legs of another gentleman, doubted that nature alone had developed their shapeliness. To satisfy himself, this skeptic pricked a handsome calf with his sword and drew blood. But the possessor of the handsome limbs, although infuriated, neither winced nor uttered a sound. His restraint under assault proved to be misguided. Disregarding the evidence of his bloodstained stocking, everybody concluded that his tailor had somehow managed to improve on nature.

It was at the Schermerhorn ball that New York society first enjoyed a difficult pleasure, the so-called "German cotillion," a dance that lasted all of two hours. In offering this elaborate novelty as a substitute for the familiar schottisches, redowas and polkas, Mrs. Schermerhorn followed a precedent established, some months earlier, at the Tuileries Palace, by the Empress Eugénie, who had forbidden them to be danced at court balls because she believed them to resemble the can-can, an obnoxiously vulgar dance as yet unknown in New York. The cotillion, approved by the Empress and introduced to New York by Mrs. Schermerhorn, became a rite which society preserved, reverently, for more than a half century. Down through the years, the élite continued to perform the cotillion, with increasingly intricate figures, at every great ball.

Charles Astor Bristed, a young grandson of John Jacob Astor, gave society the name by which it was most frequently described during the eighteen-fifties: the "upper tendom," or "upper ten thousand." Bristed amused himself by writing satirical sketches of fashionable life, and in one of these he rebuked the elect for their "arbitrary and tyrannical exercise of exclusiveness." Probably the most notable victim of this exclusiveness was ageing Cornelius Vanderbilt, who liked to be referred to as "Commodore," and who lived, socially ostracized, in fashionable Washington Place. Having begun his career as a Staten Island ferryman, he later operated steamship services on the Hudson and Long Island Sound and, after the discovery of gold in California, set up a line from New York to the West, with overland portage by way of Nicaragua. By 1853, he acknowledged that he was worth eleven million dollars which brought him a return of 25 per cent, but this formidable wealth did not counteract the effect, on a squeamish upper tendom, of his bluff manners, his reputed illiteracy, and certain ugly rumors about his domestic life. Vanderbilt was notoriously parsimonious but, exasperated by social isolation, he determined to give New York's élite an example of splendor that would shatter all precedent.

To the astonishment of everyone, he commanded the building of the first ocean-going steam yacht ever owned by an American citizen. The *North Star* was, in fact, an ocean liner, and on it, with his numerous family, his clergyman, physician and other personal retainers, the Commodore made a prolonged cruise in European waters, producing, as the newspapers forecast, a sensation second to none. The luxury of this palatial ship was overwhelming. The walls of the dining saloon were of "ligneous marble," highly polished, with panels of Naples granite. Its white ceiling had scrollwork of purple, light green and gold, surrounding medallion paintings of Columbus, Webster, Clay, Calhoun, Washington, Franklin and others. Aft of this was the main saloon, walled in rosewood and satinwood. Its rosewood furniture, carved in the style of Louis XV, was upholstered in "a new and elegant material of figured velvet plush, with a green ground filled with bouquets of flowers." There were ten principal staterooms, each decorated in different colors— green and gold, crimson and gold, orange. Every stateroom contained a large French mirrored *armoire;* the berths were "furnished with elegant silk lambrecans and lace curtains" for the protection of modesty; and the "toilet furniture" of each stateroom precisely matched its draperies and fittings. The fortunate voyagers did not have to depend, for heat, on the Commodore's explosive temper. A pleasant temperature was maintained, in the saloons and cabins, by "one of Van Horne's steam-heaters . . . a beautiful specimen of bronze trellis work, with marble top and . . . richly burnished gilding." On his return from the grand tour, having demonstrated to fashionable New York that "parvenu" might be a word of honor, the Commodore put his cruising palace into commercial service and ultimately sold her for four hundred thousand dollars. But he had set a standard for a later generation of millionaires.

Though never flexible enough to admit Commodore Vanderbilt, society gradually enlarged its membership. Nathaniel P. Willis, editor of *The Home Journal,* the favorite magazine of fashionable folk, declared that the smart set included all those "who keep carriages, live above Bleecker, are subscribers to the opera, go to Grace Church, have a town house and country house, give balls and parties." This extension of the eligible gave rise to so many problems that it became necessary to appoint an arbiter and depute to him a large measure of power. The new guardian of the social citadel was a fine-looking, portly man with a florid complexion, a natural air of command,

and a versatile mastery of all the complexities that affected the welfare of the élite. "Where Brown is found," a poem affirmed, "To fashion's eye is hallowed ground." Hallowed indeed, for "glorious Brown" not only controlled admission to the ranks of the living elect, but he likewise stood sentinel at New York's supreme portal to another and better world. Isaac Brown was not a member of society. He was the sexton of Grace Church which, as Willis so accurately said, was "the most fashionable and exclusive of our metropolitan 'Courts of Heaven.'" Brown took his immense responsibilities with appropriate seriousness, but an impish humor sometimes fractured his professional sedateness. "The Lenten season is a horridly dull season," he once remarked. "but we manage to make our funerals as entertaining as possible."

Whenever a fashionable hostess planned to give a party, she summoned Brown to a conference. He first inspected her guest list. He had an accurate knowledge of who was well or ill, who was in mourning, who had suffered financial reverses, who had friends staying with them, what socially eligible strangers were stopping at the principal hotels, what new belle had recently "come out" with such beauty or fortune as made it imperative to send a card to her family. Inspecting the guest list, Brown was able to foretell the probable acceptances and refusals, and he could always be relied on to suggest "possible and advisable enlargement of acquaintances." Brown's decision settled the problem of invitations. He likewise determined where the musicians were to be placed, in what rooms the supper was to be served, what caterer, confectioner and florist were to be employed. For his most august clients, Brown usually consented, on the evening of a great party, to function as castellan. Throughout the evening he would stand under their canopy, "wrapped in a voluminous overcoat," supervising the arrival and departure of carriages, summoning the house servants with his piercing whistle, ushering guests in and out of the house "with a courteous manner and polite word that would well become the nobleman who is Gold Stick in Waiting at the Court of Her Majesty." Brown's remarkable discretion, his infallible memory for details of lineage and financial standing, his peculiar ability to pass on the social credentials of all aspirants to inclusion among the elect, made him for two generations "an excellent Institution." Although reverence for tradition compelled him to exercise a conservative and restraining influence, he tried to adapt himself to social change. Long observation of the habits of the fashionable convinced him that they were as impatient to depart from their amusements as they were eager to arrive at them. He therefore set up a fleet of coaches and coupés which attended his clients at the opera, or at private functions, making it unnecessary for them to await the return of their own carriages, since they could step into the first Brown vehicle in line and be whirled away without delay. But there were limits to Isaac Brown's tolerance, and long after the eighteen-fifties, when vulgar new wealth was erecting palaces far uptown, he spoke for the old guard about to surrender. "I cannot undertake," he announced, "to control Society beyond Fiftieth Street."

In the autumn of 1860 tension between Southern and Northern states was becoming acute. A momentous presidential campaign was in its final phase, with four candidates in the field. The whole country was in a turmoil. Nobody felt sure that the Union would not break up. Everywhere you heard the uproar of partisan oratory, saw the red glare of great torchlight parades. But New York, as always, was a world to itself. In the rising excitement that was sweeping the nation, the metropolis succumbed to a very different furor, and people outside the sacred citadel fascinatedly watched the spectacle of society in convulsion. For New York was about to have a new experience: its first visit by royalty. This created social problems of the gravest consequence.

Royalty was traveling incognito, but this melancholy fact the elect determined to ignore. During the summer Queen Victoria had sent the young Prince of Wales on a state tour of Canada. Before his departure from London President Buchanan, a former Minister to the Court of St. James, invited the Prince to visit the United States. The Queen graciously accepted. Upon leaving the royal dominions, the Prince would drop his royal state. On his American tour he would travel under the name of Baron Renfrew. During the summer old Peter Cooper, New York's most distinguished citizen, convoked a meeting of gentlemen at the Merchants Bank to invite the Prince to the city. The Prince was nineteen, slim, fair, handsome—and deplorably frivolous. What formal hospitality should be offered to him? A number of gentlemen, probably at the instigation of their wives, proposed a splendid ball. But older, more influential leaders of the community objected to this project on moral grounds. After prolonged discussion, it was decided to honor the Prince with a banquet. A delegation of five, including John Jacob Astor III, ex-Governor Hamilton Fish and ex-Governor John A. King, was sent to Montreal to present an engrossed invitation.

The eminent delegates were dismayed by their reception. Lord Lyons, British Minister in Washington, and Major General the Honorable Robert Bruce, the Prince's governor, seemed to be upset by the engrossed document. So did the Duke of Newcastle, Minister for the Colonies and the senior member of the Prince's suite. After some tactful preliminaries they spoke frankly. Any form of hospitality would be preferable to a banquet, of which the Prince had endured too many in Canada. He was young, fond of diversion, easily bored. Could not the gentlemen from New York devise something more likely to please him? A ball, for example, since the Prince delighted in dancing? Overcoming their moral scruples, the delegates had a new invitation engrossed. It was accepted with alacrity.

Compelled against their will to give a ball, Peter Cooper's committee in New York proceeded with arrangements. The ball would be held at the Academy of Music on the night of October twelfth, and a supper room would be built, backstage, for the occasion. But who should be invited to participate in this function, the most important social event in the city's history? Obviously, only the genuinely elect. To them, unfortunately, must be added Mayor Fernando Wood and other municipal officials. The committee drew up a list of four hundred gentlemen. Upon payment of seventy dollars each of these privileged individuals would be entitled to ten invitations to the ball, three being for ladies only. Of their social discretion, the committee took a very cynical view. It ruled that the names of all prospective recipients of invitations must be submitted in advance; the committee would pass on their eligibility. Thus surrounded with an aura of exclusiveness, the Prince's ball agitated the whole of fashionable New York. Venerable gentlemen who no longer appeared in society intrigued for invitations. Ladies who aspired to enter it pleaded for them, almost on bended knees. The problem of selecting dancing partners for the Prince stirred up a tempest. Every socially eligible lady was bent on dancing with him. Husbands, fathers, brothers besieged the committee. Eventually, four thousand invitations were sent out to the ball "to be given by the Citizens of New York." The other citizens of New York were informed, through the newspapers, that on the night following the great affair they would be admitted to the Academy to view the superb decorations.

Three hundred thousand people lined Broadway, from Bowling Green to the Fifth Avenue Hotel, on the afternoon of the Prince's arrival. Municipal ceremonies engaged him at the Battery and City Hall, and as he drove up Broadway through the dusk, in an open carriage drawn by six horses, the crowds—so the Duke of Newcastle informed Queen Victoria—were "worked up almost to madness, and yet restrained within the bounds of the most perfect courtesy." He was honored by a torchlight parade of the Fire Department. He was entertained at breakfast by Mayor Wood, at "Wood Lawn," the mayor's home far out on Broadway and Seventy-seventh Street. He was driven to see the Deaf and Dumb Asylum, New York University, Cooper Institute, the Astor Library. If these buildings failed to impress him, he did not show it.

The ball, perhaps, was considered an adequate concession to the young Prince's fondness for diversion. As the poet Edmund Clarence Stedman put it:

> It was even said that his great delight
>   Established etiquette scorning
> Would not only be to dance all night
> But—once escaped from Newcastle's sight—
>   To go home with the girls in the morning!

For the gratification of this desire, however, Peter Cooper's august committee had made no provision. At nine o'clock on the night of the ball, a deputation of gentlemen arrived at the Fifth Avenue Hotel to escort the Prince to the Academy, already filled by the social élite. Among them was one fairly young man who noticed that the Prince was "obviously weary of the sexagenarians who chiefly had possession of him." He was struggling to force his hands into a pair of gloves very much too small for him, and to the young gentleman he confided a whispered explanation: "These gloves were sent me by a lady in this house, with the request that I wear them tonight; I don't know who she is. They are much too small for me, but I intend to work my hands into them if I can." The process took time, but the Prince finally succeeded. Perhaps the lady of the gloves was the heroine of a legend that persisted in New York for a half century. It was always said that on one night

GRAND BALL FOR THE PRINCE OF WALES AT THE ACADEMY OF
MUSIC, October 12, 1860

during his visit to the city the Prince eluded the vigilance of his governor, the British minister and the Duke of Newcastle—and disported himself riotously in the most luxurious brothels.

The ball opened with a *quadrille d'honneur* which was executed "with dignity and repose." Waltzes immediately followed. The Prince danced with Miss Fish, Miss Mason, Miss Fannie Butler and many others; for the pre-determined bevy of distinction this was the night of all nights. Less fortunate young ladies continually pressed about him in a manner which, as the Duke of Newcastle observed, was "not in strict accordance with good breeding." The Prince, however, did not indicate any disapproval of these aggressive beauties. The Academy was packed to suffocation, and to get into the supper room was as difficult as to get near royalty. You entered the supper room by one stage door, and left it by the other. At each of these doors a prominent citizen stood guard—John Jacob Astor III was one of them—admitting fifty people at a time. At one end of the room was a raised dais, where the royal party was served. A huge horseshoe table ran around the entire room, and behind it an army of liveried servants, elbow to elbow, filled plates and poured champagne. Even hypercritical Ward McAllister agreed that nothing could have been more successful, or better done. The Prince's ball, he de-clared, was so brilliant and beautiful that it would always be remembered by those present as one of the events of their lives.

The war ushered in a new era. Old amenities were supplanted by others, more modern and subtly refined. European habits and customs were rapidly adopted. The French chef for the first time became an almost indispensable domestic resource; "artistic" dinners replaced the obsolete solid repasts of an earlier day. Ladies were no longer satisfied by the provincial improvisations of local modistes. They had to send to Paris for everything, and the tyranny of Monsieur Worth—intransigent and perdurable—began. An inventory of the wardrobe of a young belle listed nearly three hundred necessary items costing, in the aggregate, more than twenty thousand dollars. For a single New York season her requirements included forty-five gowns for various occasions, ranging in price from eighty to twenty-five hundred dollars; seven magnificent cloaks, one of which was priced at four hundred and fifty dollars; forty-eight chemises of richly embroidered cambric with lace, or of embroidered Irish linen. Among her essential accessories were nine fans, seven jeweled combs; twenty hair nets of gold, silver, pearls and various colors; head ornaments, card cases in gold filigree and gold whist-markers; a set of Russian sables—cape, muff and boa—valued at a mere one hundred dollars. "Your pace is charming," Mrs. Lewis Colford Jones assured a young husband eager to advance his wife in society—"but can you keep it up?"

The need to keep up a charming pace imposed an unflagging effort. Rivalry was no less real for being ceremonious. Feminine social leadership was in perpetual dispute. Mrs. James I. Jones of Washington Place attempted to achieve precedence. Her dinners were exquisite; her wines perfect; her husband's Madeiras were famous. Mrs. Jones prided herself on the fact that her small dances were the acme of exclusiveness. Yet could these dances dim the luster of more enchanting novelties introduced by Mrs. William Colford Schermerhorn? The Schermerhorns, finally abandoning their ancestral mansion in Lafayette Place, built a handsome residence on Twenty-third Street west of Fifth Avenue. Its drawing rooms, picture gallery and music room were filled with notable, if disquieting, examples of European art. Mrs. Schermerhorn gave balls, not dances, and she was the first hostess in New York to have musicales featuring distinguished instrumentalists and singers. At one of these affairs, a débutante relative was greatly embarrassed "to find myself standing beside a very undressed statue and to be talking to a young man at the time." To the astonishment of New York it was demonstrated that talk—if sufficiently "polished and cultivated"—could be made a recurrent delight. An intrepid hostess endowed society with its only salon, assembling on one evening every week all its most brilliant members for conversation. This daring innovator, Mrs. Sidney Brooks, was not, however, a native New Yorker. Her peculiar inspiration could have occurred only to a Bostonian.

But the eminence of these ladies was equaled, if not exceeded, by that of Mrs. August Belmont, a woman of singular charm and beauty who, in the opinion of young men about town, was "in every sense society's queen." She was the niece of Oliver Hazard Perry, the hero of Lake Erie, the daughter of Commodore Matthew Calbraith Perry who opened Japan to American commerce. Her husband's banking house was affiliated with those of the European Rothschilds, and August Belmont had become one of the city's outstanding financial magnates. He was a short, thick-set man who walked with a patrician limp as the result of a duel that had satisfied his honor but injured his leg. Society distrusted him, partly because he cultivated a Parisian way of life. He was a collector of paintings and porcelains; he was reputed to be somewhat dissolute; his connoisseurship of horseflesh and women was considered authoritative. Belmont had a taste for society, and he conquered New York's citadel by the very sophistication which aroused its dubiety. In his home on lower Fifth Avenue there was an immense and very beautiful art gallery which also served as a ballroom, and the Belmonts entertained in regal style. Belmont had the best chef in New York, and he taught society the art of giving a perfect dinner. Old Monnot who, as manager of the New York Hotel, was an acknowledged master of this art, offered a simple explanation of Belmont's pre-eminence. Alone of fashionable New Yorkers, Monnot asserted, Belmont "makes his cook give him a good dinner every day." It was Belmont's mission to persuade society that elegance must be pervasive as well as diurnal.

Society did not require Dr. Holmes to remind it of its duty to build more stately mansions as the swift seasons rolled. It was leaving its low-vaulted past with alacrity. When he visited New York, Prince Jerome Napoleon was profoundly impressed by the "modern improvements" to be found in all the new mansions; central heating, luxurious individual bathrooms equipped with toilets, an intricate system of bells and speaking tubes connecting every room with the service quarters. The private apartments at the Tuileries, he said, were vastly inferior to those in the homes of New York's aristocracy. "They are small, wretched holes, unprovided with any of the ingenious and labor-saving contrivances which I have just seen," he remarked upon leaving one establishment, "and so uncomfortable that when I was first married I was ashamed to take my wife to them." Paris, the Prince asserted, could not rival the domestic architecture of lower Fifth Avenue and Madison Square. But the chief glory of that architecture was not yet completed at the time of his visit.

Characteristically, Leonard Jerome built his magnificent stables before erecting the palace which adjoined them. He was the most ardent votary of the new equine cult; he dazzled society with the glitter and novelty of his carriages, the costliness of his blooded horses. He excited its dubious admiration by his extravagance and assurance. Both were obvious in all his activities: his fantastic speculations, his scandalous love affairs, his incredible parties. A tall, dark man with an enormous walrus mustache, Jerome had been the publisher of a newspaper in Rochester before coming to New York and plunging into the maelstrom of Wall Street. He made, lost and again made fortunes; he was reputed to be worth more than ten million dollars. He built his palace on the corner of Madison Avenue and Twenty-sixth Street, overlooking Madison Square, a huge building of red brick faced with marble, made unique by a steep mansard roof, extremely tall windows and double porches of delicate ironwork fronting on the park. The large stables on Twenty-sixth Street were lavishly adorned with black walnut paneling, plate glass and rich carpets. On the second floor was a great hall, and there Jerome gave a ball to celebrate the opening of his palace. Society remembered this ball for the beauty of the floral decorations, the two fountains which, throughout the evening, spouted, the one champagne, the other eau de cologne, the culinary marvels disclosed at supper and breakfast.

Among the guests at this ball was Mrs. Pierre Lorillard Ronalds, a young matron widely acclaimed as the belle of the season. Such acclaim would have been sufficient to command Jerome's attention, but the lady possessed accomplishments certain to evoke his warm admiration. She drove horses with admirable grace; she sang beautifully. Never at a loss in any situation that demanded gallantry, Jerome suggested to Mrs. Ronalds the project of transforming his improvised ballroom into a private theater, so that he might ask the fashionable world to hear her sing, and see her act, in order to raise funds for the sick and wounded soldiers in military hospitals. In doing this, he assured her that he would literally bring the fashionable world to her feet, begging for tickets of admission. And so it proved. Jerome's private theater, seating six hundred, and with a fully equipped stage, was the most luxurious playhouse in New York. "As you entered you were received by liveried servants, and by them conducted to your seat, where you found yourself surrounded by a most brilliant assemblage; and on the stage, as amateur actresses supporting the fair singer, the fashionable beauties of that day." So, thirty years later, the inauguration of this "little royal theater" by Mrs. Ronalds was described by one of the audience. Thereafter, private theatricals in the Jerome theater, usually enhanced by the art of a diva or other reigning stars, became one of the most agreeable of fashionable diversions. Jerome was a generous patron of young, beautiful singers and actresses—was it not the obligation of wealth to nourish and benefit art and artists? But this particular application of the doctrine of *noblesse oblige* failed to win the unreserved approval of his wife, and Mrs. Jerome, with her three daughters, presently deserted New York and Newport for Paris.

Jerome was perhaps the only man in New York who could astound the equally imperturbable Lorenzo Delmonico, the city's premier restaurateur. Jerome arranged for a competition in dinners between himself, August Belmont and the wealthy clubman and wit William R. Travers. Each was to strive to offer the most perfect dinner ever achieved in society. "What are people coming to?" Delmonico asked a favorite patron. "Here, three gentlemen come to me and order three dinners, and each one charges me to make his dinner the best of the three. I am given an unlimited order, 'Charge what you will, but make my dinner the best.' I told my cook to call them the Silver, Gold and Diamond dinners, and have novelties at them all." The competition resulted in a tie, but Jerome's dinner was remembered because, on opening her napkin, each lady found a gold bracelet. And, years afterward, epicures recalled that the menu had included an *aspic de canvasback,* a salad of string beans with truffles, and a truffled ice cream—one of the great Lorenzo's novelties which seemed very odd but turned out to be delicious.

Indirectly, these three dinners precipitated a minor disturbance in society. Everybody who mattered now had a residence adapted to large-scale entertaining. Was not this the propitious moment to initiate a form of social reunion to be held in a quasi-public place? In all of New York there was, of course, only one such place worthy of serious consideration: the fine ballroom of Delmonico's new restaurant on Fifth Avenue and Fourteenth Street. This inspired project of resorting to the impeccable Lorenzo disguised what was, in effect, a counterrevolution. For it had become obvious that the ranks of society were being indiscriminately swollen. Was society entitled to that name if it included all who claimed the right of membership? Only by limitation, only by the practice of a rigorous exclusion would order supersede anarchy and true distinction be attained. Social union would yield social power. The genuinely august must be banded together to form a tribunal whose decrees nobody could afford to ignore. A group of such supreme dignity, of such immense prestige, could thereafter control, lead and carry on society, receive or shut out people at their pleasure.

It was the indefatigable Ward McAllister who undertook to aggregate the ultimate gods and proposed their motto: *nous nous soutenons.* His motives were not entirely disinterested. He aspired to personal social power— and how could this be achieved more easily than by being invested with deputed authority? Who was more fitted to serve as the minister, guardian and magistrate of the gods? To this end, McAllister organized a series of "cotillion dinners" at Delmonico's, restricted to seventy-five or one hundred people. As anyone might have predicted, they were a brilliant success. It was at one of these functions, after the ladies had withdrawn and the gentlemen were lingering at the horseshoe table over coffee and cigars, that the Earl of Rosebery uttered a memorable epigram. Rosebery was paying his first visit to New York and had been a guest in all the most aristocratic mansions. On the fine art of dining he therefore spoke as an experienced critic. "You Americans have made a mistake," he conjectured blandly; "your emblematic bird should have been a canvasback, not an eagle."

If McAllister was disconcerted by this protest against the ubiquity of a favorite fowl, his ruffled feelings were quickly soothed. The following morning brought him his coveted brevet of authority in the form of a poem, anonymous but destined to a social fame incompatible with its literary merits:

> There ne'er was seen so fair a sight
> As at Delmonico's last night;
> When feathers, flowers, gems and lace
> Adorned each lovely form and face;
> A garden of all thorns bereft,
> The outside world behind them left,
> They sat in order, as if 'Burke'

Had sent a message by his clerk.
And by whose magic wand is this
All conjured up? the height of bliss.
'Tis he who now before you looms—
The Autocrat of Drawing Rooms.

Had the accolade ever before been bestowed with such exquisite insight, such absolute precision of statement? In political New York effective power did not attach to high office, so in the citadel of the elect it was appropriate that the real autocrat should wear the guise of a clerk.

What were the people of the "outside world"—the mere undifferentiated masses—to make of these manifestations, so unselfishly devised to promote their material welfare and brighten their lives? Cotillion dinners were perhaps alien to their desire, certainly beyond their capacity to emulate. Yet society did not fail them; it furnished an example which they could successfully follow. As the Civil War drew to its end, Mrs. Pierre Lorillard Ronalds gave a great costume ball. The costumes were superb. Thousands of dollars were spent on floral decorations. The supper lasted until five in the morning; the last strains of music for the dancers were hushed at six. Mrs. Ronalds appeared as "Music." In her hair, she wore a harp contrived in Paris, illuminated by tiny gas jets; and only when dancing began did she remove from her person the concealed gas-containers. Mrs. Ronalds wore a short dress, and her feet were encased in scarlet boots ringed with tiny bells. As every newspaper reader knew, these were the required pedal gear of the prostitutes in John Allen's brothel on Water Street. Did witty, unconventional Mrs. Ronalds intend to present a sardonic verdict on New York society—all artificial glitter at its apex, all conspicuous vulgarity at its base?

WOMEN'S FASHIONS OF 1867, showing the store of A. T. Stewart & Company in the background, *by Goddard*

In any case, soon after her festivity the city broke out in a rash of public masked balls—at the Academy of Music, the various "assembly rooms," the French Theater on West Fourteenth Street. One of these was a *"bal d'opéra"* offered at the end of the decade by the *Société des Bals d'Artistes* and extensively reported by *The World*. The women who attended this function dressed in costumes selected to expose as much of their persons as possible; trunk hose and fleshings and ballet dresses predominated. There was no attempt on the part of the men to assume imposing or elegant disguises; most of them wore only a mask, though some resorted to cheap dominoes. By midnight the hall was crowded, the dancing floor jammed with people, and liquor was flowing freely. On the floor, women were being caught up and tossed into the air. "A young woman, rather pretty and dressed in long skirts, is thrown up and falls back into the arms of the crowd, who turn her over, envelop her head in her own skirts, and again toss her up, temporarily denuded. The more exactly this proceeding outrages decency, the better it is liked. . . . The women were bundled into the boxes and there they were fallen upon by the crew of half-drunken ruffians, and mauled, and pulled, and exhibited in the worst possible aspects, amid the jeers and laughter of the other drunken wretches upon the floor. . . . There is not a whisper of shame in the crowd. It is now drunken with liquor and its own beastliness. It whirls in mad eddies round and round. The panting women are in the delirium of excitement . . . they bound and leap like tigresses; they have lost the last sense of prudence and safety. . . . It is no longer a dance at all, but a wild series of indecent exposures, a tumultuous orgy. . . . At two o'clock this curious spectacle was at its height."

Nobody could say that the people of New York failed to improve on an example.

3

The Seamy Side

A stone's throw from crowded Broadway, eastward along Worth Street, was a region of narrow, crooked streets and dismal courts that bore names like "Murderer's Alley" and "Cow Bay." This was the Five Points, the most dangerous and depraved quarter of Manhattan. At its center was an open, triangular space of about one acre, grotesquely known as Paradise Square. Policemen entered the Five Points only in pairs, and never unarmed. Respectable New Yorkers avoided the district even in daylight. It was the citadel of a gang of criminal hoodlums who called themselves the Dead Rabbits. It was the haunt of murderers, thieves, prostitutes and receivers of stolen goods.

The streets and alleys of the Five Points lay deep in filth. They were lined by ancient tenements and low clapboarded houses in an advanced stage of decay. In cellars ten feet below the street there were "lodging houses" without ventilation or windows, overrun by rats and vermin. Tiers of bunks covered all four slimy walls. To sleep on a bunk filled with rags, or with a straw-stuffed sack, lodgers paid ten cents a night. All were welcome as long as they paid in advance. Young and old of both sexes, drunk or sober, herded together. Tenement rooms in the Five Points rented at from two to ten dollars a month. All were small, and many were inhabited by several families. "In this one room," a horrified investigator wrote, "the cooking, eating and sleeping of the whole family and their visitors are performed. Yes—and their visitors: for it is no unusual thing for a mother and her two or three daughters, all of course prostitutes, to receive their 'men' at the same time and in the same room, passing in and out and going through all the transactions of their hellish intercourse with a *sang-froid* at which devils would stand aghast."

Groceries, second-hand stores and pawnbrokers occupied the street corners of the Five Points. The last two were all operated by "fences" who bought stolen goods and disposed of them at a large profit. On every block there were a dozen or more grog-shops which sold liquor to children as well as adults. At night, most of these places opened "dance houses" in back rooms where a fiddler or two furnished music. They were always crowded with prostitutes, sailors, thieves and hoodlums. The area teemed with vagrant children half-naked, barefoot always. At all hours they could be seen rooting about in the gutters with the pigs, hungrily searching for scraps of food. Many of the boys roved the city to pick cinders, collect rags and bones, or steal. Some of them worked for Mark Maguire, a politician and owner of a notorious dive, who was known as "the king of the newsboys" because he employed five hundred lads to sell papers on the streets of the city. On mild evenings, many of the younger girls from the Five Points stood on the curbstones of Broadway, vending hot corn. Theirs was the most familiar of New York street cries: "Here's your nice hot corn, smoking hot, smoking hot, just from the pot!" The older girls from the area found employment in the sailors' dives along the East River, on Water Street, or became streetwalkers. Two pioneer social settlements—the Five Points Mission and the House of Industry—were striving to rescue residents of the area from a life of degradation.

The undisputed ruler of the Five Points was "Captain" Isaiah Rynders, a politician who for a time occupied the office of United States Marshal in New York. Rynders was a former New Orleans gambler who owned a saloon on Park Row. He had gained control of the immigrant Irish vote in the area, and he held command over the tough, dreaded Dead Rabbits gang. This

"THE TOUGHEST STREET CORNER IN THE WORLD," 1852, the Old Brewery at Five Points, *by R. E. Trebes*

THE OLD BREWERY AT THE FIVE POINTS N.Y.

made him a power in Tammany Hall. By using his gang as a mobile force to terrorize the polling places of more reputable quarters of the city during elections, Rynders helped Tammany to maintain its domination of the city government. In return, he was granted a practical legal immunity for the operations of his henchmen: owners of dives, houses of prostitution, gambling establishments and "fences," in many of which Rynders had a large financial interest.

This efficient arrangement extended to all the slum wards of the city, of which the Five Points was the toughest and most squalid. It was an arrangement benevolently fostered by Fernando Wood, a political and financial wizard who had risen to be boss of Tammany Hall. Not content with this position of influence, he had himself elected Mayor of New York. A tall, handsome, dark-haired man with an immense black mustache, Wood dressed like a fashion plate, lived in regal style on a suburban estate, and was on terms of intimacy with many prominent bankers and merchants. During Mayor Wood's administration, factional strife broke out among the Tammany leaders, splitting them into two hostile camps. The war for political supremacy that followed lifted into notoriety John Morrisey, a minor Tammany henchman, a dark, powerful giant renowned for his pugilistic skill. As a penniless youth, Morrisey had come to New York from Troy. He enlisted under Isaiah Rynders, who trained him to be an efficient gang leader, and placed him in charge of the Dead Rabbits. At the head of this gang, he had won an election for Tammany by routing, in an uptown ward, a gang employed by the rival candidate and commanded by Bill Poole, owner of a slaughterhouse on Christopher Street near the Hudson River and celebrated as a slugger under the name of "Bill the Butcher." Thereafter, Morrisey and Poole were sworn enemies. When war broke out among the Tammany leaders, Morrisey remained loyal to the "old guard," and Poole joined the insurgent faction. In these circumstances, their gangs clashed in a series of violent affrays that shocked the city. Finally, one night a group of Morrisey's gangsters tracked Bill Poole to Stanwix Hall, an ornate saloon on Broadway opposite the Metropolitan Hotel, shot him, and made their escape. Poole lingered for several days, while excitement mounted throughout the city. Then he died, and he was given a public funeral such as New York had never seen. Seven thousand members of various organizations followed Poole's hearse down Broadway on foot. Local and visiting fire brigades marched in the procession, and dirges were played by several brass bands. When this cortege returned from the cemetery, a riot broke out between Poole's gangsters and Morrisey's, which raked Broadway with gunfire, injured dozens of people, and resulted in the looting of many stores.

After Poole's murder and the riot that followed it, a wave of crime and disorder broke over the city, unchecked by Mayor Wood or his police force. As a result, in 1857 the Republican legislature drastically amended New York's charter. Abolishing the municipal police force, the legislature set up a Metropolitan Police District under a Board of Commissioners to be appointed by

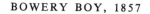

the Governor, and deprived Mayor Wood of control over the new police force. Protesting that this action was unconstitutional, the Mayor refused to disband the municipal police. A sanguinary battle between the two forces occurred at City Hall, which ended only when the Seventh Regiment surrounded the building and Mayor Wood submitted to arrest. For several months, while the constitutional issue was fought through the courts, two antagonistic police forces battled for authority in the streets of the city. This situation was an invitation to criminals and gangsters to do their worst. While the city was celebrating with fireworks on the night of Independence Day, the Dead Rabbits marched out of the Five Points and attacked the headquarters of their foes, the Bowery Boys. Rioting that night spread over downtown New York from the Bowery to Broadway. It was resumed early the next morning, when the rival gangs, returning to their battle, put to rout both forces of police. Several thousand men and women armed with guns, paving blocks, iron bars and clubs milled through the street from the Bowery to Broadway, fighting everywhere, looting houses, pillaging stores, and setting fire to buildings. The Metropolitan Police sent for Isaiah Rynders and demanded that he put a stop to the slaughter and robbery. After an unsuccessful attempt to send his Dead Rabbits back into the Five Points, Rynders advised the police to call out all troops in the city. Late at night two regiments, accompanied by the Metropolitan Police, marched into the stricken area and drove the rioters back into their slums.

By their violence and their depredations, the Bowery Boys had made that thoroughfare as well known to Americans as Broadway. Little good was reported of the broad avenue that ran northward from Chatham Square to East

Fourth Street. Infested by hoodlums, thugs and vagrants, it was squalid by day and dangerous after dark. It was lined with gin-mills and "dens of vice" frequented only by the class known as "the fancy." It was the street of down-and-outers, the last brief stop before the morgue and the Potter's Field. "Respectable people avoid the Bowery so far as possible at night. Every species of crime and vice is abroad at this time watching for its victims. Those who do not wish to fall into trouble should keep out of the way." So warned the author of a popular guidebook to the city. Naturally, most visitors to New York were bent on seeing the Bowery. As any reputable New Yorker could have told you, it was the principal boulevard of an alien city. Between it and the East River lay the dismal slums of the lower East Side, into which were herded the immigrant poor. On the Bowery, you heard foreign languages spoken more frequently than English, and when you heard English it was likely to have a thick coating of brogue. On the congested sidewalks you saw Irishmen and Germans, Italians and Slavic Jews, Frenchmen, Spaniards and a sprinkling of sad-looking Orientals. The Bowery was self-contained and self-sufficient. It had its local manners and customs, its own theaters and other places of recreation. Its turbulent life had nothing in common with that of the rest of the city.

Plays and songs and stories had been written about the Bowery Boy; artists had filled the magazines with pictures of him. He had already become a dubious hero of American folklore when the draft riots made him a civic menace, and respectable New York determined to do away with him. The Bowery Boy was not an adolescent. He was a mature tough of bellicose nature, with a taste for easily concealed lethal weapons: brass knuckles, a razor-sharp knife, a short length of iron pipe, a gun. In his leisure hours, on parade, he looked like a fancy-Dan. He wore a tall beaver hat, an inordinately long black frock coat, loud, checked, bell-bottomed pants, a vivid, floppy kerchief knotted under his collar. He wore his hair plastered down with Macassar oil, his mustache elegantly resembled a hat brush, and beneath it there jutted out, at a cocky tilt, the blackest of cigars. The girls with whom he consorted were resplendent in bright colors, short skirts, beribboned bonnets jauntily perched on the side of the head, fancy gaiters. The Bowery Boy was a plug-ugly always ready for a row, and he resented nothing more than the intrusion of outsiders into his favorite haunts.

He was certain to be a member of a volunteer fire brigade. These exclusive organizations conferred prestige, were important outposts of Tammany Hall, and could usually arrange legal immunity for their members. Was not Boss Tweed, for example, an alumnus of the famous Big Six and noted for his friendliness to all firemen? Rivalry between the various brigades ran high. They would dash to conflagrations, and fight so strenuously for the possession of fire plugs that they often neglected to extinguish the flames. Sometimes they broke open adjacent buildings under pretense of saving them, and then systematically looted the premises. There were few fires in the city without accompanying riots and robbery.

"JUMP HER BOYS, JUMP HER!" 1854, *by N. Currier*

On Saturday and Sunday nights, the Bowery was in full carnival. Along its whole length, the avenue blazed with light, rang with the music of German street bands, Italian organ grinders, itinerant harpists and violinists, the cries of street vendors, the shouts of the barkers who strove to lure the passing throng into shops. Desire must be created, and articles of commerce must be pushed. The famous Red House, a Bowery department store, put this doctrine to arresting use. They dressed up their barkers in the costumes of harlequins and had them perform as mountebanks while wooing the Bowery to come in and buy. Bankruptcy sales, fire sales, ruinous price reductions were announced by the ear-splitting barkers of cheap-jack, garishly lighted stores that sold spurious jewelry, new or second-hand clothes, flashy goods of various kinds. Among these shops, pawnbrokers' establishments were frequent, and did a huge business. So did the "exchange offices," which dealt in lottery tickets; the lotteries always paid off on Saturday nights, when tickets for forthcoming ones were first put on sale.

Every block along the Bowery showed the "transparencies" of one or more concert saloons. There were innumerable billiard parlors, either on the street level or immediately above it. Shooting galleries, open to the street and fancifully decorated, drew crowds. Even more popular, however, were the cock-pits and rat-pits to be found at Grand Street and Houston Street. At the cock-pits you could bet on the trained, spurred fowl that ripped one another to pieces. At the rat-pits you bet on the performance of terriers whose owners entered their animals in a competition of speed in killing a cage of frightened, ferocious rats.

Though the Bowery Boys and the Dead Rabbits were traditional enemies, both dreaded gangs were controlled by Democratic politicians. After Abraham Lincoln's election to the presidency, when one after another Southern state seceded from the Union, the Democrats of New York sank their factional differences to unite in opposition to a war which daily seemed more imminent. In his annual message to the city's Common Council in January, 1861, Mayor Fernando Wood declared that "disunion has become a fixed and certain fact." Accordingly, he proposed that New York secede from the United States, constitute itself a "free city" and receive "the whole and united support of the Southern States." This project met with wild enthusiasm from the Common Council. Leading Democrats throughout the North acclaimed Wood, and in New York a secret association was formed to carry out his project at a suitable time.

The outbreak of war, however, roused the city to a high pitch of patriotic excitement. Dense, cheering crowds lined Broadway as one regiment after another paraded on their way to entrain for Washington. Presently, New York took on the look of a camp; all its parks and squares were filled with barracks. As a result of a movement initiated by New York women, the United States Sanitary Commission was formed, and soon, all over the city, "thousands of women and even children devoted themselves to scraping lint, knitting socks, making garments and preparing delicacies for the sick and wounded whom they saw in perspective; and scores of the most tenderly reared and delicate young ladies volunteered their services as hospital nurses and went into training under the direction of the city's physicians."

But as the war continued, and the prospect of an early victory receded, Democratic opposition to the war grew bolder. In the summer of 1862, the Democrats called a mass meeting, attended by delegates from all over the state, to protest against its continuance. This meeting adopted resolutions strongly condemning the President and demanding that proposals for peace be submitted to the Confederacy. A similar meeting was held at Delmonico's early in February, 1863, over which Samuel F. B. Morse, inventor of the telegraph, presided. It established the Society for the Diffusion of Political Knowledge, of which Samuel J. Tilden, an eminent lawyer, was a director. Tilden spoke at the Delmonico meeting, and in *The Evening Post* William Cullen Bryant accused him of seeking to launch a revolutionary intrigue to rid the country of President Lincoln. Under Tilden's guidance the Society, as John Jay afterward said, "issued tracts defending slavery, assailing the Government, apologizing for the rebels and demanding peace." New York had become a center of Copperhead conspiracy; in Jay's words, there was "as dangerous an enemy to contend with at home as that which our armies were confronting in the field."

The political situation reflected disaffection and encouraged it. Horatio Seymour, a rabidly anti-war Democrat, had been elected Governor of New York, although the legislature was dominated by the Republicans. In 1861, Mayor Fernando Wood had been defeated for re-election because of financial scandals connected with his administration. He was replaced by George Opdyke, a wealthy importer and banker, and a Republican. But Mayor Opdyke was practically powerless; the Common Council, controlled by Democratic "Boss" William Marcy Tweed, was always able to overrule him. Tweed was no less bitterly opposed to the war than Tilden, whom he disliked, and Wood, of whom he was an avowed political enemy. Wood, out of office, was working with his brother Benjamin, a representative in Congress from New York, and Representative Clement L. Vallandigham of Ohio, who denounced the war as "a costly and bloody failure," to organize the Copperhead Democrats. In New York, their chief organ was the *Daily News,* owned by Benjamin Wood. When, in March 1863, Congress passed the Enrollment and Conscription Act, powerful forces united to make it an issue for the spreading of disaffection. One provision of the law facilitated their purpose. It exempted any drafted man from active service upon payment of three hundred dollars to secure a substitute. This clearly favored the wealthy and worked hardship on the poor.

By protesting the quotas assigned to New York, Governor Seymour succeeded in postponing application of the draft until July. The *Daily News* charged that "the evident design of those who have the Conscription Act in hand in this State is to lessen the number of Democratic votes." Governor Seymour supported this charge by asserting that Democratic districts had been discriminated against in the quotas of men to be drafted. "One out of about two and a half of our citizens," he declared, "are destined to be brought over into Messrs. Lincoln and Company's charnel house." The President's Emancipation Proclamation was likewise used to discredit the draft with the Irish, who constituted approximately one-fourth of the city's population of more than eight hundred thousand. Immigrants, they were reminded, had not crossed the Atlantic to free the slaves.

On the night of July 4th, Governor Seymour addressed a mass meeting of Democrats at the Academy of Music. Alluding to the draft, scheduled to begin exactly one week later, he threatened the Republican administration with disorder. "Remember this: that the bloody, treasonable and revolutionary doctrine of public necessity can be proclaimed by a mob as well as by a government." Boss Tweed and his henchman, District Attorney A. Oakey Hall, were among those who led the ovation which Governor Seymour's incendiary speech received. Two days before the draft was to begin in New York City, Governor Seymour left the state for a holiday in fashionable Long Branch, New Jersey.

To carry out the draft in New York, the War Department appointed, as Provost Marshal, Colonel Robert Nugent of the Sixty-ninth Regiment. Like most of that regiment, Nugent was a Democrat and of Irish extraction; his appointment was probably intended to assure the New York Irish that the draft would be fairly conducted. The city was divided into districts, in each of which was an enrollment office where names were to be drawn from revolving lottery wheels. The draft began as scheduled, on Saturday, July 11th, in the first enrollment office to be ready for operation. This was located on Third Avenue, at the corner of Forty-sixth Street. During the day, twelve hundred names were drawn. From early morning, until six o'clock when the wheel ceased turning, crowds surrounded the building. A corporal with a squad of men from the Invalid Corps and a sergeant with a dozen policemen were on duty to maintain order. No disorders occurred. On Monday, July 13th, drafting was to be resumed at the Third Avenue enrollment office, and was to begin at another office on Broadway near Twenty-eighth Street.

At an unusually early hour, groups of men and bands of women had begun to assemble, as if in accordance with a fixed plan, on Sixth Avenue and the avenues to the west. They then moved northward, stopping at every workshop and factory and compelling the workers to join them, to a vacant lot near Central Park. They were armed with clubs, iron bars, knives and other weapons. When all the bands had met at their rendezvous, they divided into two forces, marched down Fifth and Sixth Avenues to Forty-sixth Street, and turned east. Crossing Fourth Avenue, small squads cut down the telegraph poles along the tracks of the Harlem and New Haven Railway. The united forces then proceeded to the enrollment office at Forty-sixth Street and Third Avenue. Meanwhile other forces, moving northward on Second and Third Avenues from Cooper Institute, had stopped all horse-cars and were entering every shop and plant, forcing the workers to join them.

The squad of police on duty at the enrollment office were incapable of any action when, at ten o'clock, a pistol shot was heard. This was the signal for attack by the mob. A volley of paving stones crashed through the windows of the office, and the front ranks of the crowd surged in, wrecking the furniture and destroying the lottery wheel. Enraged because the drafting officers had escaped through a rear door, they set fire to the building, the upper part of which was occupied as a tenement. The adjoining buildings, similarly occupied, were soon in flames. Superintendent of Police John A. Kennedy, who

ATTENTION!

By Resolution of a large Meeting of the Merchants and Bankers of New York, held at two o'clock, at the Merchants' Exchange. Merchants are requested to close their Stores, and meet with their Employees on South side of Wall St., for immediate organization.
July 14, 2 P. M.

had hurried to the scene in civilian clothes, was recognized by members of the mob at Forty-sixth Street and Lexington Avenue, mercilessly beaten and thrown into an excavation filled with water from which he was rescued by a friend. A detachment of the Invalid Corps, arriving on the scene, tried to disperse the mob by firing a volley of blank cartridges. But, roused to fury, the mob charged the crippled veterans, beating two of them to death with their own muskets.

The disabling of Kennedy left Thomas C. Acton, head of the Board of Police Commissioners, in legal charge of the police force. Like Kennedy and the other commissioners, Acton was a Republican. Like them, he had been appointed by the Republican legislature, which still retained control of the Metropolitan Police. Acton was cool-headed and quick-witted. Convinced that the riot marked the beginning of a general outbreak that might spread to every part of the city, he ordered all police reserves to concentrate at headquarters, on Mulberry Street near Bleecker, where they would be available as a mobile force. He also ordered the city's squad of seventeen detectives to disguise themselves and mingle with the rioters. Their reports, as well as certain significant occurrences, soon made it clear that the leaders of the riot were acting under direction and that their purpose was not merely to stop the draft.

At the Broadway enrollment office, near Twenty-eighth Street, drafting had begun without disturbance. But all draft offices throughout the city were ordered closed before noon, and news of the suspension of the draft was quickly circulating. It did not stop the rioting. The main telegraph lines converging in police headquarters were cut soon after violence broke out. The mob knew nothing about these lines, and those who cut them must have been instructed by someone having full knowledge of the police telegraph system. Police telegraphers managed to splice the lines and restore communication between headquarters and the various stations. By afternoon, the rails of the New Haven and Harlem Railroads on Fourth Avenue, and those of the Hudson Railroad on Eleventh Avenue, had been torn up, isolating the city from direct approach by train. But perhaps most significant of all was an apparently minor episode. A band of rioters went to the residence of Mayor Opdyke, on Fifth Avenue, and were about to sack it when Justice George G. Barnard appeared on the stoop of the adjoining house and addressed them. Justice Barnard had been elevated to the Supreme Court by Boss Tweed, and everyone in New York knew that he was Tweed's intimate and tool. At Barnard's command, the rioters promptly abandoned their attack on Mayor Opdyke's home and withdrew.

By noon, a squad of sixty policemen sent to disperse the rioters at the Third Avenue enrollment office had been put to rout. They were attacked with clubs, iron bars, guns and pistols; stones and brickbats rained down on them from the roofs of houses. A whole block of houses was in flames. Fifty thousand rioters swarmed on Third Avenue, from Cooper Institute to Forty-sixth Street. Large bands detached themselves from this main mass. One mob sacked a block of residences on Lexington Avenue. Another attacked the enrollment office on Broadway near Twenty-eighth Street, pillaged the adjacent jewelry stores and other shops, and set fire to the entire block of buildings. A third mob, several thousand strong, stormed the large building of the Union Steam Works at Second Avenue and Twenty-first Street. This had been converted into a factory for the manufacture of military rifles, and it held great stores of arms and ammunition. The building had been occupied by thirty-five policemen, and they had armed themselves. At first they did not fire on the mob, although stones and bricks came crashing through the windows and an attempt was made to set the building on fire. But when the leader of the mob smashed through the door with a sledge hammer, they killed him. Forced to retreat, they escaped, one by one, through a hole in the rear wall of the building. The mob entered, armed itself, and set the building on fire; many were trapped by the rapid explosions which made it a roaring furnace.

Meanwhile, several thousand rioters attacked the Colored Orphan Asylum, which occupied the block on the west side of Fifth Avenue between Forty-third and Forty-fourth Streets. It was a four-story building, inhabited by more than two hundred Negro children and a staff of matrons and attendants. Foreseeing trouble, Superintendent Davis had arranged to evacuate his charges through rear doors of the institution. He was able to do this while the mob was storming the front gates. The rioters pillaged the building, destroyed all heavy furniture and equipment and set fires everywhere. When firemen arrived, the rioters beat them off. The massive institution was soon a sheet of flame. The mob then crossed Fifth Avenue and set fire to the wooden Allerton Hotel, a tavern frequented by drovers and employees of the adjacent Bull's Head Cattle Market and slaughterhouses. The Negro children who were safely evacuated from the Orphan Asylum fared far better than other members of their race. Mobs all over the city pursued, beat, and in many cases killed any Negroes they found.

Late in the afternoon, a report reached police headquarters that five thousand rioters were on their way down Broadway for the purpose of capturing and breaking up the center of police operations. Commissioner Acton detailed Sergeant Daniel Carpenter, with two hundred policemen, to go up Broadway and meet this mob. His order to Carpenter was, "Sergeant, make no

THE DRAFT RIOTS OF 1863. Police charging the rioters on Broadway

arrests." Although the mob was armed with clubs, iron bars and some firearms, Carpenter and his men charged them, cracking skulls with their clubs. The battle raged for an hour, in uproar and confusion. Then the rioters broke ranks and fled down side streets. Broadway was thickly strewn with their dead, dying and injured.

Meanwhile, Mayor Opdyke had appealed for assistance to Brigadier General Harvey Brown, commanding the garrison in the harbor forts. General Brown brought three hundred troops into the city. The Brooklyn Navy Yard sent a detachment of marines. Some soldiers and marines were detailed to guard Federal buildings which offered tempting prizes to the rioters, among them the Sub-Treasury and Arsenal. The rest were assigned to work with the police. The Navy Yard stationed two armed ships in the lower Hudson and East Rivers, where their guns covered the financial district. Mayor Opdyke urged the War Department to send additional troops to the city as quickly as possible. He requested military assistance from the governors of all nearby states. An appeal to Governor Seymour to return to the city was fruitless; the Governor did not arrive until the next day. Late in the evening, a huge mob surged across City Hall Park, smashed the windows of the *Tribune* Building, broke into it and sacked the lower floors. Police and troops, after heavy fighting, broke up this mob and cleared the district. But until late at night, in various quarters of the town, street fighting, the firing of buildings and the killing of people continued. Riot had taken on the look of revolution.

On Tuesday morning New York was a panic-stricken city. No horse-cars or omnibuses were running. No places of business or banks or factories were open. Some four hundred stalwart citizens had made their way to police headquarters to volunteer for duty, had been sworn in and furnished with clubs and badges. But terror gripped the middle classes. The few who could secure hacks and were able to pay the extortionate prices demanded set out with their families for railroad stations in Westchester or on the Hudson. Crowds hastened toward steamboat and ferry landings. Every boat, as it swung from the dock, was overloaded with people leaving a metropolis that seemed doomed to destruction. The continual clangor of fire-bells, the barking of muskets and howitzers, the flames rising all over the city and the dense pall of smoke increased a terror that spread, like a plague, from street to street. Very early in the morning large bands of rioters had assembled at strategic points in every quarter of the city north of police headquarters; mobs were at work even in such outlying districts as Yorkville, Manhattanville and Harlem. An attempt was made to burn the bridge across the Harlem River, but this failed because during the night there had been a heavy rainstorm. However, in their effort to isolate the city completely, the rioters succeeded in burning down the Weehawken Ferry buildings and docks at Forty-second Street on the Hudson River.

A fierce battle took place on Second Avenue from Twenty-first to Thirty-second Streets. Rioters not only filled the avenue, but with piles of stones and brickbats had climbed to the roofs of houses and rained their missiles on police and soldiers. The police cleared the houses of assailants by fighting their way to the roofs, then clubbing the rioters there, and throwing some headlong to the pavement. Meanwhile, the troops used howitzers and rifles with deadly effect on the mob of men and women opposing them on the avenue. The officer who took command of this engagement, Colonel O'Brien, was a well-known resident of the district. When later in the day he tried to return to his home alone, he was brutally tortured for several hours by a gang of ruffians, and finally murdered. Shortly afterward, another sharp battle took place on Second Avenue near Twenty-first Street, where there was a warehouse in which several thousand carbines were stored. The leader of the rioters, here, was a man of desperate courage. He was killed, and was found to be a young man of delicate features and fair, white skin. "Although dressed as a laborer, in dirty overalls and filthy shirt, underneath these there were fine cassimere pants, handsome rich vest, and fine linen shirt," the police afterward reported. This leader was obviously a man of far higher social position than any of his mob, and had apparently disguised himself to prevent identification by the police. His name was never learned. His corpse, during the long-drawn battle, disappeared with the bodies of many others.

Governor Seymour finally arrived in the city, went to the St. Nicholas Hotel on Broadway, then joined Mayor Opdyke at City Hall, where fifty armed policemen were holding off an angry, belligerent mass of rioters. They cheered the Governor, who addressed them as his friends, whose interests and welfare he had returned to serve. He requested them to depart peaceably. They did —to continue their work of destruction, murder and pillage. On Eighth and Ninth Avenues, mobs erected sets of barricades by lashing carts, wagons and telegraph poles together with the cut telegraph wires. The barricades extended from Thirty-seventh to Forty-third Streets, and each of them was bitterly contested with the police and troops sent to reduce them. The use of barricades in street fighting was unknown to New York, although familiar to Paris, and this fact confirmed a prevailing impression that the rioters were acting under direction.

Rioting continued, unabated, until on Thursday, July 16th, five regiments of New York troops were returned by the Army of the Potomac. By midnight of that day, the military and police were in full control of the city. By the following day thirteen regiments of regular troops were in the city. The newspapers resumed publication on Friday morning, ironically displaying a proclamation by Governor Seymour declaring the city in a state of insurrection. But the insurrection had been quelled, though without any aid from the Governor. Some twelve hundred people had been killed; the number of injured was never known; two million dollars' worth of property had been destroyed, according to conservative estimates.

Military forces remained on duty in New York until, one month after its reign of terror, the draft was resumed without disorder. The identity of the men who planned, inspired and directed the draft riot was never disclosed. And the Federal Government, after an investigation, took no action against them.

4

High, Wide and Handsome

"The papers are full of the underworld; and the people must see it everywhere, whether they seek for it or not," a widely circulated book told the nation. "The New York underworld is a very passable imitation of its Parisian original. Perhaps in some respects it has surpassed its model."

Brooding on the iniquities of the metropolis in January, 1866, Bishop Simpson of the Methodist Episcopal Church was moved to protest. He made no invidious comparisons with Paris, for he was more startled by a purely domestic equation. There were as many public prostitutes in New York as there were Methodists, he told an audience at Cooper Union, and in a sermon at St. Paul's Church he set their number at twenty thousand.

These "monstrous statements" saddened John A. Kennedy, Superintendent of Police. Was it not his duty to correct the misguided impressions of such well-meaning men as Bishop Simpson? Superintendent Kennedy ordered a census taken by the police, and issued some reassuring statistics. New York had only six hundred and twenty-one houses of prostitution, ninety-nine houses of assignation, and seventy-five concert saloons of ill repute. The number of public prostitutes was a mere thirty-three hundred, and these included seven hundred and forty-seven "waiter girls in concert and drinking saloons." There were, of course, "other women," Superintendent Kennedy acknowledged, but he had no means of determining their number, presumably large. Yet, on the whole, he felt relieved. Conditions in New York were far better than might have been expected.

But statistics were actually irrelevant. Variety, not number, was the distinctive feature of New York's life of pleasure. Its available satisfactions, as the whole nation knew, catered to every form of taste. In no other American city was temptation as perfectly adapted to the versatility of which the single-minded male is capable. The metropolitan underworld never slept; it did business round the clock in every quarter of the town; there was almost no idiosyncrasy which it failed to gratify. Day and night, at all seasons of the year, women of the town paraded Broadway from Canal Street to Madison Square. Formerly, they were never seen before dusk. But now, tripping along in the promenade of the fashionable afternoon shopping hours, they were called "streetwalkers" or "cruisers." You could distinguish them by a saucy stare, a quick backward glance of invitation cast over a trim shoulder. They loitered at the show windows of the finest shops, and before the entrances of the luxury hotels: the St. Nicholas, Metropolitan and Fifth Avenue. On sun-drenched spring days they flirted their parasols; in the early winter twilight, when Broadway was deep in snow and rang with sleigh bells, they swung their muffs with a jaunty air. You saw them in the evening, after the dinner hour, and again as the theaters were closing, moving slowly under the flare of the gaslamps; at midnight, at one, two, three or even four o'clock in the morning. On summer nights, the benches of the pleasant midtown parks—Washington

HOOKING A VICTIM, 1850, *by Serrell and Perkins*

Square, Union Square and Madison Square—were occupied by young women demurely but explicitly accessible.

For the hurried businessman, during his crowded working hours, New York had developed a peculiar institution of pleasure: the "cigar-store battery." These batteries flourished in abundance far downtown. To uninitiated passers-by, they had the appearance of bona-fide cigar stores. Their display windows were filled with cigar boxes, and inside a few cigars were actually exposed for sale. These, as misguided customers were always perplexed by discovering, were reluctantly parted with at from twenty-five to fifty cents apiece. The batteries were presided over by young women of keen discrimination, invariably able to recognize a knowing male when they saw one. To potential clients, they suggested that behind the shop, or upstairs, there were private rooms desirably occupied and that liquid refreshment was to be had at a price. Along a few blocks of Canal Street, there were seven of these establishments; on West Broadway, six; on Franklin Street, three. During the lunch hour and in the late afternoon when men were leaving their places of business the girls employed by these batteries lined up behind the display windows and solicited passers-by.

All visitors to New York wanted to see Greene Street by night, for it was the most notorious thoroughfare in the United States. Two blocks west of Broadway, extending from Canal Street northward to Clinton Place, later Eighth Street, by daylight it had the look of a decaying residential quarter lined with red-brick, low-stooped houses now grown shabby—a quiet, deserted street. Greene Street only came alive after dark. Along its whole length, on both sides, nearly every house was a brothel. Over the front doors, gaslamps blazed in bowls of tinted glass, usually red but of other colors also. On these lamps the names of the proprietor, or of the establishment, were etched in clear white: "Flora," "Lizzie," "The Gem," "The Forget-Me-Not," "Sinbad the Sailor," "The Black Crook." The houses at the lower end of Greene Street, near Canal, catered to the crews of ships docked along the Hudson River. At that end of the street, also, were the celebrated "ballrooms." These were large, low-ceilinged halls, with a platform at one end for the musicians and opposite this a long bar. Girls, being the principal attraction, were admitted free; men paid an admission of twenty-five cents. In these ballrooms, dancing and drinking was carried on until daylight, and there you could see at its best the Parisian can-can, performed by tall, long-legged girls in frilly skirts who kicked high above their heads. As you went northward along Greene Street, the quality of the brothels improved and their charges mounted. There were establishments catering to clerks and small tradesmen; up near Clinton Place were the houses for more prosperous members of the middle class. All along Greene Street the shutters were tightly closed, but here or there you could see a light peeping through from a parlor or upper room. Every house had its pianist, who entertained in the parlor where liquor was sold, and the whole street echoed with the popular music of the day.

Flora's was the most notorious, costly and well-conducted brothel in Greene Street, and had earned a sizable fortune for its proprietor. She was a handsome, middle-aged woman who dressed with the greatest elegance and had furnished her establishment with considerable luxury. Years earlier, she had become infatuated with the wayward son of a prosperous New York family, and had intrigued him into marrying her. They lived together several years, and she bore him a daughter. Then her husband became too familiar with the ladies of the house, and Flora sent him away. Or so she said; he suddenly disappeared, and no trace of him could ever be found. Flora educated her daughter at a boarding school, and the girl was kept in ignorance of her mother's history and profession. Placed to live with a respectable family as their relative, and given an attractive dowry, Flora's daughter eventually married well. Meanwhile Flora managed her business shrewdly and profitably. She was said to have excellent banking connections. She had agents in various parts of the country to recruit pretty girls for her establishment. Rumor asserted that she paid well, in the proper quarters, to be free of molestation by the police. But they had no reason to interfere with her, for breaches of decorum never occurred at Flora's. In Greene Street, that made her house unique.

There were far more luxurious establishments—called "parlor houses"— in better quarters of the city. Two of these achieved nationwide celebrity. "The Seven Sisters" took its name from a musical revue produced by Laura Keene in 1860, which achieved an unbroken run of more than two hundred and fifty performances. Appropriately, "The Seven Sisters" occupied seven adjoining brownstone residences on West Twenty-fifth Street near Seventh Avenue, which made it the largest establishment of its kind in the city. It was one of the most expensive brothels in New York, and was conducted with an almost intimidating elegance. No lamp or sign identified it, but it was known to every cab-driver and hotel clerk, and patrons of the great hotels whose arrival in the city had been noted in the newspapers usually found, in their morning mail, a chaste engraved invitation to visit "The Seven Sisters." Their reception was likely to be more cordial if they arrived in formal evening attire. The girls in this establishment—so it was promised—were cultivated, conversationally resourceful, versed in the etiquette of the best society, proficient pianists, guitarists and singers.

The establishment of Josephine Woods on Clinton Place between University Place and Broadway was smaller, less ostentatious, but professedly more select. Josie Woods, though no longer young, was a dark-haired, graceful woman of arresting beauty whose costly dresses, magnificent diamonds and fine carriage and horses were the talk of the city. Ladies who saw her at the theater, or driving in Central Park, or at Long Branch and Saratoga Springs in the summer, found it hard to believe that she actually cultivated so unspeakable a profession. She had the air of belonging in superior social circles. And in a sense she did. Her establishment received no strangers. Its clientele was drawn from New York's aristocracy, and aspirants to admission required preliminary certification. A butler answered the doorbell, but did not open the door until he had inspected the visitor through a grille. The parlors of the house were as sumptuously appointed as those of a Fifth Avenue mansion, with chairs and sofas upholstered in satin and brocade, velvet carpets, crystal chandeliers, with gilt-framed mirrors and fine paintings on the walls, with pianos and harps and marble statues on pedestals, and little tables displaying the latest books and magazines among a clutter of decorative objects in silver and enamel. In these rooms the visitor waited before being joined by Josie's girls. The establishment offered only twenty. They entered, two or three at a time, wearing evening dresses. All were beautiful, and as a collection they were remarkable for the variety of their attractions. Nothing but champagne was served in Josie's parlors; the cheapest brand sold at eight dollars a bottle. All prices in this house were extremely high. They had to be. The girls were charged from fifty to one hundred dollars a week for their rooms and board, but it was said that on a busy night any of them might earn as much as two hundred dollars. Josie Woods, a cultivated woman, disliked any allusion to the financial aspect of her hospitality. She was a gracious hostess, and was seen at her best on New Year's Day. Then, with her girls, she kept open house in the traditional manner of New York ladies, remaining at home to dispense refreshment to the gentlemen who, from noon until midnight, were engaged in paying rounds of ceremonious calls.

Before visiting Flora's on Greene Street, or one of the parlor houses further uptown, a man on pleasure bent might spend some hours drifting from one concert saloon to another. These were a new kind of resort; the Franklin Museum, in Grand Street, offering "female models, the finest formed women in the world" was the first in the field. Within a few years, some three hundred were in operation. When Superintendent Kennedy announced that only seventy-five were of ill repute wise New Yorkers acknowledged that he possessed an exceptional talent for understatement. You had only to read the advertising columns of *The Herald* to understand their appeal. The Gaieties Saloon, on Broadway near Houston Street, for example, emphasized that it employed "the prettiest waiter girls to be found in the world," maintaining "agents in all parts of the United States, England and France to engage the most accomplished young ladies. . . . Gentlemen will please call and prove our assertion to be correct. No Boys Admitted!" The advertisement also pointed out that audiences at the Gaieties were of mixed character, "respectable, though by no means stilted in manners," and that middle-aged men, with gray or even white hair, were numerous. The waiter girls, "on whose cheeks the blushes of modesty seem to be set as with the enduring pencil of the painter —these girls were not slaves, servants even—they were companions." Most of the better class concert saloons were on, or near, Broadway; the most degraded and dangerous were on William Street, Chatham Street and the Bowery, and along the perimeter of the Five Points.

On the dark streets leading off Broadway, below Bleecker, you saw the gay, blazing "transparencies" that hung out over the entrances of concert saloons, illuminating the posters which announced the names of entertainers currently performing within. Admission for gentlemen was usually twenty-five cents; ladies were admitted free. Many of these establishments were in basements. You descended the steps and found yourself in a large smoke-filled hall, where at small tables crowds of men and women were chattering and drinking. There was usually a space of clear floor on which patrons could dance between "turns" by the entertainers. At one end of the hall there was a stage for the orchestra and entertainers; an immense bar, often served by as many as a dozen bartenders, occupied one side. Nobody was permitted to drink at the bar, orders being taken from tables by the "pretty waiter girls" who were the distinctive feature of all concert saloons. From one to another place, their costume seldom varied: a low-cut bodice, very short skirts, bare legs encased in high, tasseled red boots. It was a pleasant characteristic of these resorts that a solitary male would not long suffer any want of feminine companionship.

The most elaborate, costly and refined of all concert saloons, and the only one located uptown, was the Louvre. This vast establishment was on Broadway and Twenty-third Street, overlooking fashionable Madison Square, a stone's throw from the new mansion of Mrs. William Colford Schermerhorn and the residences of other leaders of New York's exalted society. Occupying the larger part of a city block, the spacious rooms of the Louvre included a grand drinking hall with a great, ornate, mirrored bar and a sparkling fountain, a billiard parlor and smaller, more quiet lounges in which champagne only was served. The Louvre was one of the "sights" of New York, with its glittering crystal chandeliers, its tall marble columns, its walls paneled in gold and emerald and frescoed with baskets of luscious fruits and bouquets of vivid flowers. The waiter girls of the Louvre were the prettiest in the city, and their favors were highly esteemed by gilded youth. But the place was especially celebrated as the habitual resort of New York's most expensive, fashionable and beautiful *demi-mondaines* who, if in a state of transient disjunction, frequented the Louvre to win new friends and cultivate the art of real happiness.

Yet it was a concert saloon of very different type which, for two decades, had the widest fame throughout the United States. No visitor to New York would have thought of returning home without having gone at least once to Harry Hill's place on Houston Street, east of Broadway. New Yorkers considered Hill a celebrity or, as they said, a "character"—he was both unmistakably typical of the city and notably individual. A short, stocky, muscular, heavily mustached man about fifty years of age, he looked like a pugilist and had been a champion wrestler. He remained a leading figure in the sporting world, and was frequently appointed stake-holder for prizefights. Originally, he had opened his place as a "drum," or rendezvous for pugilists and wrestlers, and it continued to be the favorite resort of professional sportsmen, gamblers, politicians and the racetrack crowd. Frequently, during the winter, Hill replaced his usual entertainment by a prizefight or series of sparring matches, or gave his wrestling friends a chance to show their form. But

THE MOST NOTORIOUS DANCE-HOUSE IN AMERICA. Harry Hill's
Concert Saloon, a mecca of sporting men, criminals, politicians and prostitutes

it was his pride, as he said, that his clientele included "judges, lawyers, merchants, members of Congress and the State Legislature, doctors and other
professional men." Indeed, Hill's place catered to all classes and conditions;
there the wealthy and reputable mingled on even terms with prizefighters,
bullies, pickpockets, prostitutes, shoplifters, counterfeiters, vendors of opium
and other drugs and similar desperate characters. Yet Hill boasted that no
person was ever robbed of jewelry, watch or money while in his establishment.

Hill professed to be devoutly religious, made large gifts to charity, refused
to open his place on Sundays and closed it promptly at midnight on other
evenings. But he took a cynical view of American business civilization. American men, he claimed, were driven to bouts of dissipation by the relentless pressure of money-making, the need to take ever larger risks, the hazards of
enormous losses and spectacular reverses. Since dissipation was essential, he
considered himself a public benefactor for providing it in circumstances of
reasonable security. He kept a close watch on his prominent patrons and,
when he thought they had drunk enough or were otherwise in danger, either
sent for their friends or removed them to a private room to sober up. He
was addicted to composing rhymes, and the rules of the house, conspicuously
posted on every wall, were among his more notable poetic efforts. Reduced
to prose, they commanded: "No loud talking; no profanity, no obscene or
indecent expression will be allowed; no one drunken, and no one violating
decency, will be permitted to remain in the room; no man can sit and allow
a woman to stand; all must call for refreshments as soon as they arrive; the
call must be repeated after each dance; and if a man does not dance he must

leave." Hill did not hesitate to knock down, and then kick out into Houston Street, any violator of these rules. He kept the roughs and bullies in order; kept jealous women from tearing out one another's eyes; kept noisy drunks quiet. He walked about incessantly, shouting out, "Order! Order!—Less noise, there!—Girls, be quiet!"—or, when an entertainer was about to perform, "Attention!"

Harry Hill's place made no concession to the new taste for an atmosphere of luxury. A huge red-and-blue glass lantern identified it, and it occupied the whole of a large, shabby, two-story frame house. There were two entrances; one for men, another for women, who were admitted free. The ground-floor room, with its long bar and counter where oysters and sandwiches were sold, was reserved for Hill's sporting patrons. Upstairs was the dance hall, with a counter on one side where, after every dance, couples ordered their drinks, which were brought to the table by a waiter girl. Hill always had at least one hundred girls on hand for his patrons to dance with, and he insisted that they be well-dressed and well-behaved while in his establishment. Patrons selected their own girls; if they did not, Hill assigned them partners. It was his inflexible rule that whatever bargains were made, alliances formed, or traps set for the unwary male, no victim must be snared while at Harry Hill's; any crime to be committed must take place elsewhere. As a result, his place was distinguished as the only "reputable vile house" in New York.

In time, night prowlers came to have a keener appetite for squalor and danger. Pleasure was intensified by the thrilling possibilities of assault, robbery and the addition to liquid refreshment of knockout-drops. These were customary practices in the low concert saloons of William Street, Chatham Street and the Bowery, and they were eventually made available to reputable folk in quest of new sensations. Later, a tour of New York's night town was not complete without a visit to Billy McGlory's Armory Hall on Hester Street, near Mott, notorious as the favorite resort of gangsters, thugs and other criminals. Brawls and bloodshed were commonplace at McGlory's. The incautious visitor who came there alone might be drugged, robbed, tossed into the street and then stripped of all his clothing. McGlory, a former Five Points gangster, reinforced his staff of waiter girls with a flock of effeminate youths dressed in female attire, and made other equally dubious innovations. For the uptown clientele who visited Armory Hall in parties he installed a balcony above the dance floor. This was divided into separate compartments which could be curtained off and turned into private rooms—and it was generally understood that none of McGlory's waiter girls and boys, his entertainers, or his band of prostitutes was afflicted by any puritanical inhibitions. As an entrepreneur of pleasure, McGlory took pride in his reputation for operating the most vicious and dangerous dive in New York.

But all concert saloons were known to be in some degree dangerous. In the best of them, except for the Louvre and Harry Hill's, you were likely to have your pocket picked. If you left one of them with a girl whom you had picked up there, you might be blackmailed shortly after reaching her room; the "husband game" as it was called, was widely practiced. More probably, however, she would turn out to be the confederate of a panel-thief. The room of a girl working with a panel-thief contained a bed, a dresser and one chair, always placed near a wall, and as far from the bed as possible. The man put his clothes on this chair, since there was no other place for them. Once he was in bed and the gaslight turned out, a panel in the wall behind the chair slid quietly, the thief stretched in his arm, rifled the victim's wallet, and returned it with a few small bills intact. Since the girl always demanded payment in advance, the victim had no reason to examine his wallet before leaving her room. When afterward he discovered the robbery and complained to the police, his story would be received with skepticism. There were still a few bills in his wallet. No doubt he had spent the missing sum while drunk. Why did he come whining to the police? Hadn't he had a run for his money? For years the panel game went on unchecked.

Men of means found no difficulty in having an exciting run for their money whenever they wished. There were a dozen luxurious gambling houses where faro and roulette could be enjoyed from mid-afternoon until far into the night. Of these, the most celebrated was that operated by John Morrisey, the former gangster and pugilist. Morrisey had risen to a position of power in Tammany Hall. He was closely associated with William Marcy Tweed, Street Commissioner, boss of Tammany and political ruler of the city. Tweed later credited Morrisey with having instituted a system of repetitive voting in city elections, and with having discreetly bribed the City Council in order to secure the appointment of Tweed's henchman, Peter B. Sweeney, as City Chamberlain. Morrisey also had his fingers in high finance. He had won the friendship of

THE GEM SALOON AT 324 BROADWAY, 1853, showing Mayor Fernando Wood, *by A. Fay*

Commodore Vanderbilt at Saratoga Springs, where he operated a gambling house during the summer season. When politicians of the New York Legislature formed a conspiracy to wreck the Harlem Railroad, Morrisey acted as political agent for Vanderbilt, and subsequently profited financially when the Commodore revenged himself by creating a spectacular corner in Harlem stock.

Meanwhile, Morrisey was reputed to be making a fortune from his gambling house on Twenty-fourth Street, opposite the Fifth Avenue Hotel. It equaled the finest European casinos in luxury and splendor. The parlors were magnificently appointed. In the dining and supper rooms patrons were served, without charge, the most sumptuous meals and choicest liquors to be had in New York. The gaming rooms were at the far rear, glass-domed, carpeted in velvet, with richly brocaded walls and furniture of rosewood. Play ran high; on a memorable evening the house lost one hundred and twenty-four thousand dollars to Benjamin Wood, brother of Fernando Wood, the former mayor, and patrons often lost or won as much as ten thousand dollars at the faro table. Morrisey neither gambled nor drank. Bearded, suave in manner, soberly clad in black, he was an imposing figure; only the immense diamonds that flashed from his rings, scarf-pin, cuffs and the charms on his watch-chain suggested his profession. To annoy the censorious, fashionable neighbors who complained about his establishment, he announced his candidacy for Congress. When they declared that it would be a disgrace to be represented by a professional gambler, he had himself elected for two terms. To celebrate his victory, he bought his wife the costliest pair of opera glasses obtainable in America; they were made of gold set with diamonds and bore her monogram wrought in pearls. After retiring from Congress, Morrisey gave up his gambling house in New York, moved to Saratoga Springs and there opened a new, luxurious casino. He was twice elected State Senator and when he died, at the age of fifty-seven, members of the Legislature officiated as pallbearers, and ninteeen thousand sorrowing citizens followed his body to the grave in a downpour of rain.

Straitlaced, old fashioned New Yorkers identified such men as Hill and Morrisey with the underworld and placed them beyond the bounds of decency. Yet was it not a sign of the times, an index of the subtle moral distinctions proper to an era which valued anything "modern" and "up-to-date," that Hill and Morrisey were men of prestige? Citizens of high standing not only frequented Hill's place, they boasted of his friendship and were delighted when he indicated his esteem for them. And only pharisees would condemn Morrisey. Had he not come up the hard way from rags to riches? Was he not a man whose influence made him worth cultivating, as old Commodore Vanderbilt had shown? Who could tell when Morrisey's favor would prove useful to some business deal, to some operation the success of which might hinge upon the complaisance of Boss Tweed? Few wide-awake, aggressive businessmen refused to propitiate Morrisey if they had the chance. On any bright afternoon, you would see New York's leading men of affairs—Commodore

Vanderbilt, the banker August Belmont, the publisher Robert Bonner—gladly matching their fast horses against his in Central Park and out on the Harlem Lane.

Yet even a modern-minded society required its public scapegoats, and by common consent New York had bestowed upon two individuals the titles of wickedest man and wickedest woman. Quite understandably, both felt aggrieved. Their services to the community could not be considered superfluous. They were not unique in their professions, but merely conspicuously successful. Neither John Allen nor Madame Restell believed in the moral justice of their obloquy. Were they not in every way as reputable as the genteel society that had provided an opportunity for their careers?

John Allen kept a dance hall and fast house on Water Street, in a fine, large brick building that seemed out of place among the rookeries of the East River waterfront. He was a member of a pious, prosperous upstate family; several of his brothers were clergymen, and he had been a student at the Union Theological Seminary. But the rewards of a clergyman promised to be meager at best and, like many a young American in the eighteen-fifties, Allen's ambition was fired by the example of men who were making millions. He resolved to go into business. He went to Water Street and made a fortune of one hundred thousand dollars. His staff of twenty girls were required to wear low-cut, short scarlet dresses and red-topped boots with bells affixed to their ankles. Every evening at Allen's, it was said, "several hundred partake of the rude fun, among whom are boys and girls below twelve years of age. The atmosphere reeks with blasphemy. The women are driven to their work by imprecations, and often by blows, from their taskmaster." Yet Allen was no apostate. He subscribed to several religious magazines, and these, with various edifying tracts, were placed on the tables. There was a Bible in each of the rooms to which his girls took their clients, and Allen kept one on the bar. He liked to argue about theology with ministers who visited his place to gather material for sermons. Periodically, he assembled his staff, read to them from the Bible, preached a short sermon. Was he not as good a man as Daniel Drew, the great speculator who ruined many investors, but was known as the generous benefactor of many religious institutions? When a journalist wrote up Allen as the wickedest man in New York he was deeply affronted.

A number of prominent evangelists determined, in 1868, to bring Allen to a state of grace. One night, accompanied by several devout laymen, they descended on Allen's place, found him drunk, and proceeded to hold a long prayer meeting. The public sensation that resulted pleased Allen, and when the evangelists proposed to continue the services he agreed. Sightseers began to crowd the place, but Allen's regular clientele drifted away, to the detriment of his profits. After several months, the clergymen announced that Allen had been converted, was a reformed man, had closed his establishment and would never resume his former occupation. Meanwhile, for one month, daily revival meetings would be held in his dance hall, in which Allen would join. But while the whole city marveled at the redemption of John Allen, and at the prospect that Water Street might be brought to a better life, a cynical newspaper reporter exposed the true facts. The worthy clergymen and their devout supporters had merely made a financial deal with Allen. They had rented his place for one month at a large fee. In consideration of this payment, he was required to announce his conversion, to declare that he had freely donated the use of his property for religious purposes as an act of expiation, to make public profession of his redemption by taking part in the daily revival services. When the lease on his establishment terminated and Allen tried to re-open it, his former clients refused to patronize him. He soon retired from business, a perplexed and embittered man.

Madame Restell, unlike Allen, could neither be forced out of business nor dislodged from her large brownstone home on the northeast corner of Fifth Avenue and Fifty-second Street. She was aware of her power in the community and did not hesitate to intimate it. She declared that she had secret information concerning many eminent New Yorkers; that if she wished she could open rich and fragrant closets, and expose skeletons whose existence nobody suspected. In the city directory, and in the newspapers, Madame Restell announced herself as a professor of midwifery. She advertised her offices on Chambers and Greenwich Streets, her "infallible French female pills," her thirty years of practice, and she guaranteed "a cure at one interview." But she scarcely required this publicity. She was notorious as the most expensive abortionist in the city. As the tide of fashion ascended Fifth Avenue and drew near the street to which she had preceded it, Madame Restell was repeatedly offered fabulous sums for her property. She refused to sell.

RESIDENCE OF THE NOTORIOUS MADAME RESTELL, 1869, northeast corner of 52nd Street and Fifth Avenue

Why should the aristocracy dislike having her as a neighbor? She had done much good by preventing the misfortunes of people of position from coming to light. She had saved the reputations of many good but misguided women. She had, on the whole, increased the sum of human happiness, not diminished it.

The brownstone wash of wealth flowed up Fifth Avenue, and Madame Restell remained in her home, despised, feared, objectionably scandalous. Men remembered that twenty years earlier she had been brought to trial as a result of the death, in her former home downtown, of a girl who had been placed there for treatment. Though the evidence had been sufficient to convict her, she was acquitted. It was said that she had brought political influence to bear on the judge; that she had purchased her freedom at the cost of one hundred thousand dollars. Recalling that ancient triumph, the godly concluded that she was now too rich to be dislodged and too powerful to be eliminated from practice. They saw her, on pleasant afternoons, a hard-visaged, black-haired woman, fashionably dressed, descend the stoop of her home, enter a glittering carriage attended by two men in livery, and set off for her daily drive in Central Park. Madame Killer, she was called, the wickedest woman in town. At night, coaches frequently stopped at the side of her home, and muffled female figures would hurriedly enter the house. Sometimes, at three or four in the morning, a late reveler might see a hearse waiting at that door.

One day in 1878, a respectable, whiskered young man came to consult Madame Restell in the office which she maintained in the basement of her home. She had had some correspondence from him, and knew his story. He was desperately poor; his wife was pregnant; the birth of another child would bring them to ruin. Madame Restell gladly gave him her professional advice, and provided him with medicine and instruments for his wife. She was somewhat surprised when, ungratefully, he arrested her, identifying himself as Anthony Comstock, a crusader against vice. She sent for her carriage, and accompanied him to the Tombs. On the way, she offered him forty thousand dollars to drop his charges. He refused, but Madame Restell secured her release on bail. She returned to her Fifth Avenue home. There, early in the morning a few days later, one of her seven servants found Madame Restell's body on the floor of her bathroom, in a pool of blood. During the night, she had cut her throat. About moral issues, New Yorkers were likely to be dogmatic, however confused. A letter in *The Congregationalist* and an editorial in *The Sun* dealt with the passing of Madame Killer. Both expressed repugnance for her long, nefarious career. And both unreservedly condemned Anthony Comstock for having brought her to suicide by making her the victim of fraud.

"FIFTH AVENUE A YEAR AFTER THE DEATH OF MADAME RESTELL"

5

Tear
a Passion
to Tatters

O n an autumn morning in 1850, huge crowds lined Broadway from Canal Street south to Chambers. One of the most famous women of the age was about to arrive in New York, and everybody wanted to see her. "The visit of Jenny Lind to America," an editor declared, "is the first step in a new epoch." No singer capable of pleasing a European capital or a royal court had ever before considered coming to America. But Phineas T. Barnum, New York's greatest showman, captured the Swedish Nightingale. He offered her, so he said, more money than any singer had ever been paid anywhere. Though already fabulously wealthy, she was unable to resist the promised dazzling fortune.

Barnum brought public curiosity to a high pitch with his stories about Jenny Lind. She was the personal friend of Queen Victoria, as well as her favorite singer. Like the Queen, she was noted for piety and devotion to good works. She had endowed a home for poor girls in her native Stockholm. In England, she had donated sixty thousand dollars to charity in two months. She had given up singing opera because operatic heroines were usually abandoned women. She had refused to sing in Paris, knowing it to be a city steeped in immorality and vice. A *cantatrice* of impeccable virtue—Jenny Lind was a more amazing prodigy than any you could see in Barnum's Museum.

The *S.S. Atlantic* docked at Canal Street. On the pier were two triumphal arches bearing greetings inscribed in flowers. Under these, in solemn procession, the diva was preceded by her suite. Julius Benedict, the composer, who was to serve as her conductor and accompanist; the baritone, Signor Belletti;

Mme. Ahmansson, her companion; a secretary, a personal maid and a courier. Fat, genial Barnum rushed forward to salute his star. She was of medium height, and not a breath-taking beauty. She had a massive nose with thin nostrils "like a race-horse," as one admirer noted. He thought her eyes were her best feature; pools of "serene and lambent earnestness." Everyone was struck by her expression "of utter simplicity and goodness." She wore a hat of pale-blue silk trimmed with lace, a slate-colored dress, and a broad-cloth coat embellished with bands of velvet.

Barnum escorted Jenny Lind and her companion to his private barouche. He mounted the box beside his coachman, "as a legitimate advertisement," and between cheering crowds they were driven to the Irving House on Broadway and Chambers Street. Ten minutes after the diva entered her hotel, twenty thousand New Yorkers were milling about on Broadway. All afternoon and evening the police struggled with swelling crowds. Possibly at Barnum's suggestion, the Nightingále remained invisible. At midnight, a huge crowd still waited on Broadway. The police had to clear room for the New York Musical Fund Society who, accompanied by three hundred red-shirted volunteer firemen bearing flaring torches, came to serenade Jenny Lind. Following this unprecedented tribute, the shouts for Lind became so insistent that Barnum led her through a window to her balcony. There, she stood bowing and kissing her hands to an adoring public.

JENNY LIND AT CASTLE GARDEN, September 11, 1850, *by N. Currier*

By the night of Jenny Lind's first concert, Barnum had whipped up public excitement to fever heat. Seats for the concert were sold at auction, and the fashionable hatter John N. Genin achieved sudden notoriety by buying the first ticket for two hundred and twenty-five dollars. On the night of the concert, the doors of Castle Garden were opened at five o'clock, though the performance was not to begin until eight. The chief of police with sixty policemen tried to keep order in the immense mob that gathered in Battery Park. On the water surrounding Castle Garden hundreds of New Yorkers were bobbing about in small boats. An audience of six thousand people filled the vast auditorium. The orchestra played an overture. The baritone, Belletti, sang an aria. Then, clad in an exquisite white ball dress, Jenny Lind came on the stage. There was a salvo of applause, and the audience rose to its feet in tribute. Jenny Lind took her place beside the conductor, responded to the ovation with a deep curtsy. Benedict rapped his baton, and Jenny Lind sang the "Casta Diva" from Bellini's opera *Norma* in the original key of F—a feat never before attempted in New York. "She sings like a woman with no weakness," N. P. Willis reported; "there is plenty of soul in her singing, but no flesh and blood." She sang other selections, most notably the Swedish "Herdsman's Song," or "Echo Song," which was to become, in the United States, her most celebrated number. During the prolonged ovation that followed the concert, Jenny Lind happily brought Barnum out on the stage.

Both had good reason to feel happy. For her first concert, Jenny Lind received twelve thousand, six hundred dollars, thereby probably setting a permanent record. She donated all of this money to New York's philanthropic and cultural institutions. The volunteer firemen who honored her on the night of her arrival received three thousand dollars. Her extraordinary generosity conquered New York. "A hostile army or fleet," Philip Hone declared, "could not effect a conquest so complete." It made little difference to the public that captious critics asserted that Jenny Lind would have been the better for a little less purity, a lot more passion. Every one of her concerts was sold out far in advance. "It is amazing how people spend their money," James Fenimore Cooper grumbled to his wife. "Twenty or thirty dollars to hear Jenny are paid by those who live from hand to mouth." People were in raptures about her, he acknowledged, but—"I cannot consent to pay thirty dollars for a concert, and they are welcome to their ecstasies."

The furor caused by Jenny Lind, the golden rewards of American success, soon brought many renowned European singers and actresses to New York. Considerable interest was aroused by a personage whose worldwide celebrity derived neither from talent nor virtue. It had never occurred to Lola Montez that respectability merited her attention. This oversight made possible a career of conquest which, in six years, swept her from the *corps de ballet* of a Paris theater into a royal palace. The elderly King of Bavaria, Ludwig I, made her his mistress, gave her the title Countess Landsfeld, and permitted her to have her say about affairs of state. All Europe rang with the scandal. Eventually, the infatuated king was forced to abdicate his throne, and Lola was unceremoniously ordered to leave the country. Later she turned up in London, and was brought into court on the charge of having contracted a bigamous marriage with a wealthy young guardsman. There had been an earlier husband, mislaid in India, who now inconveniently reappeared. Lola escaped from her minor legal tribulations by returning to the Continent, and the question of her matrimonial status was soon solved by the death of both husbands. This left her, as a newspaper reported, "in the full enjoyment of that independence of all ties which was the most congenial to her nature." The diagnosis, though scarcely accurate, represented her situation when she arrived in New York.

Lola Montez was thirty-three, a woman of medium height, pleasantly plump. Those who saw her before her professional début were impressed by her creamy complexion, exquisitely regular features and large, deeply blue eyes veiled by long black lashes. Her vivacity was infectious, her demure charm was incontestible. The attractions that lured a king to his downfall were concealed by off-stage attire. But Lola revealed them when she appeared on the stage as a dancer. For her three-week engagement, prices at the theater were doubled and the pit, except for its last two rows, was converted into

"LOLA HAS COME!" Broadway Theater, 1851, *by D. C. Johnston.* A cartoon showing the effect of the notorious dancer on New York

ENTHUSIASTIC RECEPTION OF LOLA BY AN AMERICAN AUDIENCE.

reserved seats. The audiences were immense, but it was noticed that they were almost exclusively masculine. Even curiosity could not persuade the ladies of New York to risk contamination by an immoral woman. After a tour, Lola returned to New York as an actress in "a new historical drama by a gentleman of this city" entitled *Lola Montez in Bavaria*. The story was all too familiar to patrons of the fashionable Broadway Theater, and the play failed. Lola took her flamboyant past down to the Bowery Theater, where she was tumultuously applauded by the Bowery Boys. Then, once again, she went on tour.

Thereafter, New Yorkers heard about Lola, from time to time, always in connection with scandals. When, after several years, she returned to New York, there was no ovation. She lived quietly for some time in a Brooklyn boarding house, then moved into quarters on West Seventeenth Street in New York. She did her best to improve the culture of Manhattan by delivering public lectures on beauty, love, and European politics, as well as her own stormy incursion into history. These efforts were not widely appreciated. On West Seventeenth Street Lola died, early in 1861, at the age of forty-three, rescued from eternal damnation by a clergyman who was convinced of her penitence and contrition. As if to erase all memory of the fever she had roused in men, her gravestone in Greenwood Cemetery bore the unlovely name of Eliza Gilbert. Gilbert was the name of her parents who had christened her Marie Dolores Eliza Roseanne.

Four years after Lola's début in New York, the great French tragedienne, Rachel, played a brief season at the new Metropolitan Theater on Broadway and Bond Street. Dark, slender, extremely frail, on the stage Rachel declaimed poetry with a golden voice. As Phèdre, her most celebrated role, she reminded one critic of the polychromatic statues of Greece, a goddess chiseled by Phidias in ivory and gold. He was deeply moved by the contrast between the antique suggestions of her appearance and her modern portrayal of passion and woe. In her great scene, she held the audience breathless. Her burning eyes, her tragic expression, the anguished tones of her voice perfectly evoked humiliated and despairing womanhood. Yet, notwithstanding the enthusiasm of her audiences and the acclaim of the critics, many New Yorkers failed to attend Rachel's performances. Gossip about her private life, *The Herald* surmised, had kept away the circumspect and conventional.

But this moral fastidiousness was subject to strange lapses. Three years earlier, for example, scandal rather than art had packed the Broadway Theater when the tragedian Edwin Forrest played an engagement of sixty-nine performances. True, he enacted eighteen major tragic roles, including *Macbeth, Hamlet, Lear, Othello* and *Richard III*. But it was not for Forrest's heroic voice and flamboyant style that all New York turned out. It was because he had a genius for lurid drama off the stage. As a young man, Forrest had been the star of the Bowery Theater, worshiped by both the Bowery Boys and the Dead Rabbits. He remained a hero to them and when, in 1848, Forrest carried on a feud with the English actor William Charles Macready, the two rival gangs stormed uptown to drive Macready from the stage of the Astor Place Opera House. To the humiliation of New York's most eminent citizens, a riot resulted, bringing death to twenty-two people and severe injuries to many more when the Seventh Regiment fired on the mob to disperse it.

Widely condemned for his part in this disgraceful affair, Forrest immediately progressed to another scandal. Alleging infidelity on the part of his wife, the actor left her and filed suit for divorce. Mrs. Forrest promptly filed a counter-suit. This was shocking enough, but the city seethed with excitement when Nathaniel P. Willis, an old friend of both parties, became Mrs. Forrest's champion. In his magazine, *The Home Journal,* Willis published a signed statement that Forrest wished to be saved the expense of his wife's support, was jealous of her intellectual superiority, and had enlisted the kitchen and brothel in order "to throw her off like a mistress paid up to parting." Forrest added Willis' name to the growing list of co-respondents in his divorce action, and filed suit for libel against him. Then, meeting Willis in Washington Square, Forrest horsewhipped him. Additional lawsuits resulted, and the newspapers thoroughly aired Forrest's varied private life. The actor's divorce case reached a first trial, and a verdict for his wife, just before he began his engagement at the Broadway Theater. Every evening, the great tragedian offered New York audiences a singular dramatic novelty. At the conclusion of his play, he would step before the curtain to make an eloquent speech that heaped abuse on Mrs. Forrest and Willis and defended his own course of action. It was for this titillating climax that audiences jammed the theater. What could be more sensational than to hear a great actor play *Othello* in real life?

Five years later there appeared an actor who eclipsed Forrest and remained, for thirty years, America's most famous star. Edwin Booth, virtually unknown to audiences, was only twenty-four when he challenged the veteran tragedian's pre-eminence. At the head of his own company, and in New York's finest theater, he played a repertory of roles far more ambitious than any ever undertaken by Forrest. Booth was slight, darkly handsome, extremely graceful, and he astonished critics with "a rich, sonorous voice of unusual compass and flexibility." The young actor had little respect for theatrical tradition; he was a daring innovator. Unlike Forrest, he refused merely to stand and declaim his great speeches. This was the established method, and Booth discarded it. He dramatized every line of his roles, introducing a kind of realism which New Yorkers had never before seen applied to the plays of Shakespeare and other classic dramas. This roused audiences to wild enthusiasm, and by the end of his engagement Booth had established himself as the most promising of all young American actors.

Booth's spectacular success indicated how seriously New Yorkers took their theater-going. They were intolerant of mediocrity, and they had ways of making their displeasure felt. In first-class theaters, both gallery and pit booed and hissed; the more polite occupants of reserved seats merely walked out on performances which they found lacking in merit. At the old Bowery Theater, the shirt-sleeved audience was capable of breaking into a storm of riotous abuse—as every actor knew, the Bowery Boys and their girls were the most exigent of all playgoers in the city. Yet delight moved the New York public to a pitch of enthusiasm seldom exhibited in other cities. An aura of romance surrounded its reigning favorites. Crowds waited at the stage door to catch a glimpse of them. Ovations greeted them when they came on the stage. They were showered with flowers when they took curtain calls. When the veteran actor-manager James W. Wallack died, the newspapers were full of eulogy and the whole city had an air of mourning. When, toward the end of the eighteen-sixties, the old actor George Holland died, and the rector of a fashionable Fifth Avenue church, declining to hold the funeral of a player, recommended that application be made to "the little church around the corner," the public showed its anger. Eighty years later, the Church of the Transfiguration, on Twenty-ninth Street just east of Fifth Avenue, universally known to New Yorkers as "The Little Church Around the Corner," was still identified with the theatrical profession, though the reputation of Holland, whose funeral made its fame, had long passed from memory.

All during the eighteen-sixties, some fifteen principal theaters competed for public favor. Few of them ever were dark for long; there was a summer season as well as a winter one, and a favorable year could bring three million dollars into their box offices. It was an era of splendid stock companies and great stars. The extraordinary variety of New York's theatrical fare showed that it had become a cosmopolitan city. English, French, German, Italian and Spanish players found a ready welcome, and even Japanese and Chinese performers visited the metropolis. Novelties followed one another rapidly: spectacular musical extravaganzas, burlesque, or "girl shows," French opéra bouffe, or operetta, the variety show, precursor of vaudeville. In the tension preceding the Civil War, Dion Boucicault's *The Octoroon* created a new pattern of social drama. It dealt with the rankling institution of slavery, bringing to the auction block a beautiful girl unwittingly tainted by Negro blood; it thrilled audiences, and was to be successfully revived for more than forty years. The outbreak of war produced a large crop of hastily written, topical military melodramas. These gave audiences a taste for plays dealing with the American contemporary scene, which was gratified by such successful dramas as Boucicault's *The Streets of New York,* Augustin Daly's *Under the Gaslight, After Dark* and *A Flash of Lightning,* Olive Logan's *Surf, or Summer Scenes at Long Branch.* Yet native playwrights failed to dominate the New York stage. The sophisticated public preferred to be transported to the drawing rooms of London and the boudoirs of Paris. The plays of Tom Taylor and the realistic social comedies of T. W. Robertson were rushed to New York soon after their performance in London. The dramas of such Parisian favorites as Sardou and Meilhac and Halévy were quickly adapted for American stars by Daly, whose passion for the theater was to make him, at the end of the decade, a distinguished producer.

For fashionable New York it was as inevitable to subscribe for stalls at

Wallack's Theater as to have a box at the Academy of Music for opera or to select books from the shelves of the Society Library in University Place. Wallack's was a social institution, the city's premier theater, the nation's leading playhouse. New Yorkers returning from Paris insisted that the Wallack stock company was superior to that of the Comédie Francaise, and its repertory of plays far more diverting. It was the home of high comedy, not only of the classic school but of the modern, for the brilliant actor-manager Lester Wallack introduced to New York, with the plays of T. W. Robertson—*Society, Ours, Progress, Caste, Home*—a kind of natural, elegant, play of contemporary life previously unknown to American audiences.

At the beginning of the decade Wallack moved his company from Broadway and Broome Street, in the heart of the theatrical district, to a new and splendid home uptown. The new Wallack's Theater was built on the northeast corner of Broadway and Thirteenth Street, on land rented from William Backhouse Astor. It was one of the largest playhouses in the city, and in its architecture and furnishings, its handsome lobbies and lounges, represented the last word in elegance. Orchestra stalls sold for one dollar; for fifty cents you could sit in the parquet, or pit; gallery gods spent only twenty-five cents for seats in the family circle. Private boxes seating seven were on sale at seven dollars, but only parvenus occupied them. According to the inscrutable tradition of New York, to take a box for the play was even more flagrantly bad form than not to take one for the opera. The actresses and actors of Wallack's company ranked high among the city's reigning favorites. Yet Lester Wallack received only one hundred and twenty-five dollars a week. Mrs. John Hoey, the highly talented leading lady, received one hundred. Mary Gannon, whom playgoers regarded as the most beautiful and perfect of all ingénues, was paid forty dollars weekly. To play at Wallack's was the best of all passports to fame. First nights there brought out the most distinguished audience to be found in New York: the aristocracy of wealth and fashion, the leading celebrities of the stage and opera, the most beautiful *demi-mondaines,* the authors, artists and journalists of whom everyone was talking. You attended Wallack's, like the opera, as much to be seen as to see.

Old-fashioned playgoers sometimes complained that the stage was falling on evil days. They were loyal to ageing Edwin Forrest, whom the irreverent younger generation contemptuously described as "a ranter." When the veteran tragedienne, Charlotte Cushman, returned to New York after a long absence in Europe, they welcomed her with enthusiasm. Miss Cushman revived, among other plays, Shakespeare's *Henry VIII,* and on alternate evenings she assumed the roles of Queen Katharine and Cardinal Wolsey, appearing, as the Cardinal, in a full beard. Young people snickered at this whimsical performance, and were little more respectful when Miss Cushman offered a beardless but massive Romeo in what an eminent singer described as "a fine *baritone* contralto voice." But young and old playgoers alike acclaimed the Italian tragedienne Adelaide Ristori. She was no longer young, and she had never been beautiful, yet critics declared that she was "worlds in advance of any woman on the American or English stage." It was easy to see why. Ristori played in the "grand style"—she tore passion to tatters before your eyes.

Charles Dickens evoked the same kind of excitement, and for precisely the same reason. He gave thirteen readings in the handsome new Steinway Hall, on Fourteenth Street between Union Square and Irving Place, near the Academy of Music. It accommodated three thousand people. Whenever Dickens gave a reading, the hall was filled to capacity by "the intellect, the wit, the beauty, the wealth, the industrial power" of the metropolis. Meanwhile, the younger generation were hailing their own favorites, the rising stars who were innovators; the "moderns." They never had enough of Joseph Jefferson in *Rip Van Winkle*; though he was equally fine in other roles, popular demand practically limited him to this one. Young playgoers adored the sparkling little comedienne Maggie Mitchell. They created a vogue for Lotta, a pretty young girl from San Francisco who sang, played the banjo, danced breakdowns and romped through light comedy with extraordinary vivacity. But the great idol of the younger generation was Edwin Booth.

In the autumn of 1864, Edwin Booth joined his brothers, Junius Brutus and John Wilkes Booth, in a performance of *Julius Caesar* for the benefit of a fund established to erect a statue of Shakespeare in Central Park. After this performance, the three brothers separated. Edwin Booth put on a revival of *Hamlet* which achieved the unprecedented run of one hundred performances. So great was the furor over Booth's *Hamlet* that, on the last night of his engagement a committee of prominent New Yorkers came on the stage to present him with a gold medal. Booth departed for Boston, and was playing *Hamlet* there when, on April 14th, news came that his younger brother, John Wilkes Booth, had assassinated President Lincoln. Edwin Booth went into immediate retirement, as he thought, forever. But in January, 1866, the pressure of financial obligations compelled him to return to the stage. On the night of his reappearance in New York, he received an ovation from a vast cheering audience. The city had determined to show its warm affection for him, and to convince him that his brother's hideous crime must have no effect on his career. Three years later Booth opened his magnificent new theater at the southeast corner of Sixth Avenue and Twenty-third Street, designed to become a national temple of art. It was a vast, ornate house with three balconies above the orchestra, and its stage equipment was far superior to anything previously known. Scenes could be raised to the stage from below, or sink visibly before the eyes of the audience; solid side-scenes replaced the old-fashioned open side wings; backdrops were lowered, stretched on frames, from high rigging-lofts above the stage. And, for the first time in any theater, a huge fan in the basement filled the auditorium with cool air in summer and warm air in winter. The opening of Booth's Theater gave New Yorkers another playhouse which promised to rank with Wallack's as a social institution and the home of a superb repertory company.

Meanwhile, sensational novelties in theatrical fare had taken the city by storm. In 1866 *The Black Crook,* a musical spectacle of unparalleled splendor

MARIA BONFANTI, Premiere Danseuse in *The Black Crook*, 1866, *by N. Finck*

and unabashed sensuality, began its record-breaking run of nearly five hundred performances at Niblo's Garden. It was a daring ballet-show, as nearly unclad as possible, exploiting a large aggregation of *coryphées* and four lovely *premières danseuses*. "All that gold and silver and gems and light and woman's beauty can contribute to fascinate the eye and charm the sense is gathered up in this gorgeous spectacle," a sedate critic reported. From nearly all the city's pulpits there sounded dire warnings: to see *The Black Crook* was to slide far down the incline to hell. Gilded youth, and young New York in general, paid little heed, while elderly gentlemen showed an alarming tendency to imperil their souls repeatedly. Here, for the first time, was a massive display of unveiled feminine beauty. Here were infectious gaiety, dazzling scenic effects, and an incomparable ballet. What could Wallack's offer, or the Academy of Music, or even the most brazen concert saloon, that rivaled the manifold attractions of *The Black Crook*? An enchanted public ignored the protests of moralists, and the market for men's opera glasses flourished as never before.

Then, in the autumn of 1868, New York was provided with another kind of novelty: a burlesque show. The Lydia Thompson Burlesque Company played at Wood's Museum, a new theater far uptown on Broadway and Thirtieth Street, and overnight became the sensation of the season. Its major attraction was four English beauties who won immediate celebrity as the toast of the town. New York was a city of brunettes, and these girls were all radiantly blonde. Lydia Thompson was pert, blue-eyed, dashing. Pauline Markham, dark-eyed and regally statuesque, was the favorite of sophisticated men about town. Ada Harland, an exquisite dancer, and Lisa Weber, a talented singer, completed the triumphant quartette. In song and dance and skit—but, most importantly, in tights—these fascinating creatures satirized the foibles of the hour in New York, among them, to the particular pleasure of males, the "Grecian bend" or new stylish posture which fashion prescribed for ladies. In Lydia Thompson and Pauline Markham playgoers saw for the first time the "show girl"—a type that was to make theatrical history and domestic discord, a type in which, as the critic of *The Times* guardedly intimated, "nature has her own."

But nature unveiled and provocative·was being challenged by the more insidious temptations of art. To visual delights forbidden by the fashionable crinoline, opéra bouffe added the enchantment of sparkling music and vivacious wit. Coming from the boulevards of Paris at the head of rival companies, Mlles. Lucille Tostée, and Irma brought New York the delicious operettas of Offenbach. Outraged puritans fulminated in vain against their "French indecencies." The triumph of opéra bouffe was immediate, its vogue universal. In every quarter of the city—from pianos and guitars, sung, whistled—you heard the music of *La Grande Duchesse, La Belle Hélène, Barbe Bleu, La Périchole, Orphée aux Enfers* and others. The theaters in which the Parisian companies played for three seasons were always crowded. The world of fashion, the middle classes, even the very poor came again and again. New York couldn't get enough of Offenbach's lilting waltzes and haunting melodies, of the charming rival prima donnas, so "different," as people said, giving the adjective a new laudatory connotation. Tostée and Irma were piquant, sprightly, altogether adorable, and in the pantheon of masculine worship they took almost equal rank with Pauline Markham who, as a perennial cynosure, was the precursor of Lillian Russell.

Opéra bouffe was the first ᵗheatrical enterprise to feel the influence of the new finance capitalism which New York was beginning to impose on the country. A misguided native of Cincinnati, Samuel N. Pike, had built a vast white-marble opera house on the northwest corner of Eighth Avenue and Twenty-third Street. Designed to displace the Academy of Music as the home of opera, it failed to do so and was put up for sale. Nobody wanted a luxurious playhouse so remote from the precincts of fashion, and the building was eventually purchased by Jay Gould and James Fisk, the financial buccaneers who controlled the Erie Railroad. They converted the upper floors of the building into offices for their railroad. Tostée and her company were playing an engagement in the auditorium at this time, and gaudy Jim Fisk, notoriously accessible to feminine charm, was struck by an inspiration. Why not effect a corner in opéra bouffe? Applying the efficient technique which he and Gould had mastered in Wall Street, Fisk bought control of both companies and amalgamated them. Thereafter, in the million-dollar Grand Opera House, the New York public sometimes enjoyed a pleasure denied to Paris: it could hear

Tostée and Irma, on the same evening, in the same theater. Fashionable folk, driving in Central Park, were often distressed to see an imposing red-and-blue carriage flash by, and in it ponderous, disreputable Jim Fisk seated proudly between his twin divinities. New York thought it recognized an impresario when it saw one. But Jim Fisk was no impresario. He was merely the first of all "angels"—and, in the opinion of genteel New York, angel was not the word for Fisk.

When New York thought of an impresario, it pondered the vicissitudes of Max Maretzek and Maurice Strakosch who, sometimes individually and sometimes in combination, provided seasons of grand opera at the Academy of Music. Like the aristocratic directors of the Academy, the impresarios seldom had smooth sailing. Opera was essential to the fashionable, the socially elect. For where else but in the Academy's boxes—fortunately so limited in number—could you perform the obligatory rituals of public display? Was not society morally bound to show itself to the people in full regalia of ball dresses and jewels? Besides, opera was a social convenience. It filled the otherwise vacant hours before balls and late evening receptions. It enabled you to exchange brief intermission visits with your friends. It was an infallible register of social standing—you could measure the precise degree of your power, or the probable success of the débutante daughter whom you were anxiously launching, by the number of gentlemen who, during the intervals, entered your box to pay their respects. The boxes of the Academy were as competitive an institution as the Stock Exchange, as exciting in their prospects of dazzling fortune or ignominious failure—a costly parade ground for vanity and intrigue, courtship and heartbreak. Society came late and departed early, but while present it insisted upon performances of melodious old Italian operas by the greatest stars on whom, occasionally, it bestowed critical attention. Seasons of grand opera were brief and sometimes irregular; the harried impresarios made ends meet, when they could, by frequent tours.

During one starless and desperately collapsing season, Strakosch gave New York the most sensational operatic début in history. On an unfashionable night, Thanksgiving, 1859, and perhaps only because he was on the verge of failure, Strakosch thrust his young sister-in-law on the stage in a performance of *Lucia di Lammermoor*. Adelina Patti was seventeen years old, and music lovers remembered her as a child prodigy who emulated Jenny Lind. But the petite, unfledged prima donna startled the audience by her phenomenal voice and perfect art. She received an ovation, innumerable recalls, bouquets, wreaths. Overnight she became the acknowledged queen of opera, sometimes singing as often as four times a week. Two seasons later Patti left the company, and thereafter New York was not to hear her for more than twenty years.

Shortly after Patti vanished, a new operatic star conquered New York—the first American singer to become a popular idol without benefit of European prestige. Clara Louise Kellogg had studied singing as a ladylike accomplishment, with a group of society girls, but her voice was found to be of professional caliber. She was aware that a stage career would take her outside the social pale. Before making her début, she called her friends together to announce the scandalous news: "Girls, I've made up my mind to go on the stage. I know just how your people feel about it, and I want to tell you now that you needn't know me any more. You needn't speak to me, nor bow to me if you meet me in the street. I shall quite understand, and I shan't feel a bit badly. Because I think the day will come when you will be proud to know me." Miss Kellogg knew her New York. There were protests against the appearance of a young, beautiful and presumably innocent girl in works of so immoral a nature as *Rigoletto* and *La Traviata*—Boston, indeed, banned the one, and Brooklyn the other—and when, in 1863, she gave New York its first performance of *Faust,* that opera was considered daringly improper. Nevertheless, Miss Kellogg was required to sing it twenty-seven times during the season. She delighted the galleries as well as the boxes, and the massiveness of her horticultural tributes made her known as "the flower prima donna."

For lovers of music who found the immoralities of opera offensive, there were frequent performances of oratorios, usually with soloists from the Academy, by several large choral groups. Singers and instrumentalists in bewildering numbers gave concerts in Steinway Hall and smaller audience rooms every day and evening during the winter season. The already venerable Philharmonic Society offered its subscribers five or six symphony concerts every winter. The world of fashion, supporting this organization, recognized an obligation to attend its concerts; the conductors wisely played little unfamiliar music. A rival symphony orchestra was organized by Theodore Thomas, first violinist at the Academy and later to become conductor of the Chicago Symphony Orchestra. Thomas courageously attempted to create an audience for "advanced" music. At one of his concerts he gave the first New York performance of the overture to *Tristan und Isolde.* The critic of *The Times,* probably serving as spokesman for the audience, remarked, "That Wagner was thrust

THE BABY SHOW AT BARNUM'S MUSEUM, 1855

out of Munich after the production of *Tristan und Isolde* seems natural. No people could be expected to stand it. . . . We see nothing but pretentiousness and that tendency to over-elaboration which always precedes decay." But the appetite of New Yorkers for music was not appeased by the winter's plethora of concerts. On warm summer nights they flocked uptown to Terrace Garden, on Fifty-eighth Street near Third Avenue; to Central Park Gardens, on Seventh Avenue near Fifty-ninth Street; even to the remotely distant Belvedere and Lion Park, at Eighth Avenue and One Hundred and Tenth Street— where, outdoors under the trees, with refreshing drinks at hand, they could listen to popular orchestral concerts conducted by Thomas, or Carl Bergmann and Theodore Eisfeld, who in winter directed the Philharmonic.

People who sought lighter diversions were amply rewarded. Barnum's Museum, far downtown on Broadway at Ann Street, was the Mecca of all rural visitors to New York. Everyone wanted to see the celebrated midgets, General Tom Thumb, Commodore Nutt and Lavinia Warren. The country breathlessly followed a well-advertised rivalry between the General and the Commodore for the hand of Lavinia, and people were either shocked or pleased by her eventual marriage to the General in Grace Church, the most fashionable and exclusive of New York's consecrated edifices. Barnum's old Museum burned down; he built another, further up Broadway; that, too, was destroyed by fire and the great showman temporarily retired from the field.

BURNING OF BARNUM'S MUSEUM at Broadway and Ann Street, July 13,
1865, *by H. Thomas*

But the loss of Barnum's varied attractions was partly compensated by those
of Lent's New York Circus which, throughout the winter, occupied its permanent amphitheater on Fourteenth Street, opposite the Academy of Music.
And if equestriennes, high-wire artists, clowns and animals palled, you could
take in one of several minstrel shows: George Christy's, that of the brothers
Dan and Neil Bryant or that of the famous team of Kelly and Leon, famous
chiefly because of Francis Leon's daring female impersonations. But minstrel
shows were beginning to decline in popularity under the competition of "variety"—a new form of entertainment that had originated in the concert
saloons.

Variety was first introduced in Tony Pastor's Opera House, a theater on
the Bowery near Prince Street. Pastor, a former clown and a veteran entertainer in the concert saloons, was later to become the nation's leading operator
of music halls. He was a great discoverer of new, arresting talent and many
subsequently famous stars made their débuts in his Bowery music hall. But
to the sanctimonious, Pastor's was a sinful resort. Authors of books about
New York warned strangers to the city against its "dreary gaieties" and asserted that it was a place "where the mob is tickled and good taste disgusted."
Yet uptown New York eventually heard about the excellence of Pastor's
shows, and sedate citizens began risking a trip to the Bowery to see them. In
1869, the Tammany Society built a new Tammany Hall on Fourteenth Street,
near the Academy of Music. Not requiring the entire building for political
purposes, Tammany rented all but one meeting hall to a pair of enterprising

theatrical managers. They opened the building as a variety palace like the great London music halls, with bars, a restaurant, a "conversation saloon fitted up in Turkish style," a theater, a basement oyster saloon and a promenade hall. In the theater, a variety show held the stage. In the restaurant, entertainers performed. In the promenade hall, an orchestra played popular concerts. Between the hours of seven and midnight, you could enjoy all these attractions for an admission fee of fifty cents.

After the theater or opera, most middle-class New Yorkers tried to reach their homes as quickly as possible. But young men about town, if they were not going on to a ball, usually stopped for midnight supper at one of the small after-theater restaurants that catered to actors, singers, musicians and critics. The most famous of all theatrical taverns was the De Soto, on Bleecker Street east of Broadway, which served the best broiled kidneys and rarebits in the city. Edwin Booth and Joseph Jefferson went to the De Soto every night when they were playing in New York, and it had become a kind of club for the younger theatrical stars. The talk at the De Soto was always lively, and sometimes, when the crowd was in a gay mood, you would find an impromptu show in progress. To see your favorite actors "doing a turn" for their colleagues was a memorable experience that reconciled you to a long, tedious journey home on the horse-cars or crawling omnibuses in the hours before dawn.

6

Fireworks in the Parlor

IN the late eighteen-fifties, the behavior of a group of young rebels scandalized polite New York. They called themselves "the Bohemians," and they were hostile to all forms of respectability. Manhattan, they asserted, made a religion of dullness. They despised dullness. The stuffy gentility of Washington Square, the finicking proprieties observed by the "best people" who lived north of Bleecker Street—surely these invited your contempt. All the Bohemians pined for Paris, and a few of them had actually been there. They were cosmopolites by nature, if not by experience. They were dedicated, they said, "to sympathy with the finer arts, to conduct above and beyond convention." Righteous folk were alarmed by this declaration, and *The Times,* in a thundering editorial, denounced their "seductive ways" as a moral menace. This delighted the Bohemians. Wit was their favorite weapon for an attack on smugness and solemnity. They used it liberally in the *Saturday Press,* a new, irreverent literary weekly that seldom paid but somehow had caught on.

Late afternoons, and evenings after the theater, the Bohemians congregated in Charlie Pfaff's cellar restaurant, on the west side of Broadway, a few doors north of Bleecker Street. At the far end of the cellar, beneath the Broadway sidewalk, there was an alcove, a kind of vaulted cave, containing a long table and many chairs. Genial Charlie Pfaff reserved this for the Bohemian coterie. The noise of the afternoon promenade on Broadway drifted down into the cave, and at night it echoed the Niagara roar of omnibuses. The idol and poet laureate of Bohemia celebrated this meeting place in his verse:

> The vault at Pfaff's where the drinkers and laughers
>   meet to eat and drink and carouse,
> While on the walk immediately overhead past the myriad
>   feet of Broadway. . . .

He was a Jovian-looking man, with keen, steel-blue eyes and a grizzled, branching mustache and beard. He wore a suit of rough, blue-gray fabric, scorned a cravat, left his shirt unbuttoned to expose his hairy chest. His book of poems had stirred up a controversy among the critics. Polite New York shuddered at *Leaves of Grass*. It was useless for Ralph Waldo Emerson to greet Walt Whitman "at the beginning of a great career," or for the *Saturday Press* to hail him as "a great Philosopher—perhaps a great Poet—in every way an original man." Polite New York knew better.

Whitman found his sturdiest defenders among the girls who frequented the long table in Pfaff's cellar. He realized that many people would think these girls little to his credit. How could conventional folk be expected to approve of Ada Clare, for example? She was called the "queen of Bohemia," and her dubious legend had already spread as far west as Ohio. Men thought her singularly beautiful. Slender and shapely, she had an air of elegance. The black dresses she affected set off the ivory pallor of her skin, the intense blue of her eyes, her mop of short-cut, wavy golden hair. She was always vivacious, always sparkling, and she liked to sit talking far into the night, smoking one cigarette after another.

She had made the name Ada Clare so notorious that few people remembered that it was not her own. Her real name was Jane McElheny, and she came of a distinguished Southern family. Orphaned in childhood, she was brought to New York by her grandfather, and later she inherited a considerable fortune. At the age of nineteen, when her poems began appearing in the magazines, she suddenly became a literary celebrity. For a young girl to publish verse was exceptional, but not strictly taboo. Ada Clare's poems, however, shocked well-bred readers. Love was her only theme, and it inspired her with a torrid, passionate eloquence not to be condoned in a young lady. She didn't help her reputation by going on the stage, a year later, and appearing in Broadway theaters with Laura Keene and with Agnes Robertson and Dion Boucicault. But it was the prose that she began publishing—stories, sketches, little essays—which finally put her beyond the pale of respectable society. Her prose also dealt with love, its torments and frustrations and bitter disappointments. Critics praised her work. Wasn't she ardent, passionate, intellectual? Perhaps she was; nobody cared. Everybody realized that Ada Clare had been flagrantly telling the world about her sin, which should have been her shame.

She had been carrying on a love affair with the celebrated pianist Louis Moreau Gottschalk. The ladies of New York worshipped him, usually at a discreet distance. The friend of Chopin, the pupil and intimate of Berlioz, Gottschalk had returned from Paris to make a sensational American début. Sixteen New York recitals during a single season testified to his mastery, not only of the keyboard, but of the feminine heart. He was dark, handsome, fiery, and women found him irresistible. He was faithful to none of them for long. He tired of Ada Clare while she was still infatuated with him. In her stories and essays she announced her desperation, recording her humiliating efforts to invoke his pity, her obsession with suicide after these efforts failed. There was a final wretched interview in which she told Gottschalk that she was pregnant. He played a brilliant farewell concert in Brooklyn and departed for a tour of the West Indies. Ada Clare sailed for Paris to bear her child.

Paris taught her the ways of Bohemia. For the New York weeklies, she wrote bright, gossipy accounts of Parisian life. These kept her name before the public, and when she returned to the city with her child, it was as "Miss Ada Clare and son." She set up a literary salon in her home, but the socially eligible never honored it with their presence. Even the young poets who came to Pfaff's—Edmund Clarence Stedman and Thomas Bailey Aldrich, for example—had to translate Ada Clare into a conventional poetic symbol in order to express their infatuation in published verse. For New York considered Ada Clare an abandoned woman—and, instead of being contrite and repentant, she appeared to be defiantly proud of her disgrace. Walt Whitman, whom she championed vigorously, understood and appreciated her. Long afterward, he wrote about her "gay, easy, sunny, free, loose, but *not ungood* life." Perhaps what New York could not forgive was the fact that, inexplicably, all those adjectives were simultaneously true.

The dark, opulent beauty and even darker poems of Adah Isaacs Menken for a time provided Pfaff's cellar with a tragic muse. Her situation was worse than that of her friend Ada Clare. Men, famous and otherwise, wandered in and out of Adah Isaacs Menken's life with monotonous regularity. They brought her little joy; they multiplied her anxieties; and the worst nuisances of all were those who insisted on marrying her. When she was introduced to

ADAH ISAACS MENKEN AS "MAZEPPA," Broadway Theater, 1866

the Bohemian circle she fell under the spell of Whitman, published an essay in defense of the new and scandalous edition of *Leaves of Grass,* and promptly appropriated Whitman's form of free verse. The smoky air of the cellar became fiery when she recited some of her poems . . .

> I will strangle this pallid throat of mine on the sweet blood.
> I will revel in my passion. . . .

The Bohemians, listening amazedly, knew that a *femme fatale* had come among them. A few years later, in the eighteen-sixties, "the Menken," as she came to be called, achieved sensational success in London as an actress. She returned briefly to New York and startled audiences, in a play entitled *Mazeppa,* by the scantiness of her costumes and the skill of her horsemanship. Then she sailed for Europe, and afterward scandals floated back across the Atlantic. New York heard that she was the mistress of old Alexandre Dumas, author of *The Three Musketeers;* later, that she was the mistress of Algernon Charles Swinburne, a poet of reprehensibly sensual nature. People were still talking of these exploits when the newspapers announced that the adorable Menken had died in Paris, one week before the publication of her book of poems, *Infelicia*, to which she had been looking forward with pathetic eagerness. But shortly before her death she had received a visitor whose homage rejoiced her. Benign, white-bearded, world-famous and impeccably correct, Henry Wadsworth Longfellow spent an hour at her bedside, and before departing he composed a poem on love and inscribed it in her album.

The Civil War dispersed the Bohemians of Pfaff's cellar. Whitman went to Washington. Many of the others reverted to respectability. Stedman became a broker in Wall Street, Aldrich an editor in Boston; the short-story writer Fitz-James O'Brien joined the army and was killed in action. The witty, sardonic *Saturday Press* ceased publication. But the end of the Bohemian coterie did not leave New York without centers of intellectual radicalism. Outside the precinct of wealth and fashion, certain women were deliberately quickening the ferment of ideas. Their activity suggested a restlessness that could be dangerous. Did it not imply the desire for a free development that would neither ask masculine assent nor wait on masculine approval? Was it not an incentive to the further folly of an independent career? Even, perhaps, to things still worse and scarcely to be mentioned? The social desert of New York had two oases where the friction of minds was being expertly produced. Conducted by women of exceptional charm and some talent, both became widely known.

It was a lady of fashion who remarked that Mrs. Botta's Saturday-night receptions were really extraordinary. One met such celebrated people, but also such "queer" people, all mixed together; one simply couldn't tell what unsuitable contacts might result. This impression was accurate. Ralph Waldo Emerson confirmed it. He came to Mrs. Botta's whenever he visited New York, and he described her home as "the house with the expanding doors." Externally, the house did not suggest this elastic hospitality. One of a row of conventional brownstone residences on West Thirty-seventh Street, near Fifth Avenue, it was indistinguishable from the others to which celebrities were seldom invited and queer folk were never admitted. But here, for more than twenty years, Mrs. Botta had been bringing together writers, artists, musicians, actors and actresses and the most distinguished European visitors. As a young girl she had turned to teaching to support her mother and herself. She served as private secretary to Henry Clay. She lectured at The Brooklyn Academy for Women. She had published a volume of verse and, more recently, a *Handbook of Universal Literature* that eventually ran through twenty editions. In middle life she married Vincenzo Botta, an Italian philosopher and political liberal who held a professorship at New York University. Now her mission—she called it her pleasure—was to afford an opportunity for lively utterance to the widest, most varied range of minds. Millionaires and fashionable folk seemed a poor substitute for the lions of a genuinely cultivated society. Mrs. Botta's lions could all roar, more or less; they were never reduced to the absurd alternatives of chatter or silence.

So, on a Saturday night, you might hear Adelaide Ristori and Edwin Booth argue passionately about acting, with Professor Botta translating their explosive outbursts into English and Italian. You might find Emerson and Bayard Taylor earnestly discussing Bettina von Arnim, who had loved Goethe and whom they both knew well. Paul Du Chaillu would tell about darkest Africa. Sometimes you could talk with Bryant, Horace Greeley, Henry Ward Beecher. Julia Ward Howe, taking a holiday from Boston, would either give free rein to her talent for mockery, or speak with intense seriousness about the emancipation of women. Some members of a newer literary generation were always present. Edmund Clarence Stedman was already well known as a poet; so was Richard Henry Stoddard. Richard Watson Gilder would make his reputation later, and emotional Helen Hunt was to become famous as the author of *Ramona*. John W. De Forest had recently published *Miss Ravenel's Conversion,* a novel that shocked nearly all readers by presenting a woman who treated love as a pleasant, profitable game which she played wickedly, emerging unrepentant, unpunished and more prosperous than ever. De Forest frankly declared that corrupt people were more interesting than virtuous ones, and he thought postwar America was putting a premium on all forms of corruption. He had no use for the sentimental optimism cultivated by American writers; why didn't they portray the actual drift of American life? This opinion aroused protest, but Elizabeth D. B. Stoddard, the wife of the poet, agreed with De Forest. Her novel, *The Morgesons,* was a daringly realistic picture of New England and it had been as widely disapproved as his. Could it be true, as De Forest suggested, that the nation was committed to ruthless materialism, that conscience and a sense of honor were becoming obsolete?

But unusual ideas were the usual fare at these Saturday-night gatherings. At one of them, Mrs. Botta tactfully drew out a pretty Englishwoman who had recently arrived in New York from the Orient. Mrs. Anna Harriette Leonowens had spent some years at the royal court of Siam, as governess and teacher of the hereditary prince. Moreover, acquiring great influence with the King, she had succeeded in instituting many reforms in that fabulous land. Everybody wanted to hear about Anna and the King of Siam. Mrs. Leonowens told fascinating stories. She described the position of women in Siam, India and Persia. She spoke about the mysticism of the Orientals. Like them, she asked, should not the awakened soul entreat, "O Infinite, direct my feet toward thee"? Somehow, as you listened to Mrs. Leonowens, you forgot that you were in materialistic, modern New York. You even forgot that she was what people called an "advanced woman."

Some of the interesting people whom you met at Mrs. Botta's on Saturday evening were likely to turn up, on the following night, at the home of Alice and Phoebe Cary. The poet sisters, as they were known, owned a wide, low, old-fashioned house on East Twentieth Street, near Fourth Avenue, and their informal Sunday receptions were always thronged. They had come to New York from an Ohio farm as young women, without either money or formal education, determined to support themselves by writing, and they had won prestige in the literary world. Alice Cary's *Clovernook Stories,* little idylls of country life, enchanted a large audience, and her volumes of poems and ballads were widely praised. She was an indefatigable worker and under pressure of economic need she also wrote novels to be serialized in magazines, but she knew that they were poor stuff. Phoebe Cary was far less productive than her sister. She had published only two volumes of verse. Unlike Alice, who was idealistic and sentimental, Phoebe kept a tenacious grip on reality. She had a keen sense of the ludicrous side of human nature. She couldn't resist an impulse to deflate its high-flown pretensions, to expose the hypocrisy of conventional attitudes and professed beliefs. By temperament she was a disenchanter, given to puncturing cherished illusions with a thrust of wit. She wrote deadly parodies of such poets as Longfellow and Tennyson, and astringent verses about love that made old-fashioned readers uncomfortable. They preferred her fine ballads, her hymns, and the mystical religious poems that delighted John Greenleaf Whittier.

On Sunday evenings, you found the Carys in their parlor, a large room decorated in red and green, furnished with many comfortable, velvet-upholstered sofas and chairs. Later, everyone would cross the hall to have tea in the square, oak-paneled library. Alice Cary, nearing fifty, was slender and delicate. Her abundant dark hair was turning gray; she had a careworn look, an air of gentle melancholy. Phoebe, four years younger than her sister, was plump, black-haired, sprightly and addicted to wearing vivid colors. Among the men present, you were likely to see burly, smiling Phineas T. Barnum, Robert Bonner, Samuel Bowles, editor of the *Springfield Republican,* Justin McCarthy, the English writer, Stoddard and Gilder, George Ripley. Horace Greeley always came, talked for an hour or more, drank two cups of sweetened milk and water, and quietly disappeared to write his Monday-morning editorial.

But it was the women who attended these gatherings that set their tone.

Most of them, like the Carys, were engaged in some form of professional work and conventional folk, describing them as "advanced" or "strong-minded," intended no compliment. Like the Carys, they asserted that women ought to think for themselves, ought to get their opinions at first hand—not because this was their right, but because it was their duty. Preposterous as was this claim, ridicule was the wrong way to meet it. Was not the doctrine clearly subversive? Did it not threaten the very fabric of society—the institutions of marriage and family, the normal relation of the sexes, even the established economic order? If women started thinking for themselves, they were certain to wind up with the kinds of ideas you heard discussed at the Carys' on Sunday nights. They were even likely to adopt the principles expounded in *The Revolution*, that organ of the women's-rights movements which so flagrantly lived up to its inflammatory name.

There was something disconcerting about these women who were making their own way in the world. They disproved the argument that a career outside the home was bound to coarsen and brutalize any woman, in the end defeminize her. And this, too, in spite of the fact that some of them were directly —still worse, successfully—challenging masculine achievement. Could any woman seem more womanly than Fanny Fern, blonde, blue-eyed, gay and amusing though nearing her sixtieth year? Her name was far more widely known than that of her husband, the biographer James Parton, and Robert Bonner, publisher of *The Ledger,* paid her five thousand dollars a year merely to have an exclusive right to all her work. No publisher was doing as much for Parton, or any other male writer. And what was a man to think of Madame Ellen Louise Demorest? She had founded a business that now spanned the continent. From her headquarters on Broadway fashion patterns were sent out to three hundred agents throughout the country and sold to dressmakers, or to women who wished to make their own clothes in the very latest style. Moreover, she also published *The Demorest Monthly Magazine,* which was one of the most successful, with a constantly growing circulation. Every issue was a skillful blend of literature, fashion, domestic science—and, alas, social reform, as well as advanced ideas. For, unlike a sensible male, Mme. Demorest could not be content with a hugely profitable business. She held first-hand opinions and felt obliged to preach them. She went in for reforms. She was an advocate of something dangerously like women's rights. She was an aggressive champion of the cause of temperance. She was fanatically devoted to the uplift of the Negro race. Even before the war, she had insisted on employing Negro girls in her establishment, seating them among white girls and paying them the same wages. When many of her fashionable customers protested, she told them to take their business elsewhere. She refused to subordinate her convictions to her profits. Conscience overruled self-interest, as it always disastrously did in the case of reformers and martyrs. But Mme. Demorest hadn't met with disaster. Nor was she a martyr. She was an outstanding exemplar of American business enterprise at its financial best.

The most baffling of the Carys' younger friends was Kate Field. She was radiantly lovely: blue-eyed, auburn-haired, delicately formed and featured. The elegance of her clothes aroused the envy of other women. Obviously, it wasn't for lack of suitors that she remained single. Did she care for nothing but fame? Some people said so. Others, less kindly, declared that men were put off by her lively wit, her erudition, her independent spirit. Wasn't she too intelligent, too "strong-minded," for her own good? Didn't she, perhaps, arouse the resentment of even intellectual men by wounding their vanity, making them feel inferior? That she was a beauty made matters worse; they could have endured being wilted by an intelligent woman who was hard on the eyes and not quickening to the heart. But Kate Field, at thirty, was a beauty who looked ten years younger, and it was plain to see that men interested her far more than women.

Her versatility was as remarkable as her beauty. She contributed to *The Atlantic Monthly* and other magazines. She wrote a book on Charles Dickens, and another on Mme. Ristori; both had large sales. People were becoming interested in Oriental mysticism, in the supernatural, in psychic phenomena. Kate Field experimented with the planchette and automatic writing, obtained rather exceptional results, and wrote a book that attracted attention. Now, she was following Anna Dickinson, the suffragist, and Julia Ward Howe to the lecture platform, where she soon became one of the most popular and highly paid "attractions" of the lyceum circuits. Nobody who met her at the Carys' was surprised by her extraordinarily varied career in later years. She continued her journalistic work. She appeared as a concert singer. She went on the stage, in New York and London, and wrote a number of successful plays. Subsequently, in England, she earned a fortune of two hundred thousand dollars by devising a plan for spectacularly publicizing that new invention, the telephone: she sang, through the instrument, into the ear of Queen Victoria at Osborne House. She concluded that "women of discernment manage the diplomacy of business infinitely better than men."

Few people considered Susan B. Anthony and Mrs. Elizabeth Cady Stanton to be women of discernment. They often came to the Carys' and they had persuaded Phoebe Cary to serve, for a time, as a substitute editor on *The Revolution.* They were issuing their radical, defiant weekly from the "Women's Bureau," a handsome residence on East Twenty-third Street which a wealthy philanthropist, Mrs. Elizabeth B. Phelps, had equipped as a center for the intellectual, social and professional activities of New York women. Neither Miss Anthony nor Mrs. Stanton looked like the obnoxiously notorious women they actually were. You would not have taken them to be agitators, apostles of unrest, gadflies of conscience. Miss Anthony was tall, spare and plain. She had an air of severity; only her infrequent smile revealed her gracious, kindly nature and her astonishing shyness. Mrs. Stanton, white-haired and plump as a partridge, was always merry. You would have surmised her to be happily married, the exemplary mother of several children and an excellent housewife. You would have been right on all counts.

For all their air of guilelessness, these women were irrepressible fountains of subversion. Not content with spreading poisonous ideas, they were goading others, throughout the country, into joining them in militant action. Ridicule and obloquy merely increased their influence. Were they not seeking to undermine the sacred institution of marriage? Mrs. Stanton openly declared that, under American laws, the marriage relation was a false one, whether happy or unhappy. In most cases, marriage was only legalized prostitution, a state in which women could have no self-respect and men need have no respect for them. Miss Anthony asserted that women would never be able to live honestly until they were enfranchised. Then, they would no longer be obliged to sell themselves for bread, either in or out of marriage. What woman would choose to remain bound to a drunkard or libertine if she could be assured of her subsistence in any other way? Mrs. Stanton and Miss Anthony had won legislation granting married women personal control of their property and money. But this wasn't enough. Now, they were even agitating for liberalized divorce laws.

The women who frequented the Carys' Sunday parties had meanwhile been stirred to indignation by a social slight, a masculine rebuff. The New York Press Club tendered a banquet to Charles Dickens. When Jennie June, the well-known journalist, applied for a ticket, she was curtly refused; the presence of women was not desired. Smarting under this churlish treatment, she reported the incident to all her friends. Why should not women form a club of their own? She invited Mrs. Botta, Kate Field and two other friends to her home in West Fourteenth Street and laid this audacious project before them. It was received with enthusiasm, and the work of organizing began. Mrs. Botta soon withdrew because her husband disapproved so radical an enterprise. Kate Field withdrew shortly afterward, when the organizers firmly rejected her suggestion that the club attempt to secure the co-operation of men, and chose a name which she considered ridiculous. The new organization was christened "Sorosis," this name being derived from the Greek word meaning an aggregation. An initial membership of fifty was aggregated.

Perhaps the unchivalrous New York Press Club foresaw an ultimate collapse of masculine supremacy. After suitable preliminaries, it joined Sorosis in a public banquet—the first ever given in New York at which men and women sat down on equal terms, each paying their own way and sharing equally in the honors and responsibilities. Miss Anthony was among those present, and without previous warning was called upon to reply to the question, "Why don't women propose?" Smiling, she arose and spoke. "Under present conditions, it would require a good deal of assurance for a woman to say to a man, 'Please, sir, will you support me for the rest of my life?' When all avocations are open to woman and she has an opportunity to acquire a competence, she will then be in a position where it will not be humiliating for her to ask the man she loves to share her prosperity. Instead of requesting him to provide food, raiment and shelter for her, she can invite him into her home, contribute her share to the partnership and not be an utter dependent.

There will also be another advantage in this arrangement—if he proves unworthy she can ask him to walk out."

It was precisely the kind of idea you might expect from a woman who had determined to think for herself.

"WOMAN ONLY WANTS SPACE TO GROW," *by J. M'Nevin.* An impression of the "Amazonian Convention" for women's rights at Mozart Hall, 1857

7

Movers and Shakers

The Civil War brought great prosperity to Printing House Square, immediately opposite and east of the City Hall. Here, or nearby, were the plants of the city's principal newspapers. Wartime anxiety had made the reading of newspapers a nearly universal habit. To satisfy an eager demand for the latest news, the press had instituted such novel practices as the publication of "extras" and Sunday editions. Now, with the advent of peace, there was keen competition among the papers to retain and increase the swollen circulations built up during the war. The scope of news coverage was constantly expanded; the successful opening of the Atlantic cable, in 1866, enabled the press to report events in Europe almost as they happened. An equivalent expansion occurred in the publication of "feature material"—special articles, reviews of books, the drama, music and art, political comment from Washington, gossip about society, columns devoted to fashion, homemaking and other subjects of particular interest to women. As a result, journalism suddenly became an accredited profession for women of talent. Such pioneers as Margaret Fuller, Grace Greenwood and Fanny Fern were now followed by a new generation of women writers many of whom achieved national celebrity. The newspapers of New York furnished the patterns followed by the press of the entire country. Many of them were likewise read throughout the nation and exercised a powerful influence on the shaping of public opinion.

Although costs of production and distribution were mounting astronomically, it remained possible for a few men to own and control their newspapers. The major New York papers bore the unmistakable stamp of the character and personality of their publishers. Most of the publishers were also creative editors. They not only formulated policy with respect to all important questions of the day, but expressed their views by writing daily editorials and frequent leading articles. The old tradition of personal journalism still ruled and was favorable to spirited, often acrimonious, controversy.

William Cullen Bryant, who for forty years had presided over the *Evening Post,* was generally called "the Nestor of the metropolitan press." He was one of New York's outstanding public figures, whose prestige was essential to the success of all municipal ceremonies, and whose support brought prosperity to any worthy cause. Bryant had become, in effect, a civic institution, and New York scarcely remembered that he had once been the nation's most celebrated poet. He wrote little poetry now, so little that his verses on the death of President Lincoln, and the two poems which Robert Bonner commissioned him to write for *The Ledger*—at a fee, it was said, of three thousand dollars— seemed, to the younger generation, silvery echoes of a voice that belonged to the remote past. Sometimes you saw Bryant vigorously striding up Broadway, lithe and erect despite his seventy-five years, looking like an ancient patriarch with his long white hair and flowing white beard. He was austere, dignified, aloof, taciturn. "One would as soon think of taking a liberty with the Pope as with Bryant," his former colleague John Bigelow had said. Bryant was a moderate and a moralist who preached the doctrine of free trade and deplored the corruption of New York's municipal politics. He resisted the new taste for sensational journalism, .for trivial social gossip, for columns produced by women writers. *The Post* was sober, dignified, impeccably literary, and its extreme "purity of tone" made it the favorite newspaper of conservative, cultivated New Yorkers.

Younger readers—the war and postwar generations—found their spokesman in Horace Greeley. He had made *The Tribune* an intellectual catalyst, and its weekly edition was being read by the advancing tide of settlers who were following the new transcontinental railroad out on the Great Plains. "One of the first questions asked by any camp-fire," Charles Dudley Warner reported, "is, 'Did you ever *see* Horace?' " You could hardly avoid seeing Greeley in New York. He spoke at nearly every meeting held in behalf of any forward-looking cause. He was a frequent and popular lecturer. He was incorrigibly social, too, and you were likely to find him at the two houses which offered the best talk, and the most interesting people, in the city: Mrs. Botta's and the home of Alice and Phoebe Cary. The wonder was that Greeley found time to write his daily average of about two columns for *The Tribune,* and also contribute every week, to other publications, the equivalent of some six *Tribune* columns.

Greeley's eccentric appearance made him a favorite subject for the cartoonists who were forever ridiculing his radical ideas. Tall, rather stout, partly bald, his moon face was pinkish in color and framed in unkempt white whiskers worn around his throat and under his chin. His small, pale-blue eyes peered out from behind large spectacles. His black frock coat, baggy black trousers and white vest were always rumpled, his black cravat was permanently askew. He walked with a shuffling gait and he had an absent-minded air, so that if you greeted him on the street he was apt to seem little more cordial than a startled jack-rabbit. But Greeley genuinely loved his fellow-men, and he needed spectacles only because he kept his eyes fixed on the distant future. This made him the champion of youth against age, of new ideas against outworn traditions, of fruitful change against the complacent established order. Greeley was all for progress on every front, so he was invariably ahead of the times and, although he was nearing his sixtieth year, young people thought of him as their contemporary and their pathfinder. They alone, perhaps, understood that his famous maxim, "Go West, young man, and grow up with the country," implied much more than it actually said.

Greeley was driven by intellectual curiosity and he had a romantic faith in the free play of the mind. The more ideas set in circulation the better; the more radically novel those ideas, the better, too: it was this belief of Greeley's that made *The Tribune* so uniquely exciting to read. He opened his columns to planners of Utopias; could not America be made Utopian? Albert Brisbane wrote on Fourieristic collectivism; William Henry Channing wrote on socialism; various advocates of the co-operative movement expounded its principles. During the eighteen-sixties, Karl Marx contributed a weekly letter on European collectivistic theories and movements. Greeley was the first editor to cultivate the feminine audience that other editors had been neglecting. Three years after founding *The Tribune,* he brought Margaret Fuller down from Boston to serve as its literary critic and write articles on subjects of interest to women, among them a series exposing the frightful conditions that obtained in the city's public hospitals and other institutions. He also published her *Woman in the Nineteenth Century,* the first feminist manifesto to appear in America, a book loaded with intellectual dynamite. Greeley agreed with Susan B. Anthony and Elizabeth Cady Stanton that women were an exploited class. He became an active partisan of the "women's-rights movement," and frequently published articles by its leaders, though he later withdrew his support. He developed women journalists. He considered Mrs. Lucia Gilbert Calhoun, a staff member, his most effective writer. He hired brilliant, vivacious Kate Field to write long critical articles on Adelaide Ristori, travel letters from fashionable American summer resorts and from Europe and, eventually, editorials. George Ripley, the erudite founder of Brook Farm, was *The Tribune's* literary editor, and its reviews of books were outstanding. To the younger generation, Greeley's paper seemed indispensable. It was more than a mere newspaper. It was a medium for the most vital and provocative thinking of the day.

This, the most successful newspaper in New York was not. James Gordon Bennett had launched *The New York Herald* as a penny daily in 1835 from a rented cellar in Wall Street. Now *The Herald* was turned out in a white-marble building in the modern French style that Bennett had built on the site of Barnum's old Museum, on Broadway and Ann Street, and Bennett ranked among the city's foremost millionaires. At seventy-five he remained the thoroughgoing cynic that he had always been. He made no pretense of molding public opinion; he sought either to anticipate it or to follow it. In Bennett's view, any issue of a newspaper was ephemeral. The public cared nothing for what had been said yesterday, or would be said tomorrow. So he published each day's *Herald* as if there had been none before, and would be none after it. Personally, he had no principles or convictions and he did not believe that others had any, whatever they might profess. All men and all ideals were, to him, mere shams; at bottom, men were wholly selfish. No public policy was better than any other, and no subject merited very serious treatment. Bennett's object was to make as much money as possible by merchandising news and, in addition, whatever trimmings might swell his circulation. *The Herald* was not a public institution but a private enterprise conducted for profit.

In the gathering of news and its sprightly presentation, Bennett had revolutionized the New York press. *The Herald* led all other papers in the amount and variety of news which it presented. But many who read it only for that reason were offended by other characteristic features of the paper. What could you make, for example, of the heavily loaded columns of "personal" advertisements so prominently displayed? In them, you found the announcements of prostitutes. Miss Gertie Davis, formerly of Lexington Avenue, invited her friends to visit her at her specified new address. Miss Jennie Howard had left Heath's and was now located in another establishment on West Twenty-

A TYPICAL "PERSONAL" COL-
UMN from The New York *Herald*

seventh Street. You also found the amorous appeals of men attracted by some female casually seen and possibly receptive to admiration. Would the young lady in black who, with a gentleman escort, had left a downtown Fifth Avenue stage at Forty-sixth Street at ten o'clock yesterday morning, please communicate, in care of *The Herald,* at a specified box number, with the captivated male who signed his initials? The "personal" columns of *The Herald* offered an incomparable opportunity to prostitutes and recruiters for brothels, to abortionists, to blackmailers and burglars. Reputable folk agreed that they were a civic scandal. Nothing was done about it.

Bennett had been the first American journalist to realize that mass circulation could be attracted by gossip about society which, under the guise of news, publicized scandal and mocked at the elect. Wealth and fashion, in the early days of *The Herald,* feared Bennett's scurrilous abuse, and he was not above using this fear as an instrument of polite blackmail. But society had gradually become reconciled to Bennett's paper, though not to Bennett himself. And Bennett, for personal reasons, had found it advantageous to adopt a different tone. Severely snubbed by New York's fashionable circles, Mrs. Bennett had taken to living in Paris for most of the year and there she brought up their adored son and heir, his father's namesake. Young Bennett returned to New York a dandy whose tastes and habits were more sophisticated than those of any member of the inner circle. The smart set found him attractive. The elder Bennett determined that his son should have the social prestige denied to his parents. With his father's millions to back him, young Bennett laid successful siege to the citadel. Admitted to the New York Yacht Club, he entered his schooner *Henrietta,* in December, 1866, in the most spectacular race in the history of American yachting—a transatlantic run from New York to the Needles through raging winter seas for a purse of ninety thousand dollars. This event stirred up tremendous public excitement, and the circulation of *The Herald* leaped upward. When young Bennett won the race, he became a popular hero and an accredited leader of the smart set.

James Gordon Bennett the elder was grimly pleased. He relinquished active management of *The Herald* to his resplendent son, who took society with extreme seriousness and made the paper its journalistic spokesman, chronicler and defender. You never saw the elder Bennett in New York. He lived in lonely baronial state at his magnificent country home on Washington Heights, seldom opening his town house on Fifth Avenue and Thirty-eighth Street, keeping in constant touch with his son and his paper by private telegraph line. He was a solitary, imperious, vindictive old man whom few people knew, fewer still esteemed, and nobody really liked.

Henry J. Raymond, founder and editor-in-chief of *The Times,* was a familiar figure about town and popular in all circles. A short, thick-set, dark-haired, dark-whiskered man nearing his fiftieth year, he had served as an assistant to Horace Greeley before founding his own paper. Raymond was fond of social life, an enthusiastic patron of the theater, and drove a fine span of bays in the Park and on Harlem Lane. He was a gifted, facile writer

and held his staff to exacting literary standards. Raymond candidly acknowledged that he was always able to see two sides of every issue. "I always try,"
he said, "when one side is presented to look at the other and, in turning it
around, I am instinctively inclined to favor the reverse of the side I first examined." This idiosyncrasy sometimes made *The Times's* policy seem vacillating.
Raymond's major interests were politics and foreign affairs. He was an ardent
Republican, the close friend of Secretary Seward and other prominent politicians, and under his guidance *The Times* became, throughout the Civil War
and afterward, a powerful organ for the Republican administration and for
the great banking interests whose fortunes were bound up with it. You read
The Times if you were a partisan of President Lincoln and, later, of the
Radical Republicans led by grim Thaddeus Stevens, the implacable enemy of
the conquered South. You read it also for its excellent foreign correspondence,
its authoritative analysis of economic issues and political events. Raymond
died in 1869, but two years later *The Times* electrified the nation with a
sensational exposure of the Tweed Ring which had controlled, robbed and
corrupted the city of New York.

Whatever newspaper you read, you almost certainly bought *The New York
Ledger,* Robert Bonner's weekly. Its circulation stood at three hundred thousand and it claimed a million readers throughout the nation. This astonishing
success was not accidental. It had been adroitly developed by Bonner, the
Barnum of the publishing industry and an editorial genius. He often spent
as much as twenty-five thousand dollars a week in advertising *The Ledger,*
and his mode of advertising was new and sensational. He would take full
pages in *The Herald, The Tribune* and *The Times,* leave most of this costly
space blank and use only the center, or one corner, for his text. This might
be a single line, emphatically repeated: "Read Mrs. Southworth's new story
in *The Ledger.*" Or it might be a brief, provocative fragment of the story.
At first, his unconventional, extravagant advertisements exasperated most
readers. But you couldn't avoid them. They excited your curiosity and, however reluctantly, you bought the weekly. Bonner seemed always to have some
new feature that justified his advertising. As an editor, he was singularly adept
in parlor magic. He perpetually pulled irresistible rabbits out of invisible hats.

He had begun doing this soon after buying *The Ledger,* when Fanny Fern
was the literary sensation of the day. Fanny Fern was the sister of Nathaniel
P. Willis, the eminent author and editor, with whom she had quarrelled. She
wrote an autobiographical novel, *Ruth Hall,* which savagely attacked him; it
had a tremendous sale and made her famous. Bonner promptly offered her the
unprecedented fee of one thousand dollars for a story. The story came to ten
columns of his paper, but he double-leaded it so that it made twenty. Then
he advertised it prodigiously, telling the public that he had paid the incredible rate of one hundred dollars a column. This feat put *The Ledger* on
the highroad to success.

Bonner paid the highest prices of any editor in the United States, and his
list of contributors always bristled with names that were currently famous.

In *The Ledger* you found poems by Longfellow, Bryant, Alice and Phoebe Cary. There were serials by such noted novelists as Mrs. Harriet Beecher Stowe and Mrs. E. D. E. N. Southworth, or the ever popular Sylvanus Cobb, Jr. The great preacher Henry Ward Beecher wrote a series of essays for Bonner, then serialized in *The Ledger* his only novel, *Norwood; or, Village Life in New England*—a feature which added more than fifty thousand readers to the magazine's circulation. In every issue there was also more serious fare: articles by such distinguished men as the orator and statesman Edward Everett, the historian George Bancroft, the biographer James Parton, who was Fanny Fern's husband. And there were special features which Bonner devised for your edification. He ran a page of "answers to readers" which offered advice on all types of problems by men like Everett and Beecher, and various eminent lawyers, clergymen and statesmen. For chess players, there was a column originally written by Paul Morphy, the world's champion. Of one thing you could be absolutely certain: there would be nothing in *The Ledger* to offend the most delicate taste. Bonner's editorial staff had a standing order: "Take the most pious old lady in a Presbyterian church, and any word or phrase, innuendo or expression, that she would want to skip if she were reading a *Ledger* story to her grandchild, strike out."

So Mrs. Grundy was profitably enthroned in the marble building at the corner of William and Spruce Streets from which America's most popular weekly went out over the country. But did she not also preside in the kitchens of New England and the Middle West, in the lonely sod-houses of the Great Plains? Was she not still to be found behind New York's brownstone facades, the magistrate of parlors wainscoted in black walnut, where every damask chair had its antimacassar, where there was a whatnot, a square piano and a rubber plant? There, on the petticoated center table, you would see *The Ledger* with its unique blend of uplift that was never disturbing and romance that was never distasteful. Bonner was the first publisher in the United States to recognize the need for a magazine which would please the masses, but which would likewise carry names so eminent that the classes could not afford to ignore it. With his roster of celebrities, his flair for daring publicity, his immense circulation, Bonner announced the new epoch in which a diluted, antiseptic culture would be ruled by the genteel American woman.

8

The Park and Its Pleasures

Throughout the year it was in Central Park that you caught the distinctive tone of New York life. Planned by a commission of distinguished citizens headed by Washington Irving, the beautiful park was designed by Frederick Law Olmstead and Calvert Vaux. Nearly ten years of work and the expenditure of more than nine million dollars had been required to transform a barren, rocky wilderness into a rural pleasure ground. The Park was two and one-half miles long, and one-half mile wide; its area of more than eight hundred acres was double that of Hyde Park in London. Virtually completed at the end of the Civil War, the southern boundary of the Park, at Fifty-ninth Street, was on the outskirts of the city. The northern boundary, at One Hundred and Tenth Street, touched the suburb of Harlem and, beyond, overlooked a region of farms and country houses. To reach the Park from the city proper, you took the omnibuses of the Fifth Avenue Line, which stopped at Forty-second Street, and walked up the avenue. Or you could take the horse-cars on Third, Sixth, Seventh, Eighth Avenues, or on Broadway, any of which would bring you to Fifty-ninth Street.

In Central Park the world of fashion, the middle classes and the poor met, as it were, on common ground. From Christmas to the end of February, when hard frosts set in and extreme cold gripped the city, you saw flags on the omnibuses and horse cars, you heard people say, "The ball is up in the Park." This meant that the large lake north of the Mall and the pond at Fifty-ninth Street were frozen over, and that at night ice carnivals would be in progress. The Park had introduced skating as a general sport of the people, and among the wealthy it had become the vogue for both men and women. At night, the lake and the pond were brilliantly illuminated by calcium lights, and sleighs brought gay, fur-wrapped parties to speed over the ice. Temporary refreshment houses were erected every winter at both places, and there you could rent skates, or lazily sit and watch the show. At the lake, the Terrace House and the Beach House were always crowded. The Beach House was the larger, a building about one hundred and seventy-five feet in length with a spacious ladies' sitting room where chaperones could maintain their vigil in gregarious comfort. On the ice, figure skating and dancing were favorite diversions of the proficient. Occasionally you saw extraordinary feats of skill, as when a master of the new sport, on a wager, skimmed over the ice, bearing, above his head, a salver of glasses filled to the brim with wine, spilling not one drop in all his escapes from the clutches of baffled pursuers. As many as twenty thousand people skated at the lake on a frosty winter night. The brightly lit spectacle, the snow-banked hills, the trees sheathed in ice reminded travelers of resorts in Switzerland or the cities of Scandinavia.

With the advent of fine spring weather, all New York turned out in Central Park. The Mall, a stately esplanade one-quarter of a mile in length, was frequented by ladies for their afternoon walks. On Wednesdays and Saturdays, during the warm months, excellent bands gave promenade concerts in the ornate, pagodalike music pavilion near the head of the Mall, and fashionable folk, to hear them, had their carriages driven to the adjacent carriage concourse, or were deposited at the Casino on a terrace above the esplanade, and there listened to the music while enjoying an ice cream or light repast. Some forty thousand citizens less given to exclusiveness meanwhile heard the concert from benches or rented canopied rustic chairs or lolled on the grass. These pleasant musical events were not entirely the free offering of a benevolent municipality. The fund which made them possible was largely furnished by the horse-car lines—"railroads," as they were called—that profited from a large attendance.

For genteel New York, the Mall became a dominant incubator of court-

SKATING IN CENTRAL PARK, 1866, *by J. M. Culverhouse*

ship and marriage. Convention quickly established it as one of the very few public places to which a young man might take a girl unchaperoned, though a ritual taboo prevented them from entering the Casino unless they were suitably accompanied. After promenading on the Mall, they eventually descended the broad stairs at its upper end. These led to the great terrace, where two revolving fountains played. The terrace overlooked the lake, and there young people met their friends and formed parties to go boating. Mr. Dick, the concessionaire at the lake, probably knew more than any man in New York about the immediate amatory condition of the younger set. He maintained public, or "omnibus," and private, or "call" boats; and the choice between them accurately indicated the current temperature of any couple. A trip on the water to see and feed the swans—a gift from London's Worshipful Company of Vintners and Worshipful Company of Dyers—was a permitted diversion for well-bred young men and girls who, as they said, were "interested in one another" or likely to become so.

In fine weather, Central Park served as a vast parade ground for the equine cult to which all classes of the population were now fanatically devoted. There were nearly ten miles of perfect carriage road in the Park, and more than five miles of bridle paths. As a form of exercise for ladies, riding had never been socially approved in New York. Perhaps at one's country home, remote from vulgar, prying eyes, but in town—certainly not. A decade earlier, Fanny Kemble, a superb horsewoman, had aroused censorious comment by riding on Broadway—even though, as a noted actress, she was permitted idiosyncrasies denied to the genteel. Now, all this was suddenly changed; riding was sanctioned. The fashionable hour for equestriennes was before breakfast. You could see them elegantly togged out in silk hat draped with a flying veil, tight buttoned bodice and flowing skirts, a crop in one gloved hand, beautifully perched on a side-saddle.

A lady riding alone was invariably attended by a liveried groom or a riding master. But ladies were likely to ride in parties, attended by gentlemen, and always chaperoned by some young matron. And a new social occasion developed from equestrianism. On the east carriage road, at One Hundred and Sixth Street, at the head of MacGowan's Pass of Revolutionary fame, stood the buildings formerly occupied by the Roman Catholic Seminary of Mount St. Vincent. After serving as a military hospital during the War, these had been leased to Colonel Stetson, proprietor of the Astor House, and had been converted into a luxurious restaurant. It became the fashionable thing for riding parties to breakfast at Mount St. Vincent. But, according to the rigorous code of New York, this charming resort, with its fine panoramic view, was not a proper dining place. It was too remote, too secluded, and in the evening it was left to the patronage of gentlemen of rakish tastes and their abandoned feminine companions.

The great, fashionable carriage parade—so rightly considered one of the notable "sights" of the city—took place between the hours of four and five.

To view this, crowds gathered along the walk that bordered the east carriage drive from Fifty-ninth Street and Fifth Avenue to the Mall. In the continuous procession of equipages you saw everyone who counted: the aristocracy, the new smart set, the parvenus, the celebrities, the deplorably notorious. There were the dowagers whose old, conservative families—Jays, Livingstons, Stuyvesants and others—had held social power from Colonial days. They could always exercise this power if they wished, but they seldom appeared in society. They consistently avoided display; they deliberately ignored fashion. They wore an uncompromising obsoleteness as if it were the sole genuine regalia of eminence. Invisible and august, their authority was absolute. When taking the air in the Park, many of them preferred to remain concealed in their broughams, but some had progressed to public exposure in a landau. Their horses were huge, fat and slow; their coachmen and footmen, soberly liveried, were elderly; their carriages were funereally black.

The younger smart set went in for a variety of modish equipages. The victoria was establishing its superiority as a mobile display case for feminine elegance, and ladies with tiny parasols delicately poised rolled by in interminable swift succession. You saw barouches, also, roomier than the victoria and more stately, the vogue in Paris by decree of the Empress Eugénie. Mrs. August Belmont sometimes drove through the Park in her unique *demi-d'Aumont;* few knew the name of this novel vehicle which her worldly husband had appropriated from Paris. Several young ladies had taken to driving light, swift phaetons, with a groom stolidly perched on the back seat, though the first of these innovators, one of the daughters of Archibald Gracie King, had met with disapproving glares from the windows of the Union Club on her initial expedition. An occasional dogcart appeared in the procession, but this

FASHIONABLE TURNOUTS IN CENTRAL PARK, 1869, *by Thomas Worth*

odd carriage, with its two transverse seats back to back, had not yet received a certificate of fashion. It was the smart set that made a vogue of vehicular novelty. The stars of the opera and theater did not. You never saw Clara Louise Kellogg, or Maggie Mitchell, or Pauline Markham driving a phaeton; they affected the decorous victoria. The celebrated *demi-mondaines* who frequented the Louvre concert saloon appeared, in the Park, only in the most conventional of carriages. So did Josephine Wood, proprietor of the city's most exclusive brothel. And you could scarcely distinguish the equipage of Madame Restell, the notorious abortionist, from those of the most august dowagers. To a member of the smart set as original as Mrs. Pierre Lorillard Ronalds, the carriage parade must have offered a painful temptation. She had electrified Newport by appearing on the box-seat of a drag and skillfully driving a four-in-hand on crowded Bellevue Avenue. But she did not offer this exhibition of grace to the onlookers in Central Park.

Many of the onlookers were almost indifferent to the fashionable carriage parade. They had come to see another show—the procession of famous trotters that was bound for Harlem Lane. Trotting was a universal mania, a civic passion peculiar to New York. It infected all classes; even Dr. Henry Ward Beecher, the eminent Brooklyn clergyman, had succumbed and drove a fine team. Men of wealth paid fabulous prices for fast horses. When any reportedly exceptional new trotter was to be brought out and shown off, Wall Street became as excited as if a great corner was rumored. Excitement spread through the city, and many bets were made on the newcomer's performance. Stakes ran high whenever news came out that the claims of rival owners were to be settled by a race, either on Harlem Lane or at Peter Dubois' track near Macomb's Dam on the Harlem River.

Any fine afternoon you could see the wealthy horse-fanciers driving their curricles or sulkies through Central Park on their way to "the road," as they called Harlem Lane. Their horses were very unlike the sleek, showy, beautifully caparisoned animals that figured in the carriage parade. The trotters had neither beauty nor grace. They were long, lanky animals, bony, slab-sided, gawky-looking; they were bred for speed and endurance. Robert Bonner, publisher of *The Ledger,* was the most celebrated owner of trotters. Bonner owned Dexter, the world's fastest trotter; this animal had done the mile in two minutes, seventeen and one-half seconds. There were other noted horses in Bonner's stables; Young Pocahontas, Peerless, Lady Palmer, Lantern, Flatbush Maid, an animal known only as the Auburn Horse. The names of these creatures were more familiar to New Yorkers than those of most politicians, scientists or authors. Bonner was unique among horse-fanciers. Willing to pay any price for a good trotter, he was conscientiously opposed to betting and he refused to enter contests with other owners because gamblers were bound to bet on the outcome.

Old Commodore Vanderbilt was Bonner's most determined rival. He owned a dozen fine horses, of which the best and fastest were Mountain Boy, Post Boy and Mountain Maid. The old Commodore invariably began his day with a visit to his stables, and every afternoon, if the weather was favorable, he climbed into his curricle and drove a pair of trotters out to the road. Unlike Bonner, he enjoyed nothing more than gambling on the performance of his horses; and he was the most daring of drivers, habitually mocking at prudence and caution. Social leaders like August Belmont, Lewis Morris and William R. Travers maintained stables of trotters. The celebrated actor-manager Lester Wallack was almost as well known for his horses as for his theater. There were few outstanding men in the realm of finance and commerce who did not own, and drive, fast teams. For expert advice on their stables, horse-fanciers depended, successively, on two professional traders who took high rank among the city's celebrities. Hiram Woodruff was a dealer whose integrity and judgment were highly respected. When Woodruff died, his place was taken by Daniel Mace, a young man acknowledged to be the best driver in the United States and the premier authority on trotters. Men spending thirty thousand dollars or more for a horse bought only through Mace, and refused to accept the horse's time as official unless Mace had established it by driving the animal himself.

Mace was a familiar figure on Harlem Lane. You entered the Lane—later to be named St. Nicholas Avenue—from the northern end of Central Park. It ran, in an irregularly northwestern direction, across the upper part of Manhattan Island to a junction with the Bloomingdale Road, or Broadway, far out in the country at One Hundred and Sixty-eighth Street, beyond Carmansville. A branch road turning off at One Hundred and Fiftieth Street took you east to Macomb's Dam on the Harlem River, and the river road up to High Bridge. At the lower end of the Harlem Lane there were a number of inns, bars and stables; above these, "the road" passed through open fields. For a mile or more, drivers could put their horses to their best speeds. The exhilaration of driving was intense; as on Wall Street, the rule was every man for himself. Teams dashed, cut across, tore up and down the road; brushes between rivals constantly took place. Sightseers crowded the porches of the inns to watch the spectacle and participate in its excitement. When General Grant visited the city at the end of the Civil War, one of his first requests was to be taken out to Harlem Lane. He shared New York's passion for trotters, and agreed that "the road" of a late afternoon was one of the most thrilling sights in the country.

"The opening of Central Park saved horseflesh in New York," an old jockey asserted. And the flourishing equine cult led to the revival of an old sport in circumstances of unprecedented splendor. Racing—formerly carried on at Union Course and Fashion Park on Long Island—had lost all social prestige by attracting professional gamblers and a rowdy "sporting" crowd. But should not New York have its Goodwood? Should not society redeem the sport of kings? To Leonard Jerome, the answers were obvious. He bought a large tract of land in Westchester County near the town of Fordham and, with the cooperation of August Belmont and William R. Travers, founded the American Jockey Club on the British pattern, enlisting the entire smart set in this new

FAST TROTTERS ON HARLEM LANE ABOUT 1870, *by J. Cameron.*
Scene on Eighth Avenue near 137th Street showing Commodore Vanderbilt driving
Myron Perry and Daisy Burns, and Bonner driving Dexter. The Clubhouse is "Toppy"
McGuire's

association. On Jerome's two hundred and thirty acres in Westchester, the
Club laid out the most elaborate of racetracks, with a grandstand seating eight
thousand people, and a luxurious clubhouse and club stand. Largely at
Jerome's expense a great boulevard, later to be named Jerome Avenue, was
cut through from Macomb's Dam to the racetrack. The opening races at
Jerome Park were held in 1866, with General Grant in attendance, and all
fashionable New York turned out for them. Thereafter, the spring and autumn
meetings of the American Jockey Club became important events on the social
calendar, highly favored by even the most conservative, and drawing a large
popular following out from the city.

Even before inaugurating his splendid racetrack, Jerome lifted the cult of
the horse to a plane of elegance and distinction far superior to that of noisy,
competitive Harlem Lane. He was a connoisseur of horseflesh, an enthusiastic
sportsman and no misogynist. To indulge his predilections simultaneously, he
found an appropriately costly form of activity. In England, the Duke of Beau-
fort had recently attempted to revive the picturesqueness of stagecoach days
by driving a drag, or coach, and four horses. Fired by this example, Jerome
perfected himself in the art of four-in-hand driving and ordered a vehicle built.
"He turned out daily with his drag or coach loaded with beautiful women,"
Ward McAllister recalled thirty years later, "and drove to every desirable
little country inn in and about the city, where one could dine at all well, crossing ferries, and driving up Broadway with the ease and skill of a veteran whip,
which he was." But less worldly observers were shocked by Jerome's custom

of driving his coach up Fifth Avenue on Sunday mornings at the hour when the fashionable church parade was at full tide. "His horses were trained to caper and rear as they turned into the street," a censorious contemporary recorded. "Gay and laughing ladies in gorgeous costume filled the carriage. Lackeys, carefully gotten up, occupied the coupé behind. Jerome sat on the box and handled the reins. With a huge bouquet of flowers attached to his buttonhole, with white gloves, cracking his whip, and with the shouts of the party, the four horses would rush up Fifth Avenue, on toward the Park, while the populace said, one to the other, 'That is Jerome.'"

Not to be outdone, August Belmont ordered an even more costly coach, and took up the new pastime of four-in-hand driving. But Belmont and Jerome were intrepid pioneers, far in advance of the times. It was not until another decade had passed that coaching became the smartest, most exclusive diversion of New York society, having its peculiar ritual and ceremonies that were the delight of the fashionable and the astonishment of the plebeian.

PART TWO

1870-1890

**BEYOND
THE AGE OF INNOCENCE**

9

The City Marches

For years after the Civil War, elderly citizens lamented the quickening pace of change that was transforming New York. The pleasant, peaceful city of their youth had long been buried under the avalanche of progress. Few relics of it remained to reward an antiquarian interest, had one existed. But New York, always intent on the future, had little sentimental attachment to its past.

Old William Backhouse Astor, nearing his eightieth year, could testify to the relentless swiftness of change, not to be stemmed even by the city's greatest owner of real estate. In his boyhood wealth and fashion resided on the Battery. In his young manhood, daring young people had built as far north as Chambers Street. In Astor's prime, the most magnificent residence in the city was the Palladian palace of John C. Stevens, builder of steamships, set in ample grounds on College Place. Presently, fashion migrated north of Bleecker Street. In his middle age, Astor built stolid mansions for himself and his sisters on Lafayette Place. This was a wide, tree-shaded cul-de-sac, three blocks long, opening on Astor Place, renamed in his father's honor. In its aristocratic privacy, with its superb Colonnade Row, Lafayette Place was destined to permanence and would never be superseded.

But its glories had long since faded. Astor's sons built their mansions far uptown, on Fifth Avenue between Thirty-third and Thirty-fourth Streets. Much later, Astor settled his daughters and granddaughters in the same Murray Hill quarter, on Madison Avenue. Finally, over his protest, the city turned quiet Lafayette Place into a thoroughfare, cutting it through to the south. Old William Backhouse Astor reluctantly capitulated to progress. He moved to Fifth Avenue, a block north of his sons. Just below his new house, on the northwest corner of Thirty-fourth Street, his contemporary, A. T. Stewart, had built a vast, pillared, white-marble palace that exceeded, in architectural pretension and costliness, any residence in the city. Next to Astor, Stewart was the largest landowner in New York, the world's most successful merchant, and the proprietor of a huge department store. A man of solitary habits, cold, arrogant, excluded by aristocratic society as a mere tradesman, childless and almost friendless, what did he want with his splendid palace? People condemned his ostentatious extravagance. In 1876, nine years after building it, Stewart died in his marble mausoleum with its lofty picture gallery that nobody had ever entered, its magnificent, enfiladed drawing rooms where nobody was ever received. One year earlier, his neighbor William Backhouse Astor died in his far more modest new home. And already other millionaires were planning habitations of a grandeur that was to surpass the boldest dreams of Stewart and Astor. The tide of progress would sweep them even further uptown, into a wilderness of rocks and ragged truck gardens inhabited by Irish squatters and melancholy, ruminant goats.

For the city was marching northward with giant strides. William Backhouse Astor died in the new fashionable quarter, on Murray Hill, a region where, in his youth, he might have gone shooting duck and quail over coverts and thickets. But scarcely had he been laid to rest in Trinity Cemetery, far up Manhattan Island at Carmansville, when New York swept over the Harlem River to annex a large area of rural Westchester. The Annexed District, as it was called—later to become the Bronx—was still largely open country, its pleasant villages clustering along the New Haven Railroad on the east, the Port Morris branch of the New York Central on the west. The vast tract had been granted to Colonel Lewis Morris in 1676 by Governor Edmund Andros, and it still bore the name Morrisania, taken from the ancestral estate that had come down through the family. Gouverneur Morris, the Revolutionary patriot, had built a fine home there, on the Harlem Kills, and had filled it with precious objects brought from France: ancient tapestries, gilded chairs and couches, paintings and books, a rare dessert service of old Sèvres with forks and spoons of solid gold. His son and namesake still lived in the mellow old house, but the estate had shrunk to forty acres, for he had sold it off piece by piece. Directly across the Harlem from the eastern upper end of Manhattan Island was Mott Haven, where enterprising J. L. Mott had built his sprawling ironworks and a factory town. Other industries were bound to follow, and the whole of Morrisania awaited only rapid transportation to be swallowed up by the encroaching metropolis. Five years after William Backhouse Astor's death his eldest son, John Jacob Astor III, bought the remaining Morris acreage and laid it out in future building lots. He also purchased land even more remote; open fields lying along the pretty Bronx River near the rural railroad station of West Farms. New Yorkers who recalled his grandfather's visionary purchases of farms far up Manhattan Island, sixty years earlier, realized that these distant acquisitions were a portent. Someday, certainly, there would be streets and tenements and brownstone houses up in the Annexed District beyond the muddy Harlem River.

To New Yorkers returning from long sojourns in London or Paris or Rome, the city as yet seemed scarcely metropolitan. They were depressed by its architectural ugliness, its untended streets, its endless blocks of identical narrow houses, "so lacking in external dignity, so crammed with smug and suffocating upholstery." If your eyes had dwelt fondly on the gracious vistas that Baron Haussmann had opened up with his new boulevards, or on the weathered, reticent squares of Mayfair and Belgravia, what could you say about Broadway except that it was as unlovely as it was long, "filled with huddled buildings, monotonous in line and tint"? Yet patricians who had resided in foreign capitals, and were presumably free to remain there, often in the end returned to New York. They fastidiously deplored "this cramped horizontal gridiron of a town without towers, porticoes, fountains or perspectives, hide-bound in its deadly uniformity of mean ugliness"—but they settled down between Washington Square and Forty-second Street to endure a nostalgia for more beautiful cities where they felt even less at home.

Certainly the peculiar fascination of New York had little to do with what they conceived to be beauty. New York was titanic, a city of violent, bewildering contrasts. It lusted for ever greater power, greater wealth. It built only to abandon its buildings, obliterate them and build again, in a different way, for another purpose. It had succumbed to the most restless and insatiable of passions, and the results of its exorbitance confronted you everywhere. Only in New York was it impossible to distinguish the illusion of permanence from the conviction of transiency. Ceaselessly shifting, changing, growing, perpetually provisional, there was no other city like it in the world.

When arresting beauty emerged from the welter of change, Europeanized New Yorkers failed to recognize it. Europe offered neither precedent nor standard by which to judge the spectacular bridge that was flung across the East River to unite New York with Brooklyn. The Brooklyn Bridge was designed by John Roebling, who did not live to see it finished. Construction was begun in 1870, and thirteen years later the bridge was completed by the designer's son, Washington Roebling. Suspended from cables that swung from two great granite towers on opposite shores of the wide river, the bridge was acclaimed as a triumph of modern engineering and acknowledged to be one of the wonders of the world. But, architecturally, could you call it beautiful? No effort had been made to disguise its structural purpose, its modern materials, or its novel scientific principles. In fact, its design proudly embodied all these —and nothing more. No ornament softened the strong, spare lines of the bridge. No sculpture or decoration relieved the severity of the towers. The Brooklyn Bridge was uncompromisingly utilitarian. High above the river, it hung from its curving cables—a marvel, surely, but a nakedly functional marvel born of the new mechanical age that held all beauty in contempt. New Yorkers who felt the thrill of beauty only in the presence of European towers and porticoes found the Brooklyn Bridge arrogantly ugly, a defiant celebration of the raw, crude American civilization that they despised. They could not realize that it announced a new kind of beauty, indisputably native, or that it might, indeed, portend a new kind of architecture.

CELEBRATION AT THE OPENING OF BROOKLYN BRIDGE, May 24, 1883

Other New Yorkers, little concerned about aesthetics, or the esoteric science of mathematical physics upon which the Brooklyn Bridge was founded, awaited the strange experience of driving across the East River, or taking the cars at the City Hall in New York to be deposited near the City Hall in Brooklyn. The novel problem of "rapid transit" was now a civic obsession. New York had become a city of inconvenient distances. Everybody complained about the archaic horse-cars and omnibuses. A visitor from France, recording his impressions in the *Revue des Deux Mondes,* told a shocking story. He had been informed in New York that it was the practice of ladies, on entering a crowded Fifth Avenue omnibus, to seat themselves on the knees of gentlemen already placed. This was a gross falsehood, but you saw "well-dressed, well-bred New Yorkers clinging to straps, jaded, jammed, jostled, panting in the aisle of these hearselike equipages, to reach their goal." The average man spent from an hour to an hour and a half daily in going to and from his business, thereby losing an immense amount of time. And wasn't time money? The outstanding need of the city, as everyone acknowledged, was "some sure means of rapid transit between the upper and lower parts of the island."

Various plans were suggested. A group of capitalists backed the "Beach Pneumatic Tunnel." A small experimental section of this tunnel, eight feet in diameter, was built under downtown Broadway from Warren to Murray Streets. A strong blast of air, thrown out by a huge blowing machine, was forced against the rear end of a car, sending it skimming along the track like a sailboat before the wind. The enterprising capitalists claimed that they could blow twenty thousand New Yorkers every hour from the Battery to the Harlem River. A rival scheme was put forward by another group. This was called the "Arcade Railway." The plan was to construct a new underground street, twenty feet below the level of Broadway, with sidewalks and gaslamps, and to convert the cellars of existing buildings into fine shops. The center of the new street was to be laid with railroad tracks for steam trains. But the

"RAPID TRANSIT GALOP," 1875. The Third Avenue el set to music

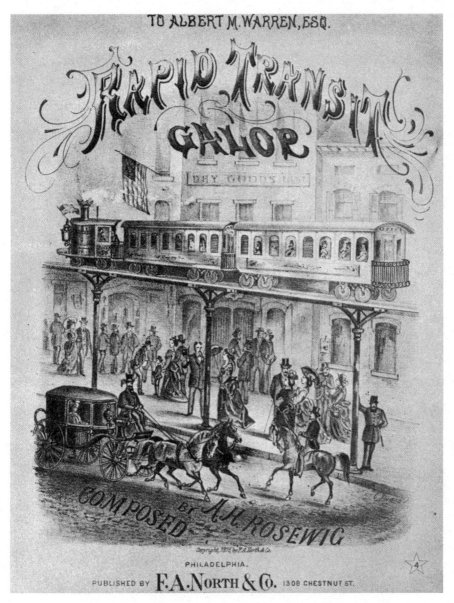

"Style" on the old Third Avenue horse cars the "Drawing Room."

PULLMAN CARS ON THE ELEVATED, 1875

plan came to nothing. John Jacob Astor III and other great landlords asserted that their buildings would collapse if digging were permitted. The Croton Water Board opposed the project because it would interfere with the city's water mains.

So New York, forbidden to burrow underground for rapid transit, went up into the air. Elevated railroads were built, radiating from the Battery, along Sixth Avenue to Central Park, along Third and Ninth Avenues—and, later, along Second Avenue—to the Harlem River. Trains drawn by steam engines rattled up and down the tracks at the alarming rate of thirty miles an hour. The engines belched sparks and smoke; ashes, water and oil dropped on pedestrians in the streets below. Horses took fright at the approach of every explosive train; the newspapers were full of reports of runaways and accidents. And terror was not exclusively equine. Nervous folk protested that cars were certain to jump the tracks and tumble into the avenues. Eugene Schuyler, a prominent citizen returning from dangerous explorations in Turkestan, made a trip out to the upper end of the Ninth Avenue line. On crossing the towering, curving trestle beyond the northern boundary of Central Park, he became ill with dread, and pleaded to be taken back to the city by boat or train or horse-car—anything rather than repeat the nerve-racking experience. Old-fashioned New Yorkers like the eminent attorney Charles F. Southmayd stoutly refused ever to ride on the elevated. Yet within a year after the elevated railroads were put in operation, five hundred houses were built north of Fiftieth Street. And the new "model" or "dumb-bell" tenements soon followed along avenues made dark and incessantly noisy by the miracle of rapid transit.

Commodore Vanderbilt likewise promoted the cause of rapid transit. To replace the old railroad depot at Fourth Avenue and Twenty-sixth Street, he built an imposing new one that straddled Fourth Avenue at Forty-second Street. Formerly, travelers had taken their seats in cars at the old depot; the cars were then drawn by horses through a tunnel under Fourth Avenue from Thirty-third to Forty-second Street, where they were coupled together and attached to a locomotive. Now, you found your train already made up at the vast new depot, which old Vanderbilt had optimistically named "Grand Central." Forty-second Street was anything but central, but nobody could deny that the new depot was grand. Its massive pavilions of red brick were embellished with ironwork painted white to resemble marble. Its spacious waiting rooms were finished in varnished woods and handsomely frescoed. The immense glass-roofed train shed furnished a common terminus for all railroad lines entering the city, and no less than eighty trains arrived and departed there every day. You could take trains for New England and the West, but you could also take "local" trains for uptown New York that stopped at stations along the line from Fifty-eighth to One Hundred and Twenty-fifth Street in Harlem. Visionaries began to speculate on the remote possibility that families of modest means might someday make their year-round homes in Westchester or Connecticut towns that were now summer resorts of the prosperous, and that men might daily "commute" from these distant habitations to busi-

GRAND CENTRAL STATION, 1885, *by L. Oram.* The Grand Union Hotel (at the right) advertised "Over 450 elegantly furnished rooms reduced to $1.00 and upward per day"

ness in the city. This vision had earlier led A. T. Stewart to project, out on Long Island, a residential community named Garden City, with fine houses set in spacious grounds and broad, tree-shaded avenues.

Well-born, well-bred, wealthy New Yorkers in childhood were taught an absolute conversational law: "Never talk about money, and think about it as little as possible." But how could people in modest circumstances obey it? In New York, you couldn't live economically with any degree of decency. In the newest uptown quarters, respectable but certainly not fashionable, you couldn't rent a house for less than eighteen hundred dollars a year. You paid your Irish cook from eighteen to twenty dollars a month. A chambermaid received from twelve to fifteen dollars monthly, and a nurse for the children the same. It was a costly matter to "change help," as everyone knew; "ladies who go to look after 'girls' in the places from which they advertise for situations, are obliged to go to the expense of hiring a carriage, it being unsafe for them to venture into these sections on foot." And the expenses of housekeeping were mounting. You paid fifty cents a pound for butter; fifty cents a dozen for eggs; sixteen cents a pound for crushed sugar; twenty-five cents a pound for fowls; thirty-five cents a pound for the choicest cuts of beef. At these rates, if your income was six thousand dollars a year, you had to economize. You couldn't afford to "entertain" very often—and New York regarded dinner parties, served to the last nicety of silver, damask, porcelain and glass, as "the touchstone of highest civilization." As one pessimistic analyst noted, the financial difficulties of life in New York "fall chiefly upon educated and refined people of moderate means."

To mitigate these difficulties, a daring experimenter offered genteel young New Yorkers a radical innovation. Patricians might have ridiculed the fantastic notions of Rutherfurd Stuyvesant had he not been the most patrician of all. His father was Lewis Rutherfurd, the gentle and learned astronomer; his mother, a descendant of the Dutch governor, transmitted the Stuyvesant fortune to him, and to requite ancestral foresight young Stuyvesant Rutherfurd promptly reversed his name. He also proposed to reverse a traditional way of life for less wealthy friends and relatives. On Eighteenth Street, near staid and well-mannered little Irving Place, he built a "French flat." Reproducing the dubious customs of Paris, the entrance to this structure was guarded by a *concierge*. Within, two staircases mounted to the upper floors, each giving access, on every floor, to a single "flat" diminutive in size and not especially sunny. To the astonishment of everybody, all the suites were rented, before completion of the building, to young couples of the most impeccable social distinction. Indeed, the list of tenants, according to one of them, produced "a very old Knickerbocker sort of effect upon the outside mind." All of them, however, were careful to refer to their new homes as "apartments," thinking that the word "flat" had a vulgar sound. But by whatever name you called it, old-fashioned folk were aghast. It seemed incredible that young people of the highest genealogical merit would consent to dwell in a building which, after all, was only a superior version of the tenements inhabited by the poor.

Where a Stuyvesant blazed the way, others were quick to follow. Paran Stevens, who collected hotels as assiduously as Commodore Vanderbilt collected railroads, soon improved on the simple pioneer example. He built the

VIADUCT OVER THE HARLEM FLATS ABOUT 1880, *by J. N. Allan*

massive Stevens House on Twenty-seventh Street. It occupied the whole block between Fifth Avenue and Broadway, and shortly afterward was transformed into the Victoria Hotel. An eight-story red-brick, marble-trimmed structure with a mansard roof, this "apartment house," as it was called, offered eighteen luxurious suites containing parlor, dining room, kitchen, butler's pantry, bedrooms, dressing rooms and bathrooms, with quarters for servants in the attic. Steam elevators lifted you to your horizontal dwelling, where all the woodwork was of fashionable black walnut and the walls were "finely frescoed and harmoniously tinted."

As yet, fashionable folk seldom ventured north of Murray Hill. But a reckless optimist built two large apartment houses on the east side of Fourth Avenue—already renamed Park Avenue—at Fifty-sixth and Fifty-seventh Streets. The district was still a wasteland of unpaved streets on which speculative builders were erecting brownstone residences for the prosperous upper middle class. On the west side of Fourth Avenue, opposite the new apartments, there remained a rocky farm where cows, goats and chickens roamed at will. One block to the south, Commodore Vanderbilt's railroad trains entered a tunnel under the avenue that kept them more or less invisible until they reached Ninety-sixth Street. A resident of Fifty-sixth Street, meeting the builder of the apartment house, complained that he was ruining the future prospects of the neighborhood. "Gentlemen," this champion of decorum asserted, "will never consent to live on mere shelves under a common roof!" The conservative upper middle class condemned aristocratic eccentricities. Failure to own your home was a confession of shabby antecedents or disreputable habits. But a taste for indecorous ways of life was spreading. Far up in the lonely reaches of the West Side—a region of almost polar remoteness unknown to fashion—capitalists were rashly investing one million dollars in the Dakota Apartments. This enormous Parisian palace overlooked Central Park from Seventy-second Street and Eighth Avenue, and in that dubious location offered its tenants the combined facilities of an apartment house and a luxury hotel. Meanwhile, above Forty-second Street, in the blocks east of Lexington Avenue and west of Sixth, the new-fangled "French flats" were being monotonously duplicated for New Yorkers who, however respectful of tradition, were economically driven to live on narrow shelves under a common roof.

Some New Yorkers of unquestionable gentility were abandoning housekeeping to live in hotels. The "downtown" hotels—the old Metropolitan, St. Nicholas and New York, the gaudy new Grand Central on Broadway at Bleecker Street, with its dining room that accommodated six hundred guests at a sitting—were "commercial" or "transient." But the Everett House on Union Square, and the neighboring Clarendon Hotel where the Grand Duke Alexis of Russia stayed during his visit to New York, were considered suitably "residential." Union Square was now given over to theaters and fine retail shops like Brentano's, the "literary emporium," and Tiffany's, where fashionable New York bought its jewelry, silverware, engraved cards and wedding invitations. All the spacious residences that formerly surrounded the pleasant little park had been adapted to trade or replaced by business buildings.

Madison Square, still lined on the east and north by aristocratic mansions, was becoming the center of metropolitan public life. Within a few blocks were to be found the newest theaters, the most luxurious hotels, the most exclusive clubs. Broadway, from Twenty-third Street down to Eighth, was known as the "Ladies' Mile," along which fashion went shopping. At Ninth Street was the block-square Italianate department store of A. T. Stewart & Company, its iron facade painted white to resemble marble. James McCreery & Company was at Eleventh Street. Arnold, Constable & Company occupied a massive white-marble building at Eighteenth Street; Lord & Taylor had recently built a vast, ornate establishment at Twentieth Street. These were the largest stores, but along the "Ladies' Mile" there were many smaller ones of high repute and equal costliness. During the afternoon "shopping hours" Broadway was blocked with victorias, landaus, broughams and coupés, and on the sidewalks there passed an incessant procession of elegantly attired women who trailed their long "walking dresses" in the accumulated urban dust.

The hotels on Madison Square were justly famous. The old Fifth Avenue retained its great prestige, and preserved traditions that endeared it to the conservative. For two bedrooms and a parlor, with full board, you paid thirty dollars a day. Immediately north of the Fifth Avenue were the Albermarle Hotel and the Hoffman House, imposing marble structures. Everyone who came to New York made at least one visit to the Hoffman House bar—if only to see its notorious principal adornment, a large painting of opulently beautiful nude women by the Parisian artist William Bouguereau. The Brunswick Hotel on Fifth Avenue and Twenty-sixth Street was the headquarters of the aristocratic "horsy set." The annual spring and autumn parades of the Coaching Club—major events in the lives of the elect that brought crowds to Fifth Avenue—assembled at the Brunswick and returned there to enjoy the bird and game dinners and rare vintages for which the hotel was celebrated among gourmets. New Yorkers asserted that any epicure could starve in perpetual indecision on Fifth Avenue and Twenty-sixth Street. For directly across the avenue from the Brunswick, Delmonico's opened a large and magnificent new restaurant, and the choice between their rival cuisines was, for a true gourmet, a problem of anguishing difficulty.

Broadway, north of Madison Square as far as Thirty-first Street, was already lined with large, new, expensive hotels. But Sixth Avenue, intersected by Broadway at Thirty-third Street, was nationally notorious. Under the roaring elevated railroad it was dingy by day and depraved by night. From Fourteenth Street northward, it had become the metropolitan night town, a gaslit carnival thoroughfare of vice. Along Sixth Avenue, and the shabby streets leading off it, were located houses of prostitution, garish saloons and restaurants, low dance halls—places like The French Madam's, The Cremorne and The Haymarket, whose evil repute had spread across the continent. In a memorable, widely publicized sermon, the celebrated Brooklyn preacher, Dr. T. De Witt Talmage, denounced this street of sin, naming it Satan's Circus. The name stuck until, some years later, a better one replaced it. Transferred from a quiet precinct to this flaming area, Police Inspector Williams, a man not disposed to ignore practical advantages, remarked that he had long been restricted to a diet of rump steak; now he was to have a generous slice of the tenderloin. Throughout the country, New York's squalid center of vice and crime became known as The Tenderloin.

Lower Fifth Avenue, between Washington and Madison Squares, remained a citadel of the aristocracy, though the flippant younger generation were beginning to refer to its inhabitants as "the cave dwellers." Millionaires like James Lenox, Levi P. Morton, Lorillard Spencer and August Belmont resisted the northward trend of fashion and refused to be dislodged from their sedate, spacious mansions, now become historic monuments in the city's social history. They did not object to the quiet, ultrafashionable Brevoort Hotel at the corner of Eighth Street—still called Clinton Place—but they resented other, less polite encroachments. Some of the old residences, in fallen glory, had been converted into expensive boarding houses. A brick mansion at the corner of Seventeenth Street flaunted a sign, "G. D. Happy, Tailor"—and the cave dwellers aggrievedly asked why this plebeian intruder was "so G— d— happy." On the northwest corner of Eighteenth Street, opposite August Belmont's handsome palace, a whole row of residences had been demolished to make way for Chickering Hall, a salesroom for pianos and a new auditorium for concerts and lectures. Notwithstanding the obduracy of the cave dwellers, people were predicting that lower Fifth Avenue, like Union Square, would soon succumb to trade.

When they spoke, nowadays, of *the* Avenue, New Yorkers meant Fifth Avenue between Madison Square and Forty-second Street, the accredited northern limit of fashion. Lined on both sides with the fine brownstone homes of the wealthy, it presented an effect of somber costliness, of almost funereal magnificence, that New York identified with splendor. Over its broad roadway, paved with cobblestones, gleaming carriages rattled and jounced to the afternoon parade in Central Park. Witty Dr. Fordyce Barker, physician to the old aristocracy of Stuyvesant Square, University Place and lower Fifth Avenue, remarked that he could not conscientiously permit his convalescent patients to take the air in their carriages, since inevitably they would be shaken up, to the great detriment of their nervous systems. But people were already talking hopefully of the new, smooth asphalt paving that returning travelers reported having seen in Paris, and some prophetic souls asserted that fashion would soon claim Fifth Avenue as far north as Central Park, and perhaps even further uptown.

Above Forty-second Street, the avenue had a ragged look. The great new Windsor Hotel, occupying the eastern block front between Forty-sixth and Forty-seventh Street, was considered inconveniently remote, though superlatively luxurious. Presently it superseded the old Fifth Avenue as the uptown center of finance, for Jay Gould built his mansion on the corner above, and in the evening frequented the Windsor to plot market strategy with other Wall Street financiers like Russell Sage, Frank Work and Addison Cammack. A few blocks north, at Fiftieth Street, just below the unfinished St. Patrick's

CONEY ISLAND ABOUT 1880

Cathedral, the tall, staid Buckingham Hotel attempted to attract conservative people far uptown. "There is no noise, no confusion of porters or waiters, no loungers or patrons of the bar who are not guests of the house," the Buckingham announced. "No attempt is made at mere display. The 'Steamboat' style is nowhere visible." Rejecting the flashy "steamboat style," the intrepid proprietors of this hotel offered single rooms, decorated in the style of the English designer Eastlake, at the modest rate of seven dollars a week. Their occupants had an unobstructed view of the vegetable gardens of Isaiah Keyser, on the west side of the avenue between Fifty-first and Fifty-second Streets, and the new brownstone Gothic St. Thomas' Church at Fifty-third. Above Fifty-ninth Street, the avenue was paved with wooden blocks, and overlooking the Park were rocky knolls from which segments had been cut away, like slices from a cheese. Far beyond the outposts of civilization, on the block front between Seventieth and Seventy-first Streets, stood the beautiful new Lenox Library designed by Richard Morris Hunt, endowed by James Lenox and filled with his priceless collections. But in their distant, lonely palace they were scarcely more accessible to the public than in the mansion on Fifth Avenue and Twelfth Street from which, for more than thirty years, James Lenox had excluded nearly all visitors.

It was, indeed, easier to visit Coney Island than to travel out to the Lenox Library, and most New Yorkers found the journey more rewarding. For one end of Coney Island had been transformed into the most pretentious of Atlantic watering places, and the other end had been made into a popular amusement park. You could go down to the Island by railroad, from Brooklyn, or take a steamboat at the Battery and sail down the harbor. Prosperous New Yorkers who formerly sent their families, for the summer, to Long

Branch and joined them only over week-ends, were now able to have their nights at the shore and return to the city, every day, refreshed for business. The splendid new resort had been brought within an hour's journey of New York.

Manhattan Beach, at the far eastern end of the Island, was the most exclusive and expensive section of the resort. Two enormous, ornate wooden hotels—the Manhattan Beach and the Oriental—had broad piazzas that looked, over lawns and flower beds, to the beach and the sea. The Oriental attracted a staid clientele. It was the summer headquarters of Senator Tom Platt, Republican boss of New York State, and was favored by members of the Union League Club. When, for the amusement of younger guests, the management introduced such novelties as tennis courts and croquet, the innovation met with considerable disapproval. The Manhattan Beach Hotel, popular from the outset with theatrical folk, was far more gay. Here, at night, concerts were given by Patrick S. Gilmore and his famous band, whose cornet soloist, Jules Levy, was universally admired. Gilmore taught his public to appreciate massive effects; he had fifty men pounding anvils when he conducted the "Anvil Chorus" from *Il Trovatore,* and he often concluded a military march with a salvo of artillery. Several times each week, the Manhattan Beach Hotel displayed the spectacular pyrotechnical set-pieces that became

THE FASHIONABLE BATHER OF 1879, from a Lord & Taylor advertisement

THE DAILY GRAPHIC: NEW YORK, SATURDAY, JUNE 14, 1879.

BATHING SUITS.

A GREAT SPECIALTY AT

LORD & TAYLOR'S, Broadway and 20th Street, N. Y.

CHEAPEST AND BEST QUALITY OF BATHING SUITS IN THE CITY.

celebrated as "Payn's fireworks"—exciting pictures of historical incidents or battles that were painted in multicolored fire. By day, the handsome bathing pavilions of the two hotels were crowded with decorously clad ladies and gentlemen who took the recommended "cure" of twenty-one immersions in the surf.

West of Manhattan Beach lay Brighton Beach, another resort with a great hotel and bathing pavilion. Brighton Beach attracted the sporting crowd drawn to the races at the Sheepshead Bay track, sponsored by the Coney Island Jockey Club, organized by a group of millionaires that included August Belmont and James R. Keene, the California plunger. Beyond Brighton Beach, to the west, Coney Island proper offered its very different enticements to a plebeian public. Sea-food restaurants and saloons, variety shows, shooting galleries, bathing pavilions, an iron pier and band concerts delighted thousands who left the heat of New York for a day or evening at the shore. Day and night the sands were crowded with bathers, and the noise of the great amusement park seemed never to cease. Everybody wanted to visit the "Wooden Elephant," a huge restaurant built in the form of an elephant, topped by a pavilion like a howdah, and having great glass eyes which, when illuminated at night, shone like beacons. So famous was this massive monument to pleasure that, for a decade and more, the phrase "seeing the elephant" signified a quest for unavowable satisfactions in disreputable quarters. The amusement park at Coney Island was, in its breezy way, a summer equivalent of the urban Tenderloin.

SHOPPING IN 1870, *by William L. Myers*

10

What Are You Going To Do About It?

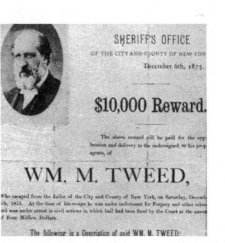

SHERIFF'S OFFICE
OF THE CITY AND COUNTY OF NEW YORK
December 6th, 1875.

$10,000 Reward.

The above reward will be paid for the apprehension and delivery to the undersigned, or his proper agents, of

WM. M. TWEED,

Who escaped from the Jailer of the City and County of New York, on Saturday, December 4th, 1875. At the time of his escape he was under indictment for Forgery and other crimes, and was under arrest in civil actions in which bail had been fixed by the Court at the amount of Four Million Dollars.

The following is a Description of said WM. M. TWEED:

O n the night of October 27, 1870, it was raining hard and steadily. The bad weather kept some New Yorkers indoors. This was a pity, because they would miss a magnificent parade. Very early in the evening thousands of loyal Democrats had assembled outside their district political clubs. Every one was handed a torch. You might have noticed that all these storm-defying citizens were wearing red shirts. This was a compliment to William Marcy Tweed, State Senator, Grand Sachem of Tammany and boss of the city. The illustrious tribune of the people had begun his political career, twenty-two years earlier, by helping to organize the celebrated "Big Six" brigade of volunteer firemen whose engine, at his suggestion, was adorned with the emblem of a ferocious tiger. The tiger seemed to be his favorite creature. It was the emblem of Tammany Hall, to which, under the driving rain, fifty thousand red-shirted citizens carrying flaring torches were marching in the largest political parade that New York had yet witnessed. The marchers had been instructed to go to the polls on Election Day, November 8th, and immediately return to their homes. No disturbances of any kind must occur at the polls or in the streets.

To older men who remembered when quite contrary instructions were the order of the day, this seemed very odd. But there were a number of reasons both for this spectacular demonstration and for the unusual instructions. Two days earlier President Grant had ordered several regiments of the army to the city, and they were quartered in the harbor forts. He had stationed two warships in the East and Hudson Rivers. He had directed the commander of the New York National Guard to have his men aid the United States Marshal and the regular troops in enforcing the election laws, should the Marshal so request. Did President Grant presume to think that he could deal with New York as if it formed part of the conquered South? Undoubtedly he remembered the acclaim that had greeted ex-Mayor Wood's proposal for secession, the strong Copperhead movement, the insurrectionary draft riot. But these did not account for his peculiar orders. He had taken military and naval precautions in response to an appeal by certain Republican leaders.

The Republican leaders had urged the President to protect the polls, if necessary, on Election Day. They asserted that Boss Tweed controlled the, metropolitan police force, that probably a majority of all Republican election inspectors were his hirelings. Under these conditions only the presence of Federal troops could assure a fair election should Tweed find the tide running against him at the polls. And there was reason to believe that this might be the case. For two years, in nearly every issue of *Harper's Weekly,* the great cartoonist Thomas Nast had been attacking Tweed as the head of a ring that was systematically looting the city. But now the effect of Nast's powerful cartoons was being immensely reinforced. George Jones, publisher of *The Times,* had joined the attack. Every day his brilliant managing editor, Louis John Jennings, was assailing Tweed and his Ring. Tweed, Jennings declared, was supported by corrupt Republican politicians whom he had put on his payroll. Without their aid, he could neither perpetuate his power nor perpetrate his thefts. Would the merciless daily bombardment of Tweed in *The*

"WHO STOLE THE PEOPLE'S MONEY?" *by Thomas Nast*

WHO STOLE THE PEOPLE'S MONEY? — DO TELL . N.Y.TIMES. 'TWAS HIM.

TWEED CARTOONS BY THOMAS NAST.

Times have any influence on the approaching election? If so, Tweed would not hesitate to steal the election. Such was the conviction of the Republican leaders who had appealed to President Grant.

But Tweed could have told them that they were wrong. There would be no need for him to steal the election. He already had it in his pocket. A careful survey had showed that the Democrats would carry the city by a perfectly safe majority. That was why orders had gone out to the red-shirted, torch-bearing marchers forbidding any violence, any destruction of ballot boxes in Republican districts on Election Day. There would be no opportunity for the President's military forces to come into the city. While the great torchlight parade was in progress, Tweed faced an enthusiastic audience in Tammany Hall. He was forty-seven years old, tall, heavily bearded, growing bald, a man of enormous bulk. His eyes glittered as coldly as the huge diamond adorning his shirt front, but his ruddy face wore a jovial expression. Tweed sat between dapper, sallow, enigmatic August Belmont and hulking, flamboyant James Fisk. In the realm of finance, Fisk and Belmont were irreconcilable enemies. Fisk, the "Prince of Erie," had appointed Tweed to the executive committee of that much plundered railroad; their relations were cordial as well as mutually profitable. Fisk had always been known as a Republican. But he cherished a deep grudge against President Grant. On Black Friday in 1869, the President had ruined the plan of Jay Gould and Fisk to effect a corner in gold. Now, from the platform of Tammany Hall, Fisk would soon announce his adherence to the Democratic Party, and his intention to have all Erie employees vote the Democratic ticket.

There were other hostilities plainly in view on the platform, no less inveterate than that of Belmont and Fisk, who merely ignored one another's presence. Ex-Governor Horatio Seymour had come to make a speech. He was the close friend and political associate of Samuel J. Tilden, Tweed's greatest enemy in the Democratic Party. Tweed had recently made it a point to humiliate Tilden publicly, and nobody doubted that Tilden would revenge himself should he ever have an opportunity. Ex-Mayor Fernando Wood was likewise present to speak. Having disbanded his Mozart Hall Democracy after a crushing defeat by Tweed, Wood was back in the Tammany fold. He was a member of Congress, now. But everyone knew that there was no love lost between Wood and Tweed. On the platform, also, were Tweed's three associates in the Ring, all Sachems of Tammany. Mayor A. Oakey Hall, known as "the Elegant Oakey," was a fashion plate, clubman and notorious playboy. He had been a journalist, had written plays, had achieved local fame as a wit and after-dinner speaker; he was also an astute lawyer. Richard B. Connolly, City Comptroller, and Peter B. Sweeny, Commissioner of Public Parks and former Chamberlain, were the other two members of the Ring.

Tweed received a frenzied ovation when he arose to speak, and his brief address was constantly interrupted by outbursts of cheers and applause. "We know and feel," he said in closing, "that although an aggressive hand is upon us, yet we must, by a judicious exercise of law and order, which is our only protection, show that it is a law-abiding and, as all the world knows, a well-governed city." Tweed intended no irony in asserting that New York was well governed. Notwithstanding the scandalous accusations made by Thomas Nast and *The Times,* the truth of his claim was being attested by many of the city's most prominent citizens, irrespective of their party affiliation. Only five months earlier there had been a municipal election to choose a Board of Aldermen. Tweed's candidates received the endorsement of the Citizens' Association, a nonpartisan organization dedicated to civic reform and purity in politics. The president of this group was old Peter Cooper, a man venerated for his philanthropies, whose personal honor was unimpeachable. "The Democratic leaders are pledged to good government and progress, and the Association has full confidence that these pledges will be kept," Cooper's group declared. Many of its members were sincerely convinced that Tweed and his Ring, all men of wealth, had "become conservative" and would therefore give up their corrupt practices. Was it not better to continue them in power than to replace them by new men who, ambitious for riches, would inevitably rob the taxpayers? This was the policy recommended by Nathaniel B. Sands, secretary of the Association and its political adviser. Sands was a Republican. He was also, by Tweed's appointment, a Tax Commissioner, receiving an annual salary of fifteen thousand dollars.

Even before the great meeting at Tammany Hall, Tweed had found a way to cope with *The Times's* allegations of wholesale theft. The newspaper constantly challenged him to have Comptroller Connolly authorize a thorough public investigation of the city's finances. Undaunted, Tweed chose six eminent citizens to undertake this inquiry and report to the public. The committee was headed by John Jacob Astor III, and among its members were Moses Taylor and Marshall O. Roberts. These gentlemen commanded vast wealth and enjoyed high repute; their colleagues were no less distinguished, though certainly less abundantly rich. Could there be any doubt of their absolute integrity? It was ridiculous to suppose any of them capable of collusion with corrupt politicians. None of them, obviously, would condone flagrant looting of the city. Whatever their findings, their report could be taken as authoritative and final, and all New York awaited it in a fever of impatience. The report was published on November 7th, 1870, just before Election Day. "We have come to the conclusion and certify," its eminent signers declared, "that the financial affairs of the city under the charge of the Comptroller are administered in a correct and faithful manner." The report was a complete vindication of Tweed and his associates. Only the most disreputable of cynics would have suggested that the honorable members of the committee were among the city's largest taxpayers, that the Tweed Ring could greatly increase their taxes should it have any good reason to do so, that it could inflict other forms of punishment scarcely more agreeable.

But moral cynicism was profoundly repugnant to New Yorkers. Conscience and conviction enlightened their verdict at the polls. They re-elected Tweed's governor, John T. Hoffman, and his mayor, "the Elegant Oakey." They didn't have to do anything about the State Legislature, where Tweed for a year had commanded a majority. He owned a large number of the Republican minority at Albany, and in New York County he actually owned the Republican machine. Naturally, the cost of "good government and progress" was not cheap. Later estimates placed it as between forty-five and seventy-five millions of dollars during the Tweed Ring's thirty months of democratic dictatorship. For the new County Court House alone taxpayers had spent more than twelve million dollars. It was the most costly public building in the United States, though far less ostentatious than the Capitol at Washington, or many another. And what could be more gratifying to Tweed than the knowledge that this monument to his glory had likewise contributed to his material welfare? Of its total cost, about nine million dollars had been siphoned into the perquisites that rewarded the Ring for their unselfish devotion to the public interest.

It was not surprising that millionaires and other prominent citizens praised Tweed, even eulogized him as a reformer. Was not innovation synonymous with progress? Was not progress the only genuine reform? Tweed, too, was a millionaire: a director of many important corporations, the president of a bank, the principal stockholder of a printing establishment which—deservedly, no doubt—received the business of public utilities, banks and many large industries, in addition to that of the city. Tweed maintained a fine home on Fifth Avenue and Forty-third Street, a yacht, an excellent stable; he had invested a large fortune in real estate. Did he not exemplify progress as well as foster it? That he was an innovator in politics nobody could deny. He applied, to public business, methods no less modern than those which had enabled such magnates as Vanderbilt, Gould and Fisk to realize their grandiose projects. In fact, they had profited by Tweed's superb efficiency, his admirably co-operative nature. If legislation was required to effect their purposes, Tweed's celebrated "Black Horse Cavalry" at the Capitol in Albany stood ready to pass it —at a price. If there was any quibbling about the price, they were equally ready to block and defeat the hoped-for measures. If the legality of any legislation had to be judicially determined, or if quick injunctions were needed to forestall hostile action from any quarter, or if important lawsuits were coming up for decision—well, the required dispensation of justice would be forthcoming from one of Tweed's eminent contributions to the State judiciary: Justices George G. Barnard and Albert Cardozo of the Supreme Court, and Justice John H. McCunn of the Superior Court.

Justice Barnard, especially, was almost as outstandingly progressive as Tweed himself. In an emergency, for example, he would hold court in the home of Josie Mansfield, Jim Fisk's mistress, where he happened to be visiting when told of the sudden need for justice. He would also, if the need was desperate, issue his judicial orders by telegraph; they could be served, within an hour or two, at any remote point in the state. And at Tweed's instigation, he simplified and perfected a political formula devised by ex-Mayor Fernando Wood. Before doubtful elections, Wood had often secured the rapid naturalization of immigrants; several hundred additional voters were sufficient for his purposes. But this was a new industrial and financial era, dedicated to quantity production—of stock-certificates, capital and, sometimes, tangible goods. Why not citizens also? Justice Barnard saw the point, and he helped Tweed, on one occasion, to make sixty thousand new citizens in twenty days.

Efficiency was the gospel of this postwar era of industrial expansion. Nobody understood this better than Boss Tweed, aware as he was of the wastefulness, the needless delays, the absurd uncertainty of traditional processes of making law and administering it. He brought the whole machinery of government up to date, adapted it to the imperative, unforeseen necessities of the time. And the Ring operated this machinery on a sound, modern business basis. Take the case of contractors, manufacturers and others who sold goods and services to New York City. The Ring told them precisely what they must charge. It also told them how much of the money they received must be returned to the Ring. The city was an insatiable purchaser, and this helped general prosperity. Keenly aware of its economic duty, the Ring deplored the infrequent periods when buying by the city slackened, and bills payable diminished. So, at such times, the Ring ordered vouchers made out to fictitious creditors. This expedient kept municipal funds in circulation. Surely it was only a financial paradox that, the faster money moved, the more it stuck to Tweed, Hall, Connolly and Sweeny.

Everybody who really counted in New York understood this process, and the fortunes of many of the best people prospered because of it. Why interfere with a mechanism so patently efficient, so generally advantageous? Even its supposed extravagance ought to be a point of pride. Did not the costliness of the Tweed Ring proclaim to the world the incalculable wealth of New York? Did it not declare that, unique among cities, New York could afford any expense to promote the welfare of its most enterprising citizens?

Many prominent New Yorkers, therefore, had reason to regret the consequences of a quarrel between Tweed and one of his subordinates. Sheriff James O'Brien presented claims against the city amounting to three hundred and fifty thousand dollars, a mere pittance. Boss Tweed disallowed them. O'Brien led a revolt against Tweed in Tammany Hall, seeking to oust the Boss. The attempt failed ignominiously, and this made O'Brien even keener for vengeance. One night in July, 1871, he delivered to *The Times* a mass of documents. They were exact transcripts from the books of Comptroller Connolly. O'Brien asserted that they would substantiate all the charges which the newspaper had been making, for nearly a year, against Tweed and the Ring. They would absolutely contradict the report made by Astor and his committee. On July 8th, 1871, *The Times* began publishing O'Brien's transcripts in daily installments; they ran for three weeks. They roused the city to a high pitch of excitement. Interviewed by a newspaper reporter, Boss Tweed angrily demanded, "Well, what are you going to do about it?"

The answer came at a citizens' mass meeting at Cooper Institute early in September. Distinguished speakers analyzed the criminal financial operations disclosed by *The Times*. Resolutions calling for the prosecution of Tweed and the Ring had been prepared in advance, and were presented to the audience by an eminent lawyer, Joseph H. Choate. "This," said Choate defiantly, "is what we are going to do about it." A Committee of Seventy was formed to carry out the program adopted at the meeting. Samuel J. Tilden and Charles

O'Conor undertook its legal direction. Justice Barnard was the first of Tweed's minions to desert him, capitulating to Tilden and the Committee. He was quickly followed by Comptroller Connolly, who appointed Andrew H. Green, a member of the Committee, as Acting Comptroller, thereby giving the prosecution access to the Ring's financial records. In the election of 1871, Tweed was returned to the State Senate, but nearly all his other candidates for public office were voted down. Thereafter, a Grand Jury began turning out criminal indictments of Tweed, his associates in the Ring and many of their beneficiaries. Tweed retained his seat in the State Senate, but resigned every other position, public and private, even being replaced as Grand Sachem of Tammany. Connolly and Sweeny fled to Europe. Justice Cardozo resigned from the Supreme Court to escape impeachment; Justices Barnard and McCunn were impeached, and removed from their judicial posts. Mayor Hall remained in office, though he, too, was under indictment. His first trial was halted by the death of a juror; his second resulted in a disagreement by the jury. Tried a third time, "the Elegant Oakey" was acquitted. Defeated for re-election as Mayor, this debonair mountebank returned to journalism and playwriting, and in 1878 himself played a role in *The Crucible,* his most successful contribution to the stage. He was the first, though not the most conspicuous, exemplar of New York's predilection for the luxury of installing a wisecracking playboy in City Hall, and thereafter rewarding him generously for the diversion he furnished.

But Tweed fell a victim to civic virtue. Conscience required a scapegoat because the incompatibility of high principle and wanton conduct—discreetly managed by many enterprising citizens—had led to scandal. A scandal of this magnitude could not be ignored. Tweed's practices had been acceptable to the righteous; it was his carelessness that they could not condone. At Tweed's first trial, the jury disagreed. At a second, he was convicted; a cumulative sentence of twelve years in prison and a fine was imposed. But a year later this verdict was overruled. Set free, he was immediately rearrested in a suit brought by the State to recover six million dollars, a share of his personal plunder for which there existed abundant evidence. By this time, Samuel J. Tilden had been elected Governor of New York and inaugurated. Tweed was confined in the Ludlow Street Jail, the debtors' prison, where he was accorded all the privileges to which so distinguished a citizen was entitled. That was how, on a visit to his home accompanied by a warden and a keeper, he managed to make his escape. After remaining in hiding near New York, he made his way to Florida in disguise, thence to Cuba, finally to Spain, where the lack of an extradition treaty promised him permanent immunity. On landing in Vigo, Tweed was recognized; a cartoon by Thomas Nast revealed his identity. The Spanish authorities delivered him to an American warship sent to bring him back to the United States. In the suit to recover six million dollars, judgment had been taken against him, but he still faced trial on many additional indictments.

Back in jail, Tweed offered a full surrender of his remaining property, and expressed a willingness to become a witness against all his former associates,

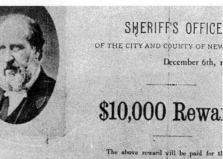

in return for assurances of mercy. Five years had passed since *The Times* had begun its exposure of the Tweed Ring. Connolly was still at liberty in Europe. Sweeny was to return and escape punishment by paying over somewhat less than four hundred thousand dollars of his personal loot. Hall, acquitted, had resigned from one of his clubs but remained a member in good standing of the others. Tilden, the great reformer, had never published the promised list of citizens revealed, by Connolly's books, to have acted in collusion with the Ring. Perhaps too many distinguished and honorable New Yorkers were implicated in the profitable avocation of looting public funds. But for Tweed, his personal enemy, Governor Tilden had no mercy.

Tweed died in jail in the Spring of 1878. Two years earlier, Tilden had been Democratic candidate for President of the United States. Many Americans believed that he had been elected and then defrauded of the high honor to which his prosecution of Tweed was a stepping-stone. Of the estimated forty-five to seventy-five million dollars which the Ring had plundered, New York City recovered approximately one million, one hundred and twenty-one thousand dollars. And it could be surmised that John Jacob Astor III's acquaintance with accounting had merely suffered a temporary lapse when, with his distinguished associates, he certified to the sound condition of the city's finances. The death of his father, William Backhouse Astor, in 1875, left him the wealthiest man in the United States. He often rewrote telegrams to save one word, and in many other ways was known to keep his vast fortune in excellent repair.

11

The Single Standard and the Double Bed

During the eighteen-seventies the structure of respectability was badly shattered. A series of scandals rocked New York. Reverberating in the press from Maine to Oregon, they were eagerly discussed by Americans everywhere. Was the metropolis only a gilded, gleaming cesspool? Had morals there utterly collapsed? Or did these scandals indicate that New York was developing new, startling moral attitudes consonant with the changing times, which it had determined to impose—like its towering fortunes, its splendors and its fashions—on the nation at large? The scandals spread over wide areas of the city's life. One involved an outstanding financier, an exemplar of American success. Another besmirched one of the strange career women who were becoming a problem, if not a portent—and its waves washed over intellectual leaders, reformers and feminists. A third was of even more spectacular significance: this scandal led directly into the pulpit of the nation's most famous and revered clergyman. As Americans read about Jim Fisk, Victoria Woodhull and Dr. Henry Ward Beecher, traditional moral standards seemed to reel and totter. Only in New York could such deplorable things happen, the righteous asserted. But each of the central figures in these scandals represented both the nation and the times.

Polite New York looked askance at Jim Fisk. Collectively, it knew him by sight and reputation, both displeasing. Individually, it tried, as far as possible, to ignore him. This was not easy. He had a passion for notoriety, a flair for acquiring and holding it. So when he registered, one summer, at the exclusive Continental Hotel in fashionable Long Branch, there was only one thing for its distinguished patrons to do. All of them hastily packed up and left the establishment. Some of them, no doubt, were compelled to return to New York on Fisk's palatial steamer, the *Plymouth Rock,* which had thirty-two suites of luxurious private apartments, a large gilded restaurant and a barroom all white marble and glittering mirrors. Characteristically, the opulence of this floating hotel was overpowering. Everything that Fisk owned, or had his hand in, had to make an overpowering effect. He was a striking figure, tall, florid, very fat. His light-brown hair was pomaded and carefully waved, his mustache waxed to fine points, and huge diamonds blazed on his frilled shirt front and pudgy fingers. Polite New York knew a vulgarian when it saw one, but it admitted that in many ways Jim Fisk was unique. He was gaudier than any other upstart, more pretentious, more recklessly indifferent to public opinion. Men of his breed were assumed to be utterly without principles, but at least they professed to have them. Jim Fisk's only principle was to have none, and make sure that everyone knew it.

Everyone knew that Fisk, with his partner, Jay Gould, had tried to bring President Grant into their plan to corner gold; Fisk had exuberantly told the story to a Congressional committee. President Grant had foiled the scheme, at the last moment. Nevertheless, Fisk and Gould made millions out of the disaster of Black Friday, which brought ruin to Wall Street and paralyzed the business of the whole country. Everyone knew, also, that the Erie Ring and the Tweed Ring were interlocking. This neat arrangement enabled Fisk and Gould, in a single year, to add more than fifty millions to the capitalization of the Erie Railroad by means of a printing press in the basement of the Grand Opera House. Most of these millions never reached the railroad's treasury, but remained in the pockets of their inspired creators. "Nothing so audacious, nothing more gigantic in the way of swindling, has ever been perpetrated in this country," upright Samuel Bowles indignantly declared in *The Springfield Republican,* "and yet it may be that Mr. Fisk and his associates have done nothing that they cannot legally justify, at least in the New York courts, several of which they seem wholly to own." Two men of Fisk's generation, Henry Adams and his brother, Charles Francis Adams, came down from Boston to investigate and write up these exploits. They called on Fisk at the Grand Opera House. To Henry Adams, it seemed obvious that all the great forces of American society were mired in one dirty cesspool of vulgar corruption. Society, he felt, was laughing a vacant and meaningless derision over its own failure. Traditional moral standards had broken down, and new ones would have to be invented. Postwar America, Adams was convinced, cared little for decency. It merely wanted a system that would work, and men who could work it. Unlike Adams, many ambitious Americans believed Fisk to be one of those men.

For Fisk, vulgar, gross and often ridiculous, was also astute and greatly daring. He had an aptitude for large affairs, and an ability to carry them through to success. Freebooting was the order of the day. If the acquisition of millions was your object, you couldn't dispense with skulduggery and fraud; you kept within the law by having the law made to suit your needs. Jim Fisk was either more cynical, or more naively honest, than other New York tycoons. He never pretended to be governed by anything but expediency and self-interest. And he conducted his life in full view of the public. All New York talked of the "Prince of Erie"—of his speculations in Wall Street, his railroad and steamship lines, his theaters, his regiment (he was Colonel of the Ninth, National Guard), his fondness for barbaric splendor, his prodigal extravagances, his love affairs. Leonard Jerome and August Belmont drove drags, four-in-hand. But Jim Fisk drove out to the Jerome Park races six-in-hand, using three pairs of white and black horses with gold-plated harnesses, mounting two Negro postilions in white livery on the leaders, and two white footmen in black livery on the back of his drag, loading the drag with the prettiest actresses from his theaters. Sometimes you saw him, in the Park, driving an outsize phaeton, or riding in his clarence, a closed carriage larger than a coupé, with a curved glass front; his was upholstered in gold cloth. Nearly always he had feminine companions, and none of them ever were ladies. Jim Fisk was married, but he maintained his wife at a convenient distance in Boston. Unlike other New York millionaires, he made no secret of keeping a mistress. Josie Mansfield lived in a fine brownstone residence back of the Grand Opera House, on Twenty-third Street between Eighth and Ninth Avenues. When Fisk entertained, his guests were invited to Miss Mansfield's home.

It was this unconventional hospitality that, in the end, led to scandal. Fisk had formed a friendship with Edward S. Stokes, the spendthrift son of a prominent, wealthy New York family. Their friendship blossomed into a joint venture in business which, for Fisk, turned out badly; Stokes repeatedly appropriated the partnership's funds. Meanwhile Fisk had introduced Stokes to his mistress, and Stokes became a constant visitor at the house on West Twenty-third Street. Like Fisk, he was a connoisseur of feminine beauty. Josie Mansfield had an exquisite figure and perfect features, large black-lashed eyes, magnificent glossy black hair. Soon all New York was snickering because the elegant dandy, Stokes, had replaced Fisk in his beautiful mistress' affections. Fisk retaliated by carrying his business dispute with Stokes into the courts. There his influence with the Tweed judiciary brought him a mollifying revenge. He had also cut off Miss Mansfield's allowance. But, like Stokes, she found financial problems exasperating, and the expenses of her establishment had to be provided for. She pleaded with Fisk for money; still infatuated, he supplied it. This detail, also, leaked out to an amused public. The town ridiculed Fisk as a cuckold who was lavishing his wealth on a flagrantly unfaithful mistress and her lover. Nettled by this reaction, Fisk again shut off the flow of funds. Then Miss Mansfield and Stokes resorted to blackmail. They threatened to publish compromising letters which Fisk had written to his mistress. Unable to redeem these by further payments, Fisk finally allowed Miss Mansfield to sue him for fifty thousand dollars which she alleged he had promised, but failed, to pay her. In answer to this suit he filed an affidavit by one of her servants, testifying that Miss Mansfield was openly living with Stokes and that they had determined to extort money from Fisk. Publication of this affidavit in the newspapers enraged both Miss Mansfield and Stokes. They brought suit against Fisk for libel.

The opening of this lawsuit occurred just when Fisk and Gould, as controlling heads of the Erie Railroad, were being subjected to the most dangerous legal attack ever made on them. The Tweed Ring had been exposed, and its members were under indictment. The Erie management could no longer rely on the Tweed judiciary to save them. The press—probably inspired by the attorneys for Miss Mansfield and Stokes—promised that trial of the libel suit would expose the financial crimes of Fisk, Gould and their confederates in the Erie Ring, and their division of Erie Railroad spoils with Tweed and his associates. In a desperate effort to avert personal disaster, Gould was seeking to reorganize the Erie directorate by adding to the board such eminent capitalists as John Jacob Astor III and August Belmont. Gould was a family man, without appetite for extramarital pleasures. Astor and Belmont were gentlemen, and in such matters gentlemen were invariably discreet. The immorality of Fisk's private life—so vulgarly and needlessly flaunted before the public—made him a luxury that Gould could no longer afford. It was unlikely that Astor and Belmont would consent to become directors of Erie while Fisk remained on the board. Besides, there was only one way to offset whatever financial revelations the scandalous lawsuit might develop. For once, Fisk had gone entirely too far. Gould peremptorily demanded Fisk's resignation from his vice-presidency and directorship of Erie. And Fisk, surprisingly, gave it.

The discarded Prince of Erie went to face his accusers in the Yorkville Police Court, on Fifty-seventh Street between Third and Lexington Avenues. The court was crowded. Policemen rustled about bringing notable visitors to reserved seats. As *The Herald* reported, Josie Mansfield looked so lovely that she created quite a flutter by her appearance. She wore lavender kid gloves, and over her magnificent dark hair was perched a jaunty little Alpine hat with a dainty green feather. Her robe was of the heaviest black silk, cut *à l'Impératrice,* and having deep flounces of black lace over Milanaise bands of white satin. A superb black-velvet mantle covered her shoulders. The glance of her lustrous eyes, the reporter noted, had "a terrible effect" when directed at the judge, jury, or any witness. The exquisite Stokes, as *The Herald* called him, "was all glorious in a new Alexis overcoat of a dull cream color"; he wore an elegant diamond ring, and swung his cane carelessly; he looked so handsome that Josie Mansfield found it difficult to take her eyes off his face. Burly Jim Fisk wore "a strange kind of blue naval uniform that fitted him wretchedly, with double rows of brass buttons"—the attire he affected as "admiral" of his steamship lines. The sympathies of the crowd were with his accusers. Perhaps for this reason, perhaps because he could not endure the obvious hatred of his estranged mistress and faithless friend, Fisk "was so discomposed that he left early."

Distracted and miserable, Fisk went to the Erie offices in the Grand Opera House. Meanwhile, word reached Ned Stokes that a Grand Jury had indicted Josie Mansfield and himself for attempted blackmail of Fisk. Late in the afternoon, Fisk drove to the new Grand Central Hotel, on Broadway at Fourth Street, presumably to visit friends who were stopping there. He went in the ladies' entrance, at some distance from the crowded lobby of the hotel, and ascended the long flight of stairs to the second floor. As he neared the top he looked up and saw Ned Stokes waiting for him, pistol in hand. Stokes fired, point blank. Fisk cried out in fear and pain, stumbled, fell down, and struggled to rise to his feet. Stokes fired again, saw Fisk fall down the staircase, and fled. Before he could leave the hotel he was seized, identified by Fisk and taken to jail. Fisk was carried to a room, where physicians worked to save his life. Gould, Tweed and Fisk's lawyers were summoned. Fisk died early the following morning. His body lay in state in the foyer of the Grand Opera House, and great crowds filed past it. After the services were read, the Ninth Regiment, with its band playing dirges, provided a solemn funeral procession. In the next issue of *Harper's Weekly,* Thomas Nast's cartoon showed Gould, Tweed and David Dudley Field—Tweed's lawyer and Fisk's—mourning at the grave of the murdered Prince of Erie, with Justice looking on. The caption read, "Dead Men Tell No Tales." Underneath were printed two lines of dialogue. Jay Gould said, "All the sins of Erie lie buried here." Justice replied, "I am not quite so blind."

Old-fashioned moralists were certain that Fisk had met the fate that he deserved. They quoted approvingly Henry Ward Beecher's denunciation of him as "the glaring meteor, abominable in his lusts and flagrant in his violation of public decency." But the generation that had come to maturity during the Civil War were inclined to disagree. Fisk had a streak of Yankee smartness and shrewdness that they admired. Hadn't he, again and again, outsmarted veteran masters like Commodore Vanderbilt and Daniel Drew? Hadn't he made his way up from being a hostler in Van Amberg's circus, a peddler in the hamlets of Vermont, to the possession of millions and the control of Erie? As for his peculiar business methods, the new generation realized that Fisk had done precisely what they would have liked to do, had they been in his place and been granted his opportunities. Even the atmosphere of profligacy that surrounded his life aroused their secret envy—the lives they led were, on the whole, irreproachably respectable, arid and dull. In refusing to be bound by the traditional moral code, in declining to become the prisoner of convention and decorum, in rejecting the easy compromise of hypocrisy, Jim Fisk had shown an intrepidity that compelled their admiration. They could not emulate him, but they did not condemn him.

This easy tolerance, which seemed so dangerously cynical to all defenders of the proprieties, indicated that the old morality was becoming obsolete. Nor were other signs lacking. You couldn't laugh away the careers of the notorious

ASSASSINATION OF JIM FISKE
by Edward S. Stokes at the Grand Central Hotel, January 6, 1872

sisters whose exploits had dazzled and bewildered New York for more than two years. They were, so to speak, feminine counterparts of Jim Fisk, absurd but formidable, rebels against prudery and defiant enemies of the established order. New York first heard about Victoria Woodhull and Tennessee Claflin when, early in 1870, as protégées of old Commodore Vanderbilt, they rented a suite of offices in Broad Street and set up in business as "lady brokers." They were young and quite beautiful. They wore their brown, curly hair cut short. Instead of the long-trained dresses decreed by fashion, they wore skirts that came only to their shoe-tops, jackets of a mannish cut, bright-colored neckties. Within a few months Woodhull, Claflin and Company, presumably on tips furnished by the Commodore, had made more than a half a million dollars in the stock market.

Why had wily old Vanderbilt taken these obscure ladies under his protection? Wall Street thought it knew the answer. Tennessee Claflin was a "magnetic healer," Victoria Woodhull a spiritualist. One soothed the aged financier's body, the other ministered to his superstitious mind. The Commodore denied that he provided the lady brokers with market tips. To the contrary; they predicted the future behavior of his railroad stocks. "Do as I do," he told a prospective speculator; "consult the spirits." And, in a generous mood, he shared with another importunate seeker for profits his latest forecast from the spirit world. New York Central common was in for a big rise, he asserted—"Mrs. Woodhull said so in a trance." It was rather hard to decide whether the bewitching sisters were advising, or being advised by, Commodore Vanderbilt. But the source of oracular wisdom was unimportant. The Commodore's prestige, backing the lady brokers, insured their success.

Clients thronged to their offices. So did the idly curious. The sisters soon posted a sign: "All Gentlemen Will Please State Their Business and Then Retire At Once." Those who obeyed this injunction, however reluctantly, were probably luckier than they knew. Tennie Claflin, among her varied talents, had the gift of turning a rising male temperature into a tangible asset. Nobody knew this better than Commodore Vanderbilt. Before setting up the sisters in business, he had married a young wife—as some said, with unseemly haste. "Didn't you promise to marry *me?*" Tennie Claflin was reported to have asked him, afterward. "Yes," the old Commodore admitted, "but the family interfered." Did Vanderbilt make reparation for his unchivalrous conduct by establishing a brokerage office where investment counsel was furnished by spooks?

If so, the reparation appeared to be considered inadequate. For it was widely rumored that Vanderbilt also put up the capital for *Woodhull and Claflin's Weekly*. The sisters launched this magazine a few months after they began stirring up the bulls and bears. Before long, its program flared across the first page: "Progress! Free Thought! Untrammeled Lives!" The *Weekly*, so another line assured readers, was "breaking the way for future generations." That was one way of putting it. A few weeks before issuing the first number of the magazine, Victoria Woodhull had published in *The Herald* a dramatic announcement offering herself as a candidate for the Presidency of the United States in the election of 1872, still distant by more than two years. New York was vastly amused. This was precisely the kind of eccentric publicity that would prevent the lady brokers from being forgotten. It was obviously contrived for the purpose of expanding their business, and it seemed to be a shrewdly spectacular method of advertising.

Nobody was surprised that the *Weekly* unreservedly supported Victoria C. Woodhull for president, and preached the cause of votes for women. Bold articles on the evils of prostitution in New York, recommending the licensing and medical inspection of prostitutes, offended the decorous and made the *Weekly* widely known. But when it began defending the practice of abortion, and advocating the doctrine of free love, there was a splutter of excitement. In the enlightened future, Victoria Woodhull declared, boundless love would prevail. Woman would feel dishonored by producing inferior children. She would consider superior offspring a necessity, and would therefore be apt to procreate only with superior men. Her sexual intercourse with others would be limited, and proper means would be taken to render it unprolific. Clearly, such views could only be proclaimed by an abandoned woman. Ugly rumors about Victoria Woodhull and Tennie Claflin were soon drifting about the city.

Anybody who visited their residence on Thirty-eighth Street, just east of Fifth Avenue, at the crest of fashionable Murray Hill, might have surmised that some of the rumors were true. Victoria Woodhull and Tennie Claflin were supporting a large, raffish household that did them little credit. There were three other sisters; all had been divorced. Two of them had children, and one had acquired a second husband. The third was a handsome spitfire, insanely jealous of the notoriety that had come to Victoria and Tennie. There was a saturnine father who had a long record as a crook. There was an illiterate mother given to explosive outbursts of temper. The family was united by a passionate affection which expressed itself most characteristically in violent brawls. Eventually, quarreling Claflins took their grievances into courtrooms where the sordid family saga was thoroughly ventilated. But for the moment their luxurious way of life depended upon discretion. Neither Victoria nor Tennie wished their pasts to be raked up, and Victoria's present marital situation was not one which polite New York would approve.

From their squalid childhood in the Middle West, the sisters had always been pariahs, forced by one or another scandal to leave whatever community they settled in. They had traveled about as fortune tellers, spiritualist mediums, "magnetic healers," vendors of spurious medicines. In Illinois, Tennie Claflin had been indicted for manslaughter; her parents had operated a hospital where she administered fake cancer cures. In Cincinnati, she figured in a blackmail case, and with Victoria was charged with keeping a house of assignation. There were similar charges in Chicago and other cities. During their wanderings, Tennie Claflin had taken a husband, then paid him to disappear when he ceased to please. Victoria, at the age of sixteen, had been married to Dr. Canning Woodhull. She bore him two children, and eventually divorced him. Later, she formed an alliance with Colonel James H. Blood, an abundantly whiskered veteran of the Civil War. The story ran that she and Colonel Blood had married, then divorced on principle; they had profound convictions on the subject of free love. But Dr. Woodhull was also a member of the household. Still infatuated, broken in health and fortune, he had returned to his former wife. Having wrecked his life, she bore him no malice. She took him in. He took care of their children. It was a chaste arrangement, but one which conventional people might easily misunderstand.

The household also included a resident philosopher. Stephen Pearl Andrews was an elderly, erudite and somewhat obscure sage. He was an irrepressible fountain of ideas, all of them radical. He was a philosophical anarchist and a mystic. He wanted to bring about a social revolution, and his zest for reforms was boundless. He preached the gospel of free love, the need for a new, superior morality. He did not reject the spiritualism professed by Victoria Woodhull and Colonel Blood. In the *Weekly,* he published the first translation of Karl Marx's *Communist Manifesto* to appear in America. The *Weekly* gave Andrews a medium in which to expound his ideas. It was a medium for Blood's ideas, also. They ran to fiscal reform; he wanted the currency to be as elastic as love. Victoria Woodhull had a weakness for men with ideas. Because her appetite for ideas could not be curbed, she often gave the impression of merely having a weakness for men. She was always glad to sign the articles written by her domestic thinkers, and this habit equipped her with quite a variety of literary styles. Presently, she had her thinkers writing speeches for her as well. She was a brilliant orator, and became a sensational success with audiences. She was a sensational success, too, with the queer intellectuals

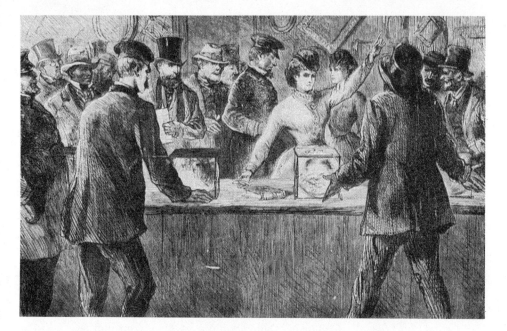

VICTORIA WOODHULL DEMANDS THE RIGHT TO VOTE, 1871

whom Andrews brought to her parlor on Murray Hill. The atmosphere, there, was thick with profound convictions, high ideals, radical theories, improbable reforms and family bickering. And the phosphorescent glow of loose morals added an odd decorative note to this salon of a presidential candidate, this rendezvous of earnest souls bent upon bringing about the regeneration of society.

Victoria Woodhull's persistent drum-beating in behalf of her candidacy provoked a mild fever of annoyance in the suffragist leaders. They had been agitating for twenty-five years, and now an unknown was stealing their thunder. If she wasn't serious, she might do irreparable damage to their cause; if she was, and the rumors about her were true, she might easily wreck it. So, rather nervously, they ignored her. This wasn't the wisest attitude to take toward the Woodhull; she had always found it intolerable. "She reminds one," a reporter wrote, "of one of the forces in nature behind the storm, or of a small splinter of the indestructible, and if her veins were opened they would be found to contain ice." He was wrong about only one detail. Whatever filled her veins was more like white-hot steel than ice.

The National Woman Suffrage Association was to hold a convention in Washington early in January, 1871. Their official policy was to demand a Constitutional amendment specifically enfranchising women. In December, Victoria Woodhull presented a memorial to Congress demanding the enactment of legislation enabling women to exercise the right of suffrage already secured to all citizens by the Fourteenth Amendment. It was a bold strategic assumption in constitutional law, and if it should win acceptance by Congress women were likely to get the vote far more readily than if a special amendment was required. This possibility had not occurred to Miss Anthony, Mrs. Stanton and the other suffrage leaders. But Victoria Woodhull hadn't dreamed it up, nor had it been suggested in a trance by one of her ghostly familiars. Her memorial was written by General Benjamin F. Butler, a member of the Judiciary Committee of the House of Representatives. Butler's political reputation was rather spotty, but even his enemies conceded that he was a man with ideas.

By a singular coincidence, Victoria Woodhull was scheduled to address the Judiciary Committee of the House on the very morning set for the opening session of the Suffrage Convention. The session was hastily postponed until afternoon. The leaders went to hear Mrs. Woodhull. Long afterward, one of Miss Anthony's friends recorded that she was "a beautiful woman, refined in appearance and plainly dressed. She read her argument in a clear, musical voice with a modest and engaging manner, captivating not only the men but the ladies, who invited her to come to their convention and repeat it." That afternoon, at the opening session of the convention, she appeared on the platform, read the "Woodhull Memorial" and reported on her meeting with the Judiciary Committee. It had been so successful that the "Woodhull Memorial" was adopted as the basis of a new program for the Suffrage Association.

In the short space of a single day Victoria Woodhull became the outstanding leader of the suffrage movement. A loud cry of anguish broke from the more puritanical suffragists, and from the men in public life who championed their cause. But Miss Anthony, Mrs. Stanton and other militant veterans never failed to recognize a principle and were always prepared to die for one. The gossip about Victoria Woodhull's past must be ignored. It was great impertinence for anyone to pry into her private affairs. "We have had women enough sacrificed to this sentimental, hypocritical prating about purity," declared Mrs. Stanton. "This is one of man's most effective engines for our division and subjugation. . . . Let us end this ignoble record and henceforth stand by womanhood. If Victoria Woodhull must be crucified, let men drive the spikes and plait the crown of thorns." For, Mrs. Stanton asserted, "her face, manner and conversation all indicate the triumph of the moral, intellectual and spiritual." If Mrs. Stanton was mistaken there was, at least, no question about the triumph of Victoria Woodhull. In New York, she lectured to enthusiastic audiences at the Mercantile Library and Cooper Institute. At a suffrage convention in Apollo Hall, she was seated on the platform between Mrs. Stanton and Mrs. Lucretia Mott, which certified to her respectability. She delivered an oration that evoked cheers from the delegates and rang through the press of the country. It was very unfortunate that, a few days later, her mother brought Colonel Blood into court, proclaiming to the world that the house on Thirty-eighth Street harbored the worst gang of free-lovers that ever lived. During the proceedings Blood, Dr. Woodhull, Victoria Woodhull and Tennie Claflin were put on the stand. When this affair was over, their shameful lives had made headlines across the continent.

In the storm of obloquy that burst over Victoria Woodhull certain savage attacks on her personal morals deeply infuriated her. One appeared in *The Independent*, the most widely circulated of religious weeklies. Its publisher was Henry C. Bowen, a pillar of Dr. Henry Ward Beecher's Plymouth Church on Brooklyn Heights, who as part owner of the church property drew a pleasant income from his pastor's fame. Another appeared in *The Christian Union*, a religious weekly edited and partly owned by Dr. Beecher. This one was written by Mrs. Harriet Beecher Stowe, the pastor's sister, a determined opponent of woman suffrage whose pious soul was revolted by the notion of free love. A third attack was made by another sister of the pastor, Catherine Beecher, equally opposed to the rights of women to be free either with their votes or their bodies. However, Mrs. Isabelle Beecher Hooker, a half-sister of the eminent preacher and the two stern moralists, was a prominent leader in the suffrage movement and a vigorous defender of Victoria Woodhull. Bowen, Dr. Beecher and his three female relatives all had some reason to be agitated by Victoria Woodhull's retort to her detractors. In her *Weekly* she promised a formal declaration of war. In New York and Brooklyn, she affirmed, civilization was festering to the bursting point. "At this very moment," she announced, "awful and herculean efforts are being made to suppress the most terrific scandal in a neighboring city which has ever astounded and convulsed any community." In an open letter to *The Times*, she declared that she did not intend to be made the scapegoat of moral hypocrites. "My judges preach against 'free love' openly, and practice it secretly. For example, I know of one man, a public teacher of eminence, who lives in concubinage with the wife of another public teacher of almost equal eminence. All three concur in denouncing offenses against morality. . . . I shall make it my business to analyze some of these lives, and will take my chances in the matter of libel suits." Bowen and Dr. Beecher knew precisely what she meant by the "terrific scandal" and neither had any doubt about the identity of the "public teacher of eminence." Measures would have to be taken to silence Victoria Woodhull.

Dr. Henry Ward Beecher, nearing sixty, was long married and the father of a family. He was the most famous preacher in the United States. Short, corpulent, moon-faced, with a mane of graying hair, he had a superb voice and great dramatic power—in the pulpit and out of it. On Sunday mornings, a squad of policemen kept order in the huge crowds that waited for hours to enter Plymouth Church. The ferries that brought thousands from New York to Brooklyn were known as "Beecher boats." All visitors to the city felt that they had to hear Dr. Beecher at least once. His eloquence was impassioned and vivid. He acted out, in tone and gesture, the anecdotes with which he illustrated his theme. He played expertly on the emotions of his hearers, moving them at will to laughter or tears. It was said that when he read from the Testament, "the idea that Jesus is speaking to them pervades the assembly." His explanation of the spell that he cast over multitudes was simple. He delivered his sermons immediately after composing them, and in a high state of excitement. "Some men like their bread cold, some like it hot," he said. "I like mine hot." This homely preference also applied to matters more delicate than either bread or sermons. Dr. Beecher's predilection for warm and wayward dalliance seemed about to plunge him into very hot water indeed. It was a form of total immersion for which he felt a personal, as well as ecclesiastical, repugnance. And there were many who, for different personal reasons, were desperately anxious to prevent the laying low of a man universally revered as a great power for good in the nation.

For Dr. Henry Ward Beecher was, in effect, a national institution. If he should be exposed as guilty of adultery—as practicing the abhorrent sin of free love—would not morality and respectability be undermined? And then, too, Dr. Beecher was big business. His religious weekly and his lecture tours were enterprises of continental scope. His high repute was of financial importance to the wealthy bondholders of tax-free Plymouth Church. Nobody was more keenly aware of this than Henry C. Bowen, who had brought Beecher to the pastorate and had given him large sums of money. Bowen detested Beecher. The pastor had seduced Bowen's first wife and, as he believed, had brought her to her death—yet Bowen did not wish Beecher to be destroyed by scandal. Neither did Theodore Tilton, though his reason was not, like Bowen's, a mercenary one. A blond, handsome young giant, Tilton was a member of Beecher's flock. Worshipping his pastor as a man of exalted spirit, he had become his favorite disciple and companion. Tilton had a strongly poetic temperament and a slender poetic talent. He was an unworldly idealist, a dedicated crusader for social reforms, an ethical visionary. Succeeding Beecher as editor of Bowen's weekly, *The Independent,* he made it the most influential religious magazine in the country. As a lecturer on the lyceum circuits, he drew large audiences. He had married Elizabeth Richards, a teacher in the Sunday school at Plymouth Church, a pretty, girlish little woman who idolized her pastor. The Tiltons had four children and a pleasant home on Brooklyn Heights. They made it a rendezvous for an intellectual circle that included Wendell Phillips, Greeley, the poet Whittier, Miss Anthony and Mrs. Stanton.

An intimate of this home, Beecher seduced Elizabeth Tilton. He taught her that "nest-hiding," as she afterward called it, was no sin; he had taught Lucy Bowen that a "paroxysmal kiss" and more obscure practices should produce no moral qualms. Elizabeth Tilton confessed her infidelity to her husband, but insisted that neither her love for him nor her purity had been blemished. Tilton, however shocked, forgave her. He tried to forgive Beecher, too. Much earlier, Bowen had told Tilton about his own betrayal by Beecher. Tilton told his story to Bowen. Shortly afterward, differences arose between them, and Beecher, aggravating these, brought about Tilton's discharge as editor of *The Independent*. With a wife and children to support and no money, Tilton turned for advice to a friend, Francis Moulton. Moulton gathered sufficient money to launch a new magazine, *The Golden Age,* for Tilton. He saw Beecher and indicated a line of action which the terrified pastor agreed to follow. The Tiltons tried to rehabilitate their marriage and home. But Tilton

surmised, with reason, that Beecher had not adhered to his promise of breaking all connection with Elizabeth Tilton. There were quarrels, and during
one of them the Tiltons told their story to Miss Anthony and Mrs. Stanton.
These ladies had no reason to love Beecher; he had repudiated his public
advocacy of the suffrage cause. They were horrified by this new and deadly
proof of Beecher's hypocrisy. Mrs. Stanton told the Tiltons' story to Victoria
Woodhull. And when she published her threat of exposure, it was Moulton
who, with Beecher's consent, sent Tilton to Victoria Woodhull to procure
her silence.

Tilton was very handsome. He was also a man of many ideas. Victoria
Woodhull later gave two contradictory accounts of their relations. She declared that "for three months we were hardly out of each other's sight. . . . He
slept every night, for three months, in my arms." She also intimated that this
was not the case; Tilton "frequently went up the stairs with me to the roof
of the house to enjoy the starlight and cool breeze on pleasant summer evenings." According to Stephen Pearl Andrews, Tilton spent his time in the
parlor with the other "radical advanced minds . . . but always with a vein of
strong dissent on his part, which led to a great deal of discussion." Some of
his time he probably spent alone. He wrote, and published as a *Golden Age
Tract,* a biography of Victoria Woodhull which not only glorified its heroine,
but lyrically endorsed her theory and practice of free love. He presided when
she lectured, in Steinway Hall, to a riotous audience on the principles of social
freedom and proudly affirmed that she was a free-lover. To Tilton's devout
readers and lyceum audiences, he seemed an apostate; his following began to
melt away. But Victoria Woodhull went on to greater triumphs. Her magazine
flourished. Her lectures drew immense audiences. People were irresistibly
curious about this beautiful, brazen adventuress who was a leader of the suffrage movement, a prophet of social revolution, a calumniator of men in high
places, an avowed spiritualist, a financier, a free-lover and an inveterate fire-
brand. Even the usual Claflin family quarrels, airing fresh scandals in courtrooms, no longer damaged her, though the reluctance of landlords to harbor
her queer household forced her to change residences with disconcerting frequency. Miss Anthony, Mrs. Stanton and Mrs. Hooker continued to champion her vigorously. The Equal Rights Party made her the first official female
candidate for the Presidency of the United States, with Frederick Douglass,
the Negro reformer, as her running mate. Tilton preferred to work for the
election of Horace Greeley. Victoria Woodhull regarded this as desertion.
It was.

Meanwhile, the attacks on her continued. Eminent suffragists who resented
having their cause associated with free love and spiritualism repudiated her.
Beecher's outraged sisters became more ferocious. Victoria Woodhull threatened Beecher by letter, demanding that he silence them. Thereafter, she met
him and later said that they had several months of intimacy during which she
saw him "frequently and alone," and that this generated a correspondence
which "was not one of mere platonic affection." Many people considered

Beecher a man of ideas, but one of the ideas he couldn't grasp was that he might quell his rambunctious sisters. So, in the end, Victoria Woodhull struck back. On November 2, 1872, *Woodhull and Claflin's Weekly* published an article entitled "The Beecher-Tilton Case." "I intend that this article shall burst like a bombshell into the ranks of the moralistic social camp," Victoria Woodhull wrote, announcing that the publishers were prepared "to take all the responsibilities of libel suits and imprisonment." Within a few hours, single copies of the *Weekly* were selling for as much as forty dollars. The article not only exposed Beecher as an adulterer, but defended him as a free-lover. "The immense physical potency of Mr. Beecher, and the indomitable urgency of his great nature for the intimacy and embraces of the noble and cultured women about him, instead of being a bad thing, as the world thinks, or thinks it thinks, or professes to think it thinks, is one of the noblest and grandest endowments of this truly great and representative man," Victoria Woodhull wrote. And she forthrightly added, "Plymouth Church has lived and fed, and the healthy vigor of public opinion for the last quarter of a century has been augmented and strengthened from the physical amativeness of Reverend Henry Ward Beecher." Beecher appreciated the defense scarcely more than the exposure. But neither then nor afterward did he sue Victoria Woodhull for libel, as she had suggested. "I tread the falsehoods into the dirt from which they spring," he said, "and go on my way rejoicing."

The pillars of Plymouth Church decided to do something more than rejoice. Anthony Comstock, a zealous suppressor of vice and defender of public morals, appealed to the United States District Attorney to arrest Victoria Woodhull and Tennie Claflin on the charge of transmitting obscene literature in the mails. The District Attorney was a leading member of Plymouth Church. The sisters were promptly arrested and jailed. They spent the better part of three months behind bars, awaiting trial. A wave of sympathy for them rose throughout the country, for people were aghast that two women should be imprisoned by the United States Government in order to vindicate the reputation of a citizen who, however eminent, refused to vindicate himself. Six months after their arrest, the indictments against the sisters were dismissed. Victoria Woodhull reprinted the Beecher-Tilton issue of the *Weekly,* and continued in the magazine to attack Beecher, Bowen and other leaders of Plymouth Church. On lecture tours, she drew tremendous audiences; the Beecher scandal had become a national obsession. She assailed the shameful hypocrisy of public opinion, the disgraceful lie of morals, conventions and manners that made people pretend to believe in principles which their conduct explicitly denied. She demanded reforms that would end the degradation of women, and urged the teaching of sexual science in the schools.

And on Dr. Henry Ward Beecher fortune also seemed to smile. Everyone knew all the alleged scandals about him, now. But the foundation of social order did not collapse. His popularity merely increased. The Sunday-morning crowds at Plymouth Church were larger than ever. Did they come to be moved when he brandished the sword of the Spirit? Or just to see this jovial, white-haired grandfather with a youthful manner who stood accused of repeated adulteries, of shameless betrayals of the faith reposed in him by his parish, his friends, and the nation at large? Did it make any difference, after all, why the crowds came to hear Beecher? Before the world and before his congregation, Beecher stood on his incorruptible righteousness. He had committed no crime. He was the hapless victim of a slander perpetrated by a prostitute, Victoria Woodhull, abetted by the degraded and immoral Tilton, a man corrupted by his association with such notoriously loose women as Victoria Woodhull, Miss Anthony, Mrs. Stanton—even Beecher's half-sister, Mrs. Isabella Beecher Hooker. Behind the scenes, a battery of eminent attorneys were working to hush up the scandal—by any means, and at any cost.

But their efforts miscarried. The Congregational clergy were aroused. Theodore Tilton had been quietly dropped from membership in Plymouth Church as one who had brought "open dishonor upon the Christian name." An ecclesiastical council was held; the moderator afterward publicly denounced Tilton as a knave and a dog. In reply, Tilton published a letter reciting all his relations with Dr. Beecher. Then Beecher appointed a committee of six prominent members of his church to investigate the "rumors, insinuations and charges" contained in Tilton's letter. And at this point Elizabeth Tilton, who had both admitted and denied her adultery, left her husband and children to vindicate Beecher. Tilton appeared before the committee, making a sworn statement of Beecher's adultery with Mrs. Tilton. Beecher denied it; he said that "she thrust her affections on me unsought." He accused Tilton and Francis Moulton of blackmail. Excitement ran high throughout the country when Beecher's committee issued a report completely exonerating their pastor. "If the secret history of this tragedy is ever brought to light," Mrs. Stanton wrote, "we shall have such revelations of diplomacy and hypocrisy in high places as to open the eyes of the people to the impossibility of securing justice for anyone when money can be used against him." And many Americans agreed. They wanted the truth established, whatever the truth might be.

Tilton brought suit against Beecher for the alienation of Mrs. Tilton's affections, announcing that if he won his suit he would accept no financial damages, though he was now a ruined man. The trial began in Brooklyn City Court early in January 1875. Nothing since the outbreak of the Civil War had excited such intense interest throughout the country as this case. Statesmen, ecclesiastics, jurists, millionaires and other prominent folk thronged the courtroom. Newspapers everywhere reported the trial at full length; many issued special supplements reproducing the voluminous correspondence that was offered in evidence. A vast pamphlet literature circulated about the country. As a witness, Beecher produced a poor impression; those who hoped that he would effect a saving miracle were disappointed. It helped little that his adoring congregation sent flowers to the courtroom in his honor. According to *The Herald,* he presented "for the investigation of scientific men a psychological problem which they must despair of solving." In *The Louisville Courier-Journal* Colonel Henry Watterson described him as "a dunghill covered with flowers." After six months of sensational testimony, the case ended with a disagreement of the jury. Plymouth Church regarded this as equivalent to an acquittal. So did Dr. Beecher. But, reviewing the case, *The Times* surmised that "sensible men throughout the country will in their hearts be compelled to acknowledge that Mr. Beecher's management of his private friendships and affairs has been entirely unworthy of his name, position and sacred calling."

There was an aftermath of church meetings, ecclesiastical councils and collateral lawsuits. They were widely publicized, but from them all Dr. Beecher emerged victorious. The "Beecher boats" continued to bring thousands to hear the great preacher every Sunday. On a long lecture tour, vast audiences turned out to hear him speak at a guaranteed fee of one thousand dollars. Three years after the trial, Elizabeth Tilton wrote a letter published by every newspaper in the land. She asserted that "the charge, brought by my husband, of adultery between myself and the Reverend Henry Ward Beecher was true, and that the lie I had lived so well the last four years had become intolerable to me." But this diminished neither the influence nor the high repute of Henry Ward Beecher. And few Americans appeared to be troubled by the spectacle "of the gospel of truth and purity being expounded by one who has so flagrantly defied its precepts."

In the circumstances, Dr. T. De Witt Talmage, Beecher's greatest rival in theological showmanship, had to find a new way of filling his cavernous Brooklyn Tabernacle, which held five thousand people and was the largest ecclesiastical building in the country. Under the protection of policemen, Dr.

RECONCILED! Puck's comment on the Beecher-Tilton Case, April 17, 1878

Talmage visited the slums of the metropolis, its dens of dissipation, gambling rooms, houses of prostitution, dance halls and concert saloons. He devoted a series of Sunday sermons to exposing "The Night Side of New York." Respectable men and women jammed the Tabernacle to learn how the dissolute lived and behaved. Dr. Talmage was severely censured, in the religious press, for pandering to the curiosity of prurient people.

His defense was one of the most profound moral observations made during the decade. Dr. Talmage asserted that he did not object to being called a sensationalist. Preaching that was not sensational, he declared, was good for nothing.

NEW YORK POLICE, 1870, *by A. Boyd Houghton*

12

The Apotheosis of Mrs. Astor

During New York's age of innocence, everyone in society knew whom you meant when you spoke of the Joneses. They were a patrician clan, and marriage had woven them into the intricate web of cousinships that united their peers. Like the Schermerhorns, Rhinelanders and other families with which they were allied, they enjoyed the benefits of an ancestral addiction to Manhattan real estate. For several generations, in a most distinguished way, the Joneses had done nothing whatever remarkable. This avoidance of note was an aristocratic ideal, the last refinement of wealth and breeding. The Joneses exemplified it. They were eminent. When one of them wilfully challenged the rule of conformity, society stood aghast.

Mrs. Mary Mason Jones committed her act of defiance at the age of seventy. She was so long a widow that only her contemporaries remembered her husband, Isaac Jones. Her power as an arbiter and her repute as a hostess had been acknowledged for more than three decades. She and her sister-in-law, Mrs. Colford Jones, had occupied adjoining, communicating residences on Broadway, opposite the New York Hotel at Waverly Place, and their dinners, balls and suppers still served as standards for the edification of youth. Innovation was scarcely to be expected from a lady of Mrs. Jones's advanced years, sedentary condition and previously blameless existence.

But, in 1871, Mrs. Jones chose to "improve" the block front on the east side of Fifth Avenue between Fifty-seventh and Fifty-eighth Streets. She built a row of residences that included, on the Fifty-seventh Street corner, a mansion for herself. Capriciously rejecting the binding convention of building in brownstone, she achieved a masterpiece of architectural audacity. Mrs. Jones's row was flagrantly Parisian. It displayed a uniform facade of pale-cream stone, with graceful balustraded pavilions, a gray-green mansard roof, and tall, wide windows which queerly opened outward like doors. Traveled New Yorkers found it reminiscent of the Champs Elysées and the Imperial court of the Tuileries. It conjured up disturbing visions of a society very unlike their own —sophisticated, dissolute, frivolous. Elderly patricians recalled that, many years before, Mrs. Jones had closed her Broadway home to make a prolonged stay in Europe. What dubious foreign influences did her new mansion commemorate? Certainly it seemed to mock at the respectable solemnities of conservative New York.

Ignoring the topography of fashion, the venerable matriarch went to live out her remaining years among the squatters' shanties, rocks and mounds of debris which, on every side, testified to her imprudence. The interior of her mansion proved to be as unconventional as its facade. Time, bringing Mrs. Jones the infirmities of age, had also invested her too prodigally with flesh. She therefore reversed the sanctified domestic arrangements of New York, had her reception rooms on the second floor, and installed herself in a suite off her entrance hall. Discarding the grim, massive furniture of her prime, she decorated her mansion in the Parisian manner. The effect was not only novel but startling. The pagan divinities that frolicked across her painted ceilings were as embarrassing as August Belmont's celebrated nude by Bouguereau. Polite New York had established the limits of permissible eccentricity. For Mrs. Jones's Parisian mansion in the wilderness, her innocently accessible bedroom, frivolous furniture and voluptuous divinities, no precedents existed. The whole affair threatened to undermine tradition, and the matriarch's immense prestige made it an especially sardonic attack on conformity.

Age and immobility did not diminish Mrs. Jones's appetite for society. The witty, intrepid old lady could fill her mansion whenever she chose, and as easily as if her invitations did not require her guests to make an almost suburban journey. She "brought out" her granddaughters, one by one, presenting them to society in a series of balls. She entertained, at dinner, those whom she considered worthy of a place on the visiting list which she could no longer put to its prescribed use. But, although susceptible to new ideas, she was inveterately prejudiced against "new people." To devise innovations was the privilege of a Jones, yet was it not her duty to condemn novelties proposed by upstarts? The case of Mrs. Paran Stevens indicated that the social situation had deteriorated alarmingly. Pondering it, old Mrs. Jones determined to rescue society, if rescue was still possible. "There is one house," she announced, "that Mrs. Stevens will never enter. I am old enough to please myself, and I do not care to extend my sufficiently large circle of acquaintances." Twenty years later, when Mrs. Jones quit her mansion for a heavenly habitation not built by her, Mrs. Stevens took possession of it. "I assure you I was actually afraid to give my consent to the lease," one of Mrs. Jones's heirs acknowledged. "I felt that I might be visited by grandmamma's reproachful spirit."

Members of the old guard like Mrs. Jones considered Mrs. Stevens a dangerous, disintegrating force. She was, so to speak, doubly anonymous. A native of barbarian Lowell, Massachusetts, she had married an obscure Bostonian who, acquiring millions in the hotel business, could only be described as a tradesman. Mrs. Stevens, a tall, handsome brunette, came to New York by way of Washington. There, foreign diplomats, lamentably ignorant of subtle republican distinctions, frequented her home. With outrageous effrontery, she made no secret of her intention to win a place in New York society. She began her siege of the citadel by violating its most inexorable law, which prohibited all formal hospitality on Sunday nights. In New York, the Sabbath was ritually dedicated to church-going, an even more stupefying dinner than usual, and nocturnal boredom. When Mrs. Stevens offered the astounding distraction of Sunday-night musicales featuring celebrated opera singers, ostracism became morally imperative. But to the dismay of conservative patricians it was found that ostracism could not be enforced. In the very highest circles there were gentlemen who had long chafed under the domestic ennui inseparable from piety. Oblivious of their duty to their church and their class, they allowed themselves to be seduced by Mrs. Stevens' superior champagne, her excellent suppers and the pleasure of hearing Mme. Christine Nilsson sing, instead of pretending to make connubial conversation at home.

A melancholy eclipse was overtaking the so-called "Faubourg Saint-Germain set," families of Colonial ancestry who had not found it worth their while to abandon their old-fashioned mansions on Stuyvesant Square and follow the "swells" to Fifth Avenue. Mrs. Lewis Morris Rutherfurd continued, from that unfashionable location, to issue decrees that were decreasingly observed, and although "she had the prettiest way in the world of putting people in their appropriate place," they often refused to stay put. Her neighbor, Mrs. Hamilton Fish, maintained a regnant attitude to society that sometimes evoked deficient appreciation. "Thursday evening last I went to my first dinner party, and never in my life was I so bored," Julia Newberry, a youthful visitor from Chicago, confided to her diary. "I had the illustrious Mr. Hamilton Fish who in spite of his having a Grandfather is little less than an idiot." The scarcely less august hospitalities of lower Fifth Avenue failed to delight young Mrs. Burton Harrison, a dweller within the citadel. Long afterward, she recalled the boredom of receptions given in "rather dreadful picture galleries where, in a glare of gaslight, we were jostled by hundreds of people standing round supper tables, from which there floated searching odors of fried oysters served with mounds of chicken salad, and accompanied by champagne that flowed like water. This ceremony accomplished, and a tour of the rooms made, there was really nothing left to do but to begin the mad rush through the upstairs dressing rooms in search of coats and hats and take one's leave."

External assault and internal skepticism showed that the life of society had reached a crisis. Were traditions of such little value that they could be quietly forgotten? Was "the concerted living up to long established standards of honor and conduct, of education and manners" to be abandoned? Conservatives acknowledged that if society was to be preserved, it must not only be made impregnable, but restored to its former high estate—especially in the opinion of its own members. In the United States, as Ward McAllister declared, "four generations of gentlemen make as good and true a gentleman as forty." But these splendid genealogical specimens could not be permitted merely to climb up their family trees and find solace in their lofty complacency. Surely they had a public duty, a higher moral obligation.

Anxiously reviewing the situation, McAllister was persuaded that society could be reorganized as a hierarchy, with all the eligible marshaled in an ascending scale of graded ranks. Centralization of control, already proving so effective in the economic sphere, was equally applicable to the social realm. After protracted daily conferences with three gentlemen of the utmost distinction, McAllister organized the Patriarchs, a committee of twenty-five gentlemen who, unquestionably, "had the right to create and lead society." "We wanted the money power," he explained, "but not in any way to be controlled by it." So Patriarchs were chosen "solely for their fitness," for they were to be vested with the sovereign's prerogative of saying "whom society shall receive, and whom society shall shut out." The Olympian list included two Astors, two Astor collaterals, two Livingstons, a Van Rensselaer, a Schermerhorn, a Rutherfurd, a Jones and a King. When published in the press, this list assured the American people that the official custodians of their pantheon "embraced not only the smart set, but the old Knickerbocker families as well."

The Patriarchs were charged not only with the duty of leading society, but also with the responsibility of creating it. How was the process of creation to be accomplished? In any critical emergency, McAllister prescribed an infallible remedy; to his mind, a ball solved all problems. So the Patriarchs were advised to create society anew by holding a series of subscription balls at Delmonico's. To each of these functions, every Patriarch had the privilege of inviting four ladies and five gentlemen on his individual responsibility. Sponsorship of guests was obviously a sacred trust, since certification by the Patriarchs had been established as the sole authentic passport to society. By making it extremely difficult to obtain an invitation to the ball, as McAllister astutely foresaw, the Patriarchs enormously enhanced its value. The prestige of society was automatically revived by competition. "Applications to be made Patriarchs poured in from all sides," McAllister noted happily; "every influence was brought to bear to secure a place in this little band, and the pressure was so great that we feared the struggle would be too fierce and engender too much rancor and bad feeling." Yet this was not solely a calculated risk; it was, in fact, the principal objective. The Patriarchs adopted a policy of fastidious exclusion. For unless they could glimpse the landscape of hell, how were the anointed to gain an awareness of salvation?

But society could not be born of multiple fatherhood alone; the feminine principle was clearly essential. So awesome, so momentous a maternity seemed beyond fallible mortal choice. Providence intervened, bringing McAllister for the first time in contact with the unique, divinely appointed candidate. He "at once recognized her ability, and felt that she would become society's leader, and that she was admirably qualified for the position." In the Cathedral of Chartres, one saw everywhere the Virgin, and nowhere any rival authority. Similarly, in the new pantheon one was blinded by the effulgence of Mrs. William Astor. Elevated to supremacy, she became the Mystic Rose about whom the greater and lesser saints revolved in their fixed orbits. Society, had it been left to the Patriarchs alone, might have been no more than an exercise in celestial mathematics, a reiterated multiplying of nine by twenty-five. But Mrs. Astor contrived a miraculous paradox. She transformed society into a secular religion. You could well say of her, as Henry Adams later said of the Virgin of Chartres, that, without the conviction of her personal presence, men would not have been inspired. By the elect, her presence was felt continuously and, for them, it made existence a perpetual liturgy.

Long frustration had prepared Mrs. William Astor for supremacy. As Caroline Schermerhorn, she had married the younger son of William Backhouse Astor. In the Astor family, precedence and fortune were transmitted to the eldest son. John Jacob Astor III inherited two-thirds of the family estate, and was head of the house. His wife outranked Mrs. William Astor; in due time his heir, William Waldorf Astor, would eclipse her son, John Jacob Astor IV. Resentful of her inferiority, Mrs. William Astor was little consoled by her husband. He disliked society and cultivated diversions which kept him almost permanently absent. Having come to consider him dispensable, she appointed Ward McAllister her counselor and chamberlain. Her first concern was to overthrow the regime of her sister-in-law. Mrs. John Jacob Astor III held unorthodox views, far in advance of the times. She cherished the odd notion of improving the standard of polite life by inviting her peers to meet celebrities from the realms of literature, the arts and the theater. She gave a dinner for Edwin Booth, a reception for Mme. Adelaide Ristori. She included among her intimates F. Hopkinson Smith, a novelist and painter. She formed *Les Causeries du Lundi,* a select group of matrons who met to hear the reading of very intellectual papers. All this—as Mrs. William Astor knew, and Ward McAllister confirmed—was profoundly wrong. Except for the illustrious dead, authors and painters merited no recognition. Like actors, they belonged to the servile classes and lived in a disreputable world. To meet them required not only a suspension of decorum, but a needlessly fatiguing mental effort. Mrs. William Astor banished them. Among the elect, conversation must be restricted to matters of genuine import. The approved topics were sufficiently absorbing. Thoughtful discussion of food, wines, horses, yachts, cotillions, marriages, villas at Newport and the solecisms of ineligibles would exclude the dangerous attraction of ideas.

The rituals devised by Mrs. Astor and McAllister were elaborate and time-consuming. On Monday and Friday nights those who had boxes at the Academy of Music attended the opera. They arrived at the end of the first act, and enjoyed the pleasure of conversing with their friends during the second inter-mission. On Monday nights they went on to the Patriarchs' Balls, the Assem-bly Balls and the Family Circle Dancing Classes, all held at Delmonico's and therefore graced by an excellent supper. This succession of festivities was interrupted, on the third Monday in January, by Mrs. William Astor's annual ball, the most sacred ceremony of the year. On that night, her mansion on Fifth Avenue and Thirty-fourth Street was ablaze with lights, and all its splen-did rooms were banked with masses of flowers. Through a wide hall, guests proceeded to the first of three connecting drawing rooms, where their hostess received them, standing before the life-size portrait which she had recently commissioned from Carolus Duran. A tall, commanding woman of formidable dignity, she was magnificently gowned by Worth. Precious antique lace draped her shoulders, edged her huge puffed sleeves. Her pointed bodice and long train were of rich dark velvet, her skirt was of satin, embroidered with pearls and silver or gold. She glittered with diamonds. Her black pompadour—later to be succeeded by an even blacker wig—was crowned by a diamond tiara and embellished by diamond stars. She wore a triple necklace of diamonds, a sunburst, a celebrated stomacher, and chains of diamonds fell from her cor-sage. Cordially greeted by this scintillant idol, her guests made their way through two more thronged drawing rooms to the spacious art gallery which served as a ballroom. Lander's costly orchestra was playing in the musicians' gallery, and the walls were hung with works of art which had acquired fame, if not merit, from Mrs. William Astor's favor. In due time supper, catered by Pinard, was served in the great dining room from an immense table where, amidst a profusion of flowers, the delicately embalmed bodies of terrapin and fowl reposed on ornate silver.

Mrs. William Astor's annual ball enabled her to assemble, simultaneously, all the carefully graded ranks of her hierarchy. Failure to be invited signified that, whatever your pretensions, you were a goat and not a sheep. This gave the ball pre-eminent significance but, since it was the most inclusive of her rites, it was not—as the unitiated supposed—the most distinguished. It was, of course, superior to her afternoon receptions. Occasionally, guests at these functions demonstrated that, as Ward McAllister declared, the Mystic Rose was not incapable of "understanding the importance and power of the new element; recognizing it, and fairly and generously awarding to it a prominent place." But this recognition was bestowed at the lowliest of her ceremonies. The most exalted of all her rites were the weekly dinner parties to which only the topmost ranks of the hierarchy were convoked. The table was illuminated by golden candelabra, decorated with golden épergnes and hundreds of *gloire de Paris* roses; a gold service, for some time unique in America, was used. The guests were seated at eight o'clock, and it was seldom before eleven that the hostess, by a slight bow to the lady facing her, intimated that the gentlemen were to be left to savor Madeira which, having anciently rounded the Cape, was now sent duly westward, and was followed by coffee and Havana cigars.

August Belmont had taught patricians the art of dining, but Mrs. William

Astor, under the tutelage of Ward McAllister, ennobled this art by dedicating it to solemn, sacred uses. Her fiat was absolute; gastronomy, formerly a mere cult, now became a holy discipline, "the ladder to social success." No heresy could be more fatal than the error of permitting two white or brown sauces to appear in sequence, or tolerating the use of truffles twice during the same dinner. Only divine favor could extenuate the crime of offering a *sorbet*— the "Roman punch" which preceded canvasbacks, woodcock, snipe, or truffled capons—flavored with rum; Maraschino or bitter almonds were mandatory. Connoisseurship bred jealousy, and, sometimes, unhappiness. Ward McAllister lost a charming friend by serving a better soup than his friend's chef could prepare. John Carr of Savannah disappeared from society when his famous "Rapid" Madeira was exhausted, and everyone knew a New York family that, after giving the most exquisite dinners, retired to Europe in the conviction of disgrace when rivals succeeded in surpassing them.

Authoritative connoisseurship could transform ignominy into honorable fame, as the case of Sam Ward proved. People said of Sam Ward that he was the only man capable of strutting when seated. Julia Ward Howe was his sister, Ward McAllister his cousin. Sam Ward was also the brother-in-law of Mrs. William Astor, but no member of the Astor family had received him for forty years. After the early death of his first wife, Emily Astor, he made an inferior marriage which turned out badly, and he compounded disgrace by permitting the Ward banking house to fail. Thereafter, Ward was involved in picturesque, but dubious, adventures on the Pacific coast, in Mexico, Central America, Paraguay and Europe, making and losing fortunes with prodigal indifference. A handsome old gentleman, now, Sam Ward was internationally known as "King of the Lobby," the most notorious of professional intermediaries between a venal Congress and the promoters who wished to purchase its favors. He was also acknowledged to be the most brilliant talker, the greatest wit of the day. He was erudite, the owner of a superb library, a discriminating collector of pictures. None of these attributes counted in his favor. It was his illustrious achievement as a gourmet that alone assured his social salvation. Nobody dared question the authority of a gentleman who, when you offered him a glass of wine, was able after one sip to identify both its provenance and its vintage, and only Astors dared to impugn his morals, or his superior gentility. Sam Ward's counsel was sought by the highest circles when there arose any delicate problem in gastronomy, for his dinners were celebrated as the most perfect ever given in Washington or New York.

A single banquet might enable one of the "new people" to leap up the ladder of social success. Edward Luckemeyer, a millionaire importer whose social ambitions were long ignored, achieved a dizzying elevation by inviting seventy-two guests to a dinner party of unprecedented beauty, magnificence and costliness. When customs duties amounting to ten thousand dollars were unexpectedly refunded by the Government, he transferred this sum to Charles Delmonico, with instructions to produce a feast that would always be remem-

Little Neck Clams	Petits pois, Tomates farcies, Pommes croquettes
Montrachet	Côtelettes de ris de veau à la parisienne
Potage tortue verte à l'anglaise	Cèpes à la bordelaise
Potage crème d'artichauts	Asperge froide en mayonnaise
Amontillado	Sorbet au Marasquin
Whitebait, Filets de bass, sauce crevettes	Pluvier rôti au cresson
Rauenthaler	*Chateau Margaux*
Concombres	Salade de laitue
Timbales à la milanaise	Fromages variés
Filet de boeuf au madère	*Old Madeira Charleston and Savannah*
Pommery sec	Bombe de glace Fraises Pêches Gâteaux
Selle d'agneau de Central Park, sauce menthe	Raisins de serre
Moët et Chandon Grand Crémant Impérial,	Café
Magnums	*Cognac et Liqueurs*

A DINNER GIVEN BY SAM WARD

bered. The banquet was held in Delmonico's large ballroom, which was almost filled by a huge oval table. This monster plateau had been transferred into an undulating landscape of flowers, in the center of which there was a thirty-foot lake where, enclosed by a delicate golden-wire network, four superb swans, brought from Prospect Park, dutifully swam. Above the sheet of water were suspended little golden cages containing rare songsters that filled the room with their music.

When gentlemen of leisure were not attending delightful weekday luncheons, stately dinners, or pleasant after-theater suppers, they could sometimes be found at their clubs. There they were technically in sanctuary. The increasingly vigilant feminine eye could not reach them; the acceleratingly dominant feminine will could not penetrate beyond the entrance. The shabby, somber old Union Club, at Twenty-first Street and Fifth Avenue, was the most aristocratic, although a group led by Alexander Hamilton and John Jacob Astor III, feeling that the Union was becoming too hospitable and democratic, founded the Knickerbocker Club to uphold an ideal of genealogical purity. Great was the scandal in society when a lady swept past the doorkeeper of the Union Club and burst into the quiet of its card room, bent upon retrieving her husband, then making a fourth at whist with three other sedate members. "An appalling silence fell on all as the members gasped and dropped the cards in their astonishment," the Club's historian recorded. "The unfortunate member—whose wife was responsible for this unheard of breach of etiquette—retained his presence of mind. Gravely he introduced his wife to his fellow members at his table. Then he turned to her and courteously and politely asked her to be seated until the rubber was ended. When this had been accomplished he offered his arm to his wife, bowed gravely to the other members and left the Club—never to set foot inside the clubhouse again."

OPENING OF THE COACHING SEASON, Fifth Avenue looking south from 27th Street, *by H. A. Ogden*

At the Union Club, talk was likely to turn on horses, ponies, hounds and foxes, for these animals were becoming indispensable adjuncts to a gentleman's leisure. The Coaching Club was a case in point. Founded by Colonel William Jay, Leonard Jerome, De Lancey Kane and other enthusiasts who wished to establish four-in-hand driving as a fashionable sport, its first public parade was held in the spring of 1876, led by the president, Colonel Jay, in bottle-green coat with gilt buttons, yellow-striped waistcoat, silk topper and boutonnière. To the Coaching Club "form" was almost as important as "family." Observance of the fine points of decorum was obligatory: the driver's apron, when not in use, had to be folded outside out; and artificial flowers were required to be affixed to the throat-latch of every horse.

Coaching became one of the most elegant diversions of the élite, and to achieve celebrity as an amateur whip was a consuming ambition of middle-aged "swells" and the younger set of "howling swells"—an ambition nearly as obsessive as that to win fame as a leader of cotillions. It led De Lancey Kane, who belonged to the numerous Astor connection, to introduce an astonishing practice. Kane began driving his coach and four from the Hotel Brunswick on Madison Square, on scheduled runs, to a country club in Westchester where the passengers had luncheon before making the return trip. Was it not, therefore, in a sense a public vehicle? If so, what was to prevent unwelcome parvenus from purchasing places, and thus insinuating themselves among their betters? Society shuddered at the prospect, but Kane was able to prove that his innovation was in the purest "form." No less an aristocrat than the Marquis of Blandford, heir of the Duke of Marlborough, had driven his coach as a public vehicle between London and Dorking—and the British ruling caste remained inviolate. Kane's equipage, known as "The Tally-ho," provided the generic name by which, to the exasperation of the Coaching Club, a gaping proletariat came to refer to all the handsome coaches which presently were being "tooled" up Fifth Avenue. And, as the years passed and the vogue for coaching flourished, people ceased being surprised that, if you were able to pay, you could enjoy the privilege of having a distinguished millionaire like Alfred G. Vanderbilt serve as your coachman because he considered this humble but expensive vocation a fashionable sport.

Fox-hunting was introduced almost simultaneously with coaching, and a number of reasons explained its strong appeal to the rich and well-born. In a civilization increasingly dominated by business, it enabled gentlemen of leisure to justify a decorative uselessness. Hunting had once been a practical occupation, and it retained an aura of common-sense reputability. Nevertheless, it was a diversion singularly suited to an aristocracy, for it permitted them to apply primitive social skills to the pursuit and slaughter of an inedible animal—thus affording opportunity for a display of prowess that served no vulgarly utilitarian end. Fox-hunting expanded the equine cult already prospering among the elect, and it brought them into intimate association with dogs whose affection—unlike that of many people—need not be attributed to social ambition. Moreover, the genealogy of both horses and dogs was absolutely controllable and, since new, anonymous people were beginning to enter society, it was pleasant to form friendships with creatures of unimpeachable pedigree.

Meanwhile James Gordon Bennett the younger, another versatile sportsman, sought to popularize polo. This ancient game was one of the British spoils of empire in India, and Bennett had acquired a knowledge of it from retired colonial administrators in England. In 1876 he brought the first polo mallets and balls to the United States. Forming teams among his friends, he taught them the rudiments of the game in a New York riding academy, then transported them in his coach to Jerome Park, where the first American match was played. The possibility of playing matches immediately after the conclusion of races soon suggested itself; the racing crowd remained to watch the new sport. Presently, succumbing to one of his more grandiose inspirations, Bennett, with Frank Gray Griswold, the ageing August Belmont and several others, formed the Westchester Polo Club, erected a clubhouse, and transported one of the Delmonicos from New York to supervise the preparation of its dinners. Under such auspices, the new sport flourished and eventually polo ponies were substituted for the unspecialized steeds which, initially, were considered adequate mounts.

These conspicuous, costly and esoteric dedications to the great outdoors gradually emerged from club talk and became eligible for conversational use in mixed society, thus extending the mental horizon of dinner parties. Though at Mrs. William Astor's table you were unlikely to meet an idea, some of the hierarchy were afflicted by a wistful reverence for the intellectual life and, at times when their sense of her awesome presence had dimmed, indulged in furtive explorations. Society, as Edith Wharton long afterward recalled, was "a little 'set' with its private catch-words, observances and amusements, and its indifference to anything outside its charmed circle." The talk of this charmed circle, she said, "was never intellectual and seldom brilliant, but it was always easy and sometimes witty." Nevertheless, some of its members occasionally wondered whether the conversation of a superior society ought not to be of superior quality. They were haunted by the tradition of eighteenth-century salons, where an aristocracy had found it possible to be both worldly and intelligent. Nobody suffered more acutely from this nostalgia for the improbable than Peter Marié, an elderly bachelor renowned as the most cultivated "exquisite," the most distinguished "beau," of the day. Fortified by a prestige second only to that of Ward McAllister, Marié determined to elevate the tone of social intercourse. He issued invitations to "an intellectual tea, on St. Valentine's Day, after the manner of the Hôtel Rambouillet." He went on to give a "remarkable dinner" for which the invitations were written in verse. The guests were requested to respond poetically, and were assured that "a beautiful prize" would be awarded to the best of their poems. Inflated with enthusiasm, Marié launched a series of dinners dedicated to reviving "the art of intellectual conversation," but these met with diminishing success and he regretfully abandoned the project.

Others, less exorbitantly ambitious than Marié, popularized the art of intellectual conversation by making it, so to speak, a spectator sport. The Thursday Evening Club was founded—this evening being sacred neither to Mrs. William Astor nor the opera—and met at the houses of different members, each of whom offered a program of edification, followed by an hour of talk among the guests, and supper. Competition, wealth and common sense eventually gave the programs an unforeseen direction. One resourceful hostess invited the club to hear Paderewski play a piano recital in her home. Mrs. Cornelius Vanderbilt, after equipping her new palace with a ballroom, hired Constant Coquelin to perform a series of "turns" on its stage—an attraction which brought out all the club members, who were delighted to enjoy the antics of France's most eminent actor but were not exposed to the social contamination of meeting him.

If Mrs. William Astor was aware that members of her hierarchy were engaging in these erratic, unsanctioned distractions, she gave no sign of disapproval. She was, in fact, preoccupied by instances of lese majesty, of ominously flagrant insubordination which, permitted to pass unpunished, would seriously threaten her supremacy. Must she defend her absolute pre-eminence in the vulgarly competitive arena of her inferiors? It seemed that she would have to, for disdain alone could not dispose of the challenges.

The first challenge came from the Vanderbilts, a dynasty that had its questionable existence beyond the horizon of her social vision. Society had denied admission to old Commodore Cornelius Vanderbilt, and it ignored the present head of the house, William Henry Vanderbilt who, having inherited ninety millions of dollars, built for himself and two of his daughters a block-long, grim, brownstone triple mansion on the west side of Fifth Avenue between

RESIDENCE OF WILLIAM K. VANDERBILT, 1882, Fifth Avenue and 52nd Street

Fifty-first and Fifty-second Streets. The magnate philosophically accepted his exclusion, but he failed to impose so appropriate a humility on the wife of his second son, William Kissam Vanderbilt. Plump, pugnacious and intrepid, Alva Vanderbilt felt herself destined to social leadership, and she determined not only to storm the citadel but overwhelm it. Retaining the eminent architect Richard Morris Hunt, she commanded that a chateau be built on the northwest corner of Fifth Avenue and Fifty-second Street to exceed in splendor the marble mausoleum of A. T. Stewart, the Parisian mansion of Mrs. Jones, and the sullen banality which Christian Herter had devised for her father-in-law.

With three million dollars at his disposal, Hunt produced the first of his masterpieces in domestic magnificence. It was inspired both by the Chateau de Blois and the mansion at Bourges of the fifteenth-century financier Jacques Coeur, the greatest upstart of the Renaissance, as one of young Mrs. Vanderbilt's friends impolitely termed him. This architectural grafting of European history on unseasoned American wealth was to influence profoundly the facades of Fifth Avenue and Newport for two generations. Only Louis H. Sullivan, the prophet of functionalism in architecture, was so ungracious as to point out that William Kissam Vanderbilt could not possibly live in his palace, "morally, mentally or spiritually, that he and his home are a paradox, a contradiction, an absurdity, a characteristically New York absurdity; that he is no part of the house, and the house no part of him."

Mrs. William Astor likewise considered young Vanderbilt and his house an absurdity, though for very different reasons, and her disrelish was increased by the laxity of her chamberlain. For while the palace was still in course of erection, Ward McAllister capitulated to its grandeur, and admitted the young Vanderbilts to the sacrosanct Patriarchs' Balls. Though Mrs. Astor did not withhold her presence when they attended, they were never presented to her. Affairs stood at this pass when, during the winter of 1883, Alva Vanderbilt announced that she would inaugurate her palace, late in March, with a fancy-dress ball. Since it was obvious that this was to be the most luxurious affair of its kind ever held in New York, the problem of costumes, as *The Times* reported, "disturbed the sleep and occupied the waking hours of social butter-flies, both male and female, for over six weeks." The great costumer, Lanou-ette, who made more than one hundred and fifty of the dresses to be worn at the ball, estimated that these had cost more than thirty thousand dollars; they had kept one hundred and forty dressmakers working, night and day, for five weeks.

There was also a flurry, in the most exalted circles, to organize quadrilles

FANCY DRESS BALL at the Residence of William K. Vanderbilt, 1883

for the occasion. In this, Mrs. Astor's daughter Caroline engaged somewhat too precipitately. When Alva Vanderbilt learned that Carrie Astor and a group of her friends had organized a "Star Quadrille," and were industriously practicing it at the Astor mansion, she expressed her sorrow to intimates of Mrs. Astor. It would be impossible for her to invite young Miss Astor to her ball; she had never met either the young lady or her mother. Faced with the alternative of disappointing her daughter or disavowing her disdain, Mrs. William Astor called for her carriage and·humiliatedly drove up Fifth Avenue. A footman in the Astor blue livery delivered her engraved calling card to a servant wearing the maroon livery of the Vanderbilts—thus admitting them to a lofty rank in the hierarchy. Immediately afterward, a Vanderbilt footman delivered the last of twelve hundred invitations at the Astor mansion.

The ball was, for Alva Vanderbilt at least, a celebration of victory, and, attired as a Venetian princess after a painting by Cabanel, she had her photograph taken with white doves hovering around her, perhaps emblematic of the enduring social peace that could be expected to result from the *entente cordiale* between Astors and Vanderbilts. The costumes were gorgeous beyond expectation. Mrs. Bradley Martin appeared as Mary Stuart, Mrs. Paran Stevens as Queen Elizabeth; the impersonation of royalty was appropriate to triumphant invasion. Mrs. Cornelius Vanderbilt, in white satin trimmed with diamonds, represented "the Electric Light." The Duc de Morny, whose title originated with the vanished Second Empire, was clad as a courtier of Louis XV. The dances were no less original than the costumes. The ball opened with a "Hobby Horse Quadrille," in which the dancers, attired in riding habits, appeared to be mounted on horses "of life size, covered with genuine hides" that had flowing manes and tails and flashing eyes; these equine effigies were attached to the waists of the dancers, whose feet were concealed by richly embroidered caparisons. Other scarcely less remarkable exhibitions of grace followed, and Henry Clews, the genial banker, reflected that, although it may not have been as costly as certain entertainments of Alexander the Great, Cleopatra, or Louis XIV, the Vanderbilt ball—reputed to have cost one-quarter of a million dollars—"when viewed from every essential standpoint, and taking into account our advanced civilization . . . was superior to any of those grand historic displays of festivity . . . more especially as the pleasure was not cloyed with any excesses like those prevalent with the ancient nobility of the old world." At Versailles, the extravagance may have been greater, but the Roi Soleil had never conceived a diversion so ineffable as the "Hobby Horse Quadrille." On the third Monday of the following January, the presence of Alva Vanderbilt and her husband was remarked at Mrs. William Astor's annual ball.

But neither peace nor certainty were, as yet, Mrs. William Astor's portion. Her sister-in-law, Mrs. John Jacob Astor III, died in 1887; John Jacob Astor III followed his wife to eternal rest three years later. This left, as head of the family, his son, William Waldorf Astor, an arrogant man who had played at politics as State Senator, had been defeated for election to Congress after a costly campaign, and had dabbled in statecraft as Minister to Italy. Pathologically sensitive, and resentful of the homage paid to his aunt, he determined that his wife should take her rightful place as *the* Mrs. Astor. Accordingly, he instructed the postmaster at Newport to deliver to his wife all letters addressed simply to "Mrs. Astor." Mrs. William Astor not only gave precisely the same instructions; before leaving New York for the summer, she deposited, as usual, her P.P.C. cards, properly bent at the corner, in the salvers of her accredited worshippers who noted that they now bore the inscription, "Mrs. Astor." All summer long, Mrs. William Waldorf Astor and her aunt, Mrs. William Astor, besought their absent friends to write to them at Newport, addressing them as "Mrs. Astor." In this war for a title, society divided: the "swells" remained faithful to their Mystic Rose; the "howling swells" favored her younger rival. By early autumn the whole nation was eagerly awaiting the outcome of this momentous conflict, which filled the press with its incessant roar. In the end, William Waldorf Astor, in a towering rage, quit his native land forever to take up residence in England, where a gentleman would be appreciated and, after long propitiation, a title might be securely bought.

At the age of sixty, Caroline Astor entered upon her apotheosis. She was more than *the* Mrs. Astor. She was the only Mrs. Astor, and there could be no greater magnificence, no more sublime destiny than that of bearing this classically simple designation, so rich in profound, mysterious meanings. No longer was she merely the central, supreme divinity of a local cult. She became the subject of a national legend, taking her permanent place in American folklore. Though she professed disdain for the press and pretended to resent any mention of her name in its columns, newspapers throughout the country faithfully recorded her imperial progress, aware that, in effect, Mrs. Astor was a national institution. Cowboys, millhands, clerks, shopkeepers, snow-bound farmers, housewives in cities and villages whose lives her activities would never touch enthusiastically followed them, for she exemplified that superior, more beautiful existence to which they all aspired.

So all the world knew that when Mrs. Astor accepted an invitation decorum required that she take precedence over all other guests. When she dined out, she was invariably placed at the right of her host. When she graced public functions with her presence, she was always "borne down by a terrible weight of precious stones," but she never failed "to scintillate for the benefit of the dim throngs that gazed in speechless awe upon her magnificence." Her preferences established amenities, her verdicts formulated etiquette for the American people. She touchingly enjoyed her unique position, but for the elect who were less opulently endowed she was capable of making considerate concessions. Thus, she gave august approval to an inferior approximation, if the genuine reality was beyond reach—"to build an addition to one's house, to be used but for one night, and to be made large enough to comfortably hold, with the house, one thousand or twelve hundred people." For not everybody could have a ballroom, and no ballroom could hope to rival that of Mrs. Astor.

It was the dimensions of her ballroom, so the world was led to believe, that in the end determined the composition of society. In the press, Ward McAllister had been intimating this for years. "Why, there are only about four hundred people in fashionable New York Society," he told reporters. "If you go outside that number you strike people who are either not at ease in a ballroom or else make other people not at ease." After long tormenting the public, which wanted its gods identified, he at last gave out the list of the sacred Four Hundred—those who had received invitations for Mrs. Astor's annual ball in 1892, the last ball to be given at her old mansion at Thirty-fourth Street.

But with the names of the Four Hundred recorded, as it were, on imperishable tablets, Mrs. Astor's apotheosis was complete. And there were few, except those beyond the pale, who agreed with the outrageous verdict of society's favorite scandal-sheet *Town Topics*: "With a pertinacity worthy of a better cause she has worn herself out in the endeavor not to be a part of Society and an aid to its advancement in worthy directions but to reign over it and have her subjects stand in awe of her power." In Mrs. Astor, many of her fellow citizens recognized the vicarious fulfillment of the American dream.

13

The Medici
Do
Their Duty

By the end of the Civil War, people of culture were saying that the time had come to establish a permanent public gallery of art in New York. Efforts to found such a gallery had been made from the last decade of the eighteenth century, but all were premature and all had failed. Was failure inevitable? John Jay, a New Yorker who wished to be proud of his city, believed that it was not. Fired by his enthusiasm, a committee was formed to launch the project, and addressed a memorial to the Union League Club urging it to assume sponsorship of the movement.

The Art Committee of the Club, headed by the publisher George Palmer Putnam, was well equipped to further the project. Remarkably enough, its members included a number of artists—the sculptor John Quincy Adams Ward, the painters Worthington Whittredge, George A. Baker and Vincent Colyer—as well as Samuel P. Avery, a respected art dealer, who was helping William H. Vanderbilt and other millionaires to form their private collections. At the instigation of this committee the Union League Club convoked a public meeting, late in 1869, to discuss the establishment of a municipal museum of art. As a result of this meeting the Metropolitan Museum of Art was organized in January, 1870, with John Taylor Johnston as president, William Cullen Bryant and General John A. Dix as vice-presidents. The trustees and executive committee were, in the main, prominent lawyers and men of affairs, but the arts were represented by the painters John F. Kensett and Eastman Johnson, the sculptor J. Q. A. Ward, the architect Richard Morris Hunt and the landscape-architect Frederick Law Olmstead, who with Calvert Vaux had designed Central Park. The president, John Taylor Johnston, was a man of wealth who had long cultivated a taste for art. Fifteen years earlier he had built the first marble mansion in the city, at the southwest corner of Fifth Avenue and Clinton Place (later, Eighth Street) and had installed an art gallery above his stable to display his collection of paintings, then among the most important in the country. On one day each week, he opened his gallery to the public, and New Yorkers were thus enabled to view such pictures as Frederick E. Church's "Niagara," and Winslow Homer's "Prisoners from the Front." For, unlike rival collectors, Johnston was interested in the work of living American painters, among whom he had a wide acquaintance. Every year in his gallery he held a reception for all artists residing in the city, and brewed for them a potent "artists' punch" whose inspirational merits Charles Astor Bristed celebrated in a widely quoted poem.

Under Johnston's presidency, it seemed likely that the new museum would fulfill Bryant's hope for a gallery dedicated to the greater works of living American artists. But this was to be indefinitely postponed. Instead, from the outset, the Metropolitan Museum was committed to the policy of forming "a more or less complete collection of objects illustrative of the History of Art from the earliest beginnings to the present time." The trustees attempted to raise, by subscription, the sum of two hundred and fifty thousand dollars to establish the museum. So tepid was the public interest that, after a year, only slightly more than one hundred thousand dollars had been secured; and in a city of millionaires only three men gave five thousand dollars or more for the cause.

Undaunted, Johnston determined to begin forming the collection which his infant museum had neither money to buy nor place to house. In 1870, a member of his executive committee, the merchant William T. Blodgett, was traveling in Europe. The outbreak of war between Prussia and France brought two private collections on the market, totaling one hundred and seventy-four paintings, principally Dutch and Flemish, but including representative works of the Italian, French, English and Spanish schools. Together, the cost ran to ten thousand dollars more than the Museum's trustees had succeeded in raising. Abetted by Johnston, who shared the financial risk, Blodgett promptly bought the pictures. Among the trustees there arose a storm of protest against this reckless extravagance, with accusations that the whole affair was a humbug and that Johnston and Blodgett had been swindled. Nevertheless, under terms which fully protected them, the trustees were finally persuaded to assume the purchase and pay for it when funds became available. With this collection as a nucleus, the Metropolitan Museum was opened, early in 1872, in a rented brownstone building on Fifth Avenue near Fifty-third Street, previously occupied by Allen Dodworth's fashionable Dancing Academy. "People were generally surprised, and agreeably so, to find what we had," Johnston recorded happily. "No one had imagined that we could make such a show, and the disposition to praise is now as general as the former disposition to depreciate."

Meanwhile, armed with petitions signed by many influential New Yorkers,

RECEPTION AT THE OPENING OF THE METROPOLITAN MU-
SEUM OF ART, 681 Fifth Avenue, February 20, 1872

representatives of the Museum persuaded Boss Tweed, and his henchman,
Peter B. Sweeny, to have the Legislature authorize New York City to erect a
museum building on public property. After prolonged debate, a site in Central
Park was chosen, between Seventy-ninth and Eighty-fourth Streets, fronting on Fifth Avenue. In 1874, ground was broken for the Museum's permanent home. But even before this, the Museum was compelled to find larger
quarters and moved into the old Douglas mansion on Fourteenth Street, between Sixth and Seventh Avenues. Once again, Johnston had acted on his
own initiative in making a purchase. This time, his acquisition illustrated the
"earliest beginnings" of the history of art. For sixty thousand dollars, he
bought a massive hoard of "antiquities" that had been excavated on the
island of Cyprus by the American consul in that remote, unknown place. The
consul, General Louis Palma di Cesnola, was not an archaeologist. A
pompous, peppery warrior, he had taken part in the Italian Revolution and
the Crimean War. Then he had emigrated to the United States and fought in
the Civil War and, having become a citizen, he was appointed to his minor
foreign post. Impressed by the notion that Cyprus was the meeting place of
ancient races, the enterprising General during six years excavated eight
thousand Phoenician, Greek, Assyrian and Egyptian tombs as well as a
Temple of Venus. The yield of all this digging totaled ten thousand objects
ranging from spearheads and bits of iridescent glass to statues from the temple.

General di Cesnola wished this collection to be kept intact and forever known by his name. "I have the pride of my race," he declared, "and that of a Discoverer who wants his name perpetuated with his work if possible." On these terms, learning that an offer had been made by the British Museum, Johnston bought the entire collection for the Metropolitan. The acquisition soon produced dramatic results.

With General di Cesnola as its director—a post which he was to hold until his death nearly twenty-five years later—the Museum, early in 1880, inaugurated its permanent home. The new building was a plain affair of red brick and tile, dominated by a huge glass roof which gave it the effect of a hothouse. Few people shared the wild optimism of the trustees, who asserted that, in the future, this ugly structure would be surrounded by architecturally superior additions which would completely conceal it from view. After the first novelty had worn off, the public might have ceased taking a trip uptown to view its collections had there not occurred a controversy and scandal which made the Museum a subject of national interest. In an art magazine, Gaston L. Feuardent, a French dealer in antiques, attacked the authenticity and value of the Cesnola collection. His specific charges were that intentionally false restorations and repairs had been made to certain objects, and that the bronzes had been provided with an artificial patina. A committee was appointed by the trustees to investigate, which in due time issued a report completely exonerating the director and his collection. This report failed to silence criticism. Incriminating articles began to appear in the press; the art critic Clarence Cook published a pamphlet charging that two statues in the collection were "a fraudulent patchwork of unrelated parts"; in *The Century* Richard Watson Gilder, after careful study, pilloried General di Cesnola "as a liar, falsifier and fraud" in a twelve-page editorial. Privately, Gilder asserted that "one of these days, instead of blaming me for what I have printed, the trustees may thank me for mercifully leaving unprinted the facts that I suppressed." The controversy, soon becoming a national sensation, led the Museum to remove the two indicted statues from their glass cases, and place them on the floor of the Grand Hall, "where they might be approached and examined in a strong light." During the next few weeks, thousands of people came to inspect the discredited statues, and "visitors washed, chiseled, cut, scraped, treated with caustic potash and other chemicals, brushed with wire brushes, and examined microscopically to their hearts' content," with the consent of the Museum authorities. Eventually, the controversy culminated in a libel suit against General di Cesnola, and a jury of laymen acquitted him of the charge of libeling his detractor. The Museum regarded this verdict as a vindication of the Cesnola collection. But the scandal had been of incalculable value. In the minds of Americans, it permanently established the Metropolitan Museum as one of the major "sights" of New York City.

Visiting the Metropolitan Museum, as the *Evening Post* noted with genuine surprise, "you feel that American art is not so bad after all. . . . The eye is really not shocked to find a Gérôme balancing an Eastman Johnson, a Troyon balancing a William Magrath, a Bouguereau balancing a Henry A. Loop." But actually, even in the loan exhibits which the Museum occasionally displayed, drawing upon the private collections of New Yorkers, there was likely to be only a scattering representation of American artists. "It has become the mode to have taste," James Jackson Jarves noted, after the Civil War. "Private galleries in New York are becoming almost as common as private stables." Years earlier, Jarves had returned from Florence with a superb collection of Italian Primitives, but nobody in New York had heard of these masters, nobody wanted them, and finally the pictures went to Yale University. The taste and knowledge of New York collectors had perhaps advanced, but when they bought "modern" paintings, they were more likely to acquire the works of Europeans than of Americans. For the opening of the Metropolitan Museum William H. Vanderbilt, whose collection was considered the finest in New York, offered the loan of ten of his pictures, and Samuel P. Avery, who had formed his collection, reported that "we took the best he had." The ten pictures chosen were Charles Jacque's "Shepherd and Flock," Jules Dupré's "Landscape," N. V. Diaz' "Forest of Fontainebleau," Jules Lefebvre's "La Sposa di Torrente," Villegas' "The Rare Vase," Erskine Nicol's "Looking for a Safe Investment"—a peculiarly appropriate title—Madou's "Flemish Cabaret," Corot's "Dance of the Nymphs," Meyer von Bremen's "What Has Mother Brought?" and Van Marcke's "Cattle."

In his earlier years, Vanderbilt had often gone down to the Studio Building on Tenth Street, west of Fifth Avenue, and had bought paintings by the artists who lived there; especially works by J. G. Brown, the highly esteemed "bootblack Raphael" who specialized in newsboys, bootblacks and other street urchins, and pictures by the equally popular S. J. Guy, who produced bright, smooth "subjects with children." But, as Avery explained, Vanderbilt "did not continue to make a collection of American pictures after he came into the possession of his fortune, since he was able to buy the best and most costly in the world. He decided, at the outset, to procure nothing that was not important." He liked pictures which told a story, "with either strong or cheerful subjects such as appeal to the imagination of the ordinary individual." He bought J. F. Millet's "The Sower" because, himself a farmer on Staten Island in his youth, he was struck by the fidelity to nature of the action of the man sowing the seed. It was the same with one of his paintings by Constant Troyon. This represented a yoke of oxen turning to leave the field after plowing. Connoisseurs praised it, but adversely criticized the action of the cattle. "Well, I don't know as much about the quality of the picture as I do about the action of those cattle," Vanderbilt remarked. "I have seen them like that thousands of times." He once sought out Rosa Bonheur at her studio in Fontainebleau, taking an interpreter along with him, intent on commissioning two paintings. The eminent artist protested that she could not, as Vanderbilt wished, produce them immediately. "Tell her I must have them," he insisted. "I'm getting to be an old man, and want to enjoy them." Rosa Bonheur burst into laughter; she was only a year younger than her patron.

A PRIVATE GALLERY OF THE PERIOD. Scene from the residence of A. T. Stewart about 1876

However, Vanderbilt received his pictures within the year. He usually got what he wanted. Admiring the minute realism of Ernest Meissonier's renditions of the military splendors of the Second Empire, he purchased seven pictures at a cost of one hundred and eighty-eight thousand dollars, and by his munificence induced the artist to paint his portrait. But Vanderbilt, who knew what he liked and had acquired a collection of paintings valued at more than one and a half million dollars, did not consider the work of American artists sufficiently "important" to grace a millionaire's gallery. To the painters and sculptors who were congregating in New York, the emergent Medici, like the Museum, offered little patronage.

New York had been a vital center of art from the beginning of the century, but now it appeared to be incubating an American renaissance. Never before had the colony of artists included so many men of remarkable talent, and never before had the creative ferment been more vigorous. A spirit of revolt was in the air, against academic tradition, against prevailing standards of taste, even against the ancient American deference to Europe in matters of art. America had come of age, and a new day had dawned. Only new forms of art could give it adequate expression. In the streets around Washington Square where the artists had chiefly settled, excitement ran high. Young painters, returning from Paris, spoke of the "revolutionaries" there who, rejected by the official Salon, were organizing their own exhibitions, refusing to be discouraged by the ridicule of eminent critics or the laughter of the public. Should not something of the kind be attempted in New York?

For New York, also, had its official Salon, the annual exhibition of the National Academy of Design. Since the end of the Civil War, the Academy was installed in a Venetian palace on the corner of Fourth Avenue and Twenty-third Street. It was a unique and powerful body, having great prestige and possessing an important social influence. It was dominated by a group of elderly members; for a generation or more the old New York families who cared for art had bought their works, sought their counsel and prized their friendship. The Academy was an old institution, founded in 1826 by Samuel F. B. Morse (who later invented the telegraph) in rebellion against the conservatism of the American Academy of Fine Arts which it soon superseded. But radicalism was no longer its note. The Academicians professed to represent American art; actually, they ruled it with an iron hand. Their exhibitions were the only stage on which rising talent could reach the public. Yet the painters who dominated the Academy were intolerant of youth and hostile to all innovation. Many of the younger Academicians—middle-aged men of growing reputation—felt that the Academy had become too conservative, too hidebound and arbitrary. The new generation of painters caustically declared that, at its exhibitions, you saw little but the same old literal still lifes, sentimental genre pictures, woolly landscapes and saccharine "ideal" heads. The Academy, they said, had become a club of distinguished patriarchs, futile, incompetent and bitterly opposed to progress. They weren't, they protested, making an issue of youth against age. The question was whether, as an artist, you were looking to the future or merely living in the past.

In the spring of 1875, the National Academy excluded from its exhibition most of the "forward-looking" painters. One of these rejected artists was Helena de Kay, the young wife of Richard Watson Gilder, who proposed to her colleagues that they hold an exhibition of their own. A meeting was held in the Gilders' home, where the daring project was submitted to John La Farge, a member of the Academy. With his collaboration, the "conspirators" arranged a show in the gallery of a prominent dealer which, to everyone's surprise, was acclaimed by the press. Two years later, when the Academy rejected a sculpture by Augustus Saint-Gaudens, another meeting was held at the Gilders' at which the Society of American Artists was formed. The new organization would not only hold exhibitions for the "forward-looking"—it determined to set up a school, the Art Students' League, in opposition to the famous one conducted by the Academy. At the first exhibition held by the new Society you might have seen the work of such prominent Academicians as La Farge, Homer D. Martin, George Inness; the sculpture of Saint-Gaudens; the painting of "new men" like Albert P. Ryder and William M. Chase. The battle lines were now clearly drawn. Over the next decade, the insurgent group increased its membership from twenty-two to more than one hundred. Old-fashioned New Yorkers with a taste for art protested that a revolution was destroying beauty. But in this clash between the old and the new a younger generation thought that they were seeing the light of dawn, and the promise of future glory.

WASHINGTON SQUARE IN THE EARLY 1880's

You could hardly escape an impression that important things were happening if you knew some of the artists whose studios were around Washington Square. The district was a kind of enclave within the city for, on the whole, the artists kept to themselves, patronized inexpensive little French and Italian restaurants south of the Square where the sauces were savory and the wine not too sour, and tried to create an oasis in what one of them, Will H. Low, called "our desert home." Those whom they considered "outsiders" were not encouraged to intrude, but few of them were as solitary, taciturn and fiercely independent as Winslow Homer. Homer's name was known to many thousands of Americans, for over a period of seventeen years he had contributed drawings to *Harper's Weekly,* and the vigorous series which he sent from the front during the Civil War were justly famous. He had been elected to the National Academy in 1865, at the age of twenty-nine, and he remained loyal to it, taking no part in the long war between Academicians and insurgents. But he didn't belong in either camp, and he knew it. He never talked about his work, and whether the public liked his paintings or not seemed indifferent to him. After the war, he had spent ten months in France without studying under any of the famous masters, or copying a single picture in the Louvre. And the paintings that he was turning out now were impressively American, not only in subject but style; you could almost say that he was inventing an American vernacular in paint.

Of all the artists working in New York, John La Farge was the most versatile, and he was expounding a revolutionary idea. He wanted architects, painters, sculptors and decorative craftsmen to work together, not only on public buildings, but in the design and decoration of homes. He wanted to change the look of American cities, and he wanted to make the arts an integral element of their life. He would have liked to bring the arts to bear on every structure that the city-dweller lived in, worked in, worshipped in, or frequented for his relaxation. Fired by this ideal, La Farge was the first American to undertake mural painting, and he had devised a method of producing opalescent glass for windows which, used most notably in churches, hung like curtains of jewels between the beholder and the light. These activities had developed, in part, from practical necessity; for a long period, La Farge made practically no money from his pictures. When his friend, the great architect Henry Hobson Richardson, gave him the opportunity to paint murals and create windows for Trinity Church in Boston, La Farge seized it eagerly. He worked there with one of Richardson's young associates, Stanford White, and he brought the young sculptor Augustus Saint-Gaudens into the project, and all three occasionally worked together thereafter.

The splendid "color church" in Boston became internationally famous, and presently La Farge was producing even more notable work for New York. He and Saint-Gaudens worked together on the interior of St. Thomas' Church on Fifth Avenue, but their beautiful decorations were lost when the building was later destroyed by fire. Alone, La Farge produced fine panels for the Church of the Incarnation on Madison Avenue, and marvelous windows for the Church of St. Paul the Apostle on Ninth Avenue and Fifty-ninth Street. His greatest achievement was the magnificent painting, "The Ascension," above the chancel of the church of that name on Fifth Avenue and Tenth Street. All the while, La Farge continued to paint pictures. "If you remember your history you will remember that the Cat Princess on retiring into private life only killed mice for fun," he told Henry Adams ruefully. "I kill mine for living, as she did before her great success. But there is always some pleasure in the hunt. . . ." The emergent Medici, after La Farge's work had become celebrated in Europe, sometimes offered him a commission. He painted decorative panels for the Madison Avenue palace of Whitelaw Reid, and did some of his finest work in glass for the Cornelius Vanderbilt chateau on Fifth Avenue and Fifty-seventh Street. But when the millionaire William C. Whitney, perhaps at the instigation of Henry Adams, proposed to become La Farge's "backer," La Farge retorted "that it made him think of the elephant who adopted the family of a heartless hen, and to take care of the chickens sat on them."

The sculptor Augustus Saint-Gaudens also took a dim view of the new millionaires as patrons of art. He liked, instead, to talk about Richard Canfield, the proprietor of celebrated gambling houses in Saratoga, Newport and New York. It was the Canfields, Saint-Gaudens said, who were actually buying works of art. Unlike his friends La Farge and Stanford White, Saint-Gaudens was not exuberant. Remarkably enough, for he was the son of an Irish mother and a French father, he had no instinct for rhetoric; he felt deeply, thought simply and seldom spoke of his own work. Brought up on the sidewalks of New York, he had studied at Cooper Institute, and had been sent to Rome and Paris for further study by two men of means. His first opportunity came when it was proposed to erect a commemorative statue of Admiral David Farragut in Madison Square Park. The committee in charge of the project wished to give the commission to J. Q. A. Ward, the most eminent of American sculptors, but Ward insisted that it be given to the unknown Saint-Gaudens. He worked on this project with Stanford White, who designed a handsome base for the statue, and they collaborated also on a tomb commissioned by the banker J. P. Morgan, a man of morose temperament who subjected them to violent rages whenever any question of money arose.

The Farragut statue, immediately acclaimed as a masterpiece, launched Saint-Gaudens on a career that was soon to make him seem, as Robert Louis Stevenson described him, "the godlike sculptor." His lovely Diana, delicately poised on the Giralda tower of Stanford White's ornate Madison Square Garden, overlooking Madison Square Park, provoked a nationwide controversy. It was the first nude female statue to achieve permanent public display in the United States and, in 1890, moralists in New York and throughout the country condemned it as an outrage, an offense against public decency. But J. P. Morgan was the largest stockholder in Madison Square Garden and, despite the clamor of protest, Saint-Gaudens' imperturbable goddess remained where she was—to become, in time, a civic favorite. When, shortly after the turn of the century, Saint-Gaudens unveiled his noble statue of General W. T. Sherman on the plaza at Fifth Avenue and Fifty-ninth Street, his prestige was so great that all criticism was silenced. Only one dissenting voice was heard. The novelist Henry James, returning to his native land after long absence, lamented that Saint-Gaudens had chosen to represent, in the dubious guise of military victory, the most splendid of all national products: the American girl.

The recognition that came to La Farge and Saint-Gaudens was long denied to Albert Pinkham Ryder, one of the founders of the Society of American Artists. Red-bearded, dreamy-eyed, shy and awkward, he looked like the visionary that he was. He lived and worked in the third-story back room of an old-fashioned house on East Eleventh Street, in a litter of canvases, packing-boxes, old magazines and newspapers, dusty furniture. "The artist," he said, "needs but a roof, a crust of bread and his easel, and all the rest God gives in abundance. He must live to paint, not paint to live." Ryder followed his own rule, content to look out over an old garden with great trees and, above the low roofs beyond, "the eternal firmament with its ever changing panorama of mystery and beauty." He felt, he said, like an inchworm swaying on the end of a twig, "trying to find something out there beyond the place on which I have a footing." This reach toward the invisible, the unattainable, was what made Ryder's paintings so disturbing. They opened doors on a spectral world where few cared to follow him. When he heard of the suicide of a hotel waiter who had lost his life's savings on a horse race, Ryder painted "Death on a Pale Horse" galloping around a race track under an ominous sky, a solitary rider in a race that would never end. Did he intend it as a kind of parable of life in New York? It made people shiver. They would have understood him far better had he painted, quite literally, the suicide of the unfortunate waiter. That would have taught a moral lesson, besides telling a story that anyone could grasp. Ryder was one of the greatest of the "new men," but even the younger generation failed to appreciate him.

JOHN ROGERS IN HIS STUDIO

They liked the work of William Chase, who returned from Europe to teach at the Art Students' League. He was among the most aggressive leaders of the "forward-looking" painters, a breezy, buoyant, energetic soul who delighted in controversy. His studio in the old Tenth Street building and, later, his home on Stuyvesant Square, became meeting places for the entire art colony. Chase earned his living as a teacher and painter of portraits—a portrait by Chase, like a Steinway grand piano, announced your affluence and your discriminating taste. But Chase, rejoicing in his astonishing technical skill, painted landscapes, still lifes, interiors, anything and everything. In their sparkling color, none of his pictures posed any difficulties or asked any questions, so in time they found a ready market. Students, flocking to him from all over the United States, wanted to learn how to paint like Chase. Most of them did. And they spread over the land a legend of the "artistic life" in New York. The shabby painters' boarding houses on Washington Square South; the romantic little table d'hôtes on Sullivan and MacDougal Streets; the old Tenth Street Studios; the pretty models who scurried across the Square: these were written up in the magazines, were described in short stories and novels. So was the Tile Club, a room on East Tenth Street decorated by Stanford White where painters like Chase, Hopkinson Smith, Swain Gifford and many others met to talk, drink beer, smoke and criticize one another's work, and to which visitors like John Singer Sargent solicited admission before coming to New York. Hearing or reading of these places, young Americans in distant towns felt that they "ought to be able to talk about art," and pined to live in a garret somewhere near Washington Square.

Yet the artist whose work was in greatest demand throughout the country, whose name was more familiar to Americans than that of any Academician or member of the Society of American Artists, played little part in New York's legendary artistic life. John Rogers lived on Twelfth Street, just west of Fifth Avenue, and in a studio behind his home was producing the celebrated "Rogers Groups" which embellished the front parlors of prosperous citizens across the continent, testifying, at moderate cost, to elegance and a love of beauty. A self-taught sculptor, Rogers, at the end of the Civil War, had exhibited in a Broadway shop a series of powerful statuettes portraying the life of the common soldier, revealing him not in his heroic moods but in his bleak daily existence, his loneliness, privation and melancholy. Highly praised by such eminent Americans as President Lincoln, Ralph Waldo Emerson and Dr. Henry Ward Beecher, these works opened a way for the "groups" which soon became a nationwide vogue.

From the outset of his career, Rogers was a daring innovator. He practiced the theories about which the younger "forward-looking" painters talked so persuasively. In his statuettes he applied a forthright realism to recording ordinary, everyday American life, making a faithful transcript of the manners, social customs, amusements, sports, domestic interests, costumes and furnishings of the day. The Rogers groups portrayed life anecdotally, always with sentiment, often with humor, sometimes with **pathos**. Such statuettes as

"Weighing the Baby," "The First Ride" or "Coming to the Parson" struck a responsive chord in the hearts of Americans who liked to believe that the lives of average men and women are the appropriate subject matter of art. But Rogers could also be profoundly serious in his interpretation of the American scene. In such statuettes as "The Foundling" and "The Charity Patient" he vigorously indicted social injustice, and in a series of statuettes dealing with the freed Negroes he expressed, like Winslow Homer, an anxious concern for these underprivileged members of American democracy.

Dedicating himself to the realistic portraiture of American life, Rogers undertook another daring innovation. Possession of "genuine works of art" was restricted to people of wealth. Why not make them available to the great masses? Rogers hit upon the notion of adding a factory to his studio and applying to his statuettes the principles of mass production and distribution. He also used the new facilities of national advertising to create a market for his wares. Rogers modeled the originals of his statuettes in clay, then passed them on to artisans in his workshop who, by means of molds, reproduced the groups in plaster, tinted them in various soft shades, and shipped them to jewelers and stationers throughout the country—to be sold, as "wedding or holiday gifts to friends," at prices ranging from ten to twenty dollars. Of the seventy-seven groups that Rogers modeled between 1860 and 1893, about one hundred thousand reproductions were enshrined in American parlors. As his market expanded, Rogers designed and sold pedestals and tables for the effective display of his works. He supplied tinting materials with which their proud possessors could restore any damaged or cracked surfaces. Like his contemporary La Farge, Rogers wanted to take art to the great public, and in this he succeeded. It was his misfortune to outlive the vogue of his work. Toward the end of the eighteen-nineties, the Rogers groups suddenly ceased to be fashionable. When the sculptor died, in 1904, at the age of seventy-three, his celebrated statuettes were being discarded. Condemned as embarrassing vestiges of esthetic naiveté, they went the way of tufted furniture, gas chandeliers, ornate whatnots and potted rubber plants. It might have pleased John Rogers to know that, forty-five years later, a unique collection of his work would be put on permanent display in a special gallery of the New-York Historical Society, and that a new generation of Americans would consider him one of the most remarkable geniuses of his time.

14

Athens by the Hudson

Among the writers and journalists, you felt the same stir of excitement that prevailed in the artists' quarter around Washington Square. New Yorkers, like other Americans, had long acknowledged the literary supremacy of Boston and its suburbs. Everybody, having played the game of "Authors," was familiar with the portraits of the great New Englanders—bearded, benign, brow on hand. It was hard to realize that these majestic figures, immortally elderly and eminent, were lapsing into silence; that twilight was falling on "the Holy Land of Boston," as William Dean Howells had called it. Greatly to their surprise, New Yorkers learned that the intellectual capital of the nation had been transferred to Manhattan Island.

This was no news to the rest of the country. It was about New York that young Americans were dreaming, if they wanted careers in literature or journalism. The most important publishers were located there, and so were the most widely read magazines. And who, even in the smallest towns, did not know about the "literary life" of the metropolis; the clubs where authors met, the homes where celebrities gathered, the banquets given in honor of distinguished English men of letters who were flocking to the United States as lecturers in order to gratify a national appetite for superior disesteem? The English etcher Seymour Haden, brother-in-law of the painter Whistler, said that New York was "a sort of Paris with practical ways about it." Nowhere were its practical ways more obvious than on the literary scene. Henry James, visiting the city after six years of residence abroad, was bewildered by one novelty. Authors were being lionized, and the competition to secure their presence was so great that they were even asked out in the morning. "People—by which I mean ladies—think nothing of asking you to come to see them before lunch," James noted amazedly. "Of course one can decline, but when many propositions of that sort come, a certain number stick." Charles Kingsley, the English novelist and poet, was equally disconcerted by New York hospitality. A committee from the Lotos Club surprised him on the deck of his ship far down the harbor. The club wished to honor him with a banquet—and he hadn't even glimpsed the Manhattan skyline. "But, gentlemen," he protested, "I am trying to view the approaches to New York. I cannot make any engagements now." The astonished lion wasn't aware that he was being introduced to the ways of the new American Athens.

In literary New York, life glittered with tempting social plums. The invitations were so numerous that, as the publisher Henry Holt ruefully observed, intending to go somewhere, you were often driven to "put it off till next week." But you never failed to turn up at the increasingly numerous ceremonial functions. You followed the excellent example of Richard Watson Gilder who, although he was "a retiring man," was usually present "at any literary event, from a feast to a funeral." Arranging a literary banquet, Edmund Clarence Stedman told a friend that the guests included at least one hundred experienced public speakers. To distribute the toasts and speeches among them was not easy. The authors, he declared, were "peculiarly sensitive as to the proper shading in the rank list." Like Mrs. Astor's world, literary society in New York took the form of a hierarchy. Nobody knew this better than Stedman. He was its supreme dictator.

Stedman was a small, blond, whiskered, affable man who looked younger than his fifty years. New Yorkers, with pardonable pride, called him "the banker poet." Wasn't it peculiarly fitting that the city's most distinguished man of letters should earn his living in Wall Street? Banking was a gentleman's profession, and literature ought to be, as Stedman himself believed. Not being a banker, but a broker, the designation exasperated him. He bitterly lamented that, instead of leading "a purely literary life," he was compelled to "work for subcommissions on the Stock Exchange." Nevertheless, his literary industry was prodigious. His long critical articles constantly appeared in all the better magazines, and were later republished in thick volumes. His magisterial verdicts poured out over the land in an incessant stream, and when his massive *Poets of America* was published, the nation gratefully accepted him as its accredited arbiter of taste.

Convinced that the older New England poets had long since fulfilled their mission, Stedman was annoyed because they also "kept others out of the ministry." Shouldn't he take over their exalted pulpit? Who had a better right to it? When poetry was required, he was always ready to rise to the occasion, whatever it might be. A college reunion, the dedication of a public building, the commemoration of an historic event moved him to graceful utterance. Eminent Americans were the more happily translated to heaven when Stedman, at their graves, offered tributes blending melancholy, consolation and elevated moral sentiments. It was no surprise to Stedman that the nation came to regard him as its "universal official poet." He deplored the base materialism of the age and invoked "the ideal." Materialistic readers praised the nobility of his *Poetical Works.* The volume of his correspondence soon became so great that he had to prepare a "manifold letter" to dispose of half of it. Yet, notwithstanding these proofs of his genius, there were skeptics who refused him the homage due a great poet. There was, for example, Elizabeth Stoddard, wife of his lifelong friend, the poet Richard Henry Stoddard. Herself an unappreciated novelist and perhaps somewhat embittered, Lizzie Stoddard ruined a pleasant evening by declaring that her husband and Stedman were "dreary failures as poets." True, Stoddard had been forced to earn his living in a post at the Custom House, as Stedman had in Wall Street; neither felt that he had ever had enough time to devote to poetry. Yet it wasn't time that they lacked, Mrs. Stoddard said. It was poetic ability.

You were likely to find Stedman and Stoddard, his inseparable companion, at the Century Club on Saturday nights, when a time-honored custom brought the members together for conversation. Founded in 1847 as an association of writers and artists, the Century had long been ruled by William Cullen Bryant, recently deceased, and had acquired prestige as the most active center of culture in the city. The club occupied an old residence on Fifteenth Street, between Fourth Avenue and Irving Place. A majority of its members had achieved eminence, if in no other way, by persistent longevity. They were gentlemen, they were conservatives, and over the Saturday-night suppers of oysters, bread and cheese they approvingly listened to Stedman condemn the spirit of the times and the new kind of literature which it was encouraging. The worship of science and the lust for wealth were destroying the love of beauty. Vulgarity held the stage; the public demanded tales of "lowly, common men," as he protested in a poem. Realism was coming into vogue. Didn't the "realists in fiction, or those in art, comprehend that from now on they will place themselves, relatively to those who work imaginatively, in the class with photographers"? "Never tell me again that you are a 'realist,'" Stedman exploded to a novelist, and he cautioned William Dean Howells that "you must not banish idealism entirely from our tastes." For among writers, as among artists, a battle was raging between traditionalists and innovators. Stedman led the forces of the old guard, striving, in his magazine articles, to disenchant the public with the new heresy, using his influence with publishers and editors to discredit the realists. Howells, editing the *Atlantic Monthly* in Boston, was their leader. If you came to New York bent upon a literary career, you either had to enlist under Stedman's banner or take your chances with the insurgent realists.

If you were a disciple of Stedman, you might hope to be invited, occasionally, to join the "charmed circle" at the venerable Century, for Stedman was a kindly, sociable soul and he had a keen sense of obligation to young writers whose work he approved. But if you belonged in the other camp you wanted to be asked to the Lotos Club. Its activities were widely reported by the press and they produced an effect of glamor. The Lotos was installed in the former mansion of a millionaire, Bradish Johnson, on Fifth Avenue and Twenty-first Street. Its members were journalists, authors, artists, actors, musicians or amateurs of the arts. Every Saturday night the club held an informal entertainment, and at these you would hear some famous actor like Joe Jefferson, or some celebrated musician, in performances which they never offered to the public. But the most notable functions of the Lotos were the banquets honoring distinguished foreign visitors, or American writers who had come into great prominence. The guests of honor always spoke "off the record" and what they said was likely to be exciting. You heard Mark Twain and Bronson Howard, the playwright who was breaking new trails in a realistic American drama; you heard W. S. Gilbert and Sir Arthur Sullivan, whose *Pinafore* had been pirated in New York; you heard Oscar Wilde, about whom the whole town was talking, and Henry Irving, the noted English actor. Sometimes, at these affairs, a controversy would break out; in any case, the general talk at the Lotos Club was always lively.

The rival literary factions met on neutral ground at the home of Richard Watson Gilder, where the debate between them was conducted on a high level of courtesy. For the writers of both schools who had already "arrived" were, with few exceptions, gentlemen who did not find literary hostility incompatible with personal friendship. Gilder usually took the exceptions in hand, and did his best to groom them socially, as well as to purify their work. He was in a position of great authority as editor of *The Century,* which he had made the most successful and influential magazine in the country. In it, he was publishing the work of Robert Louis Stevenson who, like Gilder himself, was a traditionalist and a romantic. But Gilder was also hospitable to the new realists. He published, as serials, the novels of Howells, which delighted all his readers. He published Henry James's *The Bostonians,* although it proved to be the most unpopular feature ever run in *The Century*. He daringly serialized Mark Twain's *Huckleberry Finn,* which—although he had "carefully edited" it with Twain's full consent—drew protests from many genteel readers. Gilder acknowledged that Twain was sometimes "inartistically and indefensibly coarse" but asserted that he was a good citizen and believed in the best things. Twain, with his flaming red hair and mustache, his breezy Western ways, his habit of ridiculing conventions accepted by the best people, was the most difficult of exceptions among writers who had "arrived." Gilder, like Howells, was trying to civilize him. Twain was deeply grateful.

Of all the visiting men of letters, it was Oscar Wilde who caused the greatest commotion in New York literary circles. Wilde's myth had preceded him. Everyone had seen Gilbert and Sullivan's *Patience,* which was having an enormous success at the Standard Theater. It was no secret that Gilbert had founded the character of Reginald Bunthorne, the "fleshly poet," on the witty young Irishman who had risen to celebrity in London on his epigrams, his affectations and his leadership of an "esthetic movement." Wilde

came over to lecture under the management of D'Oyly Carte, the English producer of *Patience*. The advance publicity, linking him with the operetta and exploiting his idiosyncrasies, was tremendous. From London, hundreds of letters of introduction were sent to all leading writers and fashionables in the principal American cities, many of them signed by the most distinguished names. By the time that Wilde, on the dock, told an American customs officer that he had nothing to declare but his genius, the literary hierarchy of New York was in a quandary. Should he be ignored as a mountebank, or lionized as a poet?

To genial old Sam Ward, Wilde presented a warm, enthusiastic letter from Lord Houghton. "His make-up is very extraordinary," Ward informed his sister, Julia Ward Howe; "long black hair hanging to the shoulders, brown eyes, a huge white face like a pale moon . . . a white waistcoat, black coat and knee breeches, black silk stockings and shoes with buckles. Until he speaks, you think him as uncanny as a vampire." But Ward concluded that Wilde was *"no slouch,"* and undertook to act as Wilde's sponsor and mentor.

The young poet badly needed all the influence that Ward could exercise in his behalf. Crowds gaped at him when he sauntered down Fifth Avenue wearing a Regency silk hat and a long, brownish-green overcoat, a white walking stick in his lavender-gloved hand. The diners at Delmonico's rose to stare at him whenever he entered with a party. An audience at the Standard Theater turned away from the stage when he appeared in a box to see a performance of *Patience*. His lecture at Chickering Hall sold out, and his suite at the Grand Hotel was deluged with flowers, verses, letters, invitations. Mrs. Paran Stevens gave a dinner in his honor, and other members of high society entertained him. All this could be reckoned as New York success, but Wilde craved recognition by men of letters. And from the leaders of New York's literary hierarchy he heard nothing. His letters of introduction to them produced few results. There was a good reason.

Edmund Clarence Stedman had decided that New York literary society must ostracize Wilde. "This Philistine town is making a fool of itself over Oscar Wilde. Pah!" So Stedman noted in his diary, and forthwith took measures to enforce his decree of ostracism. He declined to acknowledge two letters of introduction from Englishmen "so eminent that you would be surprised to hear their names." He refused all invitations to meet the poet. Mrs. John Bigelow, wife of the former minister to France, gave a dinner for Wilde at her home on Gramercy Park. Mrs. Botta announced him as guest of honor at one of her evening receptions. These ladies were the foremost hostesses in literary society, widely known throughout the country. They were close friends of Stedman's, and he offered them "my future opinion of the value of their courtesies to myself." One Sunday evening Mrs. Croly— Jennie June, founder of the Sorosis Club—gave a reception for Louisa May Alcott. Mrs. Stedman attended, but Stedman refused to go, fearing that Wilde would be present. Wilde appeared there, dividing the honors with the estimable author of *Little Women,* and great was Stedman's wrath when the newspapers, next morning, listed his name among the guests. All these things Stedman reported in a letter to the editor of the Boston *Transcript*. Wilde was soon to visit Boston, and the newspaper promptly published Stedman's letter, which was reprinted over the country. Wilde was a "clever humbug," Stedman announced. "So far as I know, the *genuine* writers, poets and journalists of this city have kept out of his way and are not over-pleased with the present revelation of the state of culture on Murray Hill." But Stedman's autocratic presumptions had exceeded his actual power. "I am now hesitating whether to send to my tailor for buckles and breeches and hose, or to sell my house and go to the country," he confessed angrily.

For the "Wilde case," as the newspapers called it after Stedman made it a public issue, emphasized the division between traditionalists and insurgents and hardened the determination of younger writers to contest the authority vested in Stedman and his group. As the literary capital, should not New York look to the future, break patterns rather than merely preserve them? Younger men, excluded from the sacred literary hierarchy ruled by Stedman, or admitted only to probationary rank, decried the dead hand of the past, the cult of "the ideal," the squeamish prudery being imposed on the nation's readers. An attack on authority was launched from several quarters. It progressed into open warfare and, after a decade of noisy battles that echoed over the country, the rebellion gave Americans an entirely new literature which radically changed both their thinking and their taste.

One group of innovators formed around the sprightly new humorous magazines, *Puck, Judge* and *Life,* all three of which attempted to give the country at large a light-hearted commentary on life in the metropolis. Why not give readers a panorama of the city as it really was, in all its incessant movement, its vivid contrasts, its magnificent vitality, its abundant color? New York was as unique as London or Paris and even more exciting—a magnificent subject for fiction. The older writers were ignoring it. A band of younger men began to exploit it. You were most likely to meet them in the home of Brander Matthews on East Eighteenth Street. Matthews was a native New Yorker, the son of a millionaire merchant, a witty and worldly man about town ambitious for success as a playwright, but also industriously producing articles and short stories. He had married Ada Harland, the exquisite dancer of Lydia Thompson's burlesque company, and he made his house a center for the writers who became known as the New York "local-color school." There you could meet Edgar Fawcett, who wrote satirical novels and plays about New York society; Henry Cuyler Bunner, editor of *Puck* and author of popular tales that ranged over the city from the French quarter near Washington Square to remote uptown Harlem; Mrs. Burton Harrison, a socialite whose novel *The Anglomaniacs* satirized the vulgar new-rich and became a best-seller, widely discussed. You might meet John

Ames Mitchell, the erratic painter and novelist who returned from Paris to found *Life* because his widowed mother was unhappy in France and he couldn't paint "away from the artistic atmosphere of Paris." Sometimes, at Matthews', you would encounter Stedman's godson, Henry Harland, who was writing realistic novels about the lower East Side and the prosperous Jewish families that had moved into the East Fifties and Sixties along Lexington Avenue. Harland's novels were highly praised by William Dean Howells, and his colleagues were astonished when he left New York. He emigrated to London, and there became editor of the *Yellow Book*, a magazine dedicated to the "esthetic movement."

There were also the "Bohemian" writers whose way of life and whose work scandalized their elder, more conventional colleagues. Most of them were earning a precarious living as journalists. When they were in funds, you were likely to find them at Mother Lienau's little restaurant on Fourteenth Street, opposite Steinway Hall, headquarters of the musical aristocracy, or at August Luchow's more luxurious establishment, a few doors further east. But mainly they congregated at Billy Moulds's bar on University Place near Fourteenth Street. Moulds had a weakness for impecunious writers, actors and artists. The glory of his establishment was the bean soup—hot, savory, plentiful—that formed the staple of its free lunch. At the Hoffman House bar you could eat the equivalent of a full-course dinner for the price of one drink, so varied was the assortment of dishes on the free-lunch counter. But there was one disadvantage: you were expected to tip the waiter a quarter. At Billy Moulds's place, you didn't have to tip. Moreover, if you were a regular customer and low in funds, your credit was good indefinitely. The bean soup was filling and, as Moulds said, "on the house, like a tin roof." And the bar was famous for a drink called "the razzle-dazzle," compounded of brandy, ginger ale and absinthe.

The young writers who gathered at Moulds's were fond of absinthe. They had a taste for anything exotic. They found New York exciting, and hoped to make it cosmopolitan. They liked to think of themselves as poets, pagans, rebels against morality and convention. They did their best to live up to this triple image, so other people thought them very odd indeed. The leaders of this group were Francis Saltus and his younger half-brother, Edgar, scions of a wealthy family established in New York's social citadel. They had lived for long periods in Europe, where they acquired the notion that candles should be burned at both ends. This notion had never caught on in New York, but the brothers were as willing to illuminate Fifth Avenue dinner parties as to dazzle their disciples at Moulds's bar. They, too, were missionaries of culture, which seemed to them, like the "razzle-dazzle," to be a compound of deadly intoxicants and sweetening; sin and disillusion flavored with wit. Francis Saltus wrote erotic verse that didn't have a wide circulation. Edgar Saltus, whom his friends called the "pocket Apollo," was gaining some reputation as a novelist. Readers throughout the country were pleasantly shocked by his books, which portrayed the best New York society as exemplifying the manners, and enjoying the vices, of decadent ancient Rome. Younger men like James Huneker, the music critic, Vance Thompson and Robert Chambers, who later would become a writer of best-selling novels about New York, were members of the group. They all talked about French symbolist poets and impressionist painters, about Schopenhauer, Nietzsche and Ibsen; in their articles, they introduced these exotics to puzzled readers in the hinterland. Eventually, Huneker and Thompson founded a magazine, *Mlle. New York,* which gave the country an impression of metropolitan Bohemianism.

These young writers who were thronging to New York from all over the country, the innovators who were rebelling against the genteel rule of Stedman and Gilder, found their leader in William Dean Howells. At fifty, Howells was the most widely read of American novelists, and, like Mark Twain, he was as famous in Europe as he was at home. After many years of residence in Boston, he had moved to New York, establishing himself first on Ninth Street, just west of Fifth Avenue, and later in a converted old mansion on East Seventeenth Street where the windows of his apartment looked out over Stuyvesant Square. Every month, in *Harper's,* he was waging a crusade for realism that stirred up a violent controversy among writers on both sides of the Atlantic. A stout man, with twinkling eyes and a friendly smile playing under his clipped mustache, you met him rambling about the city. For he was busily exploring all quarters of the metropolis; he had fallen in love with New York and wanted, as he told Henry James, "to use some of its vast, gay, shapeless life in my fiction." He went to fashionable teas on Fifth Avenue, and talked with a millionaire socialist whose family had a home in Newport, and whom he later met at a socialist meeting on the lower East Side. He poked about in the colorful streets east of the Bowery, in the Chinese quarter of Mott and Pell Streets. He sat in Washington Square talking with artists and immigrants, and ate in the cheap French and Italian table d'hôtes on Mac-Dougal and Sullivan Streets. He rode on the elevated to the upper West Side where streets were being cut through squatters' farms and you saw apartment houses rising among rocky hills over which pigs and goats and chickens roamed freely. Howells was fascinated by the bustle of Broadway, the theaters, the great hotels, the elegant shops with their swarms of pretty women, the sleek carriages and bob-tailed horsecars. He liked to watch the children and their nurses in Central Park, to visit the dime museums along East Fourteenth Street, to study the turmoil of Wall Street, to look at stevedores unloading the big ships that docked on noisy West Street, to see Fulton Market early in the morning when the fishing-smacks came in, to see Washington Market late at night when the farmers of Long Island and New Jersey brought in their truckloads of produce. In New York, Howells said, "one gets life in curious slices."

It was this vast, sprawling, colorful metropolitan life that Howells tried to render in *A Hazard of New Fortunes,* the first of his New York novels, the first novel ever to give Americans a realistic picture of the fabulous city. And with the publication of this immense panorama, he opened the way for a younger generation of writers to break free from the myths and taboos of smug respectability.

Within a year of the publication of Howells' novel, an ageing novelist, long forgotten by the public, died in his home on Twenty-sixth Street, just east of Fourth Avenue. And, three blocks down Fourth Avenue, a very young writer settled into makeshift lodgings to begin his career. The two men never met, but Howells had known the older man and later championed the younger; he warmly admired both. In every other respect unlike, they both rejected the myths and taboos of respectability.

You might have seen Herman Melville, occasionally, walking with his little granddaughter in Central Park. Past his seventieth year, he was still tall and stalwart, a handsome man, though his grave, preoccupied expression was rather intimidating. He had the reputation of being a recluse. Few visitors were welcome in the dark, old-fashioned house where Melville and his wife had lived for nearly thirty years. He regarded his literary career as long since ended. For more than two decades he had worked as a customs inspector, checking the cargoes of freight vessels on the Hudson River pier at Gansevoort Street. Then, made free by money which his wife inherited, he began once more to write. When younger men of letters—his neighbor Stedman, Brander Matthews and some others—formed the Authors Club, they invited him to become a member. He joined them on one evening, but never came again. At home, in his bedroom, he was trying to finish a last, short novel; a testament to the world that had forgotten him. Apparently, he had little hope that *Billy Budd* would ever be published unless he had it privately printed. Five months after completing the book he died, as he had long lived, obscurely. More than thirty years were to pass before *Billy Budd* was made available to readers.

In a bleak, cold room above the Art Students League on Twenty-third Street, east of Fourth Avenue, young Stephen Crane was writing his first novel. A pale, slim, tired-looking youth of twenty-one, he was always full of half-cynical, half-pessimistic talk, and his views on most subjects were apt to be wildly unconventional. Crane spent most of his time on the Bowery and in the adjacent slums. He came to know the people who inhabited squalid back courts, who filled the garish saloons and filthy lodging houses. At night, he sat and talked by the hour with the beaten men and forlorn painted women who haunted Union Square. The human wreckage of the great city appalled and fascinated him. What caused their degradation? Were they the victims of a cruel, callous society? Were they doomed by "a sort of cowardice," a propensity "to willingly be knocked flat and accept the licking"? If so, wasn't it because they were the product of their environment? The quarter of New York he knew best had little virtue in it, but it was dominated by the myths and taboos of respectability. Crane was "not very friendly to Christianity as seen around town." He wanted to write novels that would "show people to people as they seem to me."

He was writing *Maggie: A Girl of the Streets,* a short novel about a girl of the slums driven by her environment into prostitution. When he finished it, no publisher would accept it. Crane submitted his manuscript to Richard Watson Gilder, for *The Century;* Gilder rejected it, saying that it was cruel, and acknowledging that it was too honest for his readers. Finally, Crane borrowed money from a brother, had a paper-bound edition of his novel printed under a pseudonym, and tried to dispose of it through bookshops. This attempt also failed, and one cold night Crane used some of the copies to light a fire in his room.

Eventually, a copy of Crane's novel came into the hands of Hamlin Garland. Greatly impressed by *Maggie,* Garland invited the young writer to dinner in his Harlem apartment. Penniless and hungry, Crane tramped four miles to Garland's home and shocked his host by confessing that he would give away his literary future for thirty dollars. Garland advanced Crane some money and, more importantly, sent a copy of *Maggie* to Howells. Soon afterward, dining in a borrowed suit at Howells' home, Crane was astonished to hear his eminent senior introduce him as a writer who had sprung into life fully armed, who was capable of achieving effects beyond the power of even so great a writer as Mark Twain. Deeply stirred by Crane's story of the slums, Howells did his best to secure its publication. Yet Howells' prestige could not overcome resistance to Crane's brutal naturalism and sordid material. It was significant that Dr. Charles H. Parkhurst, engaged in a spectacular crusade against vice in New York, failed to acknowledge the copy of *Maggie* which Howells sent him. Not until after Crane's second novel, *The Red Badge of Courage,* catapulted him to fame was *Maggie* accepted by a publisher. With its republication, as historians long afterward asserted, modern American fiction was born.

15

What News

on the

Rialto?

During the mid-eighteen-seventies, an advertisement in the New York newspapers caused a mild sensation among playgoers. Augustin Daly, the celebrated producer, announced that tickets for his theater could be purchased through any district office of the Atlantic and Pacific Telegraph Company, a wire for that purpose having been installed in his box office. Many prosperous New Yorkers were equipping their homes with messenger call-boxes, so useful for the numerous occasions when you wished to reach people quickly. The call-box, a small contraption affixed to a wall, was connected by wire with the nearest district telegraph office. You turned a crank; presently, a messenger boy rang your doorbell, and you gave him your telegrams. Now, by using this device, or by sending to the telegraph office, you could secure tickets for Daly's without making a trip to the theater. This was progress indeed.

Though everybody was talking about Professor Alexander Graham Bell's new invention, the telephone, only visionaries believed that it would soon come into general use. Later that season, skeptical New Yorkers went to Chickering Hall to hear Professor Bell lecture on his marvel and demonstrate it. And Steinway Hall was sold out, far in advance, for three "Telephone Concerts" announced by the impresario Maurice Strakosch. Excellent artists performed at these concerts, but the feature that attracted audiences was a piano solo played in Philadelphia by Frederick Boskovitz and made distinctly audible in Steinway Hall by telephonic transmission. Perhaps, at some remotely future date, people might be able to enjoy concerts and operas without leaving their homes—though who, after all, would want to? Meanwhile,

UNION SQUARE IN 1882. Famous actors and actresses of the period are inset
in the margin

Harrigan and Hart, the great comedians, had discovered farcical possibilities
in "the sensation of the day" and audiences were rocking with laughter at
their skit, "The Telephone."

If you visited New York during the eighteen-eighties, you inevitably went
to the theater, for certain playhouses were nationally famous and you could
scarcely face your friends at home unless you could talk about them. Serious
drama now had the highest moral sanction; everybody knew that one of the
most successful theaters in New York, the Madison Square, was owned by
the brothers Mallory, one of whom was publisher of *The Churchman* and the
other a clergyman. Union Square had already been superseded as the theatrical center. The stretch of Broadway between Madison Square and Forty-
second Street—"the Rialto," as it was called—was a street of legend, and it
had a romantic attraction for all Americans across the continent.

This mile of the wide avenue was lined, on both sides, with luxurious hotels,
glittering bars, the city's principal theaters. At night, the lobbies of the hotels
and the facades of the theaters were beginning to be brightly illuminated by
Edison's new incandescent lamps. By contrast with their glare, the gaslights
of the street-corner lampposts seemed feeble, but it was pleasant to watch the
lamplighters making their rounds at dusk, using a long torchlike device to
open the square glass lamps, turn on the gas jets and kindle them into flame.
Long before eight o'clock, the sidewalks of the Rialto were jammed with
crowds bound for the theaters, and a continuous procession of lacquered
carriages would be drawing up in front of each of them. The little Madison
Square, just west of Broadway on Twenty-fourth Street, was renowned for its

double stage, elevated and lowered by hydraulic pressure, which made possible scene changes in less than one minute; the working of this mechanical wonder was always demonstrated to audiences after the performance. At the northwest corner of Twenty-eighth Street was the Fifth Avenue Theater, where the greatest stars brought their companies for limited engagements. On opposite sides of the Rialto at Thirtieth Street were Daly's and the new Wallack's. At Thirty-third Street there was the Standard, famous for its productions of the Gilbert and Sullivan operettas; at Thirty-fifth, the new Park Theater. Beyond, at Thirty-ninth, rose the vast yellow-brick Metropolitan Opera House, and diagonally across Broadway was the Casino, the temple of light opera. The facade and the interior of the Casino, elaborately Moorish, always impressed visitors to the city. The management also provided a singular novelty—an open-air roof garden where, on pleasant summer evenings, nightly concerts were given featuring the theater's principal players. The northernmost theater on the Rialto was the Broadway, at Forty-first Street, and elderly New Yorkers predicted that it would fail because it was too far uptown.

Down near Madison Square, the show window of Ritzman's store always drew large crowds. This was where you bought the new "cabinet-size" photographs of celebrities that everybody was collecting, and the window displayed the current "Who's Who" of international fame. But if you wished to be up to the minute in your knowledge of theatrical prestige, you went to look at the showcase of Sarony, the leading theatrical photographer, who was reputed to pay extravagant sums for the privilege of making "exclusive" portraits. This was the era of "professional beauties," and the ladies whose pulchritude Sarony exhibited today would have the whole nation talking about them tomorrow. Their careers helped to foster a new journalistic profession. They needed press agents; the naive imaginations of theatrical man-

MADISON SQUARE ABOUT 1880

agers no longer sufficed. For the public was insatiably curious about professional beauties, and it demanded revealing stories about them, the more bizarre the better. So each of these ladies acquired a personal legend. Not all of them were great actresses when appearing on stage, behind the footlights. But nearly all possessed a talent for leading vivid private lives in full view of the public. They were "personalities," perpetually surrounded by an aura of romance. They set the fashions in clothes and millinery. Women tried to imitate their figures and adopted their coiffures. The jewels they wore, the flowers they favored were discussed in every household over the land. Delmonico would identify by their names the dishes they preferred for dinner, or after-theater supper, and these culinary tributes, sedulously chronicled by the women's magazines, prompted American housewives to aggravate a national tendency to indigestion. What wonder that you went to see all the professional beauties, whenever they played, no matter what they were playing? It was scarcely necessary for them to act. They rejoiced you by being visible.

None caused more commotion than Mrs. Langtry, the "Jersey Lily." Acclaimed as the most beautiful woman in London society, she was renowned for her superb figure, her sculpturesque shoulders and arms, her incomparably exquisite complexion. Bankruptcy brought her to the English stage, and gossip linked her, all too intimately, with the Prince of Wales. An American tour was inevitable. Shortly after her widely publicized arrival in New York, the newspapers reported Lily Langtry's spectacular local conquest. Presently, the whole nation was following the progress of the infatuation of Frederick Gebhard, a wealthy bachelor socialite. He showered the Jersey Lily with flowers and jewels. He was her constant escort when she went to Delmonico's, drove in the Park, attended private parties. After playing an engagement at Wallack's Theater, Mrs. Langtry and her company went out on tour; the fact that Gebhard accompanied her caused an immense sensation. She returned, for a while, to New York, and rumor asserted that Gebhard had provided her with the luxurious residence on West Twenty-third Street where New York's young smart set paid homage to a modern Helen of Troy. Seldom had an actress played so dramatic, so passionately romantic a role in "real life"— yet the Jersey Lily was more than an actress; she was a flower of the highest English society. Unsophisticated Americans were scandalized and fascinated. Wherever Mrs. Langtry played, curiosity filled the theaters. Wherever she appeared in public, crowds followed her. The Jersey Lily's photograph, propped against a vase of cattails, was enshrined on lambrequined mantelpieces across the continent. You might have noticed that American girls were winding their tresses into the "Psyche knot" worn by Lily Langtry in the role of Galatea—when, as a cold, marble statue, she was quickened into life by love.

New York soon produced an American equivalent of the Jersey Lily. Mrs. James Brown Potter was a beautiful young matron who moved in the most exalted social circles. She had pleased society in amateur theatricals, and slightly shocked it by reciting a poem, "Ostler Joe," which made allusion to an unmarried mother. Thus encouraged, she assembled a company, engaged a handsome English actor, Kyrle Bellew, as her leading man, and embarked on a professional career. In *Life,* the rising young illustrator Charles Dana Gibson drew her descending a precipitous road from the Temple of Fame, applauded by a flock of geese attired in dress suits and top hats, with the comment, "Excuse me, Madam, but your 'social influence' is taking you in the wrong direction." Gibson's satirical drawing made Mrs. Brown Potter notorious, and she was already established as a professional beauty when, in a storm of publicity, she deserted her husband and home for more romantic opportunities. New Yorkers were amused by Oliver Herford's sly comment that "actresses will happen in the best-regulated of families," but you might have learned that several producers were expressing interest in another socialite—dark, petite, vivacious Elsie de Wolfe, a frequent guest at Ward McAllister's Patriarch Balls who, like Mrs. Potter, had achieved success in the "private theatricals" organized for the benefit of charities and expensively offered to the public in one or another theater.

Yet sedate Americans were better pleased by the swift rise to fame of Mary Anderson. In their opinion, the arresting beauty of this young Kentucky belle was enhanced by her strict obedience to all the conventions. An adoring public named her "Our Mary." Did she not exemplify the miracle of fire and innocence that all well-bred American girls were supposed to approximate? She was tall, stately, brown-haired, and her "classic profile" was even more exciting than her rich contralto voice. It made no difference that, apart from Shakespearian roles, she played only long outmoded dramas like *Ingomar.* Because of Miss Anderson, thousands of girls began taking lessons in elocution and studying the "Delsarte method" of acquiring grace in posture and

MARY ANDERSON in *Love*

movement. Eager for new conquests, "Our Mary" played for two seasons in London. Americans learned that she had won the admiration of Lord Tennyson; it was said that he would write a play for her. The famous artist G. F. Watts—a reproduction of one of his paintings adorned every American parlor —painted her portrait. Having become the darling of London society, she declined to be presented to the Prince of Wales, whose august appreciation of her beauty did not soften her disapproval of his morals. When she returned to New York, Miss Anderson enjoyed a triumph almost unprecedented. Only jaundiced skeptics denied that she was a great actress, a genius. But it was enough that she was a great beauty and—more importantly—a great lady also. If you still believed in the virtue of refinement, it was reassuring to learn that "Our Mary" would never, never act in plays "that drag one through the mire of immorality, even when they show a good lesson in the end." What was unfit to be discussed in her parlor, she said, had no proper place in the theater.

If in this you agreed with "Our Mary," and many people professed to, you often had to leave your convictions at home when you went to the theater. For the new school of "emotional actresses" about whom everybody was talking displayed no such delicate moral discrimination in their choice of plays. True, nearly all of them felt obliged to appear in the comedies and tragedies of Shakespeare. But all of them likewise played *Camille,* so that sometimes you could be moved to damp delight in any of several playhouses by stars whose fame suggested that the New York stage was now dominated by actresses, not actors, as in the past. They all played *Camille,* and they had an addiction to other French dramas whose heroines were as remarkable for moral frailty as for tempestuous eloquence. Clara Morris terrified you in *Article 47* when, with staring eyes and muttered ravings, she simulated oncoming madness and, after a hideous scene of vengeance, uttered a bloodcurdling shriek and fell to the floor, a gibbering idiot. The lovely Polish actress Helena Modjeska won your pity for a frivolous unfaithful wife in *Frou-Frou,* for a tragic lovelorn mistress in *Adrienne Lecouvreur.* Regal, handsome Fanny Davenport brought to the stage an endless procession of tarnished women. When she introduced Sardou's *Fedora* and *La Tosca,* in daring costumes created by Worth, New York's leading clergymen denounced her from their pulpits. The theater was always sold out when she performed these "indecent" plays.

Moral controversy likewise raged over Sarah Bernhardt, about whom all New York was talking for a year before her arrival in the United States. Henry James predicted her triumph in one of his London letters to *The Nation,* declaring that "she is too American not to succeed in America." She would be recognized as a kindred spirit, he said, by "the people who have brought to the highest development the arts and graces of publicity." But old-fashioned New Yorkers were affronted by all they heard about the celebrated tragedienne. Her eccentricities had become notorious. She habitually slept in a coffin padded with quilted satin. She had domesticated a lion cub and kept

it as a pet in her Paris home. She practiced sculpture, and had permitted herself to be photographed, in her studio, wearing white-velvet trousers. All this
might be forgiven were she not an immoral woman. Mlle. Bernhardt was the
mother of a young son. A London dowager, to whom she spoke affectionately about the boy, inquired whether she was married. "Pas si bête," Mlle.
Bernhardt replied smilingly. Reporters who went down the harbor to interview her filled the press with accounts of her extraordinary slenderness. "An
empty carriage drove up to the Albemarle Hotel and Mlle. Bernhardt got
out," one wag recorded. Tickets for Booth's Theater sold at a premium even
before she began her engagement. From her very first performance, Bernhardt's success was sensational. Critics acclaimed the magic of her golden
voice, the expressiveness of her face, with its crown of red-gold hair, her
supple, undulating gestures. Excitement about Bernhardt ran so high that even
the most rigorous moralists felt they had to see her. Presently, fashionable
ladies, rejecting the current styles, insisted upon having gowns that would

give them Bernhardt's "spiral silhouette"—sheathlike robes with high collars, long, tight sleeves and flaring trains. The fashionable bustle suddenly vanished. For a time slenderness, both above and below a twenty-inch waist, became the mode.

The strong partiality of French dramatists for the theme of sexual immorality, however deplorable, was taken for granted. But it was surprising to find this theme, and others no less novel, being exploited by American playwrights in dramas that purported to deal with life as it was actually being lived in New York. Realistic plays had suddenly come into vogue, and the most successful playwrights—Augustin Daly, Bronson Howard and the collaborators Henry D. De Mille and David Belasco—were putting on the stage pictures of the morals and manners of the wealthy which startled old-fashioned playgoers. For their plays revealed that, among New York's best people, traditional morality was being openly flouted and long established conventions had lost their binding force. Husbands and wives were drifting apart; men were immersed in business, women in social competition. Marital infidelity was increasing; seduction and betrayal were being condoned; the prevalence of divorce was becoming a social menace. These were the impressions you gathered from many of the plays produced at New York's two premier theaters, Daly's and the Lyceum, which had become, in effect, national institutions.

They were the city's most fashionable playhouses, the only ones for which you dressed in formal evening attire if you intended to sit in the orchestra or boxes. At his theater, Augustin Daly had organized a permanent stock company headed by vivacious, red-headed Ada Rehan and elegant John Drew, who were the exemplars of style and deportment most eagerly imitated by the younger generation. Going to Daly's was rather like attending a social function. In the long, richly furnished lobby where a Chinese boy in Oriental costume handed you your programs, you were likely to see all your friends. You met them again, between the acts, in the beautiful upstairs promenade which Daly had transformed into a theatrical museum. Occasionally Daly made lavish productions of Shakespeare's plays; so memorable were the performances of Miss Rehan, John Drew and Otis Skinner in *The Merry Wives of Windsor* and *The Taming of the Shrew* that many people attended as frequently as possible. The Lyceum Theater, on Fourth Avenue near Twenty-third Street, remote from the Rialto, was popularly called the "drawing-room home of the drama." It was a small playhouse, handsomely decorated by Louis Tiffany, where Daniel Frohman had organized a resident stock company with Georgia Cayvan as the leading lady and Herbert Kelcey as the leading man. Unlike Daly's, the Lyceum did not include the classics in its repertory, but specialized in modern realistic dramas and comedies of New York social life. Society transferred to the Lyceum its former loyalty to Wallack's. The Four Hundred went to the Lyceum, so a wit declared, to learn from the actors and actresses how they ought to behave, how they ought to furnish their homes, and how to carry their clothes.

The Casino Theater, the new luxurious temple of light opera, was the favorite haunt of gilded youth. They were always present, usually wearing the newfangled tailless evening coat, or "tuxedo," that implied the informal pleasures of a bachelor evening. You might have surmised that their attendance was not solely the result of an excessive devotion to the music of Offenbach, Johann Strauss and other popular composers. The Casino was, in fact, the city's most elegant display-case for feminine beauty. The statuesque ladies of the chorus—the "Casino girls"—were individually celebrated, and to be seen having supper with one of them was evidence of prestige as a man about town. You might aspire to personal acquaintance with one of the Casino girls, but you worshipped its bright stars humbly and remotely. They were beyond the reach of any mere "stage-door Johnny" or "champagne Charlie." They were a seductive trinity. The whole town regarded them as a civic possession, taking pride in the splendor of their beauty, in their imperious ways. Shapely Pauline Hall, stately Isabelle Urquhart, blonde, ravishing Lillian Russell—who could say which of them caused the greatest disturbance to incontinent masculine hearts? Massive floral tributes were passed to them across the footlights. The Casino lobby and the best clubs were swept by gossip of the diamonds and pearls, the carriages and horses with which hopeful adorers revealed their infatuation. Great tycoons, it was said, had pleaded for the privilege of drinking champagne from their slippers, a gesture of homage invented by Russian Grand Dukes for French ballet dancers. Each of the three had her devoted adherents. Each, as she came on the stage, was greeted with thundering applause. But already it seemed likely that Lillian Russell's fame would eclipse that of her rivals.

As a very old man, one of her youthful admirers tried to evoke the enchanting young Lillian Russell of the eighteen-eighties. Recalling her high, silvery soprano voice, he declared that "no woman except Lilli Lehmann could approach her for loveliness of song." Fifty years earlier, his image of her would not have been so notably aural. It was by her radiant, golden beauty that Lillian Russell captivated masculine New York. She was all gold and cream and rose; all slender, graceful curves; a demure expression, a flashing smile and a queenly walk. Tony Pastor had discovered her and at once starred her, at his new variety theater on Fourteenth Street, in a burlesque of *Patience*. From this, she went into the leading role of *Patience* and, after starring in other light operas, came to the Casino. Suddenly, she ran off to Europe with Edward Solomon, a composer and conductor, and returned as his wife. People said that the marriage had not turned out happily, and some years later there was gossip about the Casino's leading tenor, Signor Perugini, known in private life as Johnny Chatterton. In the pleasant basement bar of the Hotel Normandie, where gentlemen gathered during intermissions at the Casino, you might have discovered that young men about town were expressing jealousy of a tenor—a creature who, in normal circumstances, they would have thought nothing more than a superfluous larynx on legs.

All New York turned out to see the Harrigan and Hart shows, uproarious musical farces, with songs like "The Salvation Army," "The Charlestown Blues," "McNally's Row of Flats" that were played by every hurdy-gurdy in the city. Dave Braham wrote the music of these songs, for which Ned Harrigan supplied the words. He also wrote the shows and starred in them: *The Mulligan Guards* series, *Cordelia's Aspirations, Squatter Sovereignty* and many others that dealt with the social rivalries of middle-class German and Irish families on New York's East Side, with the street life of the city, with such topical issues as the long legal contest between the owners of rocky land on the East River at Seventy-second Street, and the squatters who fought to retain their shantytown. Almost as typical of New York as handsome Ned Harrigan was stentorian Maggie Cline, who played long engagements at Tony Pastor's and always sang—by request—a song about the epical fracas at Mc-Closkey's saloon: "Throw Him Down, McCloskey!" Variety had now become "smart," and you went both to Pastor's and to Koster and Bial's Music Hall on Twenty-third Street and Sixth Avenue, which had the reputation of being somewhat "fast" and became a favorite resort of men about town, writers and artists.

Times were changing, and the older generation shook their heads sadly when the ornate Booth's Theater on Twenty-third Street and Sixth Avenue was torn down to make way for McCreery's new department store while, across the street and nearer Fifth Avenue, an equally ornate building was erected for the Eden Musée. This institution soon gained the patronage of all rural visitors to the city, exercising for them the powerful attraction that Huber's Dime Museum, on East Fourteenth Street, and its several competitors, held for the city's poorer classes. The dime museums specialized in freaks, midgets, sword-swallowers, fire-eaters and human monsters of various kinds; most of them also offered variety turns; sometimes, in one or another of them, you could see the old Bowery actress Fanny Herring in scenes from the melodramas of her heyday. But the program of the Eden Musée was quite different. It contained a small variety theater, but this was the least of its glories. What country folk came to see were the lifelike waxworks, so naturally posed that sometimes you believed them to be people, and the "chamber of horrors" in which major crimes were faithfully reproduced. There was also Ajeeb, the "chess mystery." Ajeeb played against all contestants and always won. Was he a mechanically animated waxwork? Or, as many players surmised, did he conceal some unknown master of the game? To the older generation, it seemed an eloquent commentary on the times that Edwin Booth's splendid "temple of dramatic art" gave way to commerce, only to be replaced by wax figures and sensational horrors.

The new Metropolitan Opera House also impressively symbolized change. For three years before its gala inauguration in the autumn of 1883, New Yorkers watched the clash of titans which led to its erection. Like the triumphal arches of the Roman Empire, the Metropolitan commemorated victory in battle. It recorded the passing of financial and social power into new hands, the final defeat of the city's old aristocracy by the great capitalists who were masters of banks, railroads, vast industries—men like J. P. Morgan, the

Vanderbilts, George F. Baker, William Rockefeller, Jay Gould, William C. Whitney, the California multimillionaires Darius Ogden Mills and Collis P. Huntington. At the old Academy of Music there were eighteen boxes, a number insufficient to accommodate the new Medici. One of them had offered as much as thirty thousand dollars for a good box, only to be coldly refused. The old "Faubourg Saint-Germain set" was determined to exclude these up-starts. The social value of a box at the Academy was inestimable; its economic value could only be gauged by the number of millionaires who, wishing to possess a box, were denied that privilege. Affronted by the decree of ineligibility that relegated them to mere orchestra stalls in the Academy, the new Medici decided to erect their own opera house. When news of their intention reached the directors of the Academy, their chairman, August Belmont, offered to add twenty-six boxes to the venerable shrine of opera, and thereby admit the most powerful of the insurgents. This architectural appeasement, so momentous in its social implications, was haughtily rejected. Opera therefore became the symbolic, fortuitous issue that precipitated war.

The Vanderbilt family assumed leadership of the group that erected the new temple of music, and it was probably significant that, before the building was completed, young Mrs. William K. Vanderbilt, by her daring maneuver in connection with her fancy-dress ball, compelled Mrs. Astor to pay her a visit of ceremony and thus signalize her admission into the sacred Four Hundred—an accolade which not only established the social status of the Vanderbilts, but that of the opera house which they were promoting. Externally, the building was not an architectural monument of which New York could be proud. With the thrifty purpose of deriving some financial return from their costly toy, the millionaires who built the Metropolitan incorporated, in its Broadway facade, rent-producing apartments and stores. The exterior of the building was blatantly ugly. But the interior, though it reflected little more concern for esthetic considerations, demonstrated the outstanding sagacity of its architect. Josiah Cleaveland Cady had never previously designed a theater, but he had a clear understanding of the wishes of his clients. Boxes were what they wanted, and boxes he gave them. Three tiers of boxes, arrogantly rising in banks of thirty-six each, dominated the auditorium. Accommodations for the general public were provided in the orchestra stalls, a lofty balcony above the boxes, and a "family circle" so elevated that its occupants —even with the strongest opera glasses—found it difficult to maintain an illusion that they were actually witnessing a spectacle on the stage. It was certainly unfortunate that New York, where stupendous fortunes had now become almost commonplace, could not supply enough millionaires to fill three tiers of boxes at the Metropolitan. After the first season of opera, the topmost tier was eliminated. The lower tier became known as the "diamond horseshoe," and the less imposing upper tier received the commonplace designation of "golden horseshoe."

The opening of the new temple of music was preceded by intense competition for stars by Henry Abbey, the daring theatrical manager who undertook to provide opera at the Metropolitan, and Colonel James H. Mapleson, of

Her Majesty's Theater, London, the impresario of the Academy. Mapleson's brightest star was Adelina Patti, who had returned to New York, world-famous, after an absence of twenty years. Abbey provided Christine Nilsson and the tenor Italo Campanini, old favorites with New York opera-goers, and a startling new Polish coloratura soprano, Marcella Sembrich. The rival establishments opened on the same evening, thus creating a quandary for members of the social élite who had affiliations with both groups of embattled dynasties. One of these troubled spirits, Mrs. Paran Stevens, was either reluctant to prejudice her impartial position, or unable to determine which auditorium offered the greater social glory. A woman of excellent practical sense, Mrs. Stevens realized that the operas being performed were of no consequence whatever. She solved her difficult problem by dividing the evening between the Metropolitan and the Academy, thereby preserving unimpaired her hard-won social prestige. "The Goulds and the Vanderbilts and people of that ilk perfumed the air with the odor of crisp greenbacks," *The Dramatic Mirror* reported, in its account of the inauguration of the Metropolitan. "The tiers of boxes looked like cages in a menagerie of monopolists."

In a curious fashion, the first season of opera at the Metropolitan exercised a profound influence on New York's cultural history. It wound up with an estimated deficit of six hundred thousand dollars, which so discouraged the music-loving Medici that they accepted—for economic reasons only—a revolutionary proposal. Dr. Leopold Damrosch, conductor of the recently organized New York Symphony Orchestra and Oratorio Society, and a devout Wagnerian, offered to provide starless opera with singers recruited in Germany, making the works of Wagner the feature of the repertory. The Medici knew nothing about Wagner and they cared less, but unless opera in some form were given, they could not occupy their costly boxes—and for what other purpose had they built the new temple of music? Dr. Damrosch and Wagner were therefore installed in the Metropolitan, and serious lovers of modern music were introduced to the complete cycle of the *Ring des Nibelungen, Tristan und Isolde,* and *Die Meistersinger,* while bored, exasperated boxholders diverted themselves as best they could with conversation, necessarily carried on in a tone loud enough to override Wagner's inconsiderately tumultuous orchestrations.

Even the birdlike notes of Adelina Patti did not enable the Academy of Music to survive long the competition of massed millions at the Metropolitan. To celebrate the twenty-fifth anniversary of her operatic début in New York, a great torchlight procession was organized to accompany the petite prima donna from the Academy to the Windsor Hotel. It was the last fiery demonstration of a defeated aristocracy; in the spring of 1885 opera at the Academy came to an end forever. "I cannot fight Wall Street," Colonel Mapleson acknowledged; in the future, he said, the sole official home of opera would be "the new yellow brewery on Broadway." Being an Englishman, Mapleson failed to understand the cardinal principle of American finance capitalism. As John D. Rockefeller had once asserted, death solved the problem of competition; as J. P. Morgan had already demonstrated, "wasteful competition" must be replaced by the recognition of a "community of interest" by the nation's financial overlords. The principle held good for opera, as for all other enterprises in which they might be concerned.

Fortunately, the far-visioned sponsors of the new Metropolitan Opera House had anticipated the terms of a face-saving surrender. There were quite enough boxes to provide for the admission of August Belmont and the vanquished "Faubourg Saint-Germain set." And society, in New York, gratefully accepted the ethical gospel of consolidation.

PART THREE

1890–1910

GILT AND GLITTER

16

The Vertical City

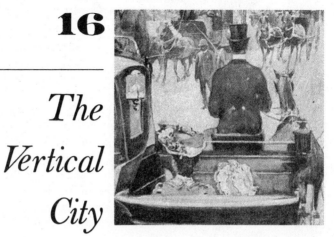

In 1890, nearly one and a half million people were living on Manhattan Island, and nearly ninety thousand had moved into the Annexed District beyond the Harlem River. Every morning, almost as many more poured into the city for the day's work. At night, they overflowed into suburban regions to sleep. They herded on cars that crossed the Brooklyn Bridge, on ferries that ploughed across the East and Hudson Rivers, and down the bay to Staten Island, on trains that thundered in and out of Grand Central Station.

The evening tide out of New York washed over a vast area. You saw tired crowds bound for the outlying quarters of Brooklyn. Throngs filled the ferry house at East Thirty-fourth Street to reach the terminus of the Long Island Railroad at Hunter's Point, and take trains for towns that were sprawling over ancient farm lands. Thousands rushed for the Staten Island Ferry to New Brighton, there to jam into trains that clattered out to Arrochar and Bowmans. The human flood swept over the Hudson into New Jersey. To Jersey City, Newark, Hoboken, Weehawken. Out to Montclair, the Oranges, Morristown. Up along the Palisades to Englewood, Leonia, Tenafly. By six o'clock, Grand Central Station looked as if a panic-stricken population were fleeing a doomed city. But this confusion was merely the nightly grim struggle to reach dinner and bed in the Annexed District; and, out beyond, in Yonkers, White Plains, Mount Vernon, New Rochelle. Wherever they lived, the home-bound masses considered themselves New Yorkers, inhabitants of the "greater city" that people were talking about, although it had, as yet, no legal existence.

This great nightly exodus from the city, scarcely conceivable a decade earlier, showed how swiftly life in New York was changing. Elderly folk were bewildered by the spirit of the times, reckless and exorbitant as never before. Everybody realized that a new era had opened, an era of illimitable progress. Science and invention were producing fresh miracles almost daily. Each morning the newspapers seemed to be announcing some dazzling project, incredible in its magnitude, extravagance and promised grandeur. Only a few years remained before the twentieth century would arrive. You didn't need the gift of prophecy to know that, before its advent, life was going to be radically different. No matter where you looked, you saw that New York was being startlingly transformed. By the time the century ran out, it was certain to become an almost unrecognizable city.

Already it seemed probable that New York was to become a city of towers, rising higher into the air than men had ever dared to imagine. By 1884, the architect Richard Morris Hunt had erected a massive new building on Park Row for Whitelaw Reid's *Tribune;* eleven stories of solid masonry, surmounted by a campanile that dominated the skyline. In the following year a younger architect, Bradford Lee Gilbert, designed the Tower Building, to be erected at 50 Broadway, on a plot twenty-one feet wide. Not only was this structure to rise to the daring height of thirteen stories, but its principle of construction was revolutionary. The laws provided that the weight of a building must be supported entirely by the thickness of its walls. Gilbert proposed "to stand a steel bridge structure on end," and months elapsed before he secured official approval of his plans. His project was so sensational that John Noble Stearns, the silk merchant who owned the land on which the structure was to be erected, expressed fears that the building would collapse.

Gilbert declared that the building would be safe in a one-hundred-mile gale, and announced that he would himself occupy its topmost floors. Most people said he was crazy. Unfavorable comment increased in volume as the structure mounted. The first seven stories were built on the steel frame; the remainder was to be of solid brick. Crowds gathered daily on Broadway to gape at the mad venture. The owner of the adjoining building became panic-stricken, sold his property, and moved from the vicinity of the new menace. One Sunday morning in 1886, when the Tower Building had reached the height of ten stories, winds of gale force struck the city, blowing at eighty miles an hour. At a safe distance from the building, crowds jammed Broadway, waiting to see the fool structure crash down into the street. Gilbert hurried downtown to see how the Tower Building was weathering the storm, a plumb line in his pocket. He climbed the ladders to the tenth story and lowered his plumb line. Not the slightest vibration was revealed; the uncompleted building was absolutely safe. As he had promised, Gilbert installed his offices on the topmost floors. He remained there until 1913, when the Tower Building was demolished.

Shortly after the sensation over the Tower Building, Joseph Pulitzer commissioned George B. Post to design a new building for *The World*. Threatened by permanent blindness, the victim always of grandiose visions that left him no peace, Pulitzer wanted a personal monument, an edifice never to be surpassed. Across Park Row from City Hall, the great *World* Building, fifteen stories high, was surmounted by a cupola with a glittering golden dome that was visible far down the bay. But before New Yorkers had ceased talking about this latest civic marvel, it had been superseded. The new principle of "steel-cage construction," as engineers called it, with which Gilbert had experimented in the first seven stories of the Tower Building, had won official sanction; the building laws had been revised. Theoretically, this principle made it possible for buildings to be carried to unpredictable heights. Bruce Price designed, for the American Surety Company, a twenty-story tower to rise on Broadway opposite Trinity Church—the city's first real "skyscraper." Every day, Trinity churchyard was thronged with people watching the gaunt steel skeleton soaring into the air. And, once again, people asserted that the project was insane. Inevitably, the building would topple over. The towerlike building, pierced by innumerable windows, was quickly filled with tenants; to have your offices there was a valuable advertisement. But presently this tower was dwarfed by another. The older generation remembered when James Gordon Bennett the elder had replaced Barnum's Museum, on the southeast corner of Broadway and Ann Street, with a white-marble French palace to house the *New York Herald*. Now the *Herald* Building was demolished to make way for the twenty-five-story St. Paul Building, designed by George B. Post. Skyscrapers soon clustered at the lower end of the island, and uptown the many-storied new hotels, rising precipitously above the street, lifted their spangles of light over the city after dark.

The new vertical city was likewise stretching out horizontally. A migration had begun to the West End, as people called it—the district west of Central Park and north of Fifty-ninth Street. For men whose places of business were far downtown, this quarter was now as accessible as Thirty-fourth Street formerly had been. You reached it on the trains of the Ninth Avenue Elevated, which ran up Sixth Avenue to Fifty-third Street, then turned westward to continue on Ninth Avenue which, above Fifty-ninth Street, had been renamed Columbus. The old Eighth Avenue line of surface cars, which formerly had sent a few horsecars, daily, as far north as One Hundred and Fifty-fifth Street, improved its service. A waiting room was erected at the Fifty-ninth Street entrance to the Park to replace the abandoned car that had served as refuge from cold and storm, and eventually the road substituted cable-cars for its horse-drawn antiques. Cable-car lines were likewise opened on Tenth Avenue, and on Western Boulevard, as Broadway north of Fifty-ninth Street had been named. Improved transportation resulted in a building boom in the West End, but certain portions of the area still had a raw, countrified appearance, although real-estate values were increasing so rapidly that only people of substantial means could consider moving there.

Development of the West End, as *The Times* reported with some surprise, had not followed the lines foreseen by the most sagacious investors in real estate. They had assumed that Central Park West and Western Boulevard were destined to be the finest private residential streets, and that West End Avenue would become the principal business thoroughfare. They were wrong on all counts. On West End Avenue more handsome private residences were being erected than on any other thoroughfare. The Elevated Railroad determined the character of Columbus Avenue, where blocks of "flats" were being built, the ground floors of which were occupied by shops. On Central Park West, the vast Dakota Apartment had exercised a notable effect. Imposing apartment houses, and towering "family hotels" like the Majestic and the Beresford were rising there, and land was being bought for the erection of churches, schools, hospitals and other public institutions. The Museum of Natural History had located on Manhattan Square; just below it, the New-York Historical Society had acquired a block front on which, eventually, to build a magnificent home for its collections. Western Boulevard—a broad avenue lined with fine trees, and having little parks along the center of its roadway—was still largely unimproved, a street of shanties, rocks and signboards. Owners of property who had assumed that it would become a street of private homes for the wealthy now expected that, in time, it would take on the character of Central Park West. But an even more splendid destiny was anticipated for Riverside Drive. Here, from Seventy-second Street to One Hundred and Twenty-fifth, a beautiful parkway had been laid out bordering the Hudson River, and at its upper end there was being erected, by public subscription, the massive granite mausoleum of President Grant. Property along the whole length of Riverside Drive was being closely held by permanent investors. With its superb view of the Hudson River and Palisades, New Yorkers felt certain that the Drive would soon be lined with palatial mansions; that, in fact, it would rival Fifth Avenue as a citadel of the aristocracy.

It seemed probable that the West End would become one of the fashionable quarters of the city, perhaps as fashionable as the stolid brownstone East Side that had been built up so much earlier. Already, if you walked about there, you noticed how different it was from the older residential districts. It was like a city in itself; it had its own distinctive social tone. The earliest speculative builders had lined the lower streets with traditional, uniform, brownstone high-stooped homes. But above Seventy-second Street, and especially along West End Avenue, handsome residences displayed facades of brick, in all shades from red to cream, and most of them eliminated the old-fashioned high stoop. They were built on the new, so-called "American basement" plan; you entered a wide reception hall on the street level, from which a curving staircase led to a salon, music room and dining room on the floor above. Most of these luxurious homes had "extensions" built out into the rear yard; these provided a butler's pantry on the ground floor, a smoking room or "den" behind the dining room, and large "boudoir bathrooms" on the upper stories. None but the wealthy could afford residences of this kind, which required many servants. And only wealthy families were able to rent suites in the great apartment houses and residential hotels that made this quarter of the city unique. The hotels were especially impressive. Their huge public rooms, resplendent with gilt and marble and murals, where liveried attendants were always ready to serve you, were designed for a way of life more ostentatious, more public in its advertised costly privacy, than any that New Yorkers had previously known. Social life in the West End was being shaped by the character of its buildings. Nowhere else in the city was there a neighborhood that so eloquently expressed the spirit of the times; the prevailing extravagance and demand for luxury; the fine, carefree sense of "easy come, easy go." Even in the least pretentious blocks of "flats" you often had to pay as much as forty dollars a month for five boxlike rooms—and although the price was absurdly high, there were few vacancies.

Beyond the West End, Morningside Heights was being made the site of a "civic Acropolis." Columbia University was moving to a tract of land on this steep ridge. Plans had been approved for the great Cathedral of St. John the Divine that eventually would crown its summit. The imposing white buildings of St. Luke's Hospital were already rising there. The National Academy of Design, surrounded by business in its Venetian palace at Fourth Avenue and Twenty-third Street, was soon to join these institutions on Morningside. North of Morningside Heights, and separated from it by the depression of Manhattan Valley at One Hundred and Twenty-fifth Street, the area as far north as the former village of Carmansville had been subdivided in building lots, but was still largely undeveloped. This region, *The Times* asserted, would be "the most attractive part of the city to anyone who is seeking a home that is somewhat suburban in character." North of it, Washington Heights still retained its rural charm. Up there, the old estates had not been split up. As *The Times* pointed out, these large holdings of land could never be subdivided and sold as building lots; the rugged nature of the terrain made such development impossible. Western Boulevard had recently been extended as far north as the heart of Washington Heights, and people considered it one of the most pleasant drives near the city.

East of Morningside Heights and below it, Harlem had been thickly built up. Like the new West End, it impressed you as being a city in itself. Its commercial artery, One Hundred and Twenty-fifth Street, offered shops in such variety that residents had little need to go downtown unless they wished to. Pleasure resorts also abounded there: beer gardens, billiard rooms, bowling alleys, restaurants. You didn't have to leave Harlem even to attend the theater, for Oscar Hammerstein had opened the imposing Harlem Opera House, where all the greatest stars played a week's engagement after concluding their Broadway appearances, and you could see them at far lower prices than you had to pay downtown. Apartment houses were beginning to rise in Harlem, along Lenox, St. Nicholas and Seventh Avenues. But, mainly, it was a community of small, middle-class homes, impeccably respectable, conservative and prosperous. On pleasant summer evenings, you saw families sitting out on their stoops, and children playing in streets seldom disturbed by traffic. You surmised that the aroma of well-cooked meals saturated the low brownstone dwellings. You could be sure that every parlor displayed an aspidistra, a "suite" of mahogany-stained furniture upholstered in velveteen, an upright piano and gilt-framed chromos and engravings on the walls. Upstairs, the principal bedroom would have a gleaming, knobby brass double bed, with cover and "pillow-shams" of crochet lace over a lining of pink or blue sateen. In these homes, pinochle was played and pyrography cultivated as a genteel art. As you walked past them you heard the strumming of mandolins and banjos, the tinkle of a piano and youthful voices singing "O, Promise Me," or "Only a Bird in a Gilded Cage."

Harlem, once a village, rejoiced in its "small-town" atmosphere. Like Brooklyn, it proudly exalted the domestic virtues, the pieties of religion, the authority of convention. It went to see sultry actresses like Fanny Davenport and Olga Nethersole when they brought French plays to the Harlem Opera House—an occasional shock was pleasant, and to reprobate sin on the stage perhaps fortified virtue. But in real life Harlem wanted nothing to do with loose morals. It distrusted the flamboyance, the ostentatious luxury of the West End. Harlemites weren't altogether pleased when a property-owner, hoping to lure fashion remotely northward, commissioned Stanford White to design two rows of stately residences on One Hundred and Thirty-eighth and One Hundred and Thirty-ninth Streets. They were dismayed when two brothers, wealthy merchants, purchased a large tract of land on One Hundred and Fifteenth Street, and there erected a costly double mansion, surrounded by spacious lawns and gardens, with private stables and a rustic "summer house." Harlem disapproved of splendor and extravagance. It took a dim view of the world of fashion, and although Fifth Avenue ran through it from Mount Morris Park to the Harlem River, Fifth Avenue had been tamed. The high cliffs of Mount Morris Park, separating Harlem from lower New York, formed the last bastion of the nineteenth century, the Victorian Age, safeguarding decency, resisting all dubious change.

Nowhere was the swiftness of change more manifest than on Fifth Avenue. Only the rough stone pavement of its roadway and the shabby, ancient horse-drawn omnibuses reminded you of the old days. After a snowfall, you still saw the "cock horse" that waited at the foot of Murray Hill to be hitched to the team of every uptown bus and help haul it over the rise to Forty-second Street. If you were in a hurry and could afford the price, you didn't take the lumbering, crowded buses. Instead you climbed into one of the shining new hansoms that lined up along Madison Square and in front of all the uptown hotels. Riding in a hansom was expensive. But you made quick time, and since these novel two-wheeled vehicles were equipped with rubber tires, the jars and jolts of your ride were greatly reduced.

All visitors to the city wanted, at least once, to ride up Fifth Avenue from Washington Square to the Metropolitan Museum, north of which the avenue still had the undeveloped look of a semi-suburban thoroughfare. Down at the Square, Stanford White's beautiful marble Washington Arch was one of the notable sights. The fine old red-brick mansions on the north side of the Square were still occupied by the descendants of their original proprietors. For a few blocks above the Square, the Avenue and the blocks directly east and west maintained their conservative residential character. But from Fourteenth Street north, business buildings had replaced the stately old homes. August Belmont, last of the obdurate "cave dwellers," had recently died. His somber mansion at Eighteenth Street, where social history had been made, was being demolished. The Lotos Club had moved further north. Aristocratic members of the Union Club felt isolated in their decrepit house at Twenty-first Street, and their desire to build a new one uptown gave rise to an incident that set New Yorkers gossiping. A committee of the Club approached their fellow-member, J. G. Wendel, with a proposal to purchase or lease the site of his ancestral home. An elderly bachelor, excessively parsimonious, Wendel lived with his sisters in a grim, decaying square house on the northwest corner of Fifth Avenue and Thirty-ninth Street. Adjoining the house on Fifth Avenue was a wide yard screened from prying eyes by a high board fence. The immense Wendel fortune was based on ownership of Manhattan real estate. Wendel never sold property; he rented it to tenants, requiring them to improve it at their own expense. Fearing that his sisters might be courted by fortune-hunters, he had in youth exacted their promise that they would never marry. Now the ageing spinsters had become recluses, never leaving their shabby old house in which the window shades were always drawn. They lavished their affection on a dog which they exercised in their spacious yard. When Wendel refused to relinquish the house and yard to the Union Club, the story went around that his sisters had exacted this financial sacrifice in belated recompense for their promise not to marry. Crowds went to stare at the world's costliest dog-run, the mansion maintained for canine residence or feminine revenge—the most expensive monument to virginity that man had ever been compelled to preserve. Outraged by this scandalous publicity, Wendel abruptly resigned from the Union Club, and thereafter left his home only to visit his equally obsolete offices.

Trade was sweeping up past the Wendel home. Madison Square, deserted by fashion, had been conquered by commerce. Old Mrs. William Colford Schermerhorn stubbornly remained in her great house on West Twenty-third Street, and visitors to the city wondered about this relic of old-fashioned grandeur, facing Stern's department store and adjoining the Eden Musée. North of Madison Square, the old brownstone residences were being altered for business or replaced by new buildings. For a dozen blocks, fine shops along the Avenue catered only to the wealthy. The display windows of art dealers, fashionable milliners, dressmakers and jewelers were among the city's most notable sights. Three celebrated new hotels emphasized the elegance of this stretch of the Avenue. At Thirtieth Street, the ten-story white-stone Holland House, renowned for its aristocratic tone, had installed the latest novelty. In every suite there was an annunciator: a dial listing innumerable services which a guest might require, with an arrow that, pointed to any item, elec-

COACH LEAVING HOLLAND HOUSE, Fifth Avenue and 30th Street

trically communicated the request to the hotel office. The Waldorf, at Thirty-third Street, was world famous for its opulent splendor, but New Yorkers already knew that it would be surpassed by the adjoining Astoria, to be erected on the Thirty-fourth Street corner. At Forty-second Street the old unused reservoir was to be demolished and replaced either by a park or a huge public library. Directly north of it, on the northwest corner of the Avenue, the tall Hotel Bristol had recently been opened. Still further north, at the entrance of Central Park, the low, red-brick Plaza Hotel, the great, fourteen-story Savoy "of an Arabian Nights magnificence within," and the luxurious New Netherland were in the very center of the new "millionaire's colony."

North of Fiftieth Street, Fifth Avenue was being transformed by the new palaces of multimillionaires. The trend of vast wealth to the east side of Fifth Avenue above Fifty-ninth Street, overlooking Central Park, had already set in, and social oracles were announcing that, from there "fashion will rule coming generations of New Yorkers." Though, at some future date, trade might cross the barrier of Forty-second Street, everybody recognized that it could never progress north of Fiftieth, for the immensely costly, grandiose homes of the Medici would neither be abandoned nor superseded. They had the look of dynastic monuments, erected to commemorate forever the glory of supreme power. Occasionally, some foreign visitor, overwhelmed by their sumptuousness, suggested that perhaps too much money had been spent on them merely to insure that enough would be, but most New Yorkers ignored this finicking criticism in their pride, sure that no other city in the world possessed a street as magnificent, as impressively beautiful, as the new Fifth Avenue.

In designing the French chateau of William K. Vanderbilt, Richard Morris Hunt had provided an example of grandeur that the Medici were resolved to equal and, if possible, to surpass. Nothing short of the replica of an historic royal or princely residence would satisfy them, and this whim was making the finest street in the newest of world capitals resonant with echoes of Renaissance France and Italy, placing a copy of Azay-le-Rideau beside a Florentine palazzo, and confronting these with an even more stupendous adaptation of Fontainebleau. William Waldorf Astor erected a cream-colored Touraine chateau on the northeast corner of Fifty-sixth Street, but abandoned the United States for England before he could occupy it. Adjoining it, on the southeast corner of Fifty-seventh Street, was the forbidding gray-stone palazzo of Collis P. Huntington, where in a red-brocaded drawing room the California railroad magnate, who in his youth had been a peddler, could relax in an adjustable easy chair controlled by levers and, if he wished, contemplate a priceless Vermeer or Rembrandt. Across Fifth Avenue, on the block front from Fifty-seventh to Fifty-eighth Street, rose the palace of Cornelius Vanderbilt. Its architect, George B. Post, had been a pupil of Hunt; he shared his master's adoration of the French Renaissance. For the grandson of rough old Commodore Vanderbilt, Post designed a massive reminiscence of Fontainebleau in red brick trimmed with gray stone, surrounded by a high, ornamental fence of wrought iron. On the Plaza side regal gates opened into a small park, through which a driveway led to a state entrance under an awesome porte-cochère. This was intended only for ceremonial occasions; for ordinary use there was a scarcely less formidable entrance on Fifty-seventh Street. The fabulous interior splendors of the palace included a marble reception hall "conspicuously larger than the Supreme Court of the United States," a vast "grand salon," an elaborately embellished "Moorish room," a great banquet hall and an immense ballroom that could be converted into a private theater.

North of the Plaza and its flamboyant new hotels, the line of grandiose buildings continued, exemplifying all architectural styles: renaissance, romanesque, baroque, rococo, classic. One of the most arresting commemorated both the power and rage of J. P. Morgan. This was the home of the Metropolitan Club, or "millionaires' club," as New Yorkers called it, on the corner of Sixtieth Street. Morgan organized this institution because the Union Club had infuriated him by declining to admit one of his partners to membership. Stanford White translated Morgan's imperial caprice into a gleaming white Italian Renaissance palace, entered from a spacious colonnaded courtyard.

Adjoining this severely classic building, on Fifth Avenue, you saw the ornate pink chateau of Elbridge T. Gerry. This was designed by Hunt, who for a decade had been filling Newport with chateaux. Before his death in 1896, Hunt added another to the glories of Fifth Avenue. For Mrs. Astor he created a white French Renaissance palace at Sixty-fifth Street. The ageing matriarch —a rose no less mystic for being visibly withered—thus provided the nation with a social capitol of appropriate splendor; in effect, an American Versailles. William Astor did not live to see the completion of this two-million-dollar edifice. But whatever grief his widow may have felt in her bereavement was doubtless somewhat assuaged by the acclaim bestowed on her new residence in newspapers throughout the country. It was not only the most celebrated private dwelling in the United States. It was a national symbol, like the White House in Washington, and it evoked nationwide curiosity and pride.

To adorn the interiors of their palaces, the Medici were pillaging Europe of art treasures. The whole nation knew that, in a single room of his Madison Avenue mansion, the sugar king Henry O. Havemeyer had hung no less than seven superb Rembrandts. But most New Yorkers were dubious about the investments of his wife who, at the instigation of the American painter Mary Cassatt, was collecting the incomprehensible paintings of French impressionists. The great tycoon William C. Whitney commissioned Stanford White to make over his recently purchased residence on Fifth Avenue and Sixty-seventh Street. Four years were required to convert the interior of this mansion into a private museum. Its gates were taken from the Palazzo Doria in Rome. Its

DRAWING ROOM OF 1906, residence of Mr. and Mrs. Harry Harkness Flagler

tremendous ballroom was ravished from a castle in Bordeaux. The ceilings of its banquet hall and drawing room had been painted, in the Renaissance, for the palaces of Genoese and Roman princes. One of the corridors was torn from a French monastery and everywhere there were windows of priceless medieval stained glass. At dinner, Whitney's multimillionaire guests found underfoot a marvelous rug on which ancient Persians had abased themselves in prayer, and they could lift their eyes from canvasbacks to an unrivaled Flemish tapestry, celebrating Roman wars no less heroic than those waged by their host in building his empire of street railways. It no longer surprised New Yorkers to learn that a Van Dyck portrait sold for fifty thousand dollars, and a celebrated Turner for the same sum. Everybody knew that dealers throughout Europe were ransacking the Continent to find treasures worthy to offer J. P. Morgan, the most renowned of all collectors of art. To the acquisition of beauty Morgan was applying the methods that had made him the supreme ruler of American finance. Relentless, insatiable, autocratic, he was pouring incalculable millions through the funnel of his desires. He had determined to gather the finest available spoils of civilization, to acquire a collection greater, more varied and far more valuable than any ever formed by a private individual. Paintings and porcelains, missals and manuscripts, rare books, miniatures, enamels, tapestries, Fragonard panels, historic furniture, the work of Renaissance goldsmiths flowed incessantly into Morgan's possession. In the cult of art foremost of the Medici, Morgan shared their conviction that art was the efflorescence of past greatness, powdered with the dust of centuries and certified by the signature of death. A later collector condensed into a single pregnant sentence the whole meaning of their sepulchral theory of esthetics. "Railroads," said Henry Clay Frick, "are the Rembrandts of investment."

The prosperous dwellers in old-fashioned brownstone houses on the East Side invested in railroads but showed no addiction to Rembrandts. Yet, within their means, they strove to appease a restless esthetic conscience by brightening up their grim homes. Carefully nurtured, floridly potted plants disappeared from front parlors. So did whatnots, marble-topped center tables and heavy "suites" of mahogany furniture upholstered in tufted brocade. Black walnut wainscoting was painted white, the walls above were paneled with moldings, and parquet floors were laid, their slippery surfaces made more perilous by small, "scatter" Oriental rugs. Gilded reproductions of Louis XVI furniture were installed; fragile chairs and sofas intricately carved, upholstered in imitation tapestry on which flirtatious shepherdesses and their swains were frozen in attitudes of gallantry beneath the uneasy posteriors of guests. There was always a *vitrine*, ornamented in ormolu and stuffed with bibelots: Chinese ivory figurines, German porcelain vases, silver snuff boxes and souvenir spoons, Royal Doulton plates, miniatures of the mistresses of French kings in gilt frames studded with rhinestones, bits of cloisonné. From pedestals of polished granite, marble busts, the work of anonymous Italian sculptors, fixed you with their blind stare. The walls displayed paintings richly framed in gold.

Only the unsophisticated cared to investigate their subjects or their signatures.

Upstairs, the "sitting room"—from which parents now fled when marriageable daughters received their friends—had acquired a decorative novelty. The "Turkish corner" or "cozy corner" was a tentlike affair of red draperies festooned on spears and embellished with scimitars. Within it, an ornamental, arabesque brass lantern failed to illuminate a divan "artistically" strewn with cushions, in front of which stood a fretted Moorish tabouret inlaid with mother of pearl. By its titilating suggestion of Oriental lasciviousness, the Turkish corner was destined to the rites of courtship. Here was accomplished the preliminary softening of young women encased in whaleboned corsets and safeguarded by equally inflexible moral taboos. Wooing was facilitated, but winning seemed to promise only loss under the regime of decorating firms that were refurbishing the brownstones. Extending their operations to the householder's bedroom, these firms advocated a scandalous innovation. They proposed to abolish the sacramental double bed and replace it by the new "twin beds" which manufacturers of fine furniture were beginning to produce. In middle-class circles, masculine resentment clashed with feminine determination to be up to date. Husbands no longer young, and perhaps only metaphysically uxorious, battled to retain the ancient hallowed symbol of wedded happiness. Clergymen and family physicians were drawn into the bitter domestic controversy. Many clergymen predicted that this innovation would weaken the holy bonds of marriage, becoming a social menace. Some physicians asserted that the old-fashioned double bed was unsanitary. Moreover, because of the fast pace and the tensions of New York life, women were now increasingly "nervous," and undisturbed sleep was certain to be therapeutic. To wives bent upon decorative renovation, this medical opinion often suggested alarming symptoms of hysteria. Prospective brides, traditionally permitted to choose the furnishings of their future homes, selected twin beds. Actually, the younger generation wondered what all the fuss was about. They surmised that two steps across a carpeted floor need not be an obstacle to bliss.

New Yorkers were becoming accustomed to the new marvels of electricity. The city's telephone system was already the largest and most efficient in the world. By 1896, it had fifteen thousand subscribers, as compared with a mere twenty-eight hundred sixteen years earlier. There were twelve central offices, or "exchanges," which handled an average total of one hundred and fifty thousand calls a day, establishing connections in about forty seconds. All subscribers were able to have "long-distance" connections, and so make calls to Boston or Washington or even Chicago, and in an effort to popularize telephone service the company had introduced "message rates," with charges rising from a minimum base of six hundred calls yearly, in accordance with actual use of the telephone. But installation of a telephone in one's home was considered a luxury, and most people, wishing to use one "uptown," went either to the nearest hotel, or to some neighborhood store whose enterprising proprietor had put in an instrument for the use, mainly, of his customers. The

THE FIRST NEW YORK TELE-
PHONE DIRECTORY, 1878

BANKS, BANKERS AND BROKERS.

Diamonds, Watches, Jewelry, Plated Ware, etc.

REAL ESTATE.

PASSE PARTOUTS

SHIP AND FREIGHT BROKERS.

RAIL ROAD TICKETS.

Bonded and Storage Warehouses.

PUBLISHERS.

INSURANCE.

CLOTHIERS.

FIRE PATROL.

COMMERCIAL AGENCIES.

SAFES AND SCALES.

HOTELS.

UMBRELLAS.

HATS.

HARDWARE.

PIPES.

KID GLOVES.

SEGARS.

TEA AND COFFEE.

FISH AND MEATS.

Produce, Cotton, Oil, and Commission Merchants.

IMPORTERS.

TAILORS' TRIMMINGS.

WEIGHERS.

DISTILLERS.

WHOLESALE GROCERS.

COLLARS & CUFFS.

PRINTERS.

SILKS AND LACES.

MILLINERY, DRY GOODS, ETC.

COAL AND IRON.

TRANSFER COMPANIES.

TRUNKS AND BAGS.

BURGLAR ALARMS.

WOOL.

Drugs, Chemicals, and Essential Oils.

device was affixed to a wall—the mouthpiece on a protruding metal neck, the earpiece to be taken from a metal cradle on the side of the box. You turned a crank lustily, lifted the earpiece, and the agreeable young woman at "central" who responded soon made your connection. Whether you spoke from a hotel or a store, anyone standing nearby could eavesdrop on your conversation, so you were likely to be very careful about discussing intimate personal affairs.

The expansion of electric lighting was scarcely less remarkable. Three companies were furnishing this service to different parts of the city. Of these, the Edison system was the largest. It supplied six thousand customers with two hundred and twenty-five thousand incandescent lamps, three thousand arc lamps, and some thirteen thousand horsepower for motors. The city had a total of three hundred and twenty-five thousand incandescent lamps and sixty-two hundred arc lights. Most of the brownstone houses were still illuminated by gas, but wealthy people who had introduced electricity for lighting purposes were able to enjoy such other conveniences as revolving electric fans to keep rooms cool in sultry weather. Already predictions were being made that cooking would be done, and houses heated, by electricity, and New Yorkers had been assured that very soon they would be "able to remain at home and enjoy the lightest note of the prima donna at the opera."

A decade earlier, New Yorkers had hopefully assumed that the elevated railroads would permanently solve the problem of rapid transit. Instead, the problem had become more urgent than ever before. In Brooklyn and up in the Annexed District, swift electric trolley cars were now flashing through the streets. But, because these required overhead wires, there was strong prejudice against their use on Manhattan Island. On the avenues having street railways, the old horse-cars were replaced by cable-cars. From windows overlooking Broadway, you saw "the curious spectacle of an apparently continuous line of roofs of cars occupying the center of the thoroughfare." But elderly people remarked that this was nothing new; forty years earlier, the same thing had been said of the old omnibuses. The cable-cars caused many accidents, especially at Fourteenth Street, where the Broadway line swung around the lower end of Union Square. This became known as "dead man's curve," for engineers asserted that the cars had to take it at high speed. Only after many pedestrians had been killed or maimed was it discovered that the engineers were wrong.

Morning and evening, the elevated trains, the cable-cars and the horse-cars that continued to jog along certain crosstown streets were all equally overcrowded. A Rapid Transit Board, set up to study the problem, revived the old idea of an underground railroad. It sent William Barclay Parsons, an eminent engineer, to study the underground rapid-transit systems of London and Paris, and devise one for New York. Parsons eventually produced plans for a "subway system" of electric trains, estimating the cost of this project at sixty million dollars. Controversy raged for several years before it was adopted. Meanwhile, for use in spring and summer, new "open cars" were

A GIBSON GIRL OF 1905. Portrait of Mrs. Charles Dana Gibson by her husband

put on the street railways. On torrid nights, New Yorkers sought relief from the heat in taking car rides. By transferring from one line to another, you could enjoy a pleasant breeze all the way from the Battery to the new amusement park at Fort George, far up on Washington Heights. In outlying regions parties were organized to take trolley rides. For these excursions the companies rented "private" cars, decorated with banners and festooned with electric lights, and the organizers usually hired a "German band" to sit on the front seats and furnish music while their blazing car sped through the night.

Old-fashioned folk were lamenting the decline of gentility, the new, rude, easy ways of the younger generation. Their daytime attire showed an increasing trend to laxity. Young men were discarding frock coats, and instead of the traditional "boiled shirt" were taking to "soft shirts" with detachable, starched cuffs and collars. When the first "rainy-daisy" skirt appeared on Broadway—clearing the ground by a scandalous six inches—newspapers ridiculed it. Yet "nice" girls quickly adopted it, and not only for wear in stormy weather. Young women wanted to look like the "Gibson girl" whose beauty Charles Dana Gibson was delineating every week in *Life*, and young men tried to resemble the square-shouldered, strong-jawed athletic "Gibson man," her inseparable companion. In their masculine "boater" hats, their mannish, high-collared shirtwaists and trimly tailored skirts, the girls were especially startling to elderly eyes. You saw them, on winter afternoons, ice skating at the new St. Nicholas Rink, on Sixty-sixth Street west of Central Park, the favorite resort of smart society when debarred by freezing weather from its usual diversion of driving in the Park; or roller skating at the Lenox

Lyceum, on Madison Avenue near Fifty-ninth Street. Winter or summer, the young girls were affecting jaunty tailored suits and an air of competent self-reliance more suggestive of proficiency in sports than of fastidious feminine elegance.

Then—as it seemed, overnight—the bicycle craze struck New York, and the whole city began pursuing happiness on wheels. Genteel conservatives deplored this new fad and were gratified when the Reverend Asa D. Blackburn, pastor of the Church of the Strangers, denounced it from his pulpit. The press commended his sermon: "You cannot serve God and skylark on a bicycle." Yet in spite of his dire warning, the young smart set took to the sport enthusiastically. They organized the Michaux Club, on Broadway near Fifty-third Street, where professional racers gave them lessons in riding single and tandem wheels. Less exclusive bicycle schools soon opened throughout the city. On fine weekday mornings feminine cyclists thronged the drives of Central Park. Lillian Russell and her friend Marie Dressler took up cycling in order to "slenderize" their figures, and on their wheels, Miss Dressler surmised, they gave "an imitation of two plump girls going somewhere in a hurry."

Miss Russell became the talk of the town. In a white serge cycling costume with stylish leg-of-mutton sleeves, you saw her pedaling up through the Park, making two circuits of the Reservoir before stopping to rest. Her bicycle was a national sensation. Entirely gold plated, its mother-of-pearl handlebars bore her monogram in diamonds and emeralds; the hubs and spokes of its wheels were set with many jewels that sparkled in the sun. A few cynics maintained that she had been provided with this luxurious machine, for purposes of publicity, by an enterprising manufacturer of bicycles. But knowing New Yorkers asserted that it was the gift of her friend "Diamond Jim" Brady. An obese, hulking figure, Brady always rode a gold-plated bicycle with silvered spokes, and on Sundays you often saw him pedaling beside Miss Russell. Sometimes, however, he rode a triple bicycle, with a beautiful girl perched behind him and his factotum, Dick Barton, on the third saddle. New Yorkers never wearied of wheeling. Young people made up parties, properly chaperoned, to ride up through the Park and along Riverside Drive to Grant's Tomb, dine at Claremont Inn, and return by night. At Claremont, in spring and summer, you could dine out of doors, in a garden strung with gay Japanese lanterns, and after dark Riverside Drive seemed alive with fireflies, so numerous were the varicolored bicycle lamps flashing under the trees.

On Sundays, many adventurous cyclists rode up to the new parks far north of the Harlem River—Van Cortlandt Park, Bronx Park and Pelham Bay Park. Near Pelham Bay Park, the Pelham Country Club, with its golf links and tennis courts, was a favorite terminus for drivers of four-in-hand coaches, and a number of wealthy New Yorkers had built year-round residences in its vicinity. Work had already begun on the project of connecting the three great parks by a chain of wide boulevards. People were already talking of a time when "the pleasure-seeker of the future shall speed on his wheel, or in his electric carriage, along miles of perfect driveway." For electric carriages had appeared on the streets of New York. The first one, especially built for "Diamond Jim" Brady, tied up traffic on Fifth Avenue for two hours when, at the alarming speed of eleven miles an hour, it was driven from Fifty-seventh Street to Madison Square. The machine terrified so many horses that, at first, the police forbade Brady to use it except late at night. But the prohibition against electric carriages had been relaxed, and it seemed likely that they would become popular with well-to-do folk.

The frightening new "horseless carriages," propelled by gasoline or steam, were quite another matter. Most New Yorkers saw them for the first time on Decoration Day in 1896, when a race was arranged by John Brisben Walker, editor of *The Cosmopolitan*, from City Hall to the fashionable Ardsley Country Club, and return, for a prize of three thousand dollars. Three American carriages, made by the Duryea brothers, competed against an imported Benz. A Duryea machine took the prize. Some harebrained visionaries predicted that horseless carriages of quality and price suitable for general use would soon be on the market. The Duryea firm presently set up a "demonstrator" in a store on Broadway, and prepared to take orders for future delivery. Their vehicle was advertised as being noiseless, odorless, free from vibration, perfectly controllable and absolutely safe; besides, while it had the handsome lines of a costly carriage, it did not have a "carriage-without-a-horse look." But New Yorkers were skeptical, and although the firm received orders for thirteen vehicles, none of these was bought by a resident of the city. Yet within three years a few millionaires provoked astonishment, rage and laughter by driving gasoline or steam cars on New York streets. The Automobile Club of America was organized, with headquarters at the Waldorf-Astoria Hotel, and in the autumn of 1899 crowds turned out to see the latest foolish fancy of the idle rich—an automobile parade that wound its precarious way from Fifth Avenue and Thirty-fourth Street to Claremont by a devious route, for the new "devil wagons" were sternly forbidden to enter Central Park. All along the route, bystanders jeeringly cried, "Get a horse!"

Meanwhile, New Yorkers had become familiar with another slogan: "Remember the Maine!" Competing for circulation, Joseph Pulitzer, owner of *The World*, and William Randolph Hearst, owner of *The Journal*, had inaugurated a form of journalism, which conservative citizens deprecated; "yellow journalism," they called it. Each of the newspaper titans determined to outdo the other in whipping up patriotic frenzy for a war with Spain. The war came. New York broke out with flags, and cheered the regiments that paraded down Fifth Avenue on their way to camp. Everywhere you heard the military marches of John Philip Sousa. Less than a week after the declaration of war, the city went wild with excitement at the news that the Spanish fleet in Manila harbor had been destroyed by a naval squadron commanded by Admiral Dewey. But a few days later, ominous news spread fear along the Atlantic coast. Another Spanish fleet, under Admiral Cervera, had left the Cape Verde Islands for an unknown westward destination. Was Cervera going to bombard New York, the Jersey coast, even Washington? Many well-to-do New Yorkers found excuses to depart from the city in haste. Three long weeks went by; the naval search for Cervera's fleet yielded no result; in New York, tension mounted rapidly. Then, to everybody's relief, it was reported that the Spanish fleet had anchored in the harbor of Santiago, Cuba. By the end of July, 1898, three months after the declaration of war, Spain was suing for peace. New Yorkers indulged in a boisterous victory celebration. Shortly afterward, matrons and young girls were crowding on trains of the Long Island Railroad to minister to the twenty thousand soldiers in the great hospital camp at Montauk Point, victims of yellow fever, malaria, typhoid and intestinal disorders.

On the first day of January, 1898, by act of the State Legislature, New York City was transformed into Greater New York. Legislative enactment trebled the city's area and nearly doubled its population. The new greater metropolis absorbed the city of Brooklyn (or Kings County) and Queens County on Long Island; the whole of Staten Island (Richmond County); and it extended as far north of the Harlem River as the boundaries of Yonkers, Mount Vernon, Pelham and New Rochelle. Under New York's new charter, this vast area was organized as the five boroughs of Manhattan, Brooklyn, Queens, Richmond and the Bronx. Elderly residents of Manhattan sentimentally lamented the passing of "little old New York." To many native New Yorkers, Brooklyn and Queens, Staten Island and the Bronx, were virtually foreign territory, never explored, though sometimes traversed in the course of expeditions to outlying cemeteries, or journeys to visit friends who lived in the suburbs. Would the new greater city remain an aggregate of independent communities, each retaining its distinctive social atmosphere, its local color? Or would there emerge, from this massive fusion of disparates, a unified city —a metropolis such as the world had never before known?

THE 400 TAKE TO THE BICYCLE, Central Park about 1895, *by B. West Clinedinst*

17

The Old Adam and the Spare Rib

Ⓞn the morning of Sunday, February 14th, 1892, the old Madison Square Presbyterian Church was comfortably filled, as usual. Among the congregation in this plain, brownstone "American Gothic" edifice you might have noticed a number of distinguished citizens. Perhaps the best known was an ageing, fragile man with keen eyes, a parchment-colored skin and a scholarly air. He was Thomas Collier Platt, the Republican "boss" of New York State. He made his city headquarters at the Fifth Avenue Hotel across the Square and issued orders to his subservient henchmen from a sofa at one end of its broad downstairs corridor, the so-called "Amen Corner" whose name symbolized his absolute dictatorship. You might have noticed that there were reporters present, though this was not remarkable. It was the custom of newspaper editors to give space, on Monday mornings, to the sermons of the city's leading clergymen. During the twelve years of his pastorate, Dr. Charles H. Parkhurst had frequently provided good copy. Tall, slender, whiskered, austere, he was an eloquent preacher, earnest but not without humor, and he had a pained sense that the life of the church had lost touch with the life of the times. He liked, therefore, to preach about contemporary issues, political, economic and social. But on this Sunday morning he had chosen his text from the Sermon on the Mount: "Ye are the salt of the earth." However edifying, it promised little that was newsworthy.

Dr. Parkhurst had been speaking for scarcely one minute when a gasp swept across the church. Then the congregation listened in astonished silence, and the reporters excitedly scratched away at their notebooks. "In its municipal life our city is thoroughly rotten . . . Every step that we take looking to the moral betterment of this city has to be taken directly in the teeth of the damnable pack of administrative bloodhounds that are fattening themselves on the ethical flesh and blood of our citizenship . . . There is not a form under which the devil disguises himself that so perplexes us in our efforts, or so bewilders us in the devising of our schemes, as the political harpies that, under the pretense of governing this city, are feeding day and night on its quivering vitals. They are a lying, perjured, rum-soaked and libidinous lot. . . . Every effort that is made to improve character in this city, every effort to make men respectable, honest, temperate and sexually clean is a direct blow between the eyes of the Mayor and his whole gang of drunken and lecherous subordinates, in this sense: that while we fight iniquity they shield and patronize it."

The excise laws, Dr. Parkhurst charged, were not being enforced. Houses of prostitution, gambling dens, notorious dives of all kinds were flourishing openly with the connivance of the police. In New York, every form of crime had its price. "All people ought to understand that crime in this city is entrenched in our municipal administration, and that what ought to be a bulwark against crime is a stronghold in its defense. . . . I should not be surprised to know that every building in this town in which gambling or prostitution or the illicit sale of liquor is carried on has immunity secured to it by a scale of police taxation that is as carefully graded and as thoroughly systematized as any that obtains in the assessment of personal property or real estate." The Mayor, the District Attorney and the police, Dr. Parkhurst declared, were linked in an "official and administrative criminality that is filthifying our entire municipal life, making New York a very hotbed of knavery, debauchery and bestiality."

Few of the clergyman's parishioners could have been better pleased by the sermon than Boss Platt. The wily old politician was neither surprised nor concerned by Dr. Parkhurst's account of unhindered, flagrant vice. This condition was familiar to every knowing New Yorker, and to most of the nation also; it had made New York the nation's principal pleasure resort. And although Platt had an occasional taste for dry theology, he preferred it, as Theodore Roosevelt later said, "wholly divorced from moral implications." On the subject of sin personal experience had taught him a certain tolerance. Earlier in his career, political opponents, having climbed up to a window of an Albany hotel, had caught him in a "compromising situation" and had briefly embarrassed him by publishing this discovery. Platt's interest in the sermon was coldly practical. He had recently declared war on Richard Croker, boss of Tammany Hall and supreme ruler of New York City. In the city, Republicans polled only about one-third of the total vote. Dr. Parkhurst, Platt surmised, might become as useful to the Republican Party as to the Lord.

Next morning, the press made Dr. Parkhurst's sermon a sensation. Excitement ran high throughout the city. Boss Croker had put Hugh J. Grant in the mayor's office because Grant, unlike most Tammany dignitaries, was rich, well-educated, well-born and satisfied by rank without power. Mayor Grant challenged Dr. Parkhurst to prove his general charges with specific evidence. District Attorney De Lancy Nicoll, scion of an old, distinguished family, smarted under Dr. Parkhurst's accusation of collusion with the criminal classes. Nicoll summoned the clergyman to appear before a Grand Jury. Dr. Parkhurst was forced to admit that he had no legal evidence to substantiate his allegations. He had based them on accounts published in the newspapers, and never contradicted by any official. The Grand Jury vigorously condemned him in a report to the Court of General Sessions, whose presiding judge issued a public statement concurring in their opinion. City officials denounced the crusading clergyman in an outburst of uncomplimentary epithets. He appeared to be thoroughly discredited.

But this humiliation merely aroused Dr. Parkhurst's native belligerence. He happened to be president of the Society for the Prevention of Crime, an association of righteous, wealthy gentlemen who, although profoundly disturbed by the degraded state of public morals, had never taken very active steps to improve them—except, perhaps, by personal example and published lamentation. To the intrepid clergyman, it was clear that the Society now had an opportunity for a livelier career. Amply provided with funds, the Society also had the benefit of expert legal counsel; one of its most aggressive members was Frank Moss, an astute, public-spirited, politically experienced attorney. Dynamic action was indicated, but probably neither Dr. Parkhurst nor his genteel colleagues foresaw the spectacular drama in which they were to play leading roles. With the support of his Society, he determined to prove his case. He intended to expose the results of Tammany's rule—the corruption of the city administration, the unholy alliance of the police with criminals and the forces of vice.

Realizing that in future he would have to speak from personal knowledge, Dr. Parkhurst undertook to journey into the hell of New York's nocturnal depravity. A zealous young parishioner, John Langdon Erving, volunteered to accompany him. But since neither of them knew the ropes, Dr. Parkhurst engaged Charles W. Gardner, a detective, to serve them as guide, at a fee of six dollars a night and expenses. Gardner studied his clients and declared that they would have to be disguised. They agreed, but Dr. Parkhurst wished to preserve his whiskers, and the detective remarked that, if due caution were taken, it would not "be necessary to harvest your lilacs at present." On the evening fixed for their first rendezvous, Gardner called for his clients and found that their disguises did not disguise them. Dr. Parkhurst was unmistakably a clergyman; Erving looked like an outmoded fashion plate. He took them to his room and proceeded to improve their makeup. Gardner began with Dr. Parkhurst. He attired the clergyman in a dirty shirt, a pair of loudly checked black-and-white trousers, a worn double-breasted reefer jacket, a tie made from the sleeve of an old red-flannel shirt. Still, Dr. Parkhurst appeared more representative of the ecclesiastical than of the sinful world, and the addition of a battered slouch hat failed to make him look sufficiently disreputable. Only when Gardner had smeared the clergyman's long, luxuriant, curly hair with laundry soap was his air of clerical austerity finally effaced. Erving was given rubber boots and a red necktie; his blond hair, parted in the middle, was suitably mussed up. Piloted by Gardner, the self-sacrificing reformers, in their undignified garb, set out on a tour of New York's "dens of vice" that continued for three weeks.

Gardner soon learned that he would have to work strenuously for his fees. Dr. Parkhurst was a very hard man to satisfy. " 'Show me something worse,' was his constant cry. He really went at his slumming work as if his heart was in his tour." In the Cherry Street saloon of Tom Summers, a notorious "fence," he downed a drink of Cherry Hill whiskey, acting, so Gardner noted, "as if he had swallowed a whole political parade—torchlights and all." He watched a stream of ten-year-old children buying pint bottles of whiskey, for ten cents, presumably to take home to their parents. In front of a sailors' dive on Water Street, three prostitutes grabbed the reformers and hauled them indoors; Dr. Parkhurst, resisting their blandishments, chatted with them amiably. The party visited a five-cent lodging house on Park Row, where the clergyman remarked—quite correctly—that the naked men lying on cots became, on Election Day, Tammany voters. Gardner took his clients to Chinese opium dens, to ordinary houses of prostitution, to houses where the prostitutes gave indecent performances, to others known as "tight houses" because all the inmates wore tights.

One incident of the tour later became celebrated because Tammany, after it had been aired in a courtroom, sought to persuade reputable citizens that Dr. Parkhurst was an evil-minded hypocrite. In the brothel run by Hattie Adams, Gardner arranged to have a "dance of nature" performed by five girls who, for furnishing this diversion, were to be paid three dollars each. When the party arrived, the girls were dressed in their usual garb and a broken-down musician, called "the Professor," sat at a piano in the parlor. Gardner blindfolded the Professor because the girls refused either to disrobe, or dance, before him. The five girls then stripped, and to a lively jig performed a dance which Gardner incorrectly described as "the can-can." Because Gardner could not dance, and Dr. Parkhurst would not if he could, Erving was compelled to represent the visitors as a dancer. As Gardner later recorded, the "dance of nature" was followed by "the celebrated 'leapfrog' episode, in which I was the frog and the others jumped over me. The Doctor sat in the corner with an unmoved face through it all, watching us and slowly sipping at a glass of beer. Hattie Adams was quite anxious to find out who Dr. Parkhurst was. I told her he was 'from the West' and was 'a gay boy.' Then Hattie tried to pull Dr. Parkhurst's whiskers, but the Doctor straightened out with such an air of dignity that she did not attempt any further familiarities."

Dr. Parkhurst's constant demand for "something worse" was apparently satisfied, according to Gardner, by a visit to the Golden Rule Pleasure Club on West Third Street. The proprietress of this establishment, a woman known as "Scotch Ann," received the party cordially and ushered them into the basement. The basement was subdivided, by flimsy partitions, into cubicles each of which contained a table and two chairs. "In each room sat a youth," Gardner later reported, "whose face was painted, eyebrows blackened, and whose airs were those of a young girl. Each person talked in a high falsetto voice, and called the others by women's names." Mystified by what he saw, Dr. Parkhurst questioned Gardner in a whisper. The detective explained. The clergyman "instantly turned on his heel and fled from the house at top speed. 'Why, I wouldn't stay in that house,' he gasped, 'for all the money in the world.' " As later investigations showed, this establishment was not unique. Similar resorts were being operated in other quarters of the city: Manila Hall, The Black Rabbit, The Palm; and Paresis Hall on Fourth Avenue between Twelfth and Thirteenth Streets. The name of this resort was grimly reminiscent of advertisements plastered on the walls of public toilets, offering the services of "Old Dr. Gray" and "Old Dr. Grindle." At Paresis Hall investigators observed, among the visitors, the captain of the precinct police station. "We saw Captain Chapman come in there," one of them testified, "and look around about two or three minutes, and then speak to the proprietor four or five minutes, and then walk out." The inference of police protection seemed not to be impossibly far-fetched.

One month after delivering his first sermon, Dr. Parkhurst carried to his pulpit a massive bundle of sworn affidavits. To his appalled congregation, he rendered an account of his journey into the Inferno. "Anyone who, with all the easily ascertainable facts in view, denies that drunkenness, gambling and licentiousness in this town are municipally protected, is either a knave or a fool," he declared. He denounced Tammany Hall as "a commercial corporation, organized in the interest of making the most possible out of its official opportunities." Tammany, he charged, had efficiently organized crime and vice for the financial profit of its hierarchy. And it embodied the tyranny of crime. He had received an immense correspondence from citizens who, abominating the whole system, assured him of their approval of his course. Many of these citizens had also stated that they did not dare sign their letters with their real names—such was their fear of the power of Tammany Hall. This astonished Dr. Parkhurst. But, during the next two years, he became inured to facts that were equally surprising. Much of the information upon which he proceeded came to him from a man who, although intimately connected with Tammany Hall, was willing to enter into a secret, silent working alliance with the clergyman and his militant organization. On the other hand, many reputable New Yorkers, of high social and financial standing, condemned his efforts to overthrow Tammany rule, actively opposed his crusade and supported, with their own prestige, the men directly responsible for the prevailing state of affairs. There was no apparent link between these gentlemen and the criminal underworld, yet they were bitterly averse to "reform." Reform, they said, "hurt business."

Assisted by a corps of private detectives and many volunteer investigators, Dr. Parkhurst continued his campaign of exposure and attack. Concentrating on the police department, he waged war from his pulpit, in the newspapers, in the courtrooms where Frank Moss diligently prosecuted cases that would establish a purchase, from the police, of immunity. Whether the purchase represented bribery of the police or blackmail and extortion practiced by them made no difference. The prosecution of these cases was not free from personal danger. After testifying, in Essex Market Court, against owners of disorderly houses in the neighborhood, the Society's agents were pursued by a mob of five hundred people. The police refused to interfere; this was the precinct of Captain William S. Devery, whom the Society had publicly accused of selling immunity. Meanwhile, in the courtroom, Frank Moss had been threatened by Max Hockstim, a Tammany henchman who owned an East Side saloon, commanded the services of a gang of thugs, and was responsible to Croker's associate, "Big Tim" Sullivan, political boss of the lower East Side.

The revelations made by Dr. Parkhurst and his Society finally yielded results. Early in 1894 the Chamber of Commerce, worried about the publicity which these revelations had received, formally asked the State Legislature to make an investigation of the city's Police Department. A municipal election was to be held in November. Albany politicians of both parties agreed that any thorough inquest into bribery and corruption would be "playing with fire." Nevertheless, Boss Tom Platt realized that the Chamber of Commerce had given him a fine chance to harass Boss Richard Croker and the Tammany organization. The opportunity was too good to pass up. Platt controlled the Legislature. So the Legislature obediently appointed a committee headed by State Senator Clarence Lexow and gave it broad powers of investigation—of which politicians naturally assumed it would not make indiscreet use. But Dr. Parkhurst, who by this time had lost all illusions about practical politics, ridiculed the probable course of the Lexow Committee. Ungratefully, he considered himself a servant of God, not an instrument of the Republican Party. Yet he was not lacking in political astuteness. By declining to co-operate with the Lexow Committee, he forced it to appoint counsel satisfactory to himself. The attorney he chose was John W. Goff, a brilliant lawyer not susceptible to political influence. As his assistants Goff named William Travers Jerome, a nephew of Leonard Jerome, and Frank Moss, counsel of Dr. Parkhurst's Society. Conducted by this trio, the Lexow investigation became a national sensation. It was like a forest fire that had got out of control. Nobody could tell where the exposures would stop—and the relentless inquisition brought terror not only to politicians, police and the underworld, but to many reputable, prominent members of the community also.

Most New Yorkers knew that the city was "wide open." On the whole, they were cosmopolitan and pleasure-loving, and many of them had no objection to leading a free-and-easy life in a free-and-easy town. The city had two pleasure districts, both nationally known. The old Tenderloin had followed the northward trend of theaters and hotels, and now embraced the area from Madison Square to Forty-eighth Street, between Fifth and Ninth Avenues. Here were located the most noted gambling resorts and brothels, the garish saloons, restaurants and dance halls where prostitutes solicited customers, the shady hotels and lodging houses where couples without luggage could hire

THE HAYMARKET, *by John Sloan*

rooms by the hour or the night. The Haymarket—which combined the attractions of a restaurant, dance hall and variety show—saw to it that you did not lack feminine companionship. The fun, like the females, was loud and lurid. All visiting firemen insisted on being taken to the Haymarket, and it was there that "Diamond Jim" Brady often entertained out-of-town friends who wanted their parties undiluted by any epicurean refinements. But Brady, the town's most conspicuous rounder, knew better than to wear any of his valuable, gaudy jewels when he went there; notwithstanding his prestige with the management and the police, he would not have been safe.

In the Tenderloin, there were brothels for the wealthy and discreet, and others that catered to a run-of-the-mill clientele. When he was assigned to the district, Police Captain Max F. Schmittberger was tipped off, by Captain Devery, not to interfere with the house operated by Georgiana Hastings. She ran a "very quiet" house; her customers included prominent millionaires, judges, city officials; she was unique in being exempt from the payment of any tribute to the police. She had political and financial influence. The Lexow Committee tried to serve a bench-warrant on her, at her house, but a judge of the criminal courts and another city official were present, and the warrant was not executed. Very different in character was the notorious brothel known as "the French madam's" and conducted by Mrs. Matilda Hermann. Mrs. Hermann had a flair for the new business technique of mass sales stimulated by artful publicity. Her house was, in fact, two adjoining houses, and so that no seeker for pleasure should fail to locate it she installed electric lamps on the front stoop. The other madams in the district immediately protested to the police; this was unfair competition. A police official suggested that they each contribute five hundred dollars to a "kitty" which would be used to compel the French madam to remove her glaring lamps. The process of removal was not accomplished quickly enough to satisfy her competitors, so they identified their establishments by enclosing the stoops with board fences —which made it easy for visitors both to recognize a brothel and enter it undetected. Meanwhile, the French madam was making a profit of from one thousand to fifteen hundred dollars a month, but in five years she had been compelled to pay more than thirty thousand dollars for protection. Unfortunately, protection did not protect her; the more she paid, the more the police extorted. One night, presumably having failed to increase her monthly payment with requisite celerity, she was arrested by a policeman who beat her up, in the street, with his club. A crowd collected, and quite naturally Mrs. Hermann was shamed by this public humiliation. Yet she was to suffer worse, for on another occasion she was arrested again, while confined to bed by illness. Taken to the police station, she was confronted by three policemen and a bootblack who swore that she had sold herself to each of them for one dollar. This aspersion on her professional status she resented more than any other indignity. Never, she assured the Lexow Committee proudly, had she sold herself for a dollar—or even for one hundred dollars. She was a business-woman, an employer, and not a prostitute.

However industrious and competent, many dealers in nocturnal pleasure found it hard to do business and earn a reasonable profit. Superintendent of Police Thomas F. Byrnes was occasionally nettled by Dr. Parkhurst's fiery denunciations, or by some especially inconsiderate exposure. At such times, he was likely to transfer many of his captains to new precincts. To the public, this process became known as a "shake-up." The madams, however, cynically described it as a "shake-down." Shortly after arriving at his station house, the new captain of police would call and demand an "initiation fee" of five hundred dollars, although this sum had been paid, for the same purpose, to each of his predecessors. Moreover, notwithstanding regular monthly payments for protection, Police Headquarters sometimes "put the bee" on the precinct captain. He would then have to raid the brothels of many of his protégées, merely as a public demonstration of official vigilance. The madams learned that such raids always occurred just after the first of the month— the date when ward men called to collect protection payments. Raids had a depressing effect on business. And the harassed champions of free enterprise found them costly, for bail had to be secured not only for the madam but for every girl in the establishment. In the Tenderloin, William R. Nelson, the

Tammany district leader, held the bail monopoly. It was a profitable sideline, because Nelson charged five dollars for every prostitute he bailed out, and his nightly average of philanthropic intercession was said to run from twenty to thirty cases. But for Nelson, the bail monopoly was mere chicken feed. He wielded absolute power in the Tenderloin, and no madam, dive owner or saloon keeper could do business there without his consent. He had to be propitiated and kept satisfied. His disfavor was disastrous. It meant being hounded out of the district.

Political influence in high quarters was the most valuable of all business assets. Police Commissioner Martin, who was Tammany leader of the district just north of the Tenderloin, was a man singularly loyal to his friends. He cautioned Captain Schmittberger not to molest Mrs. Sadie West, owner of a brothel in his bailiwick. Some of her neighbors complained that Mrs. West's house was a public nuisance. Captain Schmittberger sent an officer there to make inquiries. Although reluctant to give any information, Mrs. West told the officer that Commissioner Martin was a friend of hers, and suggested that he do nothing until he had heard from the Commissioner. That evening, Captain Schmittberger was ordered to report to the Commissioner on the following day. When he arrived at Headquarters, Schmittberger was ordered by Martin to send the officer back to Mrs. West with an apology for having disturbed her by his earlier visit—and this officially commanded mission was promptly performed. But enterprisers whose social contacts were less exalted had a merely tepid affection for Tammany Hall and the police. Miss Maud Harvey, keeper of an overnight lodging house where no questions were asked, probably expressed their secret feelings to a representative of the Lexow Committee who served her with a subpoena. She said she would have to "go and see somebody." Did she intend to go and see the police? "What, those God-damned sons of bitches?" Miss Harvey retorted. "No, the stinken bastards, I wouldn't go to them." She wondered whether the Lexow Committee would succeed in disrupting Tammany Hall. "I hope to Christ they do break up Tammany Hall," said Miss Harvey, "and I can open my house again and make some money, which I have not done in the past." Whereas many respectable citizens surmised that reform might prove bad for business, many representatives of the underworld felt that it would be good for their business. Resentment and the profit motive made them natural allies of Dr. Parkhurst. Wasn't he fighting in their behalf, whether he knew it or not?

Sporadic demonstrations of police activity, ordered by Superintendent Byrnes, were regarded as occupational hazards by the Tenderloin merchants of pleasure. "I'd be glad to know just what Dr. Parkhurst would like me to do," Captain Schmittberger complained aggrievedly to a newspaper reporter after one well-publicized raid. "I've cleaned out the Tenderloin until it looks like a Connecticut village." He had, in fact, raided twelve brothels and secured sixty prisoners who were arraigned in Jefferson Market Court. Not remarkably, Civil Justice-elect Joseph Steiner, a prominent Tammany lawyer, awaited the prisoners in court. He represented Mrs. Fannie Bennet—known in the district as "Fivepenny Fan"—and many of the others. Everything would go smoothly. The local district leader would furnish bail; the women would be able to return to work the same night; later, if any of them had to be sentenced to terms on Blackwell's Island, an additional payment would secure their release. After so spectacular a raid as this one you might have noticed that Broadway, as usual, was crowded with "cruisers"—but, instead of walking singly, as before, they promenaded in pairs and the police blandly declared that two women, innocently enjoying a constitutional after dark, could not be "picked up on suspicion." The Haymarket, as usual, was doing a prosperous business after the legal closing hour. At any hour between midnight on Saturday and midnight on Sunday, you could see men lined up at the Sixth Avenue bars, drinking without fear of police interference. The "concert halls" along the east side of Eighth Avenue held their customary Sunday night "sacred concerts" and served their patrons with liquor. A devotional song especially popular with their pious patrons was likely to be rendered, with appropriate gestures, by a buxom blonde wearing a costume notably abbreviated at top and bottom:

> Georgie, Georgie, pray give over,
> Georgie, Georgie, you're too free.
> Stop your palaver, else I'll tell Father,
> Georgie, give over and let me be.

Walking through the Tenderloin at night, you were not overwhelmed by its striking resemblance to a Connecticut village.

Nor was the downtown pleasure district—along the Bowery and adjacent streets—any more rurally virtuous in its atmosphere. A favorite resort was "Silver Dollar" Smith's glittering saloon opposite Essex Market Court, which had one thousand silver dollars embedded in its floor, a chandelier sparkling with five hundred silver dollars, and a large star and crescent behind the bar similarly adorned. You could go to Lyons' restaurant on the Bowery and see detectives, police officials and well-known politicians sitting at tables with notorious pickpockets, second-story men, dive keepers and brothel owners. Crime was a business; criminals had "position" in the world; and at Lyons' you found the criminal aristocracy consorting with members of the Tammany hierarchy. One of the most notorious of all Bowery dives was McGurk's, known as "Suicide Hall," an East Side equivalent of the Haymarket with a brothel upstairs. New, very young girls were taken to McGurk's by the "cadets," or recruiters, to be broken in, and pimps who operated on their own account set their crews of girls to work there. One night Inspector Alexander Williams, who had given the Tenderloin its name, reluctantly raided McGurk's with fifty patrolmen, arresting two hundred and fifty men and sixty women. At the Eldridge Street police station most of them were promptly bailed out, while in the street a crowd of more than one thousand people hooted and jeered. No wonder; Captain William S. Devery had recently warned the pleasure merchants of his precinct, "There is a lot of silk-stocking people coming from uptown to bulldoze you people, and if they open their mouths you stand them on their heads." On any spring or summer night you saw girls soliciting passers-by from the stoops of the brothels; a little later, in the open street, you might see pimps fighting with their girls for the money they had earned. To all this, Captain Devery had no objection. "Men that are looking for that sort of thing can find plenty of it," he remarked to a local clergyman who complained about the flagrancy of prostitution; and he had another complaining clergyman thrown out of the Eldridge Street police station.

By Dr. Parkhurst and his cohorts of reformers, prostitution was described as "the social evil." But even they conceded that their use of the definite article was inaccurate. Was not illicit gambling a "social evil" also? It flourished, unimpeded, in every quarter of the city. There were daytime gambling houses in the downtown business and financial districts. There were "pool rooms" everywhere, in which nobody played pool and neither tables, balls nor cues were ever seen; they were operated by bookmakers. There were "poker flats" catering to the thin as well as the fat pocketbook. In this sphere of the pursuit of pleasure, even the very poorest citizen and the precocious adolescent were not neglected. They were provided for in the innumerable "policy shops" controlled by "Al" Adams, where bets of a nickel or a dime were accepted on a game which a later generation of New Yorkers would know as "playing the numbers."

"Al" Adams, the "policy king," was called the meanest gambler in town. Nevertheless, he was a millionaire, a man of prestige, and he did not lack power at Tammany Hall. Tenderloin saloon keepers found it advantageous to buy their beer only from Karsh's Brewery, which Adams owned; by taking beer from him, they said, "you are all right, you will be protected." Burly, bearded, churlish, Adams had made his way up in the world from a humble start as a railroad brakeman, and he liked to compare his career with that of Andrew Carnegie, another outstanding example of American success. He was a businessman, he said, like any other; he was merely more "brilliant" than most. Sometimes he referred to himself as a "gentleman." He resented accusations that he rigged the winning numbers, or that his policy game was crooked. He was always aggrieved when stern moralists pointed out that his wealth was derived from the superstitions of the ignorant who used "dream books" to play policy, and the pocket money of schoolboys. Was pleasure an exclusive privilege of the educated, the elderly and the wealthy? Others catered to them. Adams, like the social-settlement workers, preferred to enliven the bleak existence of underprivileged people, as nearly as possible from the cradle to the grave. And he was willing to make personal sacrifices in order to indulge this philanthropic whim without interference. For Adams was said to pay, every year, more than one hundred thousand dollars to certain other brilliant businessmen who, as public spirited as himself, were devoting their lives to the affairs of Tammany Hall.

Men of wealth and position with a taste for gambling did not lack facilities.

New York had three casinos celebrated throughout the country by reason of their splendor and the affluence of their clientele. Faro, baccarat and roulette were the major attractions of these establishments, where fortunes constantly changed hands. Their proprietors ranked as men of note, whose friendship eminent citizens were proud to claim. The veteran John Daly, whose career had begun in the era of John Morrisey, ran an elegantly appointed house on Twenty-ninth Street, west of Fifth Avenue. It was the favorite resort of Elias Jackson Baldwin—the fabulous California plunger known as "Lucky" Baldwin—on his visits to New York. Many of Daly's other patrons were scarcely less spectacular. Rumor had it that Daly paid one hundred thousand dollars annually for protection, but in spite of this tax reaped enormous profits.

The New York "sporting set" and many wealthy visitors from out of town favored Frank Farrell's place, a few steps west of the Waldorf Hotel on Thirty-third Street. "Diamond Jim" Brady always took his friends and customers there, if they wanted the excitement of playing for high stakes. Farrell was an intimate friend of Captain Devery and other Tammany leaders, so his house was supposed to be reasonably safe. He commissioned Stanford White to remodel the interior of the casino at a cost of five hundred thousand dollars, and thereafter it was known as "The House with the Bronze Door" because, among its other costly decorations, White installed a massive Italian Renaissance bronze door at the rear of the entrance hall. The casino was conducted with the quiet decorum of a gentleman's club. Patrons were served an elaborate buffet supper at midnight; the finest cigars, wines and liquors were continuously available for those who wished them; no money was accepted for any of these refreshments. It was said that at least fifty thousand dollars changed hands every night. There was gossip that, on one night, a lucky patron had gathered in one hundred and sixty-five thousand dollars at the roulette table. Another player was said, on two successive evenings, to have won two hundred and ten thousand dollars—and shortly thereafter to have lost it all, and eighty thousand dollars more. Like many another purveyor of illicit pleasures, Farrell was a confirmed skeptic. He did not consider his patrons and his establishment adequately safeguarded by his personal intimacy with high dignitaries of Tammany, or by his presumably generous payments for protection. He therefore persuaded the syndicate that backed him to purchase the adjoining house, and opened up a concealed exit into it. This provided for the escape of his patrons and employees, and the possible disappearance of his equipment, if he received warning of a forthcoming raid.

No such precautions were considered necessary at the casino run by Richard Canfield. It was known to be the most exclusive resort of its kind in the world. At Canfield's you saw Vanderbilts, Whitneys and other members of the Four Hundred; statesmen like Senator Edward O. Wolcott of Colorado; Wall Street financiers like Jesse Lewisohn, the lover of Lillian Russell and a prominent figure along the "Great White Way"; and—most notorious of all —the multimillionaire John W. Gates, universally called "Bet-a-Million" Gates. Canfield's fame as "the prince of gamblers" was international. He op-

BLUE BLOODS PLAYING FOR BLUE CHIPS, a poker game of 1895, *by A. B. Wenzell*

erated the Club House at Saratoga, the Nautilus Club at Newport, and for many years had his New York establishment on Twenty-sixth Street, west of Delmonico's. When Delmonico's restaurant finally moved to a beautiful new building on the northeast corner of Fifth Avenue and Forty-fourth Street, Canfield transferred his casino to a house on Forty-fourth Street two doors east of Delmonico's. On the decoration and furnishing of this establishment, the prince of gamblers was reported to have spent about one million dollars. It was not only a palace but a museum; it contained one of the finest private art collections in the United States. In a magnificent supper room on the basement floor, patrons were served a repast from eleven o'clock onward and, although Canfield's cuisine and cellar were reputed to be the best in New York, the efforts of his chef were willingly supplemented, on request, by an order to Delmonico's which, like the supper, champagne and cigars, was served without cost. Above the supper room were a beautiful reception room and ornate private offices; in Canfield's office, a concealed safe always held five hundred thousand dollars in cash, although house losses were normally paid by check. The "public" gambling rooms were on the second story, but you seldom saw more than five or six players in them. Private rooms for patrons who wished to exceed the limits set by the house—they were the highest of any establishment in the world—occupied the third story. On the floor above was Canfield's personal apartment, the home of an art collector and bibliophile who had assembled one of the most notable libraries owned by any American.

Access to Canfield's casino was deliberately made difficult. A system of electrically controlled doors, none of which opened until the preceding one had closed, compelled patrons to pass the scrutiny of employees who identified them through peepholes. The prince of gamblers wished nobody admitted who could not afford substantial losses. He always warned patrons that the odds were heavily against them, and that although they might make an occasional "killing" they were inevitably bound to lose in the long run. Players in the public rooms usually began by purchasing five hundred dollars worth of chips; anyone who bought less was treated with faultless courtesy but, on departing, received an intimation that future visits would not be welcomed. Since the clientele was composed chiefly of multimillionaires, losses during an evening sometimes ran into the hundreds of thousands, and in the private rooms, where patrons like "Bet-a-Million" Gates often played as long as forty-eight hours without stopping, losses ran far higher. No player's name was ever spoken by any Canfield employee; patrons were addressed only by the first initial of their last names. Canfield seldom appeared in the gambling rooms or supper room of his establishment, but those patrons whom he considered personal friends could celebrate a winning, or mourn a loss, by joining him for a pint of champagne in his office, a room paneled in white mahogany inlaid with mother of pearl. The prince of gamblers never played any game of chance, though on tips furnished by his Wall Street clients he made fortunes in the stock market. The art collector never admitted his patrons to his private apartment; there, he received only the famous connoisseurs of art and bibliophiles in whose company he preferred to spend his leisure.

New Yorkers acknowledged Canfield to be one of the most fabulous figures of a fabulous era. In his early forties he was tall, heavy, clean-shaven, brown-haired; people always remembered the penetrating gaze of his dark gray eyes. He dressed with great elegance, his manners were courtly, his erudition in the fields of art and literature deeply impressed professional authorities. Yet the formal education of this professional gambler had ended in grammar school. His real education, he said, had begun when, at the age of thirty, he was imprisoned for six months as a common felon. He spent his term in jail reading assiduously and studying. Thereafter, books and art were his hobby and recreation. He said that if he could live his life over again he would become a professor of literature. Reputed to have accumulated a fortune of between five and twelve millions, he declared that he enjoyed money-making as an amusement, but valued money only because it enabled him to indulge his obsessive collector's mania. Like his friend J. P. Morgan, Canfield regarded his passion for art as his sole weakness. Unlike Morgan, however, he cleaned out other millionaires in order to patronize living artists with the proceeds. His greatest pride in life was his intimacy with James McNeill Whistler. Whistler painted Canfield's portrait under the ironical title of "His Reverence"; long afterward the picture was bought by the Cincinnati Museum. In Canfield's gambling palace you could see one of the two major collections of Whistler's work. Three of its finest paintings were later acquired by Henry Clay Frick, and in the Frick Museum could be admired by a generation of Americans to whom Canfield's name signified only a card game which the prince of gamblers had never played. But on one occasion, talking frankly with a reporter, Canfield perfectly expressed the spirit of New York during his time. "I do not know that I have any code of ethics," he said. "I do not care a rap about what other people think about me. I never did. As morals are considered by most people, I have no more than a cat. . . . So long as I can satisfy my own conscience, so long as I know that I am honest with myself, I am satisfied."

This, perhaps, was a gentleman's way of putting it. All New York considered Canfield a most distinguished gentleman, though William Travers Jerome persistently described him as a common felon. Men of high political status were apt to phrase the same creed in other terms. "Everybody is talkin' these days about Tammany growin' rich on graft," said State Senator George Washington Plunkitt, the genial philosopher of Tammany Hall, "but nobody thinks of drawin' the distinction between honest graft and dishonest graft. There's all the difference in the world between the two. Yes, many of our men have grown rich on politics. I have myself. I've made a big fortune out of the game, and I'm gettin' richer every day. But I've not gone in for dishonest graft (blackmailin' saloon keepers, disorderly people, etc.). There's an honest graft, and I'm an example of how it works. I might sum up the whole thing by sayin': 'I seen my opportunities and I took 'em.'" Richard Croker, overlord of New York, compared himself with a businessman in business: "I work for my own pocket all the time." Like many other millionaires, Croker had come up the hard way. Stern-visaged, cold-eyed, with the heavy body of a bruiser, he was a study in iron gray—hair, beard, handsome suit, hat and overcoat were all of the same dark hue. Croker, the child of poor Irish immigrants, had landed in New York in 1846, at the age of three. He had little schooling, a rough youth as a member of the Fourth Avenue Tunnel Gang, got on the city payroll in his early twenties, served as Alderman in the regime of Boss Tweed, was tried for murder after an Election Day battle and was set free because the jury disagreed. But all this was now far in the past and Croker, long boss of Tammany Hall, was a crony of eminent citizens like William C. Whitney, with whom he had in common—aside from business interests—a gentleman's pleasure in maintaining a costly racing stable. Croker had a stud-farm in Richfield Springs, and another in England, where he spent his annual holidays, and he raced his horses on both sides of the Atlantic.

Politics, Croker declared, couldn't be conducted without spoils; you had to bribe Americans to enter politics. Moreover, there had to be a boss; big business couldn't deal with a lot of officials who checked and crossed one another, and who came and went with inconvenient rapidity. "A businessman," he asserted, "wants to do business with one man, and one who is always there to remember and carry out the—business." So Croker considered himself a public servant, a man who worked for his own pocket by facilitating the progress of big business. "Police graft is dirty graft," he acknowledged in a secret conversation. "We have to stand for it. If we get big graft, and the cops and small-fry politicians know it, we can't decently kick at their petty stuff.

Can we, now? We can't be hypocrites, like the reformers who sometimes seem to me not to know that they live on graft. This I tell you, boy, and don't you ever forget it; I never have touched a cent of the dirty police graft myself."

In the end, it was exposure of the dirty police graft that put New Yorkers in a mood of high moral indignation. The Lexow Committee's eminent counsel owed their success to the bewilderment of an adolescent boy. Captain Schmittberger's oldest son had been asked at school whether the things said by the newspapers about his father were true. One night, at the dinner table, the boy asked his father to confirm or deny the reports. Shortly afterward, Captain Schmittberger went on the witness stand—and told all. A tall, handsome, powerful man, Schmittberger was the most popular police official in the city. Taken into the police force in his youth, he had been expertly trained in the "system" and, being absolutely honest, was quickly set to work collecting "protection money" or blackmail. As precinct captain of the Tenderloin, he supervised the collection of graft in the city's most profitable area, and he likewise distributed the take according to an official arrangement—keeping a portion for himself and his subordinates, passing the rest to the district inspector of police, who followed the same routine. Tammany had a regular scale of charges for police appointments. A patrolman paid three hundred dollars for his job; a sergeant, sixteen hundred dollars; the captain of a profitable district might be charged fifteen thousand dollars for his appointment—naturally, this money had to be recouped, and why should an appointment be sought except for the opportunity of making money? Police officials couldn't live decently on their official salaries. And if traction magnates and other representatives of big business were willing to pay handsomely for extra-legal privileges, why shouldn't saloon keepers, brothel owners, operators of gambling establishments do likewise?

After Captain Schmittberger had "squealed," other high police officials were persuaded to tell the Lexow Committee more than they wished to. Inspector Alexander Williams, whom New Yorkers called "Clubber" Williams because he had once remarked that there was more law at the end of a police club than in any courtroom, arrogantly told the Committee, "I am so well known here in New York that car horses nod to me mornings." He had several large bank accounts, owned a home in New York, a costly country estate in Connecticut, a yacht. Williams testified that he made his fortune speculating in real estate—in Japan. But he wasn't above "taking the pigeon from Delmonico's"—collecting the five-dollar fee which Charles Delmonico sent to the police station whenever an elaborate function was held in his restaurant, so that an officer would be assigned to duty at its entrance. The testimony of huge, illiterate Captain "Big Bill" Devery was equally damaging, and the testimony against him more so. Eventually Williams was retired "for the good of the service." Devery was dismissed from the police force, but later returned to be Chief of Police, and to delight the public in published interviews that invariably began with the phrase, "Touchin' on and appertainin' to . . . ." But many citizens lamented the resignation of Superintendent

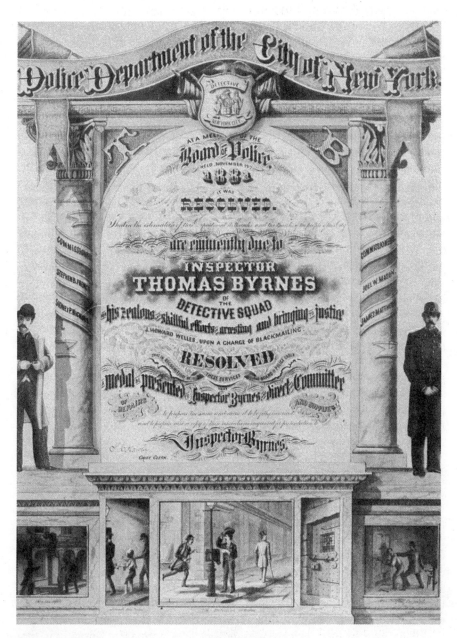

TESTIMONIAL TO INSPECTOR BYRNES

Byrnes. For Thomas F. Byrnes was the most famous detective of his time. He had established the celebrated "deadline" by fixing Fulton Street as the boundary beyond which any known criminal was forbidden to venture downtown.

He had quietly dealt with blackmailers for men prominent in Wall Street, for members of the Four Hundred. Knowing every criminal who operated in the city, he could retrieve, for people of influence, stolen jewels, pilfered wallets, the plunder taken from homes. Was it possible that Byrnes, the "terror of crooks," had plunged his hands into the "dirty police graft"? It was.

Over the many months of hearings conducted by the Lexow Committee, there were indications that a political tempest was brewing. In the Spring of 1894, Boss Croker quietly sailed for England; it was announced that he would remain there indefinitely; he had resigned the titular leadership of Tammany Hall, and had appointed, as his deputy, Thomas F. Gilroy. Public resentment against Tammany had never reached so high a temperature since the Tweed Ring was driven from power. After a mass meeting at Cooper Union the "reform" elements in the city combined into a Fusion Party which, naming William L. Strong, a banker and nominal Republican, as its candidate for Mayor, carried the municipal election in November. Mayor Strong gave the city an honest, efficient administration. Col. George E. Waring reformed the Street Cleaning Department and, as Boss Platt lamented, "no organization leader could get a place from him during his entire administration." Theodore Roosevelt, appointed to the Board of Police Commissioners, eliminated grafting officials and compelled the police to enforce laws which interfered with free access to pleasures formerly easily available. Righteousness ruled the town. But, as Roosevelt later observed, "If a reform administration honestly endeavors to carry out reform, it makes an end of itself at the end of its term and insures the return of Tammany to power."

By the summer of 1897, moral excitement had subsided. Boss Croker returned to New York, resumed his leadership of Tammany and nominated Robert A. Van Wyck, an obscure Tammany judge, as his candidate for Mayor —the first Mayor of Greater New York. Croker probably noticed a novelty injected into New York's life during his absence. The State Legislature had passed the so-called "Raines law" providing that only hotels could serve liquor on Sunday. Since saloon keepers always did excellent business on Sunday, when patrons had plenty of both leisure and money, a way around the new law was quickly found. Proprietors of saloons converted them into hotels by renting the floor above; the upstairs rooms were profitably let to transient couples; casual fornication was made easier than ever before. Downstairs, in the saloons, you couldn't have your drinks at the bar, but you enjoyed them at a table in the "ladies' room" and, since the saloon was, on Sunday, a hotel, they were accompanied by a "rat-cheese" sandwich for which no charge was made, but which nobody was expected to consume. All New York understood the joke of the "Raines-law sandwich"—a permanent "prop," as theatrical folk called it, which symbolized the immorality produced by the moral efforts of reformers. As Senator Plunkitt sagely remarked, "Reformers are mornin' glories—look lovely in the mornin' and wither up in a short time, while the regular machines go on flourishin' like fine old oaks. The fact is, a reformer can't last in politics. He can make a show for a while; but, like a rocket, he always comes down."

For the municipal campaign of 1897, Asa Bird Gardiner, Croker's candidate for District Attorney, provided the slogan that swept the city: "To Hell with Reform." On Election Day, Tammany Hall was given power over Greater New York for four years. That night, the city broke out into an exuberant celebration. From Madison Square north, on Broadway, crowds made an incessant din with tin horns and rasping rattles. Impromptu parades formed, stalling traffic, snake-dancing in the roadway, shouting the refrain of "Well, well, Reform has gone to hell." Street-vendors everywhere were selling toy tigers and little signs reading, "I told you so!" Hotels, theaters, bars and dance halls were jammed with people. The great frenzy of joy continued far into the morning.

And, all night long, the cry of "Wide Open" rang through the Tenderloin and along the Bowery.

18

Meet Me at the Waldorf

To the nation and the world, as the nineteenth century waned, the Waldorf-Astoria Hotel interpreted the spirit of New York. It symbolized the city of titanic power and inexhaustible wealth. It made credible the metropolis that had vaulted the barriers of its girdling rivers, and had begun to lift its towers into the skies. It represented the city which, driven by a gluttonous craving for beauty, was pillaging Europe and the Orient. Most of all, the Waldorf-Astoria spoke eloquently for New York's prodigal extravagance, its delight in costly pleasures, its determination to achieve a scale of luxury and splendor such as men had never before conceived. Like New York itself, the Waldorf-Astoria crystallized the improbable and fabulous. It was more than a mere hotel. It was a vast, glittering, iridescent fantasy that had been conjured up to infect millions of plain Americans with a new ideal—the aspiration to lead an expensive, gregarious life as publicly as possible.

Dedicated to creating desires which it had anticipated, and to inculcating the etiquette of their satisfaction, the Waldorf-Astoria became, in effect, a national university. Teaching the amenities of the highest social life, it wrought profound changes in the tastes, manners and customs of Americans. To citizens of Keokuk and Kokomo and Kansas City it made available, for a few weeks or days, a palace of more stupefying grandeur than any Vanderbilt chateau. To residents of New York's brownstone East Side, to Harlemites and Brooklynites and the cliff dwellers of Central Park West, it afforded an opportunity to duplicate the repast being served to members of the Four Hundred at a nearby table or—far more cheaply—to sit and watch their entrance and exit. All New York knew that, in their Fifth Avenue chateaux, Elbridge T. Gerry and Ogden Mills could entertain one hundred guests at dinner on an hour's notice. At the Waldorf-Astoria any American able to pay the price could do the same. Indeed, the anonymous citizen had at his command services, a cuisine and a décor equaled only by those of multimillionaires. As the wit Oliver Herford remarked, it was the mission of the Waldorf-Astoria to bring exclusiveness to the masses. It existed to fulfill a universal American daydream that had never before become articulate.

As a cultural institution, the influence of the Waldorf-Astoria far exceeded that of the Astor Library, established by a bequest of John Jacob Astor, founder of the dynasty. The great hotel was not, however, conceived as an Astor philanthropy. It merely commemorated the outbreak of a family feud between the founder's descendants. Before repudiating his native land and taking up permanent residence in England, William Waldorf Astor wished to revenge himself on his august aunt, Mrs. Astor. Having failed to displace her as the supreme ruler of New York society, he proposed to evict her from the home which she had made its major shrine. Her mansion occupied the southwest corner of Fifth Avenue and Thirty-fourth Street. A spacious garden separated it from the residence, on the northwest corner of Fifth Avenue and Thirty-third Street, which William Waldorf Astor had inherited from his father, John Jacob Astor III. To accomplish his vindictive purpose, William Waldorf Astor razed his father's home and, on its site, built the Waldorf Hotel.

In 1894, one year after the new hotel opened, Mrs. Astor capitulated to its dishonoring presence. She engaged Richard Morris Hunt to provide her with a new palace far uptown, remote from all plebeian caravanseries. Diplomatic negotiations followed between representatives of her son, John Jacob Astor IV, and agents of his expatriated cousin. The cousins were implacable enemies, but they shared an ancestral trait: neither disdained an accretion to his enormous wealth. The prospect of mutual advantage therefore prevailed over the fact of mutual hatred. John Jacob Astor IV agreed to build, on the site of his mother's home, another hotel—taller, more imposing, in every way more magnificent than the adjoining thirteen-story Waldorf. Designed to form an architectural unit with the Waldorf, the seventeen-story Astoria was built to be operated in conjunction with it as a single hotel. But John Jacob Astor IV protected his spleen by a monitory clause. A bond was required that, on his demand, every interior passage uniting the two buildings would be permanently walled up. Thus his mother's whim, or his own, could immediately terminate a mercenary, provisional alliance with their despised relative.

The alliance between hostile capitalists was inspired by George C. Boldt, a Philadelphia hotel keeper who had leased the Waldorf and there began his apostleship of "marvelous ways of living and luxuries hitherto unattainable." Even before revealing the marvels of the combined Waldorf-Astoria, Boldt managed to impress upon New Yorkers certain fastidious prerequisites of the higher life. If they wished to dine in the Palm Room of the Waldorf—the most exclusive of its restaurants—they would have to appear in full formal attire; white tie and tails were mandatory for gentlemen, evening gowns for ladies. This produced a flutter among the rich and well born, but the decree made a table in the Palm Room almost as desirable as a box at the Metropolitan Opera—and, presently, almost as difficult to secure. Another edict, drastically curtailing the democratic right of American freemen to look as they pleased, became a political issue in New York and the subject of a controversy in the nation's press. Waiters and other functionaries in the Waldorf's restaurants were required to have a fluent command of French and German as well as English; this was considered a legitimate demand, however capricious. But in insisting that all members of his service staff be clean-shaven, and in extending this provision to the cabmen who awaited fares at the entrance to the Waldorf, was not Boldt invading the sacred area of civil liberties guaranteed by the Constitution? Labor unions representing waiters and hack-drivers carried the issue to Governor Roswell P. Flower, himself impressively whiskered. A gubernatorial election was imminent. Warned that thirty-six thousand waiters and cabmen in the state of New York were voters, Governor Flower issued a formal statement sustaining their right to cultivate any kind of facial foliage they wished. But the prestige of connection with the Waldorf outweighed the Governor's spirited defense of personal liberty, and the ban on beards was eventually accepted. Nobody, during the long, bitter battle, drew public attention to the fact that Boldt affected a flowing mustache and trimly pointed beard.

For the unveiling of his hyphenated hostelry in the autumn of 1897, Boldt organized a function to benefit various philanthropic institutions favored by New York's élite. The appeal of sweet charity permitted the sophisticated world of fashion to gratify a curiosity scarcely avowable, because so intensely shared by millions of their undistinguished fellow-citizens. Popular curiosity was abundantly justified. Everybody had heard that the monster structure contained one thousand bedrooms and seven hundred and sixty-five private baths; that three floors were given over to public rooms and state apartments; that the chief chef, Xavier Kuesmeier, received an annual salary of ten thousand dollars—a sum so startling "for merely running a kitchen" that it evoked passionate editorials in both the American and foreign press. The Waldorf-Astoria was not only the largest hotel in the world, but the costliest in point of investment; nearly ten millions, rumor alleged, had been poured into it. Its opening, therefore, became an event of national importance, and this was officially recognized. Unable to attend the affair himself, President McKinley deputed Vice-President Garret A. Hobart to act as his personal representative.

As New Yorkers quickly realized, as Americans from every region of the country and visitors from every country of the world soon learned, there was always something going on at the Waldorf-Astoria. The vast ground floor, with its multiple restaurants and myriad public rooms, was in effect a theater offering a continuous performance in which the actors and actresses also

THE WALDORF-ASTORIA, 1896, *by Hughson Hawley*

constituted the audience. From noon until the early hours of the morning the greatest show in the city proceeded without intermission, so you went there both to see and be seen. A wide, amber-marble corridor, furnished with luxurious chairs and sofas, stretched for three hundred feet along the Thirty-fourth Street side of the hotel and became famous, the world over, as "Peacock Alley"—although it was the plumage of the female bird rather than the male that made this promenade New York's most impressive fashion show. Among the social élite, the new customs of "lunching out" and "having afternoon tea" were launched by the Waldorf-Astoria, and to dine there before attending the theater quickly became the vogue. Tables in the huge crystalline Palm Garden were sometimes engaged weeks in advance, and by seven o'clock a velvet rope, barring its entrance, informed those who dared not claim the highest prestige that they would have to find places in the equally splendid but less aristocratic Empire and Rose Rooms overlooking Fifth Avenue.

If you wished to make an impression on guests whom you were entertaining at the Waldorf-Astoria, it was essential that the *maître d'hôtel* greet you by name. A tall, heavy-set, dignified man of commanding presence, looking rather like an operatic tenor, "Oscar of the Waldorf," as he was universally known, exercised the powers of a social arbiter. To receive his salutation, to enjoy the favor of his genial, expansive smile was a kind of accolade, certifying that birth, wealth, or current celebrity entitled you to rank among the elect. Like royalty, this kindly potentate was identified by his first name alone. "If a stranger were to address me as Mr. Tschirky," he admitted, "I'm almost afraid I'd be a little confused. For I, too, you see, have fallen into the habit of thinking of myself simply as Oscar." Nobody was more thoroughly versed than Oscar in the differentiations applicable to social New York. He had been a head waiter at the Hoffman House, and was intimately acquainted with the political and sporting sets which made that establishment their headquarters. He had been associated with Delmonico's, and thus knew both the old guard and the younger smart set who inhabited the most inaccessible citadel of fashion. He applied for his position at the Waldorf before the building was completed, and Boldt, a stickler for business proprieties, demanded letters of reference. Oscar brought him one letter, accompanied by eight foolscap pages of signatures; the list of his sponsors read like a census of Mrs. Astor's world.

Boldt had made the original Waldorf fashionable by investing it with an aura of exclusiveness. As great a snob as Ward McAllister, he once privately confessed that he would prefer seeing Mrs. Astor drinking an unprofitable cup of hot water in his Palm Garden to serving a wealthy upstart with the costliest dinner that his chef could provide. But Oscar was aware that such notions had become obsolete, that the ancient social barriers were being breached. Besides, how could the vast public spaces of the Waldorf-Astoria be made to pay and yet be kept exclusive? So among the shows provided by this monster civic playhouse, you might have enjoyed a subtle drama—the effort of parvenus to establish themselves securely among the socially exalted. This drama achieved its best performance late at night, for of all social rituals celebrated at the Waldorf-Astoria, after-theater supper was the most fashionable, and therefore most popular. Frequently the consumption of lobster Newburg alone ran to eight hundred portions, and many hundred bottles of champagne washed down these and other delicacies. Feminine occupants of the Metropolitan Opera's Diamond Horseshoe arrived blazing with jewels, their pompadours crowned with tiaras or adorned by plumage that had been torn from egrets, their ermine cloaks as immaculately white as the pearl-studded shirt fronts of the gentlemen to whose superiority their effulgence so dazzlingly testified. By midnight there had congealed, around tables in the Palm Garden, the bluest blood of New York. Yet, as he recorded in his diary, Richard W. G. Welling, a prominent young socialite, saw J. P. Morgan there "with a lot of gayish women—not unusual." Sometimes you would see Lillian Russell or Anna Held or Edna May or Adele Ritchie—these exquisitely gowned queens of musical comedy drew all eyes as they swept to their tables, but their entrance perceptibly lifted aristocratic feminine eyebrows, unmoved by Morgan's equally spectacular entourage. Even more significantly you would see, in the supposedly "exclusive" Palm Garden, gold-plated aspirants from the Middle West, men like John W. Gates, William B. Leeds and Daniel G. Reid, monarchs of steel and tinplate, high-rollers whose Midas touch was more reliable than their social grace. Rumor had it that the highest social prestige was attested when Oscar personally went to a table and suggested the foods and wines to be served. But you might have noticed that he offered this delicate attention to the bluebloods, the barbarians and the beauties alike. Though disciplined in the old distinctions, Oscar was the prophet of a new era that would distinguish itself by ignoring them.

Long before New York society tired of the great, gorgeous, but too democratic hotel, it assembled there for a party which became an international sensation because of its reputedly unprecedented extravagance. The Bradley Martins, hosts at this extraordinary function, represented that "new element," the power and importance of which Mrs. Astor had graciously acknowledged some twenty years earlier. They had been favored disciples of Ward McAllister, and they had won his highest diploma by once constructing, at enormous expense, a temporary ballroom in the rear of their Twentieth Street home for use on a single evening. One winter morning late in 1896 Mrs. Martin, reading her newspaper, belatedly learned that the nation was enduring a hideous financial depression. Trade was paralyzed; the misery of the poor was acute. Naturally, Mrs. Martin recalled the cardinal principle of her mentor. McAllister had always preached that a ball effectively solved all social problems. Would not a great ball furnish an impetus to trade and thereby alleviate the hardships of the poor? Mrs. Martin determined to give one. Immediate action was essential, for affliction could not be permitted to go unchecked. Mrs. Martin decided not to await completion of the Astoria, still many months distant. She sent out twelve hundred invitations for a costume ball at the Waldorf on the night of February 10, 1897, requesting her guests to array themselves for presentation at Versailles during the reign of Louis XV.

A flurry of excitement overwhelmed the prospective guests, and for a fortnight prior to the festivity newspapers throughout the United States and in England regaled their readers with detailed accounts of the costly preparations being made for this spectacular prodigy. Like many another social savior, Mrs. Martin was ungratefully rewarded with obloquy. The rumor that more than a quarter of a million dollars was being spent on the ball brought a storm of abuse on the hostess. Editors, clergymen and politicians denounced the Bradley Martin ball as a flagrant instance of the heartless extravagance of the rich. A few days before the event, Mrs. Martin met Police Commissioner Theodore Roosevelt. "I'm very pleased that you and Mrs. Roosevelt are coming to the ball," she remarked. His reply might have daunted a less resolute philanthropist. "Oh, my wife's going because she's got her costume," Roosevelt said, "but, as one of the commissioners, I shall be outside looking after the police." For a large squad of police were being detailed to protect

New York's aggregated wealth from the possible vengeance of an outraged rabble. There were rumors that "anarchists" were planning to plant bombs at the Bradley Martin residence, and that other dissidents proposed to throw infernal machines through the windows of the Waldorf. All ground-floor windows of the hotel were boarded up, ostensibly to foil the curiosity of un-invited spectators, and a corps of Pinkerton detectives was hired to scrutinize everyone entering the hotel on the day of the ball and to mingle, that night, with the invited guests.

At prodigal expense, a large suite of the ultramodern Waldorf had been transformed into what was fondly thought to be a replica of the halls of state at Versailles during the reign of Louis XV. But society's knowledge of history had diminished since, more than forty years earlier, Mrs. William Colford Schermerhorn had attempted a similar transformation of her mansion on Great Jones Street. The guests at Mrs. Schermerhorn's ball had obediently dressed in the costumes of the pretended period and place. Mrs. Martin's guests revealed a singular propensity to anachronism. Her husband, a man of literal mind, tried to impersonate Louis XV. Mrs. Martin, with habitual wilfulness, rejected the constraints of accuracy. She chose to appear as Mary Stuart, perhaps not aware that the unhappy queen had been decapitated more than a century before Louis XV ascended his throne. To sustain this flighty illusion, she wore jewels valued at fifty thousand dollars. These included a massive ruby necklace originally owned by Marie Antoinette, and a cluster of diamond grapes that had adorned the ample person of Louis XIV. Miss Anne Morgan assumed the role of Pocahontas, in a barbaric but colorful beaded garment reportedly made by Indian squaws. The ideal of aboriginal originality likewise obsessed Richard W. G. Welling. Informed by several august dow-agers that an Indian costume "would not be *de rigueur,*" he decided to defy their prohibition. After days of research at different institutions of learning, he finally contrived to reproduce the authentic costume of an Algonquin chief. This required him to carry a tall war-pole with dangling scalps which, on the evening of the ball, could not be insinuated into a closed carriage. To the delight of crowds on Fifth Avenue, Welling drove to the Waldorf in an open victoria, looking very like one of the wooden effigies placed outside tobac-conists' shops. No less determined to achieve the inappropriately authentic, one of the Belmont brothers pleased curious spectators by dismounting from his carriage in a suit of steel armor inlaid with gold; next day, the world learned that it had cost ten thousand dollars. Mrs. Astor arrived in a costume designed by Worth. It was her amiable intention to duplicate a Van Dyck portrait, but she looked so much more like Mrs. Astor than usual that she received little credit for wearing fancy dress.

Of twelve hundred notables invited to the ball, seven hundred attended it. The wide range of their sartorial caprice inspired the hostess to an innovation. She received her guests seated on a throne placed on a high dais. Below it stood a liveried lackey who, in a loud voice, identified every guest by name, character impersonated, and historical period represented. To be rescued from the chaos of history, society required extensive footnotes.

After cultural preliminaries had been completed, the ball opened with four quadrilles rehearsed for many weeks in advance. These were followed by a cotillion lasting nearly two hours, during which jeweled favors were distributed to the participants. An elaborate supper was then served, and afterward waltzes and two-steps were enjoyed until half-past six in the morning. Three bands furnished continuous music. As Frederick Townsend Martin, brother of the host, recorded, "the power of wealth with its refinement and vulgarity, was everywhere." There had never been a greater display of jewels in New York, he asserted; "in many cases the diamond buttons worn by the men represented thousands of dollars, and the value of the historic gems worn by the ladies baffled description." To quench their thirst, the guests consumed sixty-one cases of champagne, sixty-one bottles of other wines, eleven bottles of whiskey, three bottles of brandy and approximately five hundred bottles of mineral water. Since the party was a brilliant success, Mrs. Martin undoubtedly paid with pleasure a hotel bill which came to slightly more than nine thousand dollars, covering the charges for rooms, service, refreshments and music.

THE BRADLEY MARTIN BALL, February 10, 1897, *by H. McVickar.* Mrs. Bradley Martin is shown in the oval at the top

On the following morning, the front pages of American newspapers were devoted to the Bradley Martin ball, so like "a stately court function in one of the capitals of Europe." Presently, at his Olympia Music Hall, Oscar Hammerstein produced a burlesque, *The Bradley-Radley Ball,* which amused thousands of the socially ineligible. Excoriation of the Bradley Martins continued. When New York City presumed to double their tax assessment, the unfortunate hosts decided that they had endured sufficient notoriety and determined to seek permanent refuge in England. Before going into exile, the Bradley Martins gave a farewell banquet at the Waldorf-Astoria for eighty-six guests. Breathlessly, *The World* reported the splendor with which these eminent sybarites invested the melancholy function. The total wealth possessed by the forty gentlemen present was "more than most men can grasp." There were a dozen guests having individual fortunes of ten millions or more. Nearly twice that many could reckon their means at five millions. Among the lot, fewer than a half-dozen were so undistinguished as not to be millionaires. The consorts of these gentlemen wore "enough diamond crowns to fit out all the crowned heads of Europe and have some over for Asia and Africa; there were necklaces worth one hundred thousand dollars apiece on several throats." Indeed, as *The World* summed it up, the occasion was "a delirium of wealth and an idyll of luxury and magnificence." The banquet which Oscar served to these magnificoes probably assuaged their grief at the exile of their hosts. One detail, at least, should have had an anesthetic effect. Everyone knew that the banquet cost more than one hundred and sixteen dollars a plate.

The Waldorf-Astoria transformed the art of gastronomy from a pursuit of patricians into a popular recreation. Was there any housewife in the land who failed to offer her guests a "Waldorf salad"—an ineffable composition of chopped celery, apples and walnuts, copiously drenched with mayonnaise and artistically committed to a bed of lettuce leaves? Few brides failed to receive, as wedding presents, an impressive novelty introduced by the Waldorf-Astoria, the chafing dish. In this ceremonious utensil they learned to prepare two culinary specialties of the famous hotel: chicken a la king and lobster Newburg. Gold prospectors in distant Alaska were soon demanding "Oscar sauce," a mysterious bottled condiment that the hotel made available to the nation. Through personal visits to the Waldorf-Astoria, or through published accounts of its cuisine, the democratic notion of a "swell feed" was gradually refined, polished and elevated. Oscar himself promulgated a gospel that, widely reported, announced a goal for national aspiration. "I admit frankly that when I am called upon to tempt the appetite of a cultured gastronomic organ, where eye and ear must serve as a whet, I receive my greatest delight and inspiration. Add to this order that other *carte blanche*—which lays no limit upon expenditure—then, indeed, one realizes that he has received a summons to create a work of artistic good cheer that should live in the memory of every participant. I have made it a rule, whatever the purpose of the feast, to work out my dinner with a settled design, what musicians would call *leitmotif.*" Like many other potent evangels, this seemed a trifle obscure. But

Oscar repeatedly clarified it in concrete applications that were as awesome as miracles. One of these, reported by newspapers throughout the country, deeply impressed the entire nation. Whether or not it had a *leitmotif,* its general effect was superlatively Wagnerian. The occasion was a dinner to which Randolph Guggenheimer, president of New York's Municipal Council, invited certain political associates and their wives. There were forty guests, drawn from the élite of Tammany Hall, and their "cultured gastronomic organs" were insidiously tempted by a repast which, with its accompanying wines, cost the host ten thousand dollars, or two hundred and fifty dollars a plate.

The function was held on a February evening when New York was suffering from freezing cold. Guggenheimer's guests assembled in an arbor festooned with immense clusters of hothouse grapes. Midsummer prevailed in the banquet hall, a bower of flowering rosebushes in which rare caged birds were trilling. A pool in the center of the table was banked with masses of orchids, acacias, lilies and American Beauty roses. Jeweled matchboxes for the gentlemen and jeweled perfume bottles for the ladies reposed on the napkins at every place. Elaborate *hors d'oeuvre* were followed by oyster cocktails. Then came green turtle soup, succeeded by a delicately sauced fish. A columbine of chicken was served next. After it, there was brought on a roast of mountain sheep with purée of chestnuts, jelly and two hothouse vegetables. A fancy sherbet preceded diamond-back terrapin and ruddy duck, which were followed by a fruit salad. Blue raspberries, fresh strawberries, and a vanilla mousse came next. The repast came to an end with bonbons, fruits and coffee. A fine Amontillado sherry, two very rare wines and two champagnes of superior vintage accompanied the appropriate courses, and liqueurs came on with coffee.

After accounts of this banquet had been broadcast over the land, there was no excuse for any American to be ignorant of the nature of a "genuinely deluxe meal." Obviously, it could not be duplicated by the average citizen— but the average citizen's wife began dreaming of the ten-course dinners over which, on festive occasions, she would certainly preside if and when her husband's ship came in. While awaiting its arrival she could, however, imitate the Waldorf-Astoria's practice of lighting a table with rose-shaded candles. Instead of jeweled favors for her guests, she could surprise them with a ruffled, beribboned "Jack Horner pie." The humble egg was soon being ubiquitously deviled; the salty anchovy and oily sardine were forced on reluctant native palates; sherbets achieved a common-law marriage with roasts; fruit salad became a national mental hazard; and local confectioners did a prodigious business in fancy ices that looked like mortuary monuments —rococo structures of spun sugar, lace-paper frills, satin ribbon bows, adorned with candy flowers and bisque figures. For better or worse, the Waldorf-Astoria gave "company dinner" in many American cities an entirely new look.

Masculine interest in the great new hotel centered on the Men's Café. This was a lofty, spacious hall paneled in dark wood, liberally provided with tables around which there were grouped comfortable armchairs. A huge, four-sided mahogany bar served by eight bartenders dominated the room, and its repertory of liquid refreshments ran to nearly five hundred different concoctions. Not far from the bar a "free-lunch" table offered Virginia hams, Vermont turkeys, various hot delicacies in casseroles and a temptingly assorted cold buffet. After the Stock Exchange closed, at three o'clock, the Men's Café became an uptown extension of Wall Street. Between the hours of four and seven you were likely to see men whose operations in the stock market were making financial history, and others who were consolidating companies into gigantic "trusts" controlling entire industries. Occasionally, J. P. Morgan honored the Men's Café with his presence. "Morgan, the great financial Gorgon," as a popular song described him, usually sat at a table alone, looking like a Colossus; glowering, grim, red-faced, with restless, dark, burning eyes. Taciturn, enigmatic Henry Clay Frick and "Smiling Charlie" Schwab, partners of Andrew Carnegie, were frequently there. So was Judge William Henry Moore, a suave, cultivated gentleman who had already created three great trusts in steel, matches and biscuits. People were already beginning to speak of Judge Elbert H. Gary, a cold, precise, astute corporation lawyer from Chicago, as a coming man. With Morgan's approval and support, Gary had combined large steel interests into the Federal Steel Company, a two-hundred-million-dollar trust which was Carnegie's most formidable competitor. And even earlier, with John W. Gates, Gary had formed the wire-nail trust, building this consolidation in the Waldorf-Astoria—in the Men's Café, in the elaborate suite upstairs for which Gates was said to pay twenty thousand dollars a year, in the private dining rooms and parlors where Gates and his crowd often gambled all night and far into the next day.

The Waldorf-Astoria was a rallying point for big business, which Gates so picturesquely exemplified that the general public found it hard to distinguish between big business and big gambling. To Gates himself, the possibility of such a distinction might never have occurred. To gamble for stakes higher than the human imagination had ever before conceived was not only his amusement but his vocation. He liked to risk immense sums—and it made little difference to him whether he bet on the success of an industrial "trust," the turn of a card, the fleetness of a horse, the course of the stock market, the progress of two raindrops down a windowpane, or engaged in a prolonged trial of luck at poker, baccarat or roulette. A tall, stout man, heavily mustached, his loud joviality masked a ruthless will. Crude and vulgar, his lack of breeding disconcerted polite folk. J. P. Morgan couldn't abide him, and in the end excluded him from the billion-dollar United States Steel Corporation —the greatest of all "trusts," a project which Gates dreamed up, one evening, while dining with some of his cronies in the Men's Café.

The grandiose alone appealed to Gates, and this made him a symbol of the times. In the minds of New Yorkers he became inseparably identified with the Waldorf-Astoria; the vast, glittering hotel was the most appropriate of

THE WALDORF BAR, *by W. A. Rogers.* "Bet-a-Million" Gates in the right foreground

domiciles for an imagination capable of dealing in nothing less than superlatives. One night when Gates and some of his cronies were playing poker, having set the limit of bets at one thousand dollars, Judge Gary sent word that he would like to join the game. "Tell Judge Gary," said Gates, "that the game is going to be so high it would be over his head." And, on another occasion, after a convivial, luxurious dinner, Gates and his crowd began playing baccarat. When the session terminated, at five in the morning, more than one million dollars had changed hands. Gates's wife sometimes lacked sympathy with her husband's favorite recreation, which kept him absent for unpredictable hours. If, on his return, he reported heavy losses, there was apt to be a scene, and on the following day Gates usually made amends with a handsome trinket, a necklace or diamond brooch for which he paid fifty thousand dollars or more. But if Gates had made a killing, Mrs. Gates cheerfully celebrated good fortune. In their huge, ornate apartment, George Boldt had installed a pantry containing a small range. Mrs. Gates would make coffee, whip up a batter, and prepare the flapjacks that had been her husband's favorite fare in their ungilded youth. To these occasions, the cuisine of the Waldorf-Astoria was inadequate.

New York society was only briefly faithful to the mammoth hotel. To ultrafashionable circles the presence of an indiscriminate throng soon became distasteful. Even before William Waldorf Astor had built the Waldorf, an enterprising caterer, Louis Sherry, opened a restaurant on Fifth Avenue and Thirty-sixth Street and won away from Delmonico's the Patriarchs' and Assembly balls. Shortly after the Waldorf-Astoria was completed, Sherry commissioned Stanford White to design a new, more splendid establishment to be built on the southwest corner of Forty-fourth Street. Diagonally across the avenue, on the northeast corner, Delmonico's erected a handsome building and moved into it. Deliberately rejecting the ostentatious magnificence of the Waldorf-Astoria, Sherry's and Delmonico's achieved an atmosphere of quiet elegance, and attempted to maintain a reputation for social exclusiveness. It was at Sherry's, one Sunday night, that Mrs. Stuyvesant Fish and Mrs. Burke Roche launched a minor social revolution. In London, they had seen aristocratic ladies dining in fashionable restaurants, on the Sabbath, hatless and wearing low-cut evening dresses. Resolving to flout New York tradition, they caused a sensation at Sherry's by appearing with heads uncovered, in gowns that offered a shameless exposure of flesh. The innovation was widely disapproved; even the press deplored this scandalous example set by two members of the highest social rank. But Mrs. Astor was diplomatically persuaded to confound all critics and rescue her errant subjects from obloquy. With a fine sense of *noblesse oblige,* she broke her rule of never dining in a public place. On a Sunday night she swept regally into Sherry's on the arm of Harry Lehr. To the amazement of the fashionables who were dining there, Mrs. Astor was wearing "a coquettish raiment of white satin, with the tiniest headdress, and her famous pearls." The momentous issue, as everybody realized, was settled forever.

19

Storm Over Olympus

$\mathbb{A}$t Grace Church, on a wintry day in 1895, they were celebrating the obsequies of pompous, paunchy Ward McAllister. The Grand Chamberlain, the autocrat of drawing rooms, the discoverer of the Mystic Rose and inventor of the Four Hundred had passed to his eternal reward at the age of sixty-eight. You might have expected the entire celestial hierarchy to assemble in final tribute to their mentor and chief of protocol. But it was startling to see how little his memory was honored. Society ignored the dead lion. Only five Patriarchs, only a handful of the lesser elect attended his funeral. The general public crowded into the church out of curiosity, and the band of musicians that had played at all the balls which he arranged attended in a body. It was their last public appearance; these masters of discreet harmony were disbanding.

Indeed, in society, harmony had perished and discretion appeared to be obsolete. McAllister's star was already waning when, five years before his death, he published *Society as I Have Found It,* a fatuous volume of memoirs that brought about his eclipse in a storm of laughter. In *Life* there appeared a cartoon of a policeman reporting to his captain with two drunks in formal evening attire. "What's that you've got, O'Hara?" the captain inquired "Society as Oi have found it, sorr!" With utter seriousness, with portentous solemnity, McAllister had inadvertently held New York's élite up to ridicule. His downfall was instantaneous and irrevocable. Society writhed while the nation giggled. Having committed the unpardonable sin, McAllister was promptly repudiated by his disciples. "McAllister is a discharged servant. That is all," Stuyvesant Fish informed the press when asked whether, as usual, the durable arbiter of elegance was assuming direction of a great ball. This cashiering was a symptom of the increasing boredom of the elect. Perhaps the nature of their diversions was ineffable, but a suspicion that they were tedious could not be suppressed. Two years after McAllister's unlamented death the Patriarchs whom he had constituted a quarter of a century earlier held their last ball at Sherry's. Then, preferring to abdicate rather than appease the relentless new dispensation, they too disbanded. Was not suicide more honorable than surrender?

The tocsin of revolution had rung out in Sherry's only a few months before, and its reverberations were still alarming conservatives throughout the country. Herbert Barnum Seeley, a nephew of the late Phineas T. Barnum, was a man of means who led a muted existence on the outer fringes of the social citadel. He craved recognition; he coveted the accolade; he aspired to the fame of a man about town. The approaching marriage of his brother gave him an opportunity to move toward his goal. He determined to give a bachelor dinner at Sherry's in honor of the prospective bridegroom. Inviting some fifty gentlemen of established social position, he hinted that they would be diverted with original entertainment. Originality as conceived by a descendant of the great showman was scarcely to be ignored, and his invitations were accepted with alacrity. Unfortunately Seeley had inherited none of his uncle's astuteness in dealing with theatrical agents. He made a contract with one, then canceled it in favor of another who promised to supply superior talent at a lower price. His frugality proved to be misguided. The aggrieved agent whose contract Seeley revoked decided to have his revenge. On the night of the banquet, accompanied by several professional colleagues, he presented himself to Captain Chapman at the Tenderloin police station. Obscene, disorderly, unlawful doings were taking place at Sherry's, Captain Chapman was told. Before a drunken, lustful crowd of the idle rich, women were dancing "in the altogether." One tearful complainant, afterward identified as a vaudeville agent, asserted that his "daughter" was undoubtedly being forced, against her will, to divest herself of the ultimate safeguards of chastity. The horrified Czar of the Tenderloin listened no longer. With six detectives he raced to Sherry's, broke into that sacred resort of patriarchs and matriarchs, appeared before Seeley and his appalled guests. Alas, not a single specimen of nude femininity was to be found. After pronouncing a stern warning, Captain Chapman and his detectives withdrew.

But the scandalous story broke in the yellow press. Seeley and his unfortunate guests—some of them married men—became nationally notorious. It developed that the performer whom Captain Chapman sought to apprehend was none other than Little Egypt, a buxom cultural missionary who, at the Columbian Exposition in Chicago, had titillated unsophisticated Americans by introducing the stomach dance, or "hoochy-koochy." Had she—as the yellow press alleged—exhibited this exotic depravity to Seeley and his guests, clad in nothing at all, and elevated on a Sherry banquet table? The whole nation wondered. In the end, Little Egypt issued a public statement. She had not danced "in the altogether," although it had been her intention to do so, merely to satisfy her esthetic impulses. After Captain Chapman's unmannerly intrusion, she had danced, but clad in a Zouave jacket and a pair of lace drawers. An encore was demanded, and she was preparing to "throw everything overboard" when, unnerved by Chapman's warning, she abandoned that pleasant project and merely repeated her first dance. Art had suffered; Seeley and his guests had been deprived of a unique experience; but the puritanical morals of the police had triumphed. The scandal of the Seeley banquet rang through the press during many weeks. Americans discounted the testimony of "the sinuous Oriental dancing woman." And Herbert Barnum Seeley, no longer even on the periphery of society, but no longer obscure, was credited with achieving "the gayest, raciest dinner ever given in New York."

Yet, as many knowing New Yorkers surmised, the peculiar primacy of Seeley's banquet may have been exaggerated. There were rumors afloat about two other functions which surpassed it. Oddly enough, both involved the use of that innocent social resource of provincial hostesses—the Jack Horner pie. A story was going round that a wealthy bachelor, James L. Breese, had given a dinner and used a huge Jack Horner pie as the centerpiece of his table. At an appropriate moment the confection opened and from it emerged, to dance on the table, a young woman worthy of contemplation if for no other reason than because she was "covered only by the ceiling." The second savory bit of gossip related to a birthday supper allegedly tendered "Diamond Jim" Brady by Stanford White, in his studio high in the tower of Madison Square Garden. What common denominator of taste united gross, gaudy, illiterate Brady and the famous architect, whose erudition and fine esthetic sensibility were praised by all his friends? Both men had a weakness for outstanding exemplars of feminine pulchritude, especially if their charm was not spoiled by wearisome inhibitions. On the occasion of the rumored supper party, Brady and ten other men joined White after the theater. When dessert was to be served, so the story ran, waiters brought on an immense Jack Horner pie, in lieu of a birthday cake. This was set on the table. A red ribbon was handed to Brady, a white ribbon to each of the other guests and the host. When the ribbons were pulled a beautiful girl arose from the pie. Brady's red ribbon was fastened to her arm, and this encouraged him to reel it in. Instantly, the lovely creature revealed that she was as destitute of inhibitions as of apparel. Unkind comment on the host's parsimony was made by the other guests, for in the highest circles a prodigal distribution of "favors" was customary on occasions of exceptional festivity. After a few moments, White clapped his hands. The doors opened. Unadorned even by ribbons, eleven girls pranced in to placate the disappointed connoisseurs.

Though she did not adopt these dubious innovations, Mrs. Astor made certain concessions to social progress. She gave a dinner for Mrs. Potter Palmer of Chicago, a city deplorably located somewhere beyond the Hudson and unvisited by her. Convinced that a vast social wilderness stretched westward from Central Park to the Pacific Ocean, Mrs. Astor made the astonishing discovery that not all of its inhabitants were Indians, or the descendants of fur-trappers employed by her husband's grandfather. But she believed that progress must be governed by propriety. She resolutely opposed the new vogue of bridge-whist as an after-dinner relaxation. Following the old custom, she relied upon the conversation of her guests to provide entertainment when they had left her table. As *The Times* explained, she continued "to wield the only scepter possible in a democratic country—that of womanly kindliness, refinement, discretion and tact." Yet her subjects betrayed symptoms of restiveness and ennui. Her daughter-in-law, the exquisite Mrs. John Jacob Astor IV, favored more sparkling parties and more amusing people, and at her balls was likely to offset the stately elegance of a cotillion with a program of songs by Mme. Melba, Mme. Nordica, or some equally luminous star of the Metropolitan Opera. Richard W. G. Welling attended one of Mrs. Astor's afternoon receptions and found there "all the plain, good people whom she keeps on her list and whom young Mrs. Jack Astor *excludes*. The smart ones stayed away, mostly." When, before, had anyone—smart, or not—ignored the imperial summons? And when had any hostess dared to exclude people, however plain and good and possibly dull, whom Mrs. Astor ennobled by keeping on her list?

Americans at large, convinced that her new palace was the nation's social capitol, persistently affirmed that Mrs. Astor's annual ball was the most important of social events. A dense aura of universal faith surrounded this holiest of rituals, and the most cynical apostates succumbed to its contagion. Even for infidels the sacramental ceremony retained its awesome significance. Life held no more bitter mortification than failure to receive a command

SOCIETY TAKES ITS PLEASURE IN THE PARK, 1892. General Logan, Jr., and his wife, *by Louis Maurer*

to participate. Year after year, the hierarchy assembled for solemn worship of the Mystic Rose. In her magnificent shrine, standing beneath the portrait by Carolus Duran, blazing with diamonds, robed by Worth with a vestment of velvet and old lace embroidered in gold or silver, she accepted the homage of the faithful and the merely superstitious. Nearing her seventieth year, wigged and wrinkled and withered, she nevertheless seemed immortal, like a mummy or an idol that time had ironically preserved instead of destroying. The traditional liturgy of quadrilles and cotillion continued to be performed. The figures became more complicated, the favors more costly. But the old guard were aware of the changes. At one end of the immense gilded ballroom, a large divan stood on a dais, known to the elect as "the Throne." Who would share its august but inextensible surface with Mrs. Astor, her daughter and daughter-in-law? There was an annual "throne list." Inclusion signified the ultimate beatitude. At one ball, failing to receive a place on the throne, Mrs. John Drexel—a dowager of impeccable ancestry—burst into noisy tears and fled, crushed by her public humiliation. The throne was a novelty, a recognition of the need—amidst increasing vulgarity and a rising indifference to discrimination—of maintaining the aristocratic principle. Mrs. Ogden Mills, arrogant descendant of the landed Livingstons, had pronounced her own verdict: "There are really only twenty families in New York." Mrs. Astor, whose Schermerhorn ancestors had derived their wealth from commerce, acknowledged the doctrine but rejected the census. The guest list of her ball defined the sacred hierarchy; her dinner list of one hundred and fifty names determined the inner circle. Who was Mrs. Ogden Mills that she should presume to designate the most exalted? Mrs. Astor's throne accommodated far fewer than twenty. It was perhaps unfortunate that the measurement of mortal buttocks should be the final determinant.

Even more remarkable a novelty than her throne was Mrs. Astor's new chamberlain, McAllister's successor. He was her principal concession to social progress. His investiture expressed her tacit admission that manners and morals were changing, that dignity, ceremonious formality and fastidious standards were becoming obsolete. Socially, at least, she invented Harry Lehr. She created him to arrest the dangerous blight of boredom and restlessness attacking her world. Under her supervision he would discipline the new taste for frivolity, the new cult of the bizarre. Harry Lehr was her latest stratagem and only fatal illusion. How could she foresee that this prodigy of her old age would become the most affectionate of traitors, engaging in a conspiracy against her? Blond, plump, petulant, waspish, with a fluty voice and a mincing gait, Harry Lehr was an opportunist who had resolved to live by his wits. Lacking wealth, abhorring work, craving luxury, his elevation to the office of major-domo for Mrs. Astor endowed him with social power, which he turned to profitable account. Fashionable tailors, haberdashers, jewelers, florists, hotels and restaurants gladly supplied his wants without cost, assuming that his patronage would bring them the wealthiest clientele. George Kessler, agent for a noted French champagne, paid Lehr six thousand dollars a year to fill the cellars of society with it. "I make a career of being popular," Lehr declared with unaccustomed candor. And he said, of Ward McAllister, "He was the voice crying in the wilderness who prepared the way for me."

McAllister had taught society that extravagance must be conspicuous. Lehr was attuned to the new times. He realized that the sillier extravagance became, the more arresting its effect. He had a talent for female impersonation and drew on a well-stocked wardrobe of wigs and dresses to exercise it. It may have been this talent which most recommended him to Mrs. Stuyvesant Fish, a very distinguished dowager. For in her softer moods, which were infrequent, Mrs. Fish also impersonated the feminine. Stanford White created for her a magnificent palace on the northwest corner of Madison Avenue and Seventy-eighth Street, in the Venetian style. Society called it the "palace of the doges," without perceiving the famous architect's malice. The doges were the chief magistrates of the republic of Venice—but they had no real power. In her palace, Mrs. Fish commanded the installation of a splendid Gothic bedroom at prodigal cost. After it had been completed, she refused to sleep in it, but had another bed put in her adjoining dressing room; she was intimidated by the authentic. She was intimidated by her butler. He, too, was authentic; he had served in English ducal families, a fact which he never failed to impress on all with whom he came in contact. Morton had only one failing, a fine taste in wines. On a day when Mrs. Fish had unexpectedly invited many guests for luncheon, Morton was moved to alcoholic acerbity. "I suppose that because you happen to be Mrs. Stuyvesant Fish, you think you can drive up and down the Avenue inviting whom you like to the house," he informed her. "Well, let me tell you, you can't. Sixteen is my limit, and if you ask any more they go hungry!" The next day, Morton was dismissed, although on that evening Mrs. Fish was giving a large dinner party. His revenge was exquisitely subtle. He merely unscrewed the whole of the Fish gold dinner service into three hundred separate pieces and jumbled them into a single heap on the dining-room floor.

Mrs. Fish abhorred dullness even more than Dr. Parkhurst abominated sin. Like him, she felt a call. Like him, she embarked on a crusade. Quick-tempered, malicious, easily bored and incapable of enduring monotony, she proposed to purge society of its stodginess. How more amusingly than by compelling society to make itself absurd? She was reputed to be witty, though her wit usually took the form of imaginative insult. "Make yourself perfectly at home," she greeted a group of dinner guests. "And, believe me, there is no one who wishes you there more heartily than I do." She welcomed another company of friends with the remark, "Well, here you all are, older faces and younger clothes." To a gentleman who paid his respects at one of her parties, she said, "Oh, how do you do! I had quite forgotten I asked you." Bored by one of her own parties, she terminated it at an early hour by ordering the orchestra to play "Home Sweet Home" continuously until her guests had taken the hint; still playing, it followed the last lingering revelers downstairs to the front door. "I'm so tired of being hypocritically polite," she complained to one of her intimates. She preferred to be spontaneously rude. With whim and malice as her only guides, she made bad manners so fashionable that they came to seem good.

In Harry Lehr, Mrs. Fish recognized a kindred spirit. They were both astute, cynical judges of their environment; they saw how easily it could be dominated by insolence, spite and savage ways. "Mrs. Astor is an elderly woman," Mrs. Fish observed blandly, and determined to seize the scepter. With Lehr's aid, she launched a palace revolution. For Mrs. Astor's ten-course banquets, she substituted dinners served in fifty minutes flat. For after-dinner conversation, she substituted professional entertainers or noisy ragtime bands. One night, in her ballroom, a troupe from the circus performed and a baby elephant circulated among the guests passing out peanuts. On another evening, the chorus of a musical comedy went through its dance routines, and boys dressed as cats distributed favors which, to the horror of the ladies, turned out to be lively white mice. This, perhaps, was Mrs. Fish's commentary on the favors bestowed at a great ball given by Mrs. Pembroke Jones— diamond bangles and diamond scarf-pins. She never saw any reason to dispute Harry Lehr's verdict on New York society: "I saw that most human beings are fools, and that the best way to live harmoniously with them and make them like you is to pander to their stupidity. They want to be entertained, to be made to laugh. They will overlook almost anything so long as you amuse them."

Together, Mrs. Fish and Lehr perfected techniques of sophisticated silliness that captivated the elect. They sponsored a dinner party for dolls at which everyone conversed in baby-talk, and gave a banquet for one hundred dogs at which, it was said, the owner of the guest of honor decorated his unpedigreed pet with a diamond collar costing fifteen thousand dollars. On another occasion, they invited a large party to dinner, announcing as the guest of honor Prince del Drago, an unknown foreign friend of the Chicago speculator Joseph Leiter. When the guests had assembled, Leiter arrived holding by the hand a small monkey attired in full evening dress, and at the table the creature was seated in the place of honor usually reserved for Mrs. Astor. As a result of this function, Mrs. Fish and Lehr were accused by the press of having "held up American society to ridicule." Far from being fatal, this indictment gave added luster to their bloodless reign of terror.

Contemplating the twilight of her long reign, the treachery of her chamberlain and the disintegration of her hierarchy, Mrs. Astor gave an unprecedented interview to a newspaper reporter. "I am not vain enough to believe that New York will not be able to get along without me," she announced to the American people. "Many women will rise up to fill my place. But I hope that my influence will be felt in one thing, and that is, in discountenancing the undignified methods employed by certain New York women to attract a following. They have given entertainments that belonged under a circus tent rather than in a gentlewoman's house." Her influence continued to be felt at the Metropolitan Opera, on Monday nights, when the fashionable world assembled to do its duty by art and put itself on display to the populace. Fortunately Mrs. Fish detested music and seldom attended, so her aura of mild lunacy, her perfume of sawdust and tanbark never pervaded the cavernous red-and-gold auditorium except when *Aida* was performed, and refractory, moth-eaten animals were led across the stage. Realizing that the plebeian public, however interested in the performance on the stage, was excited by the performance being given in the horseshoes, the management helpfully provided diagrams showing the location of every box and identifying its proprietor. Thus the audience was enabled to recognize its favorite non-professional stars.

Eyes always turned first to Mrs. Astor's box. The public had come to venerate the gallant old lady, and was almost as proud of her presence as it was eager to see her celebrated diamond stomacher and tiara. None of the current boxholders carried fantasy to the perfection formerly cultivated by Mrs. Louis Hammersley, who had had the walls and ceiling of the salon behind her box entirely concealed by festoons of orchids. Nevertheless, during intermissions, in a blaze of light, the two tiers of boxes made a brave show. Every woman wore full regalia, and in the matter of gown and jewels attempted to outshine her neighbors. Diamond tiaras, ropes of pearls, enormous sapphires and emeralds accented the superb upholstery turned out by Worth or Callot or Paquin. The most vexatious problem confronting these ladies, as one of them acknowledged, was to devise some novel way of displaying a profusion of jewels. Mrs. John Drexel therefore ceased to carry her priceless pearls beneath her multiple chins. She had them reset in a wide band which belted her waist, diagonally crossed her imposing bosom and shoulder, and descended her back. Mrs. Frederick Vanderbilt, having heard that Venetian beauties of the Renaissance liked to toy with a single jewel at the end of a chain, decided to wear one dangling at her feet. She progressed to her box kicking a great uncut ruby or sapphire attached to her waist by a rope of pearls. This was invisible to the audience when she was seated, a fact which gave her whim an added touch of distinction, for what could be more impressive than the studied concealment of so extravagant an ornament? More conscientious in the performance of her parade duty was another lady who, in order to exhibit her gowns and jewels adequately, had an unusually high chair built for her box so that the maximum of her expansive, glittering torso would be visible. Any of these ladies would have agreed with Mrs. O. H. P. Belmont, the former Alva Vanderbilt. "I know of no profession, art, or trade that women are working in today," she declared, "as taxing on mental resource as being a leader of society."

Mental resource was severely taxed by two intrepid women who were creating a vogue for the most improbable of diversions—brilliant talk. Miss Elsie de Wolfe and Miss Elisabeth Marbury had installed themselves in Washington Irving's old home, far downtown on the southwest corner of Irving Place and Seventeenth Street, and their Sunday-afternoon parties were already famous. Fat, jolly Miss Marbury was a play-broker and literary agent. She represented many eminent writers, and visiting European celebrities habitually made her their social impresario. Miss de Wolfe, having won acclaim as an amateur actress, had gone on the stage and become one of Charles Frohman's stars. Not content with her fame as the best-dressed woman on the American stage, she deserted this profession to embark on a new career as an interior decorator—and millionaires were finding her notions of elegance far more costly than their own untutored, wistful dreams of splendor. Elegance was apparent in the little French drawing room, the marble-paved hall, the ivory-and-yellow dining room which, on Sunday afternoons, overflowed with painters and poets and politicians, singers and actresses, authors and playwrights. "You never know whom you are going to meet at Bessie's and Elsie's," William C. Whitney told his friends, "but you can always be sure that they will be interesting and that you will have a good time."

So society clamored to be invited to parties that were given in order to produce the friction of ideas, where anybody who could contribute to the play of minds was welcome, be it Sarah Bernhardt, Paderewski, or Theodore Roosevelt. Cynical old Henry Adams found the house filled by a mad cyclone of people and was dazzled by their brilliancy. Even Mrs. Astor was deeply impressed by the social novelty of intelligence. "I am having a Bohemian party, too," she told Miss de Wolfe and, when asked upon whom she relied to give it a Bohemian atmosphere, showed her adaptability to the new vogue. "Why, J. P. Morgan," she replied, "and Edith Wharton."

Not being gifted with prevision, the guests of Miss Marbury and Miss de Wolfe could not know the true fame of one of their captive, foreign lions. (Somewhat later he would figure in Marcel Proust's great novel, *Remembrance of Things Past,* as the Baron de Charlus.) Nevertheless, his visit to New York caused a flutter in the sophisticated smart set. Society, inured to the female impersonations of Harry Lehr, was slightly disconcerted by the eccentricities of Comte Robert de Montesquiou. A member of the highest

SOCIETY PATRONIZES AN ARTIST, 1892, *by Charles Dana Gibson*

French nobility, an autocrat of Paris salons, a poet and a celebrated deviser of exotic parties, he had been imported by Miss Marbury to lecture to fashionable ladies. His distinguished lineage made him a social prize for the elect, always responsive to European titles. Montesquiou's conversation sparkled; his insolence and haughtiness were appreciated in exclusive circles. Fashionable ladies concealed their surprise at his appearance—he rouged his cheeks and lips, beaded his eyelashes with mascara, wore corsets. He appraised them critically as hostesses, but his interest in them as women was humiliatingly deficient. Worse still, he took no pains to disguise the violence of his emotions, or the nature of his love affairs.

A connoisseur of exotic revels, Montesquiou might have approved the project conceived by James Hazen Hyde, who had just come into the fortune amassed by his father as president of the Equitable Life Assurance Society. He determined to give a costume ball which would eclipse in splendor any function of the kind ever held in New York. He enlisted the talents of Stanford White, who transformed Sherry's large ballroom into a reproduction of the Hall of Mirrors at Versailles, with its floor carpeted in rose petals and its walls embellished by thousands of orchids. The guests were requested to wear court costume; waiters and other attendants were attired in the livery and perukes of royal lackeys. The celebrated actress Gabrielle Réjane was brought from France to emerge from a sedan chair and recite some verse. At supper, caviar and diamond-back terrapin were on the menu, and only the costliest of champagnes were served. All in all, the host could scarcely doubt that he had achieved his ambition. As he had proudly announced that the function was costing him two hundred thousand dollars, its success seemed inevitable. But the costly fantasy was widely reported by the press, with a tone of extreme disapproval. Public confidence in insurance companies was seriously weakened, and an official investigation of their affairs soon followed. As a result, James Hazen Hyde found it expedient hastily to take up residence in Paris.

However indifferent to public opinion, society was nervously susceptible to blackmail. Its apprehensiveness was profitably exploited by Colonel William D'Alton Mann, a patriarchal, debonair veteran of the Civil War who had a strong addiction to experiment. Colonel Mann was a familiar figure along Fifth Avenue, a kindly-looking old gentleman who wore a flowing white beard, a red bow tie and a clerical frock coat, who had a fondness for cats and always carried lump-sugar in his pocket for hapless truck horses. His air of benevolence was, unfortunately, deceptive. Colonel Mann was the publisher of *Town Topics,* a weekly magazine of social gossip, and the terror of society. He had devised means of securing peculiarly discreditable tidbits of scandal about the elect. His Newport correspondent gained access to their homes in the guise of a musician. His news of Fifth Avenue palaces was obtained by discreet payment to servants. He gathered occasional items from mischievous tattlers like Harry Lehr, and many from social climbers with grudges to pay off. It was Colonel Mann's boast that his office safe held the reputations of the Four Hundred. When finally opened, it contained only a few bottles of brandy. But fear had filled it with alarming ghosts and hideous skeletons.

Much of the information that Colonel Mann acquired was never printed in *Town Topics*. He derived his income from a product of high social value: silence. When he published a massive, ornamental volume entitled *Fads and Fancies of Representative Americans,* the eminent socialites whose biographies it featured were happy to pay fifteen hundred dollars a copy in order to have their private fads and fancies go unrecorded. As a matter of policy Colonel Mann was always willing to accept munificent loans from prominent gentlemen whose dismal secrets had come to his attention. The loans were usually made freely, and no vulgar revelations followed. People who refused to pay for silence found their peccadilloes reported in *Town Topics* with embarrassing frankness. In his innocent literary commerce, Colonel Mann had the financial and legal support of an eminent jurist, Justice Joseph M. Deuel.

After many years of prosperity, this estimable partnership was publicly attacked by *Collier's Weekly*. Justice Deuel promptly brought suit for libel, and society anxiously awaited the trial. The evidence produced, and the facts elicited in court, proved to be sensational. Twelve respected millionaires—among them such astute financiers as J. P. Morgan, William C. Whitney, William K. Vanderbilt, James R. Keene and John W. Gates—had been snared by Colonel Mann and his partner for loans aggregating nearly two hundred thousand dollars. The Equitable Life Assurance Society had come through with a loan almost as large, to the advantage of James Hazen Hyde. *Town Topics* maintained an editorial list of sacred bulls, gentlemen of singularly acute perception whose gracious availability to an occasional "touch" made them immune from attack in its columns. On the charge of libel, the jury returned a verdict of acquittal. Society rejoiced that Colonel Mann was discredited and his power broken. But the doughty old censor of the morals of the élite had perfected a form of journalism which, in later years, would continue to plague Americans whose prominence made their private lives of interest to the public.

Meanwhile, by what was destined to be her final imperial gesture, Mrs. Astor had provoked comment throughout the country. The visit to New York of H.R.H. Prince Louis of Battenberg stimulated her flagging energy and she determined to give a banquet in his honor. Surely to this stately ceremony she would command all of the inner circle, the impeccable one hundred and fifty whose rotative presence at her dinner table signified their salvation. Failure to be included among them, as the Reverend Charles Wilbur de Lyon Nichols had lately reminded a skeptical world, "virtually debars one from eminent leadership in that surpassing coterie known as national and international American society." The sensation was immense when the press announced that Mrs. Astor had invited only seventy-nine guests to meet Prince Louis at dinner. In the yellow journals, columns were devoted to detailed appraisal of the eligibility of those who were so signally honored. Had Mrs. Astor arbitrarily created a new, supereminent rank within the ancient hierarchy? This portentous question remained forever unanswered. Time at last vanquished her indomitable spirit, mercifully clouded her weary mind. Unaware that her long reign had ended, she did not lay aside her scepter; she bore it into the world of illusion that gradually enveloped her. Still erect, still bravely gowned and jeweled, she stood beneath her portrait— quite alone; greeting imaginary guests long dead, conversing cordially with phantoms of the most illustrious social eminence. In the autumn of 1908, Mrs. Astor died at the age of seventy-seven.

Chilly gusts were stripping the trees of Central Park. A rain of shriveled leaves fell on the great crowd waiting in silence along Fifth Avenue. The massive iron and glass portals of the Astor palace slowly opened. A flower-mantled coffin was borne out and deposited in its hearse. As the doors of the hearse closed, an epoch passed into history. Presently, the crowd melted away.

FIFTH AVENUE IN 1902, looking south from 34th Street, *by C. K. Linson*

20

Are There Any More at Home Like You?

When dusk crept into New York, the Gay White Way blazed up. Streaking the night sky with a lurid glare, it summoned all Americans to revelry. A two-mile stretch of din and dazzle, Broadway between Madison and Longacre Squares held carnival for the whole country. It was the national highway of pleasure, saturated in legend, and the exploits of its transient sovereigns often seemed as fabulous as those of the ancient gods. The pulse of Broadway throbbed everywhere on the continent. The Gay White Way was a fever in the blood of Americans, breeding hallucinations of forbidden delights. Bouguereau's celebrated nude in the Hoffman House bar presided over one end of this street of joy. At the other end, the luminous griffin on Rector's lobster palace stood sentinel until the last hansoms rattled off under the sunrise, carrying the last night-hawks to sleep. New Yorkers, at the turn of the century, asserted that the intersection of Broadway and Forty-second Street was the crossroad of the world.

The Gay White Way was a city in itself, the domain of a society that flourished through the night but dissolved at dawn. By day, its members recognized no affiliation; they moved in widely separated orbits. Evening revived their collective unity. They became citizens of Broadway, dwellers in the city of beautiful nonsense. Here they met on common ground—Wall Street financiers, industrial magnates, gilded fractions of the Four Hundred, gaudy playboys, journalists, celebrities from the Bohemia of the arts, the greatest stars of the theater, gamblers, jockeys, pugilists, professional beauties, chorus girls, kept women—notorious votaries of pleasure, the cynosures of a vast, prosperous public. Mingling with the crowds that surged up and down Broadway under the garish lights you saw streetwalkers and confidence men; "guns," or thieves; "dips," or pickpockets; "moll-buzzers" who rifled women's handbags; panhandlers, dope-fiends, male prostitutes; detectives whom the underworld called "fly-cops" or "elbows." Rural visitors to the city stood gaping at the windows of the white-tiled Childs' restaurants, where white-clad conjurers perpetually juggled flapjacks. Sometimes, above the din and clatter you heard the tunes of old, familiar hymns sung to the blare of a trumpet, the clash of cymbals, the rattle and tinkle of tambourines. Into the heedless nightly bedlam the Salvation Army hopefully brought its mission of redemption.

To spend a night on the Gay White Way in classic style you began with cocktails, dined, took in a show, had supper at Rector's and wound up your festal excursion with breakfast at Jack's. Fulfillment of this program with adequate attention to all its ceremonies required a hard head, a fat pocketbook and the dedicated use of some ten hours. For a tour of the cocktail route you set out from the Hoffman House bar, crossing Broadway to Delmonico's old stand. Louis Martin had transformed it into a Parisian restaurant. Among its attractions was a café with comfortable *banquettes,* marble-topped tables, and an atmosphere of exotic impropriety, for ladies

THE HOFFMAN HOUSE BAR. A poster of the period showing the much-married Nat Goodwin in the right foreground; Tony Pastor with cane; Grover Cleveland and Chauncey Depew in the central foreground, with Buffalo Bill behind them

were served liquor if escorted by gentlemen. At Martin's the problem of masculine solitude could easily be solved. The foyer was hospitable to well-groomed ladies who seldom disdained invitations to an evening of diversion. If you preferred to continue on your way alone, you drifted northward to the bars of the Gilsey, Grand and Imperial Hotels; to Haan's famous "sample room" on Herald Square; to the bar of the Normandie Hotel. On the southwest corner of Forty-second Street, George Considine's Metropole, with a restaurant-bar opening on three streets, was a favorite rendezvous for theatrical people. Early in the new century, the old St. Cloud Hotel, directly across Broadway, was demolished and replaced by the Hotel Knickerbocker. The immense bar of the Knickerbocker, adorned by Maxfield Parrish's mural of Old King Cole, became known to the nation as the "Forty-second Street Country Club." North of the Knickerbocker, the cocktail route ended at the bar of the new Hotel Astor on the west side of Longacre Square.

You could dine sumptuously at either of these hotels. Or, if you wished to mingle with the "sporting crowd," you went to Shanley's lobster palace on Longacre Square. But if you were entertaining a Broadway beauty and intended to "make a splash" you gave her dinner at Martin's, or at Louis Bustanoby's Café des Beaux Arts, over on Sixth Avenue and Fortieth Street, restaurants celebrated not only for their impeccable cuisine but for their popularity with the notables of the Gay White Way. To break into the smart set of Broadway, as into that of Fifth Avenue, it was essential to be seen in the right places at the right times. What "little girl" or "cutie," newly come from Omaha or Cincinnati or Worcester, did not hope to rise to fame and fortune on her looks, to rival such regnant beauties as Anna Robinson, Frankie Bailey, or the members of the *Florodora* sextette? Naturally, she wanted to appear, to "make an entrance," during dinner hour at Martin's or Bustanoby's. These restaurants were artfully contrived showcases for feminine beauty, and in them soft music was dispensed by little bands of Hungarian gypsies. A liberal tip, and appropriate advance notice, persuaded the gypsy fiddler to meet you at the door, to play to your fair companion as she walked slowly to the table in time with his music, while forks were suspended in the air, conversation ceased, and all eyes were fixed upon her. This was known as making an entrance. To see it carried off with the greatest éclat, you had only to watch the progress to her table of any star of musical comedy, preceded by a smiling headwaiter, followed by the fiddler playing her latest song hit—Lillian Russell, for example, majestically, radiantly moving along the central aisle between tables with her long train flowing behind her, bowing to right and left, the layered silks that sheathed her whispering as she passed, while the gypsy band strummed John "Honey" Stromberg's "When Chloe Sings a Song," or "Come Down, Ma Evenin' Star." It was a sight never to be forgotten.

Long after the brightly lighted marquees of the theaters were darkened, the Gay White Way was jammed with hansoms, coupés, broughams, all bound uptown to Rector's, a long, low, yellow building on the east side of

Longacre Square between Forty-third and Forty-fourth Streets. For the society of Broadway, Rector's had the unique prestige that Mrs. Astor's palace had for the society of Fifth Avenue. It was the supreme shrine of the cult of pleasure, and the privilege of occupying a table there for after-theater supper certified that you had arrived, that you were worthy of sharing the highest rite celebrated by Broadway's élite. Such was the international fame of Rector's that its name was never inscribed on the building, which was identified only by the electrically illuminated griffin suspended from its facade. It was the American cathedral of froth and frivolity, the terminus of the primrose path, the tabernacle of that small hot bird and large cold bottle which, to the nation at large, symbolized the life of the Gay White Way—a life emancipated from conventions, a life that had broken the moral tyranny of Mrs. Grundy. Everybody understood the implications of the last line of Eugene Walter's torrid drama, *The Easiest Way,* which told the story of a kept woman. Miss Frances Starr enacted its unhappy heroine, Laura Murdock, deserted at last both by the man who had kept her and the man whom she loved. "Dress up my body and paint my face," Laura Murdock bade her maid: "I'm going to Rector's to make a hit—and to hell with the rest."

The presiding geniuses of this national gate to perdition were Charles Rector and his son George, a tubby, jovial young man who liked to boast that Rector's was "the center of the web spun by the benevolent spider of Manhattan in its effort to snare the genius, ability and beauty of America." Charles Rector had begun his career as the driver of a horse-car on the Second Avenue line. Later, conducting a sea-food restaurant in Chicago, he became famous as the man who had parlayed a fifteen-cent oyster stew into a million dollars. After he had opened his New York restaurant, Charles Rector withdrew his son from Cornell University and sent him to Paris, at the demand of "Diamond Jim" Brady, to master the closely guarded secret of the exquisitely delicate sauce that enveloped filet of sole à la Marguery. On his return with the mysterious formula, young George Rector became his father's partner, the accredited greeter and herald of the Gay White Way, whose genial recognition conferred the rights of citizenship. By midnight, Rector's was always crowded. It was a spacious establishment, walled in mirrors from floor to ceiling, richly decorated in green and gold, lighted by sparkling crystal chandeliers. For the favored élite there were one hundred tables on the ground floor. Seventy-five additional tables upstairs provided for the patronage of the less illustrious. The value of being seen at Rector's could be measured financially. The Christmas tips of Paul Perret, the head waiter, often ran as high as twenty thousand dollars. And Jerry Pelton, the coat-room boy who had started working there at a salary of fifteen dollars a week, was soon paying Rector's five thousand dollars a year for the privilege of guarding the outer apparel of customers.

Like his protégé, George Rector, "Diamond Jim" Brady had a unique, official position in the world of Broadway. People called him the king of the Gay White Way, though actually he held multiple posts and exercised powers that far exceeded those of his purely decorative royalty. He was Broadway's master of revels, its oracle and arbiter, its greatest host, its premier angel and philanthropist, its outstanding playboy, its most benevolent, authoritative pander. All America knew James Buchanan Brady by sight as well as reputation—he had seen to that. A master of personal publicity, he had purposefully made himself a living legend. The son of a West Street saloon keeper, thrown on his own resources in childhood, without formal education and almost illiterate, Brady had become a multimillionaire. He was a super-salesman of railroad equipment, and an unusually successful Wall Street speculator. His fortune was rated at twelve million, his annual income at one million. Reproached by George Rector for being a soft touch, for letting himself be trimmed by sycophants, male and female, Brady replied gravely, "Being a sucker is fun—if you can afford it." It was much the same with his gaudy sets of enormous gems—he had thirty sets, each composed of twenty items, and collectively they included more than twenty thousand diamonds, of varying size and shape, as well as six thousand other precious stones. Decked out in one of his matching sets of jewels, Brady looked like an ex-cursion steamer at twilight. "Them as has 'em, wears 'em," he explained. His jewels, his prodigal spending, his uncouth manner, his sulphurous private life flagrantly exposed to public view were elements of an apparatus of publicity that returned enormous profits.

"Diamond Jim" even exploited his monstrous aspect, his gargantuan appetite. He tipped the scales at nearly two hundred and fifty pounds; his majestic stomach began at his collar bone, beneath triple chins, and swelled in an opulent curve toward his massive legs. His huge purple-red face was chiefly remarkable for a pair of small, close-set, shrewd porcine eyes, a heavy, undershot, pugnacious jaw with bulldog jowls. Buried in that ugly flesh was a kindly, boyish smile. "Diamond Jim" did not smoke, nor did he consume any alcohol; his favorite drink was freshly squeezed orange juice, of which he often swallowed four gallons during a meal. He was a marathon eater. George Rector described him as "the best twenty-five customers we had." Wilson Mizner, a playboy who had connections with the criminal underworld and achieved Broadway celebrity as a wit, said that Brady liked his oysters sprinkled with clams, and his steaks smothered in veal cutlets. This was hardly an exaggeration. At Rector's, with an oversize napkin tied around his neck, Brady would polish off four dozen oysters, a dozen hard-shell crabs, six or seven giant lobsters, a large steak, a tray of French pastry and coffee. "Whenever I sit down to a meal," he once said, "I always make it a point to leave just four inches between my stummick and the edge of the table. And then, when I can feel 'em rubbin' together pretty hard, I *know* I've had enough." Broadway, having its own peculiar standards, regarded "Diamond Jim" as more of a gourmet than a gourmand. It also considered him a great gentleman.

Brady was an inveterate "first-nighter" at the theater, and producers always reserved for him the same pair of front-row seats on the aisle. After an opening night he would come on to supper at Rector's with his mistress, Edna McCauley, a handsome blonde who had been a department store salesgirl until "Diamond Jim" picked her up in Peacock Alley. Usually they would be joined by Lillian Russell and her lover, Jesse Lewisohn. Though her figure was now matronly, Miss Russell's golden loveliness had not tarnished and, after two decades of stardom in light opera, she still reigned as the perennial queen of American beauty. "Why do people marry Lillian Russell?" the matinée-idol Charles Richman once asked. In girlhood, she had married the musical director Harry Braham and quickly divorced him. Later, she had eloped with the British composer Edward Solomon, married him, discovered that he was a bigamist and divorced him, too. There had been the unfortunate episode of the tenor Perugini who, lacking any sexual interest in women, married her to advance his career; after sensational ructions, Miss Russell secured a third divorce. But men still wanted to marry her. Jesse Lewisohn was squandering millions on her, providing a private car whenever she went on tour and, when she was playing in New York, keeping a special train in readiness to transport her to her Long Island estate at any moment she wished to go there. Miss Russell and Lewisohn, Miss McCauley and "Diamond Jim" were an inseparable quartet, and all Broadway extolled their ideal friendship.

Yet within a few years this happy association was to break up. Miss Russell left New York for a prolonged tour. Before her departure, Jesse Lewisohn was stricken with a mysterious, wasting malady. Ordered by his physician to leave New York for a rest-cure in the country, he went to Brady's farm in New Jersey. Brady, worried by his pal's illness, sent Miss McCauley out to the farm to nurse him. On one of Brady's week-end visits there, Lewisohn and Miss McCauley announced that they had fallen in love and intended to marry. After a terrifying outburst of rage, Brady returned to New York. Within a few days, Lewisohn and Miss McCauley sailed for Europe. During the ten years of their affair, Edna McCauley had steadfastly refused to marry Brady; nobody knew why. "There ain't a woman on this earth who'd marry an ugly-looking guy like me," he said, when it was all over. He knew that people, seeing Miss Russell in his company, dubbed them "Beauty and the Beast."

But this explosive disruption—as embarrassing to Broadway as the Astor divorce to Fifth Avenue—was still in the future. Meanwhile Miss Russell, pampered and portly, was the brightest of a constellation of stars whom the comedians Joe Weber and Lew Fields were displaying at their little Music Hall adjoining Daly's Theater. The silvery voice that once effortlessly achieved eight high C's at every performance of an operetta—Mme. Nellie Melba went backstage to remonstrate with Miss Russell, protesting that at the Metropolitan she was not required to produce half as many high C's in a week—had now clouded. Yet it was startling to hear Miss Russell sing "coon songs," to see her, as the curtain lifted, reposing in bed, wearing a plug hat, or in male attire smoking a cigarette. So great was the demand for

LILLIAN RUSSELL, *by A. C. Learned*

first-night seats at the Music Hall that they were invariably auctioned off, with boxes sometimes bringing as much as five hundred dollars. Weber and Fields evoked gales of laughter with their absurd travesties of current Broadway successes. But they gave playgoers an even more novel delight—the largest, shapeliest and prettiest chorus line that New York had ever seen.

The Music Hall chorus girls were Broadway celebrities, noted for their incendiary effect on the most gelid of masculine connoisseurs. The superb, peerless legs of Miss Frankie Bailey, an irreplaceable treasure of the public domain, were registered for copyright at the Library of Congress. They were not only catnip to men; they became a national verbal affliction. If a man wished to bestow lavish praise on a lady's ankles, he merely alluded to her "Frankie Baileys." When, amply skirted, Miss Bailey swept into Rector's for supper, every man in the place mentally divested her of all obstructive envelopments. In fleshings, her legs had the grandeur of a major scenic phenomenon, and who would wish to fence the Grand Canyon or dry up Niagara Falls? However incomparable, Miss Bailey was only one of a bevy, and the calorific charms of Miss Bonnie Magin, Miss Goldie Mohr, Miss Aimee Angeles, Miss Mabel Barrison and Miss Vera Morris had made these damsels almost as famous. "Who wouldn't be a Weber and Fields papa?"

De Wolf Hopper asked Music Hall audiences. It was the most superfluous of questions.

You would have noticed, at Rector's for supper, a young man who was already envisaging bigger and better chorus lines. Florenz Ziegfeld was tall, slim, dark; women said he had "a Mephistophelian look." A woman was presently to suggest the idea that enabled him to turn American businessmen into bedazzled, carnivorous Fausts. It was because she usually accompanied him to Rector's that you noticed Ziegfeld. She was his first prodigal experiment. She was also his wife. Anna Held had been the reigning favorite of Paris and London music halls when Ziegfeld brought her to New York and, almost overnight, made her a sensational success in musical comedy. A young French girl, small, slender, brunette, she had exquisite features, a magnificent complexion and a vivacious manner. In an era of great beauties, Ziegfeld surmised, beauty alone was not enough; he endowed Anna Held with a legend. "Won't You Come and Play Wiz Me?" she sang archly, and this naughty invitation took the town by storm. Presently, Americans were electrified by the news that Miss Held's beautiful body profited by daily immersion in a bathtub full of milk. This queer, exotic luxury set off a nationwide controversy. Everyone read about the efforts of a Brooklyn dairyman to collect an unpaid milk bill. The milk he delivered, Ziegfeld blandly announced, was sour. For Miss Held's ceremonial purification it had to be expedited, still warm, from the cow. Scarcely had the public digested this novel idea when a more provocative story leaked out. At a supper party there had occurred a scientific debate as to how many consecutive kisses two pairs of lips could exchange before paralysis set in. One of the guests wagered that he could kiss Miss Held two hundred times with sustained ardor. Her lips were red and bewitching, her unselfish devotion to science was extreme, but the experiment ended after one hundred and fifty-two kisses; the fortunate gentleman reeled away, dazed by an excess of bliss. Was it any wonder that a hush fell on Rector's as Anna Held made her entrance, wearing a daring Parisian gown, a large hat liberally plumed, and jewels that were as incandescent as her captivating eyes?

Musical comedy was enjoying a tremendous vogue and, year after year, its newly discovered bright stars came to Rector's from the theater. There was petite, ash-blonde Edna May who, after two years as a chorus girl earning fifteen dollars a week, became the toast of the town in *The Belle of New York,* playing a Salvation Army lassie, singing her way to fame with a song which went, "They never proceed to follow that light but they always follow me. . . ." Miss May duplicated her success in London, and soon married a millionaire, Oscar Lewisohn, brother of Lillian Russell's lover. Retiring from the stage, she laid siege to London society, and Broadway laughed over a story that floated back. Her father, a former Syracuse postman, went to visit her and, at a very smart dinner party, was asked about his profession. Smiling reassuringly at his worried daughter, he replied, "At home, they call me a man of letters." Even more alluring than Miss May, the crowd at Rector's asserted, was auburn-haired, sprightly Adele Ritchie, whom they named "the Dresden china doll." Gilded youth flocked to the Fifth Avenue Theater when she starred in *A Runaway Girl,* heaping the stage with flowers after she sang "Oh, Listen to the Band," gorgeously arrayed in a gown of white brocaded satin, trimmed with pearl passementerie and flounced with Duchesse lace.

Yet neither Miss Held, Miss May nor Miss Ritchie caused a furor comparable to that produced by six lovely chorus girls who became more illustrious than any star of the musical stage. They were the original *Florodora* sextette, and it was to see them, and their successors, that for more than five hundred nights New Yorkers filled the Casino Theater. Many prominent hierarchs of the Gay White Way, including Stanford White and Frederick Gebhard, retained orchestra seats for every performance of *Florodora,* arriving when the sextette came on and departing after the last encore. The six tall, queenly girls, perfectly matched in height, wore frilly, pleated pink walking costumes, large black picture hats, long black gloves, and carried parasols. Six youths in gray cutaways and top hats saluted them: "Tell me, pretty maiden, are there any more at home like you?" The six beauties demurely responded, "There are a few, kind sir," and linked arms with the men. They smiled, posed gracefully, tapped the stage with their parasols, and swished in stately fashion from one side of the proscenium to the other.

This was all, but the audience always went wild; there were never fewer than six encores. The Misses Margaret Walker, Vaughn Texsmith, Marie Wilson, Marjorie Relyea, Agnes Wayburn and Daisy Green achieved financial, as well as artistic, success. They played the field, scoring their triumphs at Rector's as well as the Casino. Miss Wilson accepted a stock-market tip from James R. Keane, partner of J. P. Morgan, ran it up to seven hundred and fifty thousand dollars, then married Frederick Gebhard, who twenty years earlier had scandalized the country by his love affair with Lily Langtry. Miss Texsmith married Isaac J. Hall, a millionaire silk manufacturer. Miss Green married a wealthy financier from Denver. Miss Wayburn divorced Ned Wayburn, a well-known theatrical director, to marry a diamond magnate from South Africa. Miss Relyea married Richard Davis Holmes, nephew of Andrew Carnegie. Holmes dropped dead of excitement one night before the curtain rose at the Casino. Subsequently, Miss Relyea married a Wall Street broker. Before *Florodora* rounded out its first year, this record created the durable legend that every member of the "original" sextette had married a millionaire. The possibility of so affluent a destiny was not to be resisted. All over the land, young girls developed an ambition to find employment in the chorus lines of Broadway musicals. As a preparation for life, it seemed superior to the best of fashionable finishing-schools, for in the chorus a girl learned by doing— and she was paid fifteen dollars a week while exhibiting her talents and exercising her wits.

So beauty continued to stream into Rector's: beauty already in full career; beauty beginning its quest for a gold-plated future. The members of the original *Florodora* sextette came there. So did most of the seventy-nine girls

SOUVENIR ALBUM OF *FLORODORA*, 1900

who replaced them before the show closed its first run. There were other girls, like Nina Farrington and Anna Robinson, whose excursions behind the footlights were not dictated by economic necessity, whose appearances on the stage gave a pleasingly amateur effect to what unkind people might have considered a professional calling. Miss Robinson was not only an arresting beauty; she knew how to dress with the greatest elegance when in funds, and funds were seldom lacking. She did well for herself in New York, but even better as a result of taking a holiday in London, where an Australian millionaire expressed his admiration with jewels worth nearly a million dollars. None of the crowd at Rector's could have foreseen that she would eventually die penniless in the psychopathic ward of Bellevue Hospital. There was dark, demure Evelyn Nesbit, a chorus girl in *Florodora,* though never a member of the sextette. Stanford White admired her, and so did Harry Kendall Thaw, an erratic millionaire playboy from Pittsburgh. Thaw married her. One night when White was having supper alone at Rector's, Thaw also came there alone. He looked nervously around the room until his glance fell on White. He turned very pale, reached toward his hip pocket, hesitated, then left the restaurant. A few nights later, on the roof garden of Madison Square Garden, Thaw shot and killed Stanford White. Another girl frequently seen at Rector's was handsome Nan Patterson, a replacement for one of the original sextette in *Florodora.* One night she had supper there with Caesar Young, a wealthy bookmaker. The couple departed in a hansom. While riding uptown, Young was shot and killed. Stunning Miss Patterson was acquitted of the charge of murder.

The big spenders who frequented Rector's were addicted to champagne, a fact of importance to two personages of the Gay White Way. George Kessler and Mannie Chappelle were wine agents. Kessler, a tall, dark-bearded man of distinguished appearance, represented Moët et Chandon's champagne. Chappelle, white-haired and dapper, represented Mumm's. When these gentlemen arrived for supper on the same evening, Rector's took on the air of a competitive arena. Their task was to persuade the spenders to start the evening on their products, and thus set an example for others. So Kessler would choose a strategic table occupied by a party presided over by "Diamond Jim" Brady, or Stanford White, or Frank Gould, or Larry Waterbury, the polo player, or Charles Thorley, the Fifth Avenue florist, or any of a half-dozen Wall Street men. Presently there would arrive at the chosen table, with Kessler's compliments, two quarts of Moët et Chandon. Within a few moments Chappelle would send to the same table, with his compliments, three quarts of Mumm's to displace his rival's gift. The process often continued until Kessler and Chappelle were supplying wine for nearly every table in the restaurant. This delicately philanthropic gesture, however, always paid off well. Once the customers had been primed, they began buying champagne liberally, and continued as long as they remained in the restaurant. In the end, his largess at Rector's helped to make Kessler a millionaire, and he retired to a fine estate in England to lead the life of a country gentleman.

One of the major attractions of supper at Rector's was the opportunity to see, at close range, the leading personalities of the American theater. Actresses and actors, dramatists, producers, composers all gathered there. "While others were forced to pay to see theatrical stars," George Rector noted, "the theatrical headliners paid to see Rector's." When Anna Held launched Florenz Ziegfeld on his life work by nagging him into producing a revue featuring young, beautiful girls in lavish but abbreviated costumes, and Ziegfeld, naming the roof of the New York Theater the *"Jardin de Paris,"* put on the *Follies of 1907,* the hit of the show was a song entitled "If a Table at Rector's Could Talk." Had tables at Rector's become miraculously articulate, they might have begun by talking about the group of people whose professional careers and private lives, conducted on both sides of the Atlantic, made them New York's earliest bright "international set." It was of these people that Wilson Mizner, returning to Rector's after a long absence from New York, remarked, "The same old faces. But they're paired off differently." Their uncouplings and new conjunctions were professional as well as personal. The human scenery of their lives shifted with bewildering rapidity. But, disproving the proverb, most of these perpetually rolling stones were richly acquisitive. Nearly all of them acquired romantic legends, and many acquired fortunes likewise.

Outstanding among them was Maxine Elliott, whom the younger generation held to be the only serious rival of Lillian Russell as queen of beauty. Miss

Elliott's stately figure, her classic profile, raven hair and magnificent dark eyes were universally acclaimed, her portraits were eagerly collected. Crowds filled the theaters wherever she played, and gathered at stage doors to see her arrivals and departures. It was not only her extraordinary beauty that attracted them, but the aura of splendor that surrounded her. New Yorkers, inured to the caprices of celebrated actresses, were astonished by her exploits. She was even more exigent than Mrs. Patrick Campbell, the famous English star who, playing in a theater on Forty-second Street and distracted by the rumble of traffic, commanded that a block of roadway be covered with tanbark. "I wouldn't *dream* of moving from New York to Philadelphia, even, unless it was in my private car," Miss Elliott confided to Miss Billie Burke, a very young star. She did everything on the grand scale, maintaining a town house in London and an English country estate in addition to her American establishments. Married for a time to the comedian Nat Goodwin, an indefatigable collector of beautiful wives, she evoked from him the reminiscent comment, "Being married to Maxine is like being married to a Roman senator." But the chilling implications of this tribute did not accord with her legend. Gossip persistently affirmed that Miss Elliott was the mistress of J. P. Morgan. It was also said that she had captivated King Edward VII, and that this conquest had been commemorated by the gift of a fabulous gold dinner service. These rumors added to her glamor, and in both London and New York she moved in exalted social circles. "I may sit below the salt sometimes, dear, but I'm *there*," she remarked. Knowing New Yorkers surmised that if Miss Elliott ever sat below the salt it was only because a mistake had been made in placing the salt-cellar.

Charles Frohman, the great tycoon of the American theater, the star-maker, was often to be seen at Rector's. Short, tubby, bald, laconic, he controlled an empire that spanned the American continent and extended to England. Sometimes he arrived for supper accompanied by one of his principal players— Viola Allen or Virginia Harned, exquisite Ethel Barrymore with, perhaps, her brother Jack, whom women considered the handsomest man on the stage, or their uncle John Drew, the national model of masculine elegance. But these occasions were exceptional, for Frohman held the odd theory that the illusions of the theater would be shattered if the public saw too much of its favorites offstage, or knew too much about them. As a result Miss Maude Adams, the most august of his stars, was not only invisible but enveloped by a veil of mystery. She was, in a way, Frohman's personal romantic legend. Everybody believed that he was in love with her; many people asserted that they were secretly married, although Frohman lived, as a bachelor, in a hotel. He had persuaded the Scottish author, James M. Barrie, to dramatize his novel, *The Little Minister,* for Miss Adams. The play, achieving three thousand performances in the United States, catapulted her to fame. Thereafter, Barrie never wrote another novel; instead, he turned out play after play for Maude Adams. "He wanted me to be a playwright, and I wanted to be a novelist," Barrie said of Frohman. "All those years I fought him on that. He always won. . . ."

In this amiable battle, the tubby little tycoon probably conceived himself as a medieval knight riding out to joust for his adored lady. Yet he couldn't help distilling gold from romance. His victory over Barrie earned fortunes for him, for the reluctant playwright, and for the most highly paid but closely shrouded of American actresses.

Frequently at Rector's with Frohman, you saw Clyde Fitch, the most celebrated and successful of American playwrights, who once had four plays running simultaneously in New York, and whose annual income was said to exceed a quarter of a million dollars. Fitch was a small, slender, dark-haired man, an esthete whose magnificent home on Fortieth Street near Park Avenue was a private museum of art, whose breakfast parties brought together writers, artists, the brightest stars of the stage and a sprinkling of society folk. Fitch's drawing room comedies dealt with New York society and portrayed women of fashion, marvelously gowned and jeweled, in settings of ostentatious luxury. The feminine public adored his plays. But the women who thronged to see them—the rich, new rich, and those who hoped to become rich—seldom noticed that Fitch's heroines, for all their supposed elegance and fastidiousness, were essentially trivial and mean. His heroines were possessive and acquisitive snobs. They were unscrupulous liars, monsters of jealousy, climbers ruthlessly bent on social advancement. They were extravagant wasters whose exorbitant demands often drove their menfolk to bankruptcy, disgrace and suicide. Fitch catered to women of fashion, but he despised them. He complained bitterly, also, about his actresses and actors. They knew nothing of the usages of good society; he had to teach them manners, diction, demeanor; he had to select their stage attire. Once, when rehearsing a scene that required a profusion of flowers, Fitch compelled a horrified producer to send to the nearest florist for a thousand dollars' worth of fresh roses. It was precisely the kind of gesture that the crowd at Rector's admired.

Fitch was the restaurant's most eminent man of letters. But other writers came there: handsome Richard Harding Davis, the novelists David Graham Phillips and Rex Beach, even timid, furtive O. Henry, whom few of the other celebrities ever identified. And, nearly every evening, you might have seen jolly, rotund Victor Herbert, America's best loved composer, who lured the soprano Fritzi Scheff away from the Metropolitan Opera to play a snare drum and sing "Kiss Me Again" in *Mlle. Modiste.* In that operetta, Herbert gave the Gay White Way its second theme song: "I Want What I Want When I Want It." Sometimes William Pruette, who sang it in the theater, would rumble it out at Rector's, and the whole supper crowd would join in the chorus, accentuating every "want" with a bang of the fist on the table.

Sitting at one of the best tables, and often accompanied by a well-known beauty, you would have seen a man whose grotesquely short body, enormous bald head and funereal expression gave him a curiously sinister aspect. His reputation was even more sinister. He was "Little Abe" Hummel, the most notorious criminal lawyer in the United States. An indefatigable first-nighter, party-giver, and free-and-easy spender, Hummel was the intimate friend and attorney of many famous actresses, actors and other notables of the Gay White Way. But he was likewise the favorite adviser of the criminal underworld, and rumor had it that he often planned the operations of vice-rings, thieves, confidence men, gangsters and their mobs. Everybody knew that he was an astute blackmailer. He systematically persuaded Broadway damsels to sign affidavits that they had been seduced by prominent men. The victims, or their attorneys, would be summoned to his office, and were usually glad to pay whatever amount Hummel required to destroy the incriminating documents. Hummel's partner, William F. Howe, was known in the underworld as "the mouthpiece," Hummel as "the brain"; the Gay White Way affectionately called him "Little Abe, the light of the Tenderloin." Friendly and generous, he was personally likable, and neither his dubious ethics nor his profitable rascality made him any the less popular with Broadway's smart set. Other representatives of the underworld aristocracy also made their way to Rector's for supper—Shang Draper, Bud Hauser, "Doc" Waterbury, "Doc" Owens. They were good company, George Rector said, out of office hours. They always behaved discreetly at Rector's. In a way, they gave the place a tone. Rector's, after the theater, incubated what a later generation was to call café society.

When Rector's began emptying out, the real nighthawks moved over to Jack's, on Sixth Avenue, opposite the new Hippodrome, for breakfast. How, in flagrant defiance of the law, John Dunstan kept his bartenders busy all night, nobody ever knew. It was generally believed that a sizable portion of the yield of his gold mine on Forty-third Street found its way to Tammany Hall. Jack's was a large place, simple in its décor, where Irish waiters who looked like pugilists served hearty food and heady liquor. Clams or oysters, lobsters or crabs in any of a dozen styles, steaks, chops, kidneys. But the most popular fare for a night-ending breakfast was scrambled eggs with Irish bacon, accompanied by champagne, and topped off by a large pot of steaming, strong coffee. Having therewith fortified yourself, you were ready to take your cutie home. Outside Jack's, as the dawn broke on Sixth Avenue and the milk wagons rattled by, you found the last of the sea-going hackmen: Ten-cent Dan, Gas-House Sam, Bounding Dick, Tenderloin Bill, Frank the Gyp. Their scale of prices depended upon your sobriety and your knowledge of Manhattan topography. They were agreeable outlaws who enjoyed trimming the prosperous, ignorant and inebriated. Their ambition was to give you a "runaround," or show you the sunrise in Central Park. Some of them were not above rolling and frisking a solitary drunk. But if you were "wise," they knew it, and treated you accordingly. And, reaching your bed as millions of New Yorkers were bound for their day's work, you could repeat the Gay White Way's favorite aphorism: "It's a great life—if you don't weaken."

21

Cosmopolis Under the El

At Rector's temple of pleasure and perdition any patron willing to spend twenty dollars on a supper party for five was able to include in his hospitality two bottles of champagne and a round of cigars. The lower end of Orchard Street, near East Broadway, was less than three miles distant from Longacre Square. Down there were two restaurants scarcely less popular than Rector's, though very unlike it. One of these establishments served a dinner of soup, meat stew, bread, pickles, pie and a "schooner" of beer for thirteen cents. Its neighboring competitor charged fifteen cents for a similar dinner, and offered two schooners of beer and a cigar, or cigarette, as an extra inducement. But the thirteen-cent restaurant had an edge on its rival. To many customers, two cents made a vital difference. Most of them were Polish Jews, fugitives from pogroms in their native land. In New York, they labored long hours in "sweatshops" and herded in squalid, overcrowded tenements. Tenement families often had to take in lodgers to make ends meet. A lodger, as some of them said, could "live like a lord" for twenty-five cents a day.

Prosperous New Yorkers couldn't tell whether this statement was ironical, or merely grotesque. To them, existence in the slums had the look of social misery. Dire mass poverty was all too visible. Men, women and many children worked for eighteen hours a day at low wages. Ceaseless privation, widespread disease and helpless ignorance were obvious to anyone who cared to investigate. Sociologists asserted that no other city in the world had so many dark, windowless rooms, so many persons crowded on the acre, so many families deprived of light and air. Nobody knew how many thousands of the desperately poor lived in ancient rookeries, accessible only through narrow back alleys, hidden behind the gaunt tenements that lined teeming slum streets. To a million children these streets, or the tenement roofs, offered their only playgrounds. Was it any wonder that cruelty, violence, sordid vice flourished, or that crime prospered? Enlightened philanthropists declared that the slums of New York, notorious throughout the country, were a disgrace to the nation's largest, wealthiest city. Yet if existence there revealed undeniable social misery, it likewise spoke eloquently of indefeasible human hope.

Nothing was more characteristic of New York than the rapid degeneration into slums of areas formerly fashionable, or inhabited by the prosperous middle classes. The fine "Colonial" houses of Cherry Hill, where George Washington had lived after his inauguration as president, were a festering slum. So was formerly aristocratic Chelsea, now the center of a district known as Hell's Kitchen that extended from Twenty-third to Fortieth Streets between Seventh Avenue and the Hudson River. Bond Street, once the citadel of elegance, was tenanted by rag-pickers. The neat brownstone residences of East Harlem had been subdivided until rooms were no larger than closets, or they had given way to tall tenements. The district was now called Little Italy. On Sixty-third Street, in the shadow of the gas tanks on the East River, the homes of middle-class families were replaced by densely populated buildings known as Battle Row. The slums had followed the lines of the elevated railroads, and block after block of "flats" had sunk to the level of tenements. You couldn't distinguish a "flat" from a tenement by its facade; brass railings and intricately carved brownstone were not incompatible with dark, dingy rooms, hideous overcrowding, accumulated filth and infestation by vermin. The most trustworthy distinction was a closed front door. A locked entrance and a janitor indicated that the first step had been taken to secure privacy. This suggested that the building was a "flat," not a tenement. Lack of privacy was the chief curse of the tenement. The dark, dirty hall that served as a highway for all the world by day and by night, that furnished a refuge for hoodlums, was the tenement's most conspicuous feature. Below Houston Street, the doorbell and janitor had become virtually extinct. So, although the slums had spread over the city, many New Yorkers maintained that they were confined to the area south of Fourteenth Street.

Journalists named this region the "melting pot," for there a vast immigrant population was supposedly being made American. Yet the fusion of nationalities was less obvious than their persistently maintained identity, their continuing separateness. The slums below Fourteenth Street were, in fact, Cosmopolis. They harbored swarming colonies, all foreign in language, customs, institutions; some, even in costume. Between the Bowery and the East River was the congested "ghetto" inhabited by Russian, Polish and Rumanian Jews. There you saw venerable, scholarly-looking men, patriarchally bearded, wearing skullcaps and long-skirted kaftans; elderly women who shaved their heads and wore the traditional wig. The signs on the shops were in Hebrew characters, and you heard Yiddish spoken more frequently than English on the

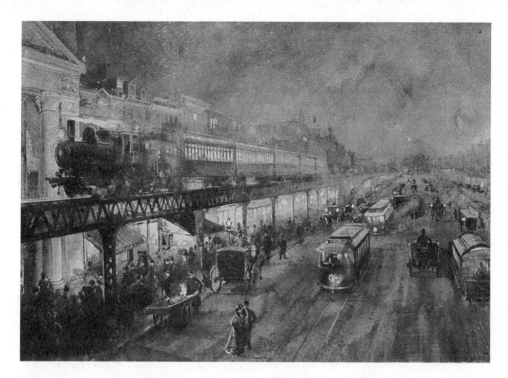

THE BOWERY AT NIGHT, 1895, *by W. Louis Sonntag, Jr.*

noisy, thronged streets. In two small rooms of a six-story tenement it would not be unusual to find a "family" of father, mother, twelve children and six lodgers.

West of the Bowery, you passed into Italy. The colorful Italian quarter had spread uptown from the rookeries of Mulberry Bend as far as the decrepit buildings on Thompson and Sullivan Streets, south of Washington Square. The Negroes who had formerly occupied these buildings had been driven northward by the Italian incursion. They had migrated to Seventh Avenue in the Thirties; to Ninth Avenue in the Fifties, a district soon to become known as San Juan Hill, because of the bravery of Negro troops in the Spanish-American War. In the sprawling Italian quarter, as in southern Italy, life was lived on the street in mild weather. Whenever the sun shone, everybody turned out on the sidewalks to carry on their household work, their bargaining, love-making or mere idling. Hucksters' and peddlers' carts made two rows of booths in the roadways; on the sidewalks, ash barrels served for counters.

Below the Italian quarter, opening off Chatham Square, Chinatown was squeezed between Pell and Mott Streets, bisected by twisting, narrow Doyers Street. Here you saw no women. The older men wore Chinese costume and pigtails. The walls of buildings were plastered with red-and-white posters bearing Chinese characters in orange and black. Silence, a sullen stare, an air of distrust greeted the too curious visitor. Southeast of Chinatown was the district inhabited by the Greek colony. Down near the Battery, on Greenwich and Washington Streets, where Turks, Syrians and Arabs had settled, you found coffee houses and bazaars like those of the Levant. North of the Bowery and east of Third Avenue lay Little Germany. Along Second Avenue, near St. Mark's Place, a stone's throw from the grave of Peter Stuyvesant, was Little Hungary, with its brightly lighted cafés where gypsy musicians played, where, on summer nights, the sidewalk terraces were crowded. Further up Second Avenue, clustering about the huge cigar factories in which they earned their livelihood, were colonies of Bohemians. Many of them carried on their trade in their tenement homes. By working from dawn to midnight a man and wife might produce three thousand cigars a week, and be paid at the most fifteen dollars.

To explore these quarters of the city was an adventure on foreign soil. Only the facades of the buildings persuaded you that you were actually on Manhattan Island, reminded you that nowhere else could you become an alien so abruptly and diversely. It gave you an odd feeling to learn that many dwellers in the area below Fourteenth Street passed their lives without ever once crossing that barrier, or seeing the wonderful modern city that lay north of it. New York had become a metropolis virtually invisible, if not unknown, to millions of its own residents. Yet the segregation of the downtown slums from the life of uptown Manhattan was more apparent than real. The two regions, however insulated from one another socially, were vitally connected.

Nothing seemed more remote from the world of the tenements than that of the palaces on Fifth Avenue. But Mrs. Astor's annual ball was nourished by the income derived from immense tracts of slum property. Her world included many members of Trinity Church, which drew huge revenues from ownership of houses unfit for human habitation. An intricate network connected the slums with the office of Boss Richard Croker in Tammany Hall. This network crossed the lines which linked the slums to the society of the Gay White Way. The underworld celebrities who frequented Rector's, the vice-rings whose operations were so ably safeguarded by "Little Abe" Hummel, were native to the blighted area south of Fourteenth Street. Hardworking residents of the Jewish quarter formed no part of the audiences at Broadway theaters. But many of them took pride in the legendary fame of Weber and Fields. They knew that short, explosive Joe Weber and lank, dead-pan Lew Fields were children of the tenements, had begun their careers as little boys playing a "Dutch act" in Bowery dime museums. They had heard, too, about bearded, silk-hatted Oscar Hammerstein, builder of theaters, producer of operas, eccentric genius and shrewd businessman who was said to be reaping a fortune from an *Amerikaner* amusement called vaudeville in a new theater named the Victoria. They knew that Hammerstein had got his start as a cigar-maker. Weber, Fields, Hammerstein—they had risen to fame, to fabulous financial success, from dire poverty, and now they were accepted, honored, by the great ones of this strange new world. The knowledge was like a beacon of hope. It proved that the gateway of opportunity had not closed.

And there were other connections that bridged the seemingly impassible divide of Fourteenth Street. New York's most important manufacturing industry was the mass production of ready-made clothing, and this was founded on the "ghetto." If, late at night, you rode uptown from Chatham Square on the Second Avenue elevated, every window of the big tenements, lining both sides of the way like continuous brick walls, gave you a glimpse of men and women hunched over sewing machines or, half-naked, wearily pressing garments in a cloud of hot steam. The elevated was a gangway through a vast workroom where multitudes were forever laboring, morning, noon and night. But had not the rich factory owners and the prosperous "sweaters," or subcontractors, themselves started as sweated "hands"? To some observers, improvement in the dreadful living conditions that prevailed on the lower East Side seemed the more remote because of the dumb acceptance of these conditions by the East Side itself.

The fact remained that three-quarters of the city's population lived in tenements. Wasn't the misery that darkened their lives a threat to democracy, and a challenge to conscience? Nobody felt this more deeply, more aggrievedly, than Jacob A. Riis, a talented writer on the staff of *The Sun,* assigned by that newspaper to cover Police Headquarters. Himself an immigrant from Denmark, Riis had experienced many of the hardships familiar to the foreign-born poor. Writing stories of crime for his newspaper, he made it his business tirelessly to investigate conditions in the slums. Appalled by what he saw and learned, his indignation boiled up in a book, *How The Other Half Lives.* This blistering exposure shocked the city and the nation; with his new prestige, Riis became a powerful, insistent crusader for reform. A similar sense of personal, moral responsibility afflicted a young graduate trained nurse. Called one day on an errand of mercy to a squalid rear tenement on Ludlow Street, Miss Lillian D. Wald was aghast at the unsuspected horrors suddenly revealed to her. All the maladjustments of social and economic relations seemed epitomized by what she saw during a brief walk, and what she found at the end of it. She was convinced that the conditions she had discovered were tolerated only because, like herself, uptown New Yorkers did not know about them; she felt challenged to learn about them, and to tell. Presently, with her friend Miss Mary M. Brewster, she went to live in the heart of the "ghetto." Identifying themselves with the neighborhood, socially and as citizens, they established a volunteer district-nursing service, then opened the Henry Street Settlement. By virtue of her experience in all forms of social welfare—gained by the experimental, trial-and-error method of meeting problems as they arose—Miss Wald soon achieved national celebrity. Insisting on group co-operation within the neighborhood, she overcame the apathy and helpless acquiescence of its residents. The "house on Henry Street" developed social services that later became municipal functions. It initiated progressive social legislation. It provided a forum where representatives of labor, management and government met to discuss and solve controversial problems. A similar experiment was undertaken by John Lovejoy Elliott, a young university graduate who moved into Hell's Kitchen while engaged in an investigation of the city's sweatshops.

He remained there to establish the Hudson Guild, a settlement dedicated to teaching people to help themselves and each other. In this gang-terrorized slum Elliott managed to weld together into an efficient working team priests, tradesmen, teachers, longshoremen, truck drivers, seamen, office workers and factory hands from the many nationalities composing its population, creating a neighborhood spirit which in time reshaped the community.

In the East Side cafés where foreign intellectuals debated how to emancipate the American workers whose language they seldom understood, many political radicals received their education. Among them was a short, stocky, exceedingly plain woman who looked like a strong-minded, respectable housewife. Emma Goldman was strong-minded, no housewife, and anything but respectable. Her prim white shirtwaist and black skirt disguised a proletarian Aspasia whose stormy love affairs, kindled by private passion, invariably turned into public demonstrations of a theory. She was a philosophical anarchist, and she detested both capitalists and reformers. She was also a woman with a mission; she had consecrated her life to helping bring about the proletarian revolution. In the cafés, there was much talk of the class struggle and the workers' revolution. How could it best be expedited? Grim, heavily bearded Johann Most, a political exile from Europe, preached the gospel of terrorism; he had published a pamphlet on the science of revolutionary warfare. Most was Emma Goldman's mentor. All this kind of talk went to the head of Alexander Berkman, an intense, scholarly young radical. He was Miss Goldman's lover. During a bitter strike at the Homestead plant of the Carnegie Steel Company, in which several workers had been shot, Berkman made an unsuccessful attempt to assassinate Carnegie's partner, Henry Clay Frick. Overnight, Miss Goldman became nationally notorious as "Red Emma" and thereafter was closely watched by the police. She achieved further notoriety when a demented youth, Leon Czolgosz, assassinated President McKinley, and it developed that, under an assumed name, he had talked with her several times before setting out on his murderous venture. She was ignorant of his intention, and innocent of complicity in his crime. She wanted to bring about the revolution—but she abhorred cruelty, even when practiced by the victims of cruelty.

Anarchism made few converts in the East Side cafés, but socialism was quite another matter. It promised a more equitable distribution of wealth, and in crowded tenement homes where children could not be excluded from any discussion even the youngsters had decided opinions on the subject. Looking in on one of the children's clubs at the Henry Street Settlement, Miss Wald heard a fiery debate on socialism. "The millionaires sit around the table eating sponge cake, and the bakers are down in the cellar baking it," a twelve-year-old boy declared. "But the day will come,"·he continued, pointing an accusing finger at the universe, "when the bakers will come up from their cellar and say, 'Gentlemen, bake your own sponge cake!'" Admiring this impressive oratory, Miss Wald had a guilty sense that the settlement was probably responsible for the picture of licentious living summed up in the consumption of sponge cake—the settlement's most popular juvenile treat, with ice cream added on great occasions. But she realized that the boy's argument reflected discussions overheard at home. However poor, tenement families in the Jewish quarter were reading *The Forward,* a socialist daily newspaper published in Yiddish. Founded by members of labor unions and "intellectuals," it was edited by Abraham Cahan, a brilliant young writer whose stories of "ghetto" life had already been translated into English and were being read "uptown."

Undaunted by the stubborn resistance of their employers, the workers were organizing trade unions. In the cafés, you heard much talk about two young women residents of the neighborhood. Miss Rose Schneiderman, working ten hours a day as a capmaker, had organized a women's union in her trade. Women workers, she preached, must stand together, not only for their own rights, but in behalf of those who would come after them. Miss Fannia M. Cohn, a garment worker, was eloquently demanding a crusade against the sweatshop. This was admirable, everybody agreed. But what about another project that seemed to be an obsession with her? She was forever discussing a program of adult education—nothing less than a workers' university would do!—to be conducted by the unions for the benefit of their members. It seemed fantastically visionary, and even the most optimistic unionists could not foresee that Miss Cohn would eventually carry it through on a scale that far exceeded her early ambitions.

Meanwhile, nobody could deny that the intellectual and literary life of the "ghetto" was running at full tide. Even "uptowners" who understood no Yiddish made the long journey downtown to see the great actor, Jacob Adler, play Shylock. And the same thing occurred when Adler performed the powerful dramas written by Jacob Gordin: *The Jewish King Lear, God, Man and the Devil, The Wild Man.* Gordin's plays dealt with such problems of "ghetto" life as the conflict of ideals between the older, immigrant generation and their children, born in the new land and thoroughly Americanized. Among younger writers, Mary Antin was presently to write in English *The Promised Land,* a memorable study of the hardships suffered by immigrants, and Abraham Cahan would soon afterward use English to tell, in a notable novel, *The Rise of David Levinsky,* the story of progress from hardship to material success. In the Jewish quarter a love of art was so obstinate that even extreme poverty could not quench it. A company of Russian actors headed by Alla Nazimova and Paul Orleneff came to New York, opened at the Herald Square Theater and failed to attract the Gay White Way. Should these talented players be permitted to lack an audience? In the cafés of the East Side, Miss Emma Goldman and others raised enough money to hire the shabby old Third Avenue Theater on East Third Street, and the company was installed there. Shortly afterward uptown intellectuals, dramatic critics and Broadway stars were flocking down to see Nazimova play Ibsen's *Ghosts* and *The Master Builder* in Russian. One year later, playing *Hedda Gabler* in English on Broadway, she began her long, prosperous career as an American star.

Walking about the lower East Side, you would have noticed the many "nickelodeons" where moving pictures were being shown—the cheapest amusement of the poor. Their recessed fronts were plastered with posters vividly suggesting the excitement, adventure and beauty that five cents would buy. As dusk fell, electric lights blazed out their names: "The Family," "The Cosy," "The Jewel," "The Bijou Dream." A former garment worker, William Fox, owned fifteen of these establishments. A former fur cutter, Marcus Loew, had set out to acquire a chain of nickelodeons. He had taken into partnership another furrier, Adolph Zuckor, and they made money rapidly. Now, Zuckor had gone on his own as the proprietor of a picture house on Fourteenth Street, and was already dreaming of making pictures that would be longer, more like the plays that drew crowds into the theaters on Broadway. Factory workers who had known Fox and Loew and Zuckor in the days of their poverty envied them their present dazzling success. But nobody foresaw that these men were to become, within a very few years, millionaires, absolute masters of vast, powerful industrial empires. And would anybody have believed that they were to help bring about profound changes in American culture? Not even David Wark Griffith, who was producing "canned drama" for the Biograph Company in their studios on Fourteenth Street, saw any future in the flickers, although he was giving the humble audiences of the nickelodeons such fare as

KOSTER & BIAL'S MUSIC HALL

Thirty-fourth Street, Herald Square.

KOSTER, BIAL & CO., ... Proprietors
ALBERT BIAL, . . . Sole Manager.
W. A. McConnell, ... Business Manager.

Week Commencing Monday Evening, April 20, 1896.

Evenings, 8:15   Saturday Matinee, 2:15

THIS PROGRAMME is subject to alterations
at the discretion of the management.

1 OVERTURE,   "Masaniello,"   Auber

2   WM. OLSCHANSKY
              The Russian Clown

3   CORA CASELLI
              Eccentric Dancer.

4   THE THREE DELEVINES
       In their original act "Satanic Gambols"

5   PAULINETTI and PICO
    The Athletic Gymnast and Gymnastic Comedian.

         MONS. and MME.
6   DUCREUX-CERALDUC
              French Duettists,

7   THE BROTHERS HORN
    Assisted by MISS CHARLOTTE HALLETT
              "London Life,"

    THOMAS A. EDISON'S LATEST MARVEL

8   THE VITASCOPE,

    Presenting selections from the following:

"Sea Waves," "Umbrella Dance," "The Barber Shop," "Burlesque Boxing," "Monroe Doctrine," "A Boxing Bout," "Venice, showing Gondolas," "Kaiser Wilhelm, reviewing his troops," "Skirt Dance," "Butterfly Dance," "The Bar Room," "Cuba Libre."

INTERMISSION . 10 MINUTES

IN THE GRAND PROMENADE
Dr. Leo Sommer's Blue Hungarian Band.

Programme continued on next page.

Shakespeare's *Taming of the Shrew,* Tolstoy's *Resurrection* and Browning's
Pippa Passes on films that ran for less than fourteen minutes. And Griffith's
most popular star, a golden-curled girl whom audiences knew only as "Little
Mary," was delighted whenever she could secure theatrical engagements under
her stage name, Mary Pickford. Obviously, motion pictures would never be
anything more than a cheap show catering only to the poor and ignorant.

The bitter rivalry of two underworld celebrities for a long time kept the
region south of Fourteenth Street in a condition of terror and turmoil. "Monk"
Eastman and Paul Kelly were gang leaders who controlled mobs of plug-uglies
and killers. Both were useful to Tammany Hall, had influence with its rulers,
and were protected in their operations by its district leaders in the slums. Monk
Eastman made his headquarters in a dive on Chrystie Street near the Bowery.
Short, bull-necked, with cauliflower ears, a broken nose and a scarred face,
he was proud of his ferocious aspect. He had a fondness for pets—cats and
pigeons especially—and owned a bird-and-animal store on Broome Street.
This was his hobby. His income was derived from houses of prostitution and
gambling joints; the operations of his guns, dips and blackjackers; the hire of
thugs whom he provided to citizens who had grudges to pay off, and for whose
services—from minor disability to murder—he charged fixed rates according
to the injuries inflicted.

Eastman's rival, Paul Kelly, was of Italian origin; his real name was Paul
Vaccarelli. He, too, had an honest business as a front; he owned and operated
the gaudy New Brighton saloon and dance hall on Great Jones Street, and
made his headquarters there. But his money-making enterprises were the same
as Eastman's. Unlike Eastman, Kelly was not disfigured. He was a dark, soft-

spoken, dapper little man who conversed fluently in English, Italian, French and Spanish, who enjoyed discussing art and the higher things of life, who wore expensive, conservative clothes. Kelly's gang was said to number fifteen hundred members; Eastman's roster was put at twelve hundred. For a period of more than two years, these overlords of crime conducted relentless war on one another, each deploying squads to raid the other's enterprises and destroy them, or merely to do battle with guns and blackjacks on the streets. The hostile armies even invaded the balls held at Walhalla and New Irving Halls by local political and "social" clubs, shooting out their mortal enmity without regard to the safety of innocent pleasure-seekers. These affrays had cost the lives of some thirty gangsters when, one night, a prolonged gunfight occurred on Second Avenue and Rivington Street, under the elevated railroad, in which more than one hundred gangsters of the rival clans were engaged. Finally quelled by large detachments of police, this battle, with its high toll of dead and wounded, made headlines in all the newspapers. Officials of Tammany acted promptly, informing Eastman and Kelly that their reign of terror was impairing their political usefulness and must stop. Tom Foley, a Tammany potentate, arranged a meeting between the rival overlords and acted as mediator between them in patching up a truce. To celebrate the peace, Foley gave a ball for both gangs at which Eastman and Kelly, having ostentatiously shaken hands before their assembled followers, retired with Foley to a box and amiably viewed the subsequent rituals of friendship.

By the terrorized residents of the Lower East Side, news of Foley's diplomatic victory was received with a certain skepticism. They were scarcely to be blamed for taking a dim view of the efficacy of Tammany intervention. And as things turned out, they were right. The gang war was soon resumed. But although Eastman was eventually sent to prison and Paul Kelly's prestige and power evaporated, other gangsters succeeded them. Big Jack Zelig, one of Eastman's favorite pupils and lieutenants, became the most notorious. A redoubtable killer, Zelig was described by the fly-cops of the "front office"— Police Headquarters—as the toughest man in the world. Not content with his pickings on the East Side, Zelig moved his gang in on the Gay White Way. There, he sold his peculiar services to the owners of pretentious gambling establishments. He furnished gunmen for their protection; assigned thugs to intimidate their competitors by wrecking raids, personal injury and the beating up of customers; and in behalf of his clients did a general business in stabbing, shooting, bomb-throwing and murder. Zelig prospered until, for the sum of two thousand dollars, he accepted the commission to murder Herman Rosenthal, proprietor of a gambling house on West Forty-fifth Street near Broadway, who had taken into partnership Police Lieutenant Charles Becker, head of the Gambling Squad, but had subsequently quarreled with him. Becker, threatened with exposure by Rosenthal, wanted him blotted out. Arrangements for the murder were made with Zelig by Becker and Bald Jack Rose, another gambler. Zelig deputed four of his gunmen to carry out the job, which they did, early one morning, in front of Considine's Metropole. The gunmen were later apprehended, and Lieutenant Becker was arrested. In their trials, Zelig was expected to be a star witness for the District Attorney; he had already testified before the Grand Jury. But on the day before his scheduled appearance in court, Zelig was shot and killed by another gangster. The underworld lamented his passing. He had made crime big business, put it on a respectable industrial basis. The lessons he had taught were to bear rich fruit within a very few years.

PART FOUR

1910–1930

THE FESTIVE ERA

22

The City of Fantasy

For more than two decades New Yorkers were deafened by the chatter of invisible machine guns. In one or another quarter, automatic riveters kept up a ceaseless fusillade. Like human spiders dangling in space, workmen were spinning delicate webs of steel ever higher into the air. The era of super-skyscrapers had opened. Once again, you could watch New York being transformed. Seen from the bay on a sunny morning, Manhattan became an island of glittering pinnacles, a mirage of clustered, slender shafts plumed with steam. Veiled, at its base, by a gossamer of dust perpetually suspended in the air, the island seemed to float on mist. The reality contrived by engineers resembled an illusion conjured up by poets.

Cloud-cathedrals of the religion of Success—to the world they symbolized New York. Appropriately, the earliest of these new shrines displaced one raised by an older faith. The Madison Square Presbyterian Church was torn down. On its site, a fifty-story campanile announced the insurance of life as a promise of salvation. High above the greenery of Madison Square Park, the great illuminated clock of the Metropolitan Tower preached the gospel that time is money. Overriding the roar of Manhattan, a carillon rang out every passing quarter hour. Below City Hall Park, the rose-colored Singer Building, thrusting its forty-seven stories toward heaven, commemorated the minutes and hours which, threaded through the needles of sewing machines, were being stitched into homemade finery by millions of women. Nearby, the Woolworth Building soared sixty stories above Broadway. A Gothic spire, turreted, gilded, intricately carved, it affirmed the fertility of the lowly dime, declared the glory of an empire of bazaars where pins and perfumes, gumdrops, shoelaces, kitchenware and kickshaws were transmuted into billions of dollars.

At the lower end of Manhattan, the vaulting towers pressed closer and closer together. Capitols of realms of finance, oil, insurance, shipping, communications, transportation, irrelevantly crowned by Greek temples, Aztec pyramids, Egyptian obelisks that were never to be seen from the streets. Monolithic office buildings tenanted by brokers, lawyers, exporters, great corporations. Into the deep canyons of the streets, the daylight came grudgingly; the sun touched them only momentarily. Behind clifflike walls, lights blazed throughout the day. Presently, zoning laws were passed, and a new style of architecture developed. Towers now ascended in a series of terraced setbacks. At night, floodlights outlined their broken perpendiculars and from their apexes, in golden lanterns, searchlights coldly swept the skies. Over the years, the super-skyscrapers marched northward, massing near Pennsylvania Station and Grand Central, deploying along Fifth Avenue, bordering Central Park on the south and west. Twilight enveloped the city in a violet haze. The monster buildings lost their substantiality, their finials lacquered by the setting sun, their bases shrouded by the encroaching darkness. From an uptown terrace, looking southward, you saw New York flare up in an enchanted geometry of lights.

LOWER MANHATTAN,
by Louis Lozowick

It was characteristic of New York that the vast railroad terminals suggested neither arrivals nor departures, that the trains which justified their erection were buried far underground. Immense public concourses with labyrinthine arcades of shops, they disgorged their multitudes of "commuters" every morning, sucked them back again in the exhausted, feverish late afternoon. Externally, Pennsylvania Station resembled an ancient Roman, Doric temple; but if prayers were ever muttered there they were addressed only to the great god Prosperity, dispenser of livelihood. So that this temple might bring within the metropolitan area all of northeastern New Jersey, so that all of Long Island might become, in effect, a suburb of the city, sandhogs had drilled tunnels beneath the Hudson and East Rivers. And now the daytime New Yorker might reside as far away as Philadelphia, never seeing by night the city where he worked unless, detained long overtime, he chose to sleep in one of the huge, impersonal, two-thousand-room hotels that eventually surrounded the station.

Externally, the Grand Central Terminal resembled a Palace of Industry in some nonexistent World's Fair. But was not New York itself becoming the universal exposition, the world's international playground? Through this glittering, resonant gallery commuters were catapulted into the city from far up the Hudson Valley, from Westchester, from Bridgeport and New Haven in Connecticut. Proper Bostonians came down for a day of shopping in New York, or to attend decorous directorial meetings where everybody voted in the affirmative—and sedately returned on the Merchants' Limited to find repose on beds undisturbed by vulgar excitement since the Tea Party. Other visitors, like old-fashioned New Yorkers, marveled at the changes wrought by the building of the terminal. Lower Park Avenue, with its smoking open cut and clangor of steam engines, its fringe of disused breweries, livery stables and ancient factories, was roofed over and transformed into an esplanade bordered by luxury hotels and splendid apartment houses. Gradually Park Avenue extended its arrogant magnificence, its costly, pampered residential exclusiveness for nearly three miles northward, to sink at last into the misery of East Harlem slums. Meanwhile, around Grand Central, a midtown business area was in process of development. Towering transient hotels, enormous office buildings with daytime populations as large as those of cities mushroomed about the terminal, to culminate, after fifteen years, in the fifty-three-story Lincoln Building, the fifty-six-story Chanin Building, the seventy-seven-story Chrysler Tower that stabbed, with its gigantic metal hypodermic needle, the racing clouds. On Madison Avenue the Ritz-Carlton Hotel, opened in 1910 to anticipate remotely future concepts of grandeur, gradually took on an air of conservatism. Like an elegant, high-bred dowager, it lifted supercilious eyebrows at the antics of a younger generation—at raccoon coats and rakish roadsters; at stag-lines vouched for but often dubiously rowdy; at débutantes for whom introduction to the ways of the world seemed the most superfluous of rites.

Even more spectacular than these changes were those produced by the long awaited achievement of rapid transit. The first section of New York's subway system, opened in 1904, ran up the East Side from City Hall to Grand Central, thence westward across Forty-second Street to Times Square (the former Longacre Square), thence northward on Broadway to One Hundred and Forty-fifth Street. As the years passed, this system was greatly expanded and altered. Eventually, trains sped under the East River far into Brooklyn, northward to Washington Heights, beneath the Harlem River far out into the East and West Bronx. Before 1930, a second system linked Manhattan with Brooklyn and Queens; a third system, already under construction, would run the length of Manhattan's West Side, penetrate into Brooklyn and, by another line, reach out into Long Island as far as Jamaica. The results of rapid transit became evident in changes that occurred in the city's population. In 1910, New York was a city of nearly four million, eight hundred thousand people. Nearly half of them—somewhat more than two million, three hundred thousand—were concentrated on Manhattan Island. Brooklyn had nearly one million, seven hundred thousand residents. The Bronx had fewer than a half-million; Queens, slightly more than a quarter of a million; Richmond (Staten Island) had fewer than one hundred thousand residents. Twenty years later, with a total population of nearly seven millions, the residential distribution of New York's inhabitants had drastically changed. The population of Manhattan had decreased to one million, eight hundred thousand. Brooklyn had more than two and one-half million residents. The Bronx had more than one million and a quarter; Queens, more than one million. But Staten Island, still linked with Manhattan only by ferry, had little more than one hundred and fifty thousand residents. It remained predominantly rural—the only part of New York City where farming and truck-gardening were important, profitable sources of livelihood.

In less than two decades, rapid transit radically altered the life of the average New Yorker of modest means. He might pass his working hours on the fiftieth floor of a skyscraper, but to reach it from home and return there he was likely to spend as much as one and one-half hours every day underground, standing on his feet, tightly squeezed into an overcrowded subway train that hurtled him five miles, ten miles in either direction. The extraordinary diversity of New York was nowhere more evident than in the outlying regions of the city. Washington Heights was a quarter of serried apartment houses, sidewalks congested with baby carriages by day, deserted by pedestrians at night except on Broadway, the community Main Street. To the north, across the Harlem River, Riverdale, in the West Bronx, had the look of a garden city, a landscaped caprice of wealthy folk defiantly resisting encroachment by the conquering armies of financial mediocrity. The East Bronx was plebeian and populous. For some distance along the Grand Concourse, a wide, parked boulevard running northward, you saw tall, pretentious apartment houses; there was also a massive, ornate hotel. But the inspiration to grandeur quickly exhausted itself. Most avenues in the East Bronx were lined with blocks of flats, scarcely distinguishable from one another. The cross streets displayed solid rows of brick two-family dwellings, all exactly alike.

Its vast, sprawling monotony gave the East Bronx an effect of harshness, of joylessness. It represented financial and social progress from the swarming lower East Side of Manhattan. It was the first stop on a circuitous road of aspiration that might subsequently lead to Washington Heights, then to Riverside Drive, West End Avenue or Central Park West, and ultimately reach Park Avenue.

Across the East River from midtown Manhattan, the borough of Queens quickly lost its suburban character. Large-scale development of real estate made Queens an area of vivid contrasts. Sunnyside, a community of genteel small homes, was designed for people of modest means but refined taste. The tall, efficient, regimented apartment houses of Jackson Heights, the landscaped colonies of Forest Hills and Kew Gardens catered to the prosperous classes. But Queens also contained dreary miles of squat houses, as featureless as kennels, erected to provide accommodations for workers in the great mechanized industrial plants which were concentrating there.

Brooklyn—the multiple bedroom of New York—seemed a separate city: the plain, respectable, domestic neighbor of a frivolous, spendthrift beauty. To Brooklynites, Manhattan was New York. Residents of Manhattan, always the most parochial of New Yorkers, were likely to be totally ignorant of Brooklyn. It existed on the fringe of their consciousness as a *terra incognita* or an immense bewilderment. It stretched over an area nearly three times as large as Manhattan, which it far surpassed in population. To Manhattanites it remained a vague region lying between the East River and the Atlantic Ocean at Coney Island, a human reservoir that released its floods into the subway during the early morning rush-hour and drew them back during the evening one. But Brooklyn was no less various than Manhattan. On quiet Columbia Heights, overhanging the East River, you were back in the early nineteenth century, the era of merchant-princes whose clippers voyaged to the Orient; the wharves and warehouses far below still received cargoes of spices whose pungent odors drifted up to old, spacious red-brick residences. Tall hotels and apartment houses were rising on the Heights, where at night the hoarse voices of ships betrayed a sleepless harbor. There were super-skyscrapers in downtown Brooklyn; the area around Borough Hall roared with traffic and bustled with crowds. There were slums as wretched as those of Manhattan in Williamsburg, Brownsville, Red Hook. But out in Flatbush, or down in Bay Ridge along the Lower Bay, you saw mile after mile of pleasant streets lined with snug, small houses, each having a little grass plot, a porch, a sunroom. These districts gave you the peculiar quality of Brooklyn. It was a metropolitan anachronism, a militant citadel of homes.

A permanent home was the aspiration of Brooklynites; for residents of Manhattan the concept was rapidly becoming obsolete. In 1916 William Dean Howells, nearing his eightieth year but always a faithful observer of New York life, published *The Daughter of the Storage,* a story telling of the marriage of a young couple in the storage-warehouse where their first meeting and subsequent courtship had taken place—their respective families were perpetually either "going into storage" or coming out of it. The first of October was "moving day," and in the residential quarters of Manhattan you saw, on nearly every street, the huge, gaily painted, lumbering vans that announced a restless annual migration to new domiciles, probably soon to be abandoned in their turn. The poor had always lived in tenements because they had to, and families of modest means had long been accustomed to dwelling in flats. But the increasing trend to a migratory existence was especially pronounced among the prosperous classes. It indicated that more and more New Yorkers, presumably able to afford the advantages of a private residence, were deserting their homes for the new, modern apartment houses that were being built on both the West and East Sides. Even the very wealthy had begun to share this predilection for diminished responsibility and greater convenience. In 1910, a huge building of luxury apartments had been erected at Fifth Avenue and Eighty-first Street, consisting of eighteen- and twenty-room suites renting for as much as twenty-five thousand dollars a year—and it had been fully rented even before construction was finished.

Old-fashioned moralists were appalled by the obsolescence of the old-fashioned home. It was a symptom of the changing mores, changing only for the worse. Among the "best people" divorce no longer resulted in social ostracism; it was fully sanctioned. Even more significant and far more dangerous was the new independence being claimed by women. A few years earlier, a group of society and professional women had founded the Colony Club, building for it on Madison Avenue a magnificent home designed by Stanford White and furnished by Miss Elsie de Wolfe. Not only did this institution offer facilities for transient residence, but it was actually equipped with a bar. Denounced from the pulpits of the city and deplored by many eminent citizens in the newspapers, the outrageous enterprise persisted in flourishing, and ladies of the highest social standing happily identified themselves with its defiance of sanctified conventions. Conservatives received another nasty shock when, not long afterward, the Waldorf-Astoria Hotel announced that ladies unaccompanied by gentlemen would be served, at any hour, in its restaurants. At the aristocratic new Plaza Hotel, a leader of the smart set produced consternation by taking a cigarette from her jeweled case and puffing it before the assembled diners. Another distinguished lady narrowly escaped being asked to leave Sherry's when, instead of seeking the privacy of a retiring room, she nonchalantly "touched up" her face at a table, in full view of everybody. But presently you saw women smoking in the public rooms of such fashionable hotels as the Plaza, St. Regis and Ritz-Carlton. The minor—and formerly secret—rites of beautification were being openly performed. A new diversion, the *"thé dansant,"* brought respectable matrons to hotels in the late afternoon, to dance with anonymous young men hired by the management and, all too frequently, to substitute cocktails for tea. In ultrasmart circles the plump and pretty pupils of extravagance, as H. G. Wells termed them, were beginning to question the eternal verity of the "double standard." Conversationally, the ancient chastity belt had deplorably slipped. The stylish new "hobble-skirt" was an ominous symbol. Though by binding their knees it condemned women to watch their step, it suggested latent pliancy above the kneecap.

Meanwhile, feminine insurgency found a dramatic outlet in the suffrage movement, which enlisted women from all ranks of society. Miss Anthony and Mrs. Stanton had died, but new leaders had taken their places: Mrs. Harriott Stanton Blatch, daughter of the pioneer crusader; Mrs. Carrie Chapman Catt; Miss Alice Paul and Miss Lucy Burns—rebellious, aggressive young women who were advocating the adoption of militant tactics developed by the English suffragettes. Nearing her sixtieth year, bored by easy triumphs in the world of fashion, Mrs. O. H. P. Belmont, the former Alva Vanderbilt, turned to the suffrage movement as a promising form of belligerency. In 1912, she determined to give New York a spectacular demonstration of the movement's strength. Led by Miss Inez Milholland, a renowned beauty, and marshaled by Mrs. Belmont, a long parade of white-clad feminists marched down Fifth Avenue from Fifty-ninth Street to Washington Square— socialites, businesswomen, trade unionists, factory workers, housewives. Crowds lined the Avenue to see these fanatical "new women," who were undisturbed by ridicule, who brazenly asserted their equality with men.

Five years later, when the United States entered the World War, this assertion suddenly became a fact. Débutantes and young matrons flocked into the motor corps organized by the National League for Woman's Service. You saw them, smartly uniformed, driving staff cars and ambulances about the city at all hours of the day and night. Women replaced absent men in business offices, banks, department stores, factories; they filled the numerous wartime agencies set up by the Federal Government. The emergency shattered traditions and swept conventions into the discard. The younger generation achieved its emancipation without any struggle.

New Yorkers turned out on Fifth Avenue to cheer parades of departing troops. They heard rumors of German submarines entering the harbor; then, of a steel net sealing off the Narrows. In restaurants, and in the theaters, they stood while orchestras played the national anthems of all the Allies. They watched the great camouflaged transports steam down the Hudson River. Fifth Avenue became the Avenue of the Allies, its buildings streaming with flags. On November 7, 1918, a report of the end of hostilities swept the city into delirious celebration. Business suddenly came to a standstill. Millions of people poured into the streets, shouting, singing, blowing tin horns, snakedancing. Young girls kissed every man in uniform they encountered. Fifth Avenue was closed to traffic; the crowds there and on Broadway were so dense that people could scarcely move. From windows high up in office buildings a blizzard of torn paper and ticker tape fell on the wild hilarity of the streets. Ships and tugboats in the rivers blew hoarse, continuous blasts. Drivers of stalled automobiles tootled their horns, and the noise of playful backfiring was like a cannonade. But the report that war had ended proved to be premature. Four days later, before dawn, New Yorkers were awakened by the screeching of sirens, the din of factory whistles and church bells. This time, the report was true. The great carnival of joy was repeated. Thereafter, celebrations were numerous. All New York turned out to welcome the troops returning from France. Regiments paraded up Fifth Avenue—under a massive triumphal plaster arch at Madison Square; past a queer commemorative court of pylons in front of the Public Library; finally, under a "curtain of jewels" suspended above the Avenue from two tall white pillars. At night, in the play of colored searchlights, this sparkling curtain was very effective.

The drapery of glass beads, glittering like gems under artfully tinted light, was a prophetic symbol of the new era—the era of peace, prosperity and Prohibition. Prosperity was registered down on Broad Street, in an imposing white building that resembled an ancient Greek temple. The Stock Exchange was being swamped by an "unprecedented bull market." Serious recessions were to occur; then there began the long, dazzling boom that altered life for everybody. Prohibition was ushered in by a final melancholy binge. On the last night of legal drinking, New Yorkers crowded into corner saloons, into the cafés and supper rooms of hotels, into hot spots along Broadway's roaring Forties, joylessly awaiting the midnight hour that would inaugurate a future of deprivation and drought. Prosperous citizens had stocked up on liquor at soaring prices, but even millionaires could not acquire supplies adequate to last a lifetime. As midnight approached, people drank copiously but solemnly. Some shed tears over the extinction of all gaiety. Some pleaded for souvenirs of an epoch about to pass into history—a champagne glass, an ice bucket. In the crowd around the four-sided bar of the Waldorf-Astoria, a man sadly sang "Auld Lang Syne" and the oldest bartender wept. Nobody surmised that New York was not to be permanently arid. Nobody foresaw the giddy, glittering era of speakeasies and night clubs, the crystallization of a café society, the rise of a new plutocracy dominated by bootleggers, gangsters and racketeers.

Wherever you looked in New York, you saw how rapidly life was changing. People expressed alarm at the defiant revolt of the younger generation. If your concern was paternal, the flapper was a problem. Otherwise, she was a pleasure. Jauntily feather-footed in her unfastened galoshes, her flesh-colored stockings rolled below the knee and her skirt barely touching it, slender and boyish, the flapper came in to the tune of "I'll Say She Does"—and frequently she did. Her seniors soon caught on. The women you saw shopping on Fifth Avenue didn't suggest matrimony and motherhood. Their shingled hair was peroxided or hennaed, their eyebrows were plucked and penciled, their eyelids were beaded, their cheeks and lips were piquantly rouged. Except for their silver-fox or mink jackets, the sum of what they wore could almost have been packed into their handbags. Smart leather-goods shops were advertising the novelty of an "overnight case." It seemed a primary requisite for women who, in the current phrase, were bent on "leading their own lives." One index of the moral revolution was a spreading masculine perplexity. How could you tell a "respectable woman" from one who wasn't?

EASTER EVE, WASHINGTON
SQUARE, *by John Sloan*

Sex appeared to be a ubiquitous commodity, as accessible as chewing gum. Amateur competition drove the streetwalkers indoors, except around Times Square.

At night, the former Gay White Way was dark and deserted. Old citadels of pleasure, like the Hoffman House and Martin's, had given way to business, which conquered Broadway as far north as Forty-second Street, where the Hotel Knickerbocker was presently converted into an office building. Times Square—with its immense electric signs, its fantasy of multicolored lights that raced and tumbled and danced and jetted into iridescent spray—was the center of nocturnal amusement. Broadway and Seventh Avenue, up through the roaring Forties and into the Fifties, were dominated by grandiose new movie palaces. The theaters were now to be found in the cross streets between Sixth and Eighth Avenues. Madison Square Garden was demolished to make way for an insurance skyscraper; a new sports arena was erected at Eighth Avenue and Fiftieth Street, inheriting the famous but now inaccurate name. Vaudeville was fighting a losing battle at the Palace Theater, last of its kind, which soon would succumb to the movies. On Broadway, and on Seventh Avenue, there were great public dance halls where you bought tickets, at a dime a dance, to cavort on a few inches of floor while embracing one of the large staff of girl "taxi-dancers." From the lower East Side, the enterprising brothers Minsky transported burlesque to Broadway, and a strip-tease queen became the newest idol of sophisticates.

Social change swiftly transformed Fifth Avenue during the postwar decade. Prohibition and the uptown trend of business closed Delmonico's, the city's most celebrated restaurant, after nearly a century of existence; its handsome building was replaced by a skyscraper. Sherry's—for a generation the scene of society's most spectacular fantasies—was converted to the uses of a great financial institution. But Louis Sherry's name was perpetuated by a corporation which, in addition to other enterprises, opened a new restaurant on Park Avenue. Smart society celebrated the nubility of its daughters in the Crystal Room of the Ritz-Carlton, and with a sigh of relief deputed to Miss Juliana Cutting the powers which its parents had vested in Ward McAllister. An elderly lady of impeccable lineage, assured position and imperious manner, Miss Cutting became a professional Cerberus, an industry as well as an institution. In the raffish, anarchic new era of gate-crashers, hip-flasks, and dubious parvenus, she regulated the social careers of the youthful élite, maintaining carefully graded lists of débutantes and stag-lines, circulating her chosen protégées through all the best parties, providing the thousand or more guests considered essential to a successful ball, and guaranteeing them an eligibility frequently contradicted by their singular behavior.

Meanwhile the tide of commerce flowed up Fifth Avenue as far as Fifty-ninth Street. Palaces of the Medici, built in the hope of permanence, fell to the wreckers and were replaced by skyscrapers and fashionable shops. The Renaissance chateau which Richard Morris Hunt designed for William K. Vanderbilt, the adjoining one erected for his son by Stanford White, the Florentine palazzo of Collis P. Huntington, were demolished. When past her eightieth year, Mrs. Cornelius Vanderbilt II sold her massive reminiscence of Fontainebleau for seven million dollars. Some of its interior glories went to embellish a motion-picture theater in the Middle West, but the aged chatelaine, determined to save its ornamental wrought-iron palisade from

FIFTH AVENUE CRITICS, *by John Sloan*

desecration, insisted that this be sunk in the Atlantic Ocean. Only the forbidding brownstone mansion of William Henry Vanderbilt resisted destruction. Occupied by Mrs. Cornelius Vanderbilt III, dowager empress of Mrs. Astor's shattered realm, it resembled a tasteless cenotaph. Sometimes you might have seen a red-velvet carpet unrolled at its entrance, a relic of more stately days which announced that Mrs. Vanderbilt was receiving the bearers of seventy-five august names who, according to her irreverent son, composed her primary list of the elect and "the backbone of American society." Oldest and ugliest of the Medicean dynastic monuments, the Vanderbilt mansion was a shrine dedicated to archaic rituals and fading splendor.

At Fifty-ninth Street the lofty Sherry-Netherland and Savoy-Plaza supplanted flamboyant hotels erected there during the eighteen-nineties. The long vista of palaces that fronted on Central Park soon passed into history. Wreckers razed the chateau from which Mrs. Astor had ruled society, the chateau to which Elbridge T. Gerry was able to invite one hundred dinner guests at a moment's notice. Northward along the Avenue, tall apartment houses displaced the imposing residences of multimillionaires. It was characteristic of the period that two of these numbered among their tenants Arnold Rothstein, financial genius of the underworld plutocracy, and Dutch Schultz, its outstanding local monopolist. Examples of the architecture of grandeur still survived, and some were inhabited by their owners. Mrs. Hamilton McK. Twombly, granddaughter of Commodore Vanderbilt, occupied the ninety-room residence which she had erected in her old age; she was reputed to pay her chef twenty-five thousand dollars a year. But most of the remaining mansions passed into the possession of schools, professional associations and other quasi-public enterprises. Or, like that of William C. Whitney, they were eventually shuttered and relegated to caretakers. After the death of the great tycoon's son, Harry Payne Whitney, his widow, the sculptress Gertrude Vanderbilt Whitney, preferred to reside in a studio on West Eighth Street. Only the imperial residence of Henry Clay Frick, preserved intact as a museum, would illustrate, for future generations, the way of life of the Medici.

The rich, old and new, took to new forms of existence. They moved into penthouses on the summits of towering buildings, duplex or triplex apartments having landscaped terraces that suggested the hanging gardens of Babylon. Or, wishing complete freedom from responsibility, they moved into costly apartment hotels where checkbook and pen were the only requisites for homemaking in four rooms or forty. One penthouse hostess offered her dinner guests the novelty of corn harvested from her "little farm" on the thirty-second floor. It no longer surprised people to be invited, by a wealthy dowager, to parties in her "little Gothic nest" high up in the Ritz Tower. The late-afternoon cocktail party, a new social institution, became the most popular form of hospitality. You might find your hostess installed in a five-room furnished suite at a luxurious hotel, its walls practically invisible under her aggregated Vermeers, Rembrandts and Italian primitives. These were indisputably more authentic than her Scotch and gin. But they seldom received even conversational attention from her guests—young Hapsburgs, anxious to please; hawklike White Russian princesses; insolent Hollywood stars; a darkly sinister torch-singer; a sprinkling of docile intellectuals and dashing débutantes; a few petulant gigolos and a large number of anonymous, agreeable people with vaguely familiar faces. At cocktail parties, the promise that "everybody is coming" was likely to be fulfilled more prodigally than the hostess intended. Guests thought nothing of bringing a few friends without requesting permission. In the beneficent alcoholic glow, nobody minded anything too much. Thimble-bellied drinkers were pleasantly led to bathrooms to be sick. Whenever possible, pugnacious ones were hustled into elevators before a fracas developed. Those who passed out were magnanimously ignored. The festivities, beginning at six o'clock, sometimes ran far into the following morning. "I want to give a really *bad* party," a character in one of Scott Fitzgerald's novels announced. "I want to give a party where there's a brawl and seductions and people going home with their feelings hurt and women passing out in the *cabinet de toilette.*" Of all desires, this was the easiest to gratify. Parties often turned out that way without any effort.

The residential transformation of Manhattan produced some odd results. One was the conversion of a slum into New York's most fashionable quarter. Past the tenements of Third, Second and First Avenues, on the edge of the East River and overshadowed by noisy Queensboro Bridge, several blocks of ancient, decaying brownstone dwellings lined the deserted continuation of Avenue A. The two blocks between Fifty-seventh and Fifty-ninth Streets were known as Sutton Place. It was here, on the northeast corner of Fifty-seventh Street, that Mrs. W. K. Vanderbilt chose to erect a handsome Georgian residence when she abandoned her Fifth Avenue chateau. Her friends Miss Anne Morgan and Miss Elisabeth Marbury bought and rebuilt the adjoining houses. Presently, wealth and fashion followed the trail blazed by these patrician pioneers into Sutton Place, into quaint Riverview Terrace, high above the East River between Fifty-eighth and Fifty-ninth Streets, into the old dwellings on Sutton Place South that were remodeled as small, expensive apartments. Great apartment houses soon encroached on this exclusive precinct. A "Sutton Place address"—a generic term indicating that you had migrated as far east as possible somewhere in the Fifties—placed you among the knowing who considered Fifth Avenue absurdly passé and Park Avenue vulgarly ostentatious. From their windows and terraces in this quarter, residents had a view of the traffic-laden East River, the municipal institutions on Welfare Island, the serrated skyline of factory-fringed Williamsburg and Long Island City. This vista was far inferior to that of the Hudson from Riverside Drive. But fashion had always condemned the West Side as unfashionable. So it surged into Beekman Place, a blighted relic of middle-class mid-Victorianism, creating there a colony of millionaires, people of the theater, highly paid artists and writers. It rehabilitated two rows of decrepit houses near Second Avenue, making their back yards a pretty communal garden, and Turtle Bay became identified with elegant sophistication. Throughout this ultrasmart area, there remained many gaunt tenements and old "cold-water" flats. In its juxtaposition of wealth and poverty the reclaimed slum achieved an irony unique even in New York.

On the cross streets of both the East and West Sides, the old "private houses" formerly sacred to one-family occupancy were profitably converted into multiple dwellings. On the fashionable East Side, you saw the grim brownstone residences shorn of their high stoops, their faces bravely painted, made over into stylish warrens, each of their rooms becoming a single self-contained apartment equipped with colored, tiled bath and electric kitchenette tucked away in one-time closets. A studio couch, a "modernistic" chest, some chromium-plated chairs, one or two Victorian pieces picked up in Third Avenue antique shops and subsequently "pickled," a mirror-topped cocktail table, a few aluminum pudding molds affixed to the walls, one of which was usually painted in a color different from the others—served to make these miniature habitations modishly "amusing." This was the adjective in vogue. It connoted mild deprecation, smart up-to-dateness and the current equivalent of an obsolete gentility. A one-room home on the East Side placed you among the prosperous, able to afford a monthly rental of more than one hundred dollars. On the West Side rentals were considerably lower, the word "amusing" was applicable chiefly to motion-picture shows, and pudding molds were confined to the kitchen. Many of the old homes, shabby and peeling, were lodging houses renting furnished rooms by the week or month. Many others had been converted into small apartments with a minimum of expenditure. Battered garbage cans on the sidewalks, milk bottles and brown-paper bags of food on the window sills, an air of suspended animation between the morning and evening rush hours, gave the long West Side streets their characteristic quality. These houses harbored "white-collar" office workers and business girls who bought their food in the ubiquitous delicatessen stores and prepared it on electric plates concealed on closet shelves; who were skilled in the use of bathroom clotheslines and electric irons; who took summer holidays at camps in the Catskills and derived their winter dreams from the neighborhood movie theaters.

Down on the Stock Exchange, a runaway bull market testified to limitless prosperity. Along with the wealthy, the middle classes plunged happily into the maelstrom of speculation. Clerks, housewives, taxi-drivers, shopkeepers, teachers, waiters in speakeasies were buying stocks on margin; the portal to riches stood invitingly open, and all America was storming through it. Announcement was made that John D. Rockefeller, Jr., had leased from Columbia University the tract of land bounded by Fifth and Sixth Avenues, between Forty-eighth and Fifty-first Streets, and would there erect a fabulous business and entertainment center, with a magnificent new opera house to replace the outdated old Metropolitan. Shortly afterward, it was announced that the Waldorf-Astoria Hotel would be closed and demolished, to make way for the tallest structure in the world—an office building rising to a height of one hundred and two stories, surmounted by a mooring-mast for dirigibles. Plans had been drawn for a new Waldorf-Astoria Hotel, forty-seven stories high, to be built on the square block bounded by Park and Lexington Avenues, from Forty-ninth to Fiftieth Streets. These projects were in tune with the spirit of the times. Nevertheless, as newspapers attested in sentimental, nostalgic articles, New York lamented the passing of the gaudy, stately old Waldorf-Astoria; its disappearance marked the end of an era.

And presently the age of fantasy was over. Down in the colonnaded temple on Broad Street an ominous recession had been followed by a rapid recovery. On October 24, 1929, the stock market crashed. Five days later, panic gripped the city and spread out over the nation as all financial values collapsed, and the gigantic structure of prosperity fell into ruins. While banks failed and bread lines lengthened and apple-sellers shivered on street-corners, the gleaming, white Empire State Building, projected by confidence, rose as a monument to hope.

TIMES SQUARE IN 1927, *by E. H. Suydam*

23

Paint, Protest and Parties

In New York, whatever seemed most unlikely was often bound to happen. So, characteristically, a rebellion against gentility broke out in the last remaining stronghold of conservatism. Resisting architectural change, the quarter around Washington Square preserved the atmosphere of an earlier, vanished city. The spacious Georgian mansions on the north side of the Square retained their traditional dignity. Some were occupied by the children of their builders, aged ladies and gentlemen so fiercely conservative that they rejected the automobile and drove up Fifth Avenue in victorias or barouches. Along the Square, and in the cross streets immediately north of it, silvered plates affixed to front doors bore names that ran far back in the city's history: Rhinelander, Stewart, Van Rensselaer, Jones.

For many years, painters and writers had resided among these patricians. They filled the old Tenth Street Studios and the newer studio buildings on Fifth Avenue and Twelfth Street. They lived in the pleasant red-brick houses lining quiet streets east and west of the Avenue. Eventually, they took over the stables of Washington Mews and MacDougal Alley, transforming these into studio homes. The south side of Washington Square, long deserted by patricians, had been a center of Bohemian life for two generations. A number of eminent artists had their studios in the Renaissance tower of the Judson Memorial Church designed by Stanford White. Most of the old homes had sunk to the shabby estate of rooming houses. One of these, conducted by an amiable Frenchwoman, Mme. Catherine Branchard, was already famous because it had harbored so many well-known writers in their impecunious youth. But even cheaper lodgings were to be found in Greenwich Village. In that forgotten backwater west of Sixth Avenue you could rent a room for as little as twelve dollars a month. The streets of Greenwich Village had been laid out on a diagonal to the north-south axis of Manhattan before the checkerboard street plan of the island was mapped early in the nineteenth century. It was a maze where even native New Yorkers lost their way in confusion, a labyrinth of narrow, twisting streets that seemed to cross and recross one another without ever arriving anywhere. In the Village, West Twelfth and West Fourth Streets improbably met. Most of the streets had names rather than numbers, and were lined by old, low, dormered red-brick houses slowly crumbling to decay; houses innocent of modern conveniences, with large, stately rooms. There were quaint cul-de-sacs like Milligan Place and Patchin Place, and odd byways like Minetta Lane. In its picturesque decrepitude, part slum, part shabby-genteel, the Village was curiously isolated from the roaring modern city that surrounded it. Presently, artists and writers, social radicals of all kinds, young people from all over the country who hoped to make careers in New York found congenial refuge there. Life in the Village was simple and cheap. It was a place where people were free to "be themselves."

It was the painters who first proclaimed a revolution in the arts. In his little gallery on the top floor of a brownstone building at 291 Fifth Avenue, the photographer Alfred Stieglitz showed the work of some American artists whose canvases looked like nothing that anybody had ever seen before and of some Europeans whose pictures were even more queerly incomprehensible. A shy, fragile little man, Stieglitz hectored the visitors who came to his tiny gallery to gape or laugh at "the craziest painters in America." He had an evangelical fire and fervor when he preached about Modern Art, about the Spirit of Life, about the Wonder of Things—somehow, you knew that he capitalized the initial letters—and his eloquence brought about conversions. When a Washington millionaire, Duncan Phillips, began collecting the paintings of John Marin, Stieglitz scored a public victory. Meanwhile, he kept his other protégés from starving, buying their work himself when nobody else would and laying the foundations of a collection which, forty years later, was to enrich a number of American museums, notably, New York's Metropolitan. In the studio on West Eighth Street where she practiced sculpture, Gertrude Vanderbilt Whitney held exhibitions of the work of unknown young artists. She had already determined to establish there a museum of American art chiefly devoted to living painters and sculptors. But the most ominous portent of revolution was a collective show put on by eight painters whose pictures, derided by the critics and scandalizing the public, won them the name of "the Ash Can School."

They gloried in the name. They despised all academic conventions. They detested the slick, "pretty-pretty" pictures exhibited by fashionable dealers, liked by a public which wanted to avoid all "unpleasant" aspects of life. Robert Henri, leader of the eight rebels, invented their battle cry: "Don't imitate; be yourself!" Of the others, John Sloan, William J. Glackens, George

WASHINGTON SQUARE: A holiday in the park, by *William J. Glackens;*
Courtesy, Museum of Modern Art

Luks and Everett Shinn had been newspaper illustrators, pictorial reporters of
city life in the raw. They lived near Washington Square, or in the Village.
They wanted to record the look and feeling of New York's workaday exist-

ence; the humor and squalor of streets and back alleys by day and by night; the drinkers in neighborhood bars, the crowded gallery of a vaudeville theater, frowsy women reeling out their wash on tenement clotheslines, shopgirls hurrying home from work. They weren't squeamish, and several of them had a talent for ribaldry which got expressed on their canvases. They relished the seamy side of New York life, and they painted it realistically, with an effect of cynical satire that displeased sentimentalists and provoked controversy whenever they held an exhibition.

The rebellious eight soon attracted adherents. Among these were Jerome Myers, who found a romantic aspect of New York in the streets, cafés and theaters of the lower East Side; Walt Kuhn, who painted the backstage life of theater and circus; George W. Bellows, whose favorite subject was prizefights. They joined Arthur B. Davies, one of the derided eight, in organizing an art exhibition which soon had New York in an uproar that spread over the country. The International Exhibition of Modern Art opened, early in the winter of 1913, at the armory of the Sixty-ninth Regiment on Park Avenue and Thirty-fourth Street. This "Armory Show" put on view sixteen hundred paintings and sculptures by American and European artists. Its emblem, significantly, was the pine tree symbolic of the American Revolution. Yet it was not the work of American rebels, but that of European experimenters, which made the show sensational. Outrage and protest flared up in newspaper headlines. Cubism, futurism, post-impressionism became issues in a battle that engaged the general public. Critics blasted at the baffling "Nude Descending a Staircase," by Marcel Duchamp; Constantin Brancusi's roughly hewn block, "The Kiss"; the distorted, crudely colored nudes of Henri Matisse; the incomprehensible vagaries of Pablo Picasso and Francis Picabia. Obviously these were the work of degenerates or imposters. Conservative New Yorkers spluttered and raged. Some demanded that the show be closed by the police, on the ground of obscenity. After all, hadn't Anthony Comstock raided the Art Students League with far less provocation? Theodore Roosevelt, who seldom lacked strong convictions on any subject, condemned all "modernists" as lunatics. Francis Picabia, whose paintings were one of the storm centers of the show, explained that modern art was "the objectivity of a subjectivity"—a definition that was hotly debated as being either profound or absurd. The famous tenor Enrico Caruso went to the armory, delightedly drew caricatures of cubist art and scattered them to a boisterous crowd. From early morning until late at night the exhibition was jammed with visitors, puzzled or exasperated or enthusiastic. Whatever their emotions, nearly all of them emerged in a belligerent mood. Everybody seemed to realize that this affair was making history. Even those who denounced the show most bitterly acknowledged that it was dynamite.

The revolutionary pine tree, emblem of the Armory Show, also symbolized the new spirit abroad in Greenwich Village. To the horror of patrician residents, people now included in the Village the quarter around Washington Square. For the Village wasn't merely a neighborhood. It was also a state of mind. It was hell-bent for change; "the old ways must go, and with them their priests." It wanted to precipitate another American revolution. Not only in art and literature. In morals—in social institutions and economics and politics. Even sex, presumably the oldest thing in the world, was taking on seriously revolutionary implications. A current story illustrated the difference between the Village and the rest of America. At the Ferrer School, a center of light and learning conducted by anarchists, where Robert Henri and George Bellows taught art and many distinguished writers gave lectures, one speaker had given a lecture on the new theories about sex. At the end of his address, an earnest little cloakmaker rose from her chair and indignantly announced, "Comrade Speaker, you talk about revolution, but I been in this here sexual movement for over twelve years, and I ain't seen no progress yet." The Ferrer School was not a Village institution, and in the Village they knew better. For the Village not only had an insatiable appetite for new theories—it put all of them into practice as quickly as possible. There was, for example, the case of young Max Eastman, a propagandist for the causes of suffrage and labor, and beautiful, mysterious Ida Rauh, a refugee from uptown brownstone wealth. They had fallen in love; disappointingly, they had married. But on the mail-box of their Charles Street flat appeared their two names, precisely as though they were unwed. The newspapers had blown up this fact into a scandal. Yet

THE HOTEL LAFAYETTE, *by John Sloan*

scarcely a year later Floyd Dell, a Chicago literary critic who moved into the Village to write fiction and poetry, was sharing an apartment with a girl, living with her "in sin" quite publicly. This was as it should be—a companionship of two artists who knew that it might not last long, though they hoped it would last forever. In the Village you didn't rest on professing your convictions; you felt obliged to demonstrate them in action. And since it was obvious that every attractive idea ought to be adopted, you were likely to lead a richly varied life. Though monogamy might be your hope and a final philosophy your object, your path was apt to be littered with abandoned lovers and discarded ideas. But wasn't this precisely what progress implied? Should life be anything but a perpetual experiment, a continuous use of freedom?

Freedom, experiment, change—these were the keynotes struck by Mabel Dodge's celebrated "Evenings." Pretty, plump Mrs. Dodge was a personage. Other people were intense—it was a quality highly approved—but she carried intensity to a pitch that astonished everyone. There seemed never to be enough "causes" to satisfy her ardor. She acquired and fostered them with impartial affection: the new art, the new poetry, birth control, free speech, the unemployed, the I. W. W., psychoanalysis. A woman of wealth, Mrs. Dodge came to Washington Square from long residence in Europe, cherishing a notion but seeking a mission. She believed that one must just let life express itself in whatever form it will. Her mission suddenly became clear; she would persuade life to express itself faster. Perhaps she could upset America, dynamite New York, bring ruin to the old order of things. The first step was "to get people together so that they can tell each other that they think." Of course, they must be people who "believe in life." Mrs. Dodge installed herself on one floor of a decaying mansion on the corner of Fifth Avenue and Ninth Street. She set out to dynamite New York from a beautiful white drawing room filled with delicate French furniture, illuminated by an ornate Venetian chandelier, and adorned with modern paintings, Persian miniatures and a collection of antique colored glass.

In Mrs. Dodge's drawing room daring projects were incubated. The Armory Show was developed there. So was the great pageant held in Madison Square Garden to dramatize the bitter strike of workers in the silk mills of Paterson, New Jersey, a strike organized by the militant, hated I. W. W. Handsome young John Reed wrote the pageant enacted by two thousand strikers. His Harvard classmate, Robert Edmond Jones, designed the scenery for it and staged it. Fifteen thousand New Yorkers turned out to see it, and high up on the Garden Tower the letters I. W. W. blazed in red electric lights which the police failed to extinguish. At Mrs. Dodge's gatherings, the air was always "vibrant with intellectual excitement, and electrical with the appearance of new ideas and dawning changes." You could listen to Emma Goldman preaching anarchism. Or hear "Big Bill" Haywood, leader of the I. W. W., and Elizabeth Gurley Flynn, the fiery "Wobbly Joan of Arc," expound the doctrine of syndicalism. When an "Evening" was devoted to the new art, modernist painters like Marsden Hartley or John Marin made it sound quite as explosive as the doctrines of the political radicals. Naturally, the queer theories of Dr. Sigmund Freud came up for discussion. Gnomelike Dr. A. A. Brill, the master's disciple and translator, was asked to elucidate them. Several guests got up and left, because they were either disturbed or incensed by his assertions about the subconscious, and the startling elements of one's personality that behavior revealed to the initiated. You might hear Mrs. Margaret Sanger also. She had been imprisoned for her birth-control crusade. She spoke as an ardent propagandist for the joys of the flesh, ridiculing the traditional sense of sin, explaining the physical possibilities of "sex expression." Gentle Hutchins Hapgood asserted that many brave young American women were conscientiously practicing free love, "adapting themselves in this way to life, and thus doing their share towards a final disintegration of the community." At Mrs. Dodge's "Evenings" you couldn't help believing that "the old ways were about over, and the new ways all to create."

Nobody doubted it at the Liberal Club, the Village's chief intellectual center, on MacDougal Street south of the Square. The leading spirit there was Henrietta Rodman, an earnest, reckless idealist who was constantly discovering new schemes for the betterment of the world. Miss Rodman was a teacher in a public high school, and the municipal authorities found her hard to cope with, for she couldn't be intimidated. What were they to do with a rebel who agitated for suffrage, went in for free love, associated with anarchists and socialists, crusaded for the reform of dress, demonstrating her theories by cropping her hair and going about hatless, clad in flowing robes and sandals? At the Liberal Club you were likely to meet the literary set, the artist crowd, and several different groups of political radicals. Though they shared a desire to upset the established order, they disagreed violently about programs of salvation. Since everybody acknowledged that nothing was more important than a program, controversy seldom died down. Ideas exploded with a noise that soon began to be heard across the continent. Speakers often came to the Liberal Club directly from jail, having defied the law in some spectacular public demonstration of their convictions. Members of the Club listened enthusiastically. They were conscientious protesters. They tried to dream up offenses that would carry them to prison and martyrdom in behalf of their principles; that was a principle, too. Even the poets and painters yearned to provoke Mrs. Grundy into calling the police. How better could they prove that art was revolutionary?

But this thesis scarcely required any assistance from the police. Every issue of *The Masses* proclaimed it, and *The Masses* was rapidly making the Village nationally famous. With headquarters in a converted store on Greenwich Avenue, which Villagers liked to call the Boul' Mich', this magazine was a cooperative venture run by a group of writers and artists. Among the writers on its board were John Reed, Louis Untermeyer and Mary Heaton Vorse. The artist members included John Sloan, George Bellows, Stuart Davis and fat, genial Art Young, whose powerful social cartoons were a regular feature. Edited by Max Eastman and Floyd Dell, *The Masses* professed to be "a revolutionary and not a reform magazine." It had no respect for the respectables; it was searching for "true causes"; and its policy was to conciliate nobody, not even its readers. After pondering a typical issue, one cynical newspaper columnist concluded:

> They draw nude women for *The Masses*
> Thick, fat, ungainly lasses—
> How does that help the working classes?

The poetry and fiction published by the magazine were little less disconcerting than its nudes or its political opinions. Its roster of contributors heralded a literary renaissance: Sherwood Anderson, Carl Sandburg, Edgar Lee Masters, Upton Sinclair; and, in time, Edna St. Vincent Millay, John Dos Passos, E. E. Cummings. At monthly editorial meetings, contributions for the next issue were put to a vote of the board and debate about them always ran high. This democratic practice exasperated Hippolyte Havel, a volcanic little anarchist. "Bourgeois pigs!" he blazed out at one meeting. "Voting! Voting on poetry! Poetry is something from the soul! You can't vote on poetry!"

Perpetually in need of funds, *The Masses* staged an annual benefit costume ball at Webster Hall, on East Eleventh Street, a gay and riotous celebration where intellectuals masqueraded and then went to hail the dawn, with appropriate ceremonies, in Washington Square. Inspired by these revels, the Liberal Club followed suit with their Pagan Routs—so named by Floyd Dell —where the high-jinks of Village nymphs and satyrs soon attracted sightseers from uptown Manhattan. One night a group of pranksters succeeded in climbing to the top of Washington Arch, undetected by the police, to proclaim the free republic of Greenwich Village, a Utopia dedicated, as one Villager later said, to "socialism, sex, poetry, conversation, dawn-greeting, anything so long as it was taboo in the Middle West."

Since costume balls were fun, why not try amateur theatricals? The painter Everett Shinn had already written two witty burlesques and produced them in his studio. The Liberal Club set up a movable stage and began experimenting with programs of one-act plays written and acted by members. John Reed contributed several. Floyd Dell wrote a series of comedies that satirized "modern" ideas, "radical" behavior and the "causes" which kept the Liberal Club and *The Masses* in a continuous ferment. This levity shocked consecrated radicals like Miss Rodman, but amused others whose idealism was less vulnerable. The Village was aware that its rebellious nonconformity had a humorous aspect. It enjoyed having its most serious convictions mocked at by one of its most prominent rebels. The success of Dell's comedies led to experiments with more serious plays. Presently, a group headed by Robert Edmond Jones, Philip Moeller and Edward Goodman organized a company called The Washington Square Players. It offered one production at the Liberal Club, and the outlook for a Village theater seemed hopeful. But the ambitious producers had visions of a larger, wealthier audience. They deserted the Village for a theater far uptown, in fashionable East Fifty-seventh Street, and some years

CURTAIN TIME, *by Carlos Anderson*

later reorganized their company under the name of The Theater Guild. Meanwhile, the amateur performances at the Liberal Club suggested a project to George Cram Cook and his wife, Susan Glaspell.

Cook and Miss Glaspell had recently come to the Village from Iowa, and were living in Milligan Place. They often dined at Polly's restaurant, in the basement under the Liberal Club, and Cook sometimes joined the crowd at the Working Girls' Home, on the corner of Greenwich Avenue and Christopher Street. These were the favorite Village hangouts. Polly Holliday, who ran the restaurant, looked like a madonna and came from the staid town of Evanston, Illinois. She was an anarchist, philosophically so orthodox that she could not be persuaded to join the Liberal Club; she considered all organizations equally illegitimate. Her partner in the restaurant was Hippolyte Havel, the eccentric little anarchist; he cooked the food, waited on table, and argued with the patrons, often denouncing them to their faces as "bourgeois pigs." The atmosphere of the Working Girls' Home was very different. It was a comfortable, old-fashioned saloon, run by a genial Irishman named Luke O'Connor. Many years earlier, when he was stranded and broke in New York, John Masefield had worked there, and O'Connor had a photograph of the now celebrated poet hanging above the bar. This connection with literary fame inclined O'Connor to take a tolerant view of Village writers and artists. He provided them with a nourishing free lunch and extended generous credit, so the Working Girls' Home was always crowded.

The Liberal Club's program of plays incited Susan Glaspell and "Jig" Cook, as his friends called him, to try their hands at playwriting. With some other

Villagers, they went up to Provincetown, on Cape Cod, during the summer, and produced their plays very simply on a porch. The next year, they took an abandoned wharf and rebuilt it as a small theater. Word reached them that a young Villager had arrived in Provincetown with a trunkful of plays. Said Miss Glaspell, "Well, tell him we don't need a trunkful, but ask him to bring one." The unknown playwright came over to read his play aloud; he was a tall, lean, dark man with burning eyes; his name was Eugene O'Neill. Two of his plays were accepted and produced that summer. Cook and Miss Glaspell were convinced that they had discovered a genius. Cook was a middle-aged romantic, an incurable idealist who had never found a congenial vocation. But now he determined to establish an art theater dedicated to a form of drama as experimental, as revolutionary, as the new painting, poetry and fiction. Returning to New York, he rented a ramshackle stable on MacDougal Street, adjoining the Liberal Club, converted it into The Playwrights' Theater, assembled a company of actors in the Village as The Provincetown Players, and launched a venture that soon achieved celebrity. The Provincetown Playhouse, as it came to be called, produced the works of many young playwrights, but it was chiefly to see the early plays of O'Neill that audiences came from all over New York to sit on hard benches in a dim, narrow stable and watch a company of gifted amateurs perform on a stage little larger than a handkerchief.

An early recruit to the company of amateurs was a young girl who came to the Village from Vassar College, and settled in a bleak room on Waverly Place to write poetry while seeking to earn her living as an actress. Slender, red-haired, undeniably pretty, Edna St. Vincent Millay captivated the Villagers with her frivolous ways, her gaiety, her delight in life. She wanted to live fearlessly and fully, at whatever cost, and it was this attitude, expressed in her verse, that made her the idol of youth all over the land. She invoked the lovely light of a candle burned at both ends, all too quickly consumed. She wrote bitter-sweet, skeptical love songs which made her the accredited spokesman of a generation that seemed resolved to purchase its wisdom at "the booth where folly holds her fair."

Presently, the claim of some residents that the Village had become "the cradle of modern American culture" seemed beyond dispute. Willa Cather, whose novels everybody was reading, lived there. Theodore Dreiser, who had been living uptown, moved into a studio on ·West Tenth Street. A large, awkward, friendly man, he had a great zest for serious conversation, and at his parties Kirah Markham, a dark, statuesque beauty, presided over the punch bowl in a setting lit by flickering candles and dull lamps. At Dreiser's you might hear Edgar Lee Masters read his *Spoon River* poems, or you might find a crowd gathered around ouija boards to receive communications from the supernatural realm. Sherwood Anderson made long visits from Chicago, a stout, florid man who seemed permanently perplexed but was nevertheless persistently oracular. The poet Edwin Arlington Robinson spent much of his time in the Village. Tall, thin, slightly stooped, Robinson had a storklike, scholarly look. Incurably shy, he was a legendary recluse, and you needed long acquaintance to break down his habitual reserve. Sometimes you saw him dining at Regnaneschi's table d'hôte, near Jefferson Market Court, with one or two friends. But he had a curious prejudice against sitting at a table with more than three people; he thought it "uncivilized." Occasionally Miss Amy Lowell came down to the Village from Boston, to read her verse to an audience of young poets. A massive, masculine-looking woman, armed with a huge portfolio, a battered reading lamp, an impressive repertory of profanity and a case of very black cigars, she usually managed to turn an evening of poetry into a furious brawl where a half-dozen quarrels were going on at once. She had a taste for battle and she didn't think much of any art that failed to provoke a row.

Some of the battles that convulsed the Village rang out over the nation. Censorship, in one or another guise, initiated many of them, lifting into high relief the conflict between conservatives and radicals. Even before the United States entered the First World War, *The Masses* was constantly in trouble with the authorities. With the advent of war, it was suppressed by the Department of Justice; its editors were indicted, and twice brought to trial, under the Espionage Act. Meanwhile, the Society for the Suppression of Vice had banned the sale of Theodore Dreiser's novel *The "Genius,"* and under the leadership of H. L. Mencken American liberals launched a crusade to establish the freedom of writers. In courtrooms where pacifists were standing trial you would have seen Miss Millay who, hating war as bitterly as they did, came to comfort them by reciting her poems while juries decided on their cases.

By the end of the war, the Village had become nationally famous as New York's "Latin Quarter." The best advertised of American Bohemias, it was a lure to sightseers and a destination for all types of eccentrics. Even the look of the Village had changed. It was no longer insulated from the city. The West Side subway, with a station in the very heart of the Village, made it as accessible as Times Square. Traffic roared up and down the wide swath of Seventh Avenue, which had been extended through the middle of the quarter, leaving the hideous scars of partly demolished buildings on both sides. Antique shops flourished on Eighth Street, Christopher Street and Greenwich Avenue. Everywhere you saw "quaint" basement tearooms, with names like The Purple Pup, The Mad Hatter, The Mousetrap. In many of these, "poets" recited their works by candlelight and gullible tourists absorbed "art." Sheridan Square, with its subway station, was the center of a profitable tourist trade. A new, pretentious, modern theater was erected there, and *The Greenwich Village Follies* played, at Broadway prices, to uptown audiences. There, also, young Don Dickerman opened his Pirate's Den, a tourist night spot having a coffin as a signboard, waiters and musicians dressed as buccaneers, cutlasses and blunderbusses hanging on the walls. When Polly Holliday abandoned MacDougal Street and the radicals to open a large, "bourgeois" restaurant nearby, old Villagers felt that the end had come. It was a bitter thing, Floyd Dell said, to look at the new generation of "professional Villagers," playing their antics in public for pay, and realize that this was the kind of person one was supposed, by the public, to be.

The earlier groups of Villagers were rebels and radicals on principle; even their defiant love affairs were conducted in the light of some social theory, deliberately adopted. To be immoral for the sake of a higher morality was a program they understood. But they were appalled by the new settlers whose only principle, they thought, was to have no principles whatever. At the height of their fame, "Jig" Cook disbanded the Provincetown Players; when they achieved popular success, he was convinced that they had failed. Eugene O'Neill's plays were being produced on Broadway. "Jig" Cook and Miss Glaspell left the Village to pursue the ideal in Greece. Mrs. Dodge, after a tempestuous love affair with John Reed and a marriage to the painter Maurice Sterne, departed for Taos, New Mexico, and a new mission among the Pueblo Indians. John Reed, after helping to found the Communist Party, went to Russia, died there, and was buried as a hero in Moscow's Red Square. Miss Millay married and went to live in the Berkshire Hills. Many of the other early settlers migrated to Westchester, or Montparnasse, or the French Riviera. The Village, Floyd Dell lamented, had become a showplace where there was no longer any privacy from the vulgar stares of an uptown rabble. It had advertised its freedom and happiness too well, and shrewd enterprisers were providing cheap substitutes for tourists who wouldn't know the difference.

The new gathering places boasted of "atmosphere" and exploited "characters." On Washington Square South, Guido Bruno, a huge blond Czech, conducted a widely publicized "garret" where self-styled geniuses performed for awed Philistines. Grace Godwin operated a rival garret nearby. Romany Marie, a former member of Miss Goldman's anarchist group, opened a dimly lighted rendezvous where nothing more conspiratorial than fortune-telling and gypsy music was offered. There you saw bobbed-haired Village girls wearing the batik smocks, scarves and blouses they had bought from Peter Mijer, who came to the Village from Java, bringing this new craft which presently became a vogue that swept over the whole country. Wandering through the village restaurants, Bobby Edwards, a tall, emaciated man wearing large, shell-rimmed eyeglasses, strummed his ukulele and sang his comic songs. Tiny Tim, a pale youth with long black hair, went about selling his "soul candy"—each package contained one of the poems which he no longer tried to have printed in magazines. "Old Man" Clivette was another character who made a profession of failure. As a painter in Paris, he was reputed to have gained some prestige. But in the Village he presided over an institution known as the Bazaar de Junk, insulting the tourists who came to buy the weird objects offered for sale, or attend the evening "readings" held there. Some Villagers asserted that Joe Gould was an unrecognized genius. A little man, bald, scantily bearded, with the air of a college professor, Gould was writing an interminable work, either autobiography or history, of which no fragment was ever published. Was Baroness Elsa von Freytag von Loringhoven a genius or a madwoman? Margaret Anderson, of *The Little Review*, published the

GREENWICH VILLAGE CAFETERIA, *by Paul Cadmus; Courtesy, Museum*
of Modern Art

Baroness' verses, and declared her to be "the only figure of our generation
who deserves the epithet extraordinary." Penniless, often starving, she lived
in two tenement rooms with three dogs, painting and writing verse and parad-
ing the Village streets in eccentric costumes which frequently caused her to
be arrested. Once she shaved her head and lacquered it bright vermilion. To a
benefit concert for *The Little Review* held at the Provincetown Playhouse, she
came attired in a trailing blue-green dress, carrying a peacock-feather fan, her
face powdered yellow, her lips painted black, a canceled postage stamp affixed
to one cheek, and wearing, for a hat, an inverted coal-scuttle. Introduced to
the singer who had performed, the Baroness asked her why she sang. "I sing
for humanity," the singer replied. Contemptuously, the Baroness boomed out,
"I wouldn't lift a leg for humanity." In a way, this declaration summed up
the attitude of many of the newer Villagers.

The younger writers and painters who had settled in the Village with in-
tentions of serious work soon learned to avoid the more publicized gathering
places. Many of them rallied around *The Little Review,* which handsome
Margaret Anderson and stout, forthright Jane Heap had transferred from
Chicago to New York. This eclectic publication, dedicated to the work of the
literary advance guard, was the most influential of a series of little magazines

which had sprung up in the Village, had briefly flourished there but had usually died for want of support. Unlike its predecessors, *The Little Review* found readers throughout the United States, and even in Europe. In part this was due to the fact that every issue carried an installment of James Joyce's *Ulysses,* the publication of which kept its intrepid editors under constant attack by the Society for the Suppression of Vice. But Miss Anderson and Miss Heap were dauntless, and you would not have surmised that they never had a week when their morning coffee was assured, or that it was not unusual for them to live for three days at a time on biscuits because they had no money for other food.

In their apartment, in an old house on Sixteenth Street just west of Fifth Avenue, you heard the best talk to be had in New York, and sometimes the most exciting music also, for Miss Anderson was a talented pianist, and the *Little Review* circle included advance-guard musicians as well as writers and painters. The large living room in Sixteenth Street, with its gold-papered walls and old mahogany furniture and blue divan swung from the ceiling on heavy black chains, was an oasis for creative minds, and there you were likely to meet young writers whose work was blazing new trails for their con- temporaries: the brilliant, unhappy poet Hart Crane; tall, slim, auburn- haired Djuna Barnes, an innovator in both verse and prose; the poet Lola Ridge. Presently, however, *The Little Review* was suppressed, and Miss An- derson and Miss Heap transferred it to the more favorable climate of Paris. Another magazine thereafter maintained the Village's repute as a citadel of culture. Generously subsidized, and domiciled on West Thirteenth Street, *The Dial* became the accredited champion of the advance guard. Its roster of contributors included many eminent European writers and artists. But it also published the early work of some Americans identified with the Village either by residence or affiliation; among them, Marianne Moore, Glenway Wescott and William Carlos Williams.

However, by the nineteen-twenties, if you wished to see celebrities, you didn't look for them in the Village. The largest constellation could always be found, during the lunch hour, at a hotel on West Forty-fourth Street near Sixth Avenue. The Algonquin was a rendezvous of "sophisticates" unique in New York, and its fame had traveled far and wide over the land. The Village prided itself on striking the note of the future, on being in advance of the times; it wore poverty and frustration as badges of honor. But the Algonquin spoke vigorously for the present, and its keynote was success. Lunch there had become an institution of the city's theatrical, journalistic and literary worlds. The general public went to gape at its current favorites as, a genera- tion earlier, it had gone first to the Waldorf-Astoria and then to Rector's. Elegant, suave, witty Frank Case conducted the Algonquin as if it were a salon or a club. He was a lover of good talk and, in his own right, as much a celebrity as any of his eminent guests. Georges Jacques, the head waiter who presided urbanely over the Rose Room, did duty as the intelligentsia's Dun and Bradstreet. His decision on your request for a table placed you either among the "haves" or the "have nots." If you deserved admittance, the location of your table indicated your prestige rating. "No diplomat in Vienna was ever more adroit than Georges," Jim Tully declared. "He seats people according to their stations. And each writer seated feels as august as the Pope, though he be hidden so far behind a post that he could not be found by the Nobel committee."

But, as everyone knew, the real rulers of this noonday Vatican assembled at the Round Table. They lunched together daily, and rumor credited them with formidable power. They were more arbitrary than Mrs. Astor in the days of her supreme authority, and nobody would have dared to crash the triple barriers of their exclusiveness. They detested bores; they cherished violent antipathies; their genius for verbal assassination was notorious. Was not the Round Table a kind of stock market, establishing the daily values of professional reputations? The coterie included men who were notably shaping public opinion. There were critics and columnists whose verdicts could make or break: Alexander Woollcott, Heywood Broun, Franklin P. Adams, Robert Benchley, Deems Taylor. There was Harold Ross, editor of *The New Yorker*, a new, highly influential weekly. The playwrights George S. Kaufman, Marc Connelly and Robert Sherwood were prominent members of the group. So were best-selling novelists Edna Ferber and Alice Duer Miller, and Dorothy Parker, who was gaining celebrity for her barbed light verse and ironical short stories. Viewing the array of talent usually present at the Round Table, Frank Ward O'Malley once remarked that if an explosion occurred and blew the coterie into eternity, American literature would stop dead—for twenty-four hours.

This was probably a jaundiced appraisal. So, too, was the comment that the coterie lived by one another's wits. Certainly wit, at least in the public mind, was their common hallmark. They invented the wisecrack, and the fast comeback that topped it. Some of their wisecracks were genially malicious. But the best were intended to draw blood and inject a drop of poison; to rate with this coterie, the victim had to produce a lethal retort. Not only did the group give a new turn to American humor, but they exemplified an attitude of skepticism soon widely adopted. Reacting against solemnity, pretentiousness, smugness, they helped to create a vogue for the flippant and cynical. Sophisticates had to be bright and knowing and up to date at any cost; how otherwise could you distinguish them from mere highbrows or sourpusses?

In addition to the Round Table perennials, the Rose Room always staged a dazzling show of theatrical and literary notables. Where else would you have found, on a typical day, Ethel Barrymore, Jane Cowl, Marilyn Miller, Tallulah Bankhead, Laurette Taylor, Gertrude Lawrence, Noel Coward; perhaps, for good measure, Lillian Gish, Mary Pickford and Douglas Fairbanks? Sooner or later, you also saw most of the famous writers. Sinclair Lewis, Joseph Hergesheimer, Carl Van Vechten, Gertrude Atherton and handsome Fannie Hurst. The rising young stars: Scott Fitzgerald, Louis

Bromfield, Robert Nathan. Ruddy, jovial Irvin Cobb and massive Hendrik van Loon. Elinor Wylie, whose beauty caused even more commotion than her fine poems, or the delicate fantasies which she called novels. The writers whose short stories were being featured in current magazines: Katherine Brush, Thyra Winslow, Donn Byrne, Konrad Bercovici, who looked like a ferocious Balkan bandit, but was all kindliness; ebullient Charles Brackett. Occasionally you might see H. L. Mencken and George Jean Nathan, who had made *The American Mercury* the intelligentsia's favorite magazine. Such leading reviewers of books as Harry Hansen, Burton Rascoe and Ernest Boyd were seldom absent. No wonder that ambitious young writers tried to wangle invitations to the Rose Room. One of them dedicated his first novel to twenty prominent Algonquinites, identified only by their initials; his entire literary education had been acquired by table-hopping. It was easy to understand why Mrs. Atherton and Joseph Hergesheimer wrote up the Algonquin in best-selling novels. The wonder was that more novelists didn't make copy of it. New York had never before had a playground for so many lively minds bent on gaiety, and delighting in the antics of a cockeyed world.

The cult of gaiety, the general sense of fun, found an outlet in parties. Every day at six o'clock the round began; if you wished, you could keep going until long after dawn. An aura of turbulence and violence, an overtone of madness put a premium on conduct that was exuberantly bizarre. Of the more spectacular forms of hedonism, blond, handsome Scott Fitzgerald and his pretty, tawny-haired wife, Zelda, ranked as creators. It was therefore in character for Fitzgerald to jump into the Pulitzer Fountain in front of the Plaza Hotel; to try to disrobe himself in a theater during the performance of a revue; and, when sufficiently drunk, to get into fights with waiters in speakeasies, or other guests at parties. On one occasion, with a group of acquaintances, the Fitzgeralds embarked on a tour of night clubs that led from Broadway to Washington Square and up through Harlem. At five in the morning, the revelers arrived at Childs' on Fifth Avenue and Fifty-seventh Street, for breakfast. When this ritual had been concluded, it seemed time for the party to break up. Fitzgerald, however, was in no mood to go home—home was the place where you dressed to go out. He herded a few loyal spirits into a taxicab and rattled them off downtown. As it turned out, their destination was the morgue, and the end of their evening's gaiety was an inspection of cadavers.

24

Some Liked It Hot

It was the rise of the cabaret and the sudden outbreak of a dance craze that radically altered New York's night life. In less than six months, the old "lobster-palace society" faded out and its historic citadel was demolished. When Rector's famous griffin ceased to blaze above Times Square an era passed into history. Moralists who had formerly denounced the establishment as a temple of sin began speaking of it as a vanished stronghold of propriety. In retrospect Rector's seemed, like Mrs. Astor's ballroom, a symbol of social conservatism. Even Julian Street, light-hearted chronicler of Broadway pleasures and no puritan, was aghast at the changes. He warned his readers throughout the nation that the cabarets had brought into being "a social mixture such as was never before dreamed of in this country—a hodge-podge of people in which respectable young married and unmarried women, and even débutantes, dance, not only under the same roof, but in the same room with women of the town." The new "cabaret society" was a genuinely democratic group, dedicated to liberty, equality and fraternity. In its frantic, joyous night prowling you saw Fifth Avenue dowagers and gilded youth; Broadway stars; showgirls, prostitutes, gigolos; Tenderloin big shots, tycoons of brothels and gambling houses; Tammany politicians and Wall Street playboys.

To Captain Jim Churchill, proprietor of one of Broadway's gaudier lobster palaces, the new vogue was an old story. A retired police officer of long experience, he remembered dives like Billy McGlory's and McGurk's Suicide Hall. "They'll 'can' this cabaret stuff," he prophesied. "It's just 'joint' stuff." But to stay in business, Churchill had to move with the times. Reluctantly, he sank his moral prejudices and converted his restaurant into a cabaret. In a cabaret, little tables were massed around a large central space, where a show was put on by singers and teams of professional dancers, and where the patrons also danced. No matter where you went, you saw couples leaving their tables, their food and champagne to push onto the dance floor. There, locked in a tight embrace, they moved through the startling figures of the Texas Tommy, the bunny hug, the grizzly bear, the turkey trot, the one-step, or the tango. Never before had well-bred people seen—much less performed—such flagrantly salacious contortions. Yet, as a popular song declared, "everybody's doing it." At Louis Martin's Café de l'Opéra, on Broadway and Forty-second Street, the spacious ground-floor restaurant was deserted after midnight. But the gilded, mirrored cabaret and ballroom upstairs was always crowded. So were the dancing rooms at Bustanoby's, in Thirty-ninth Street; at Murray's ornate Roman Gardens, on Forty-second Street west of Times Square; at Maxim's, at the Cafe Madrid. In John Reisenweber's establishment just below Columbus Circle, three floors were given over to dancing. George Rector, in his new place on Broadway a block north of Columbus Circle, opened a ballroom which featured a *"souper* Tabarin." New Yorkers were happily unaware that the *Bal Tabarin,* in Paris, was a dive. In the feverish, festive winter of 1913, Manhattan night life centered on restaurants which, in effect, were merely public dance halls of a more expensive kind than those frequented by the working classes.

The cabarets and the scandalous "modern dances" set off a hurricane of protest. Outraged conservatives, clergymen, educators, social workers, editors of newspapers joined in a massive attack. They were stirred to wrath by "vice," by "immorality," openly condoned and participated in by New York's "best people"—with a shameless abandon never before conceivable. Few of these enraged protesters foresaw that the new night life and the new dances were to help bring about a revolution in morals, manners, fashions in clothes, social customs. But some clergymen expounded the prophetic significance of an immense painting displayed in the blue, gold and black marble splendor of Louis Martin's Café de l'Opéra—a French and fleshly representation of the Fall of Babylon. Yet, notwithstanding the violent storm of denunciation, the dance craze persisted, became endemic. At all the cabarets you saw lines of men and women, in full evening attire, held back by a velvet rope and a stern head waiter who was busily checking their names against his list of advance reservations.

How had it all started? A season or two earlier, in *The Hen Pecks,* a Broadway musical, Blossom Seeley, a raucous young singer, put over a song called "Toddling the Todolo" and, as an encore, danced the Texas Tommy, long familiar on San Francisco's Barbary Coast. Then, out of New York's Tin Pan Alley—West Twenty-eighth Street between Broadway and Sixth Avenue—there had come a song which quickly swept over the continent. You heard "Alexander's Rag-time Band" wherever you went, and its snappy rhythm made you want to shake your shoulders and your feet. Its composer, Irving

BURLYCUE, *by Kyra Markham*

Berlin, was the son of an immigrant Russian cantor who had settled on the lower East Side. Before rising to the comparative dignity of Tin Pan Alley, young Berlin had earned his living as a "'singing waiter" in "Nigger Mike" Salter's saloon and Jimmy Kelly's Chatham Club, notorious Chinatown dives. Ragtime, however, was no novelty. It had been made popular, for nearly a decade, by Negro composers, musicians and singers—and Bert Williams, most famous of the singers, had been starred for three years in the *Follies* by Florenz Ziegfeld. The song writers of Tin Pan Alley, and other people interested in genuine ragtime, had long been dining, on Sunday evenings, at a small hotel on West Fifty-third Street, under the elevated, operated for members of his own race by Jimmie Marshall, an accomplished Negro. Marshall's was famous as the New York headquarters for Negro talent. There, on Sunday nights, you saw the actors, musicians, composers, vaudeville headliners—such celebrated performers as Ada Overton Walker, Abbie Mitchell, Bert Williams, such successful song writing teams as Bob Cole and J. Rosamund Johnson, who, among many other hits, had produced "Under the Bamboo Tree"; Alex Rogers and Will Marion Cook, who put out "Bon Bon Buddy, the Chocolate Drop." You saw Ford Dabney and James Reese Europe, who had organized and trained Negro orchestras; Will Dixon, the "dancing conductor"; "Buddy" Gilmore, the trick tap-drummer. On Sunday nights, at dinner, these stars performed for the pleasure of their friends. Marshall's had a cabaret long before Broadway ever heard the word. If you went to Marshall's you knew about a new, unorthodox form of Negro music, called "jazz," which had come up from the honky-tonks of Storyville in New Orleans. You knew about an entirely new genre of Negro songs, the "blues," which had been set down by William C. Handy, a band leader and composer who was working on Beale Street, in Memphis, Tennessee.

Jazz and the blues first leaked out into Manhattan from Marshall's. As early as 1905, a playing-dancing-singing Negro band was organized there as "The Memphis Students." They used banjos, mandolins, guitars, saxophones and drums in combination, and were given star billing at Hammerstein's Victoria Theater, the Metropolitan Opera House of vaudeville. Five years later, Jim Europe gathered all the professional Negro band players into a chartered organization, The Clef Club, which did a tremendous business in supplying bands for private parties. In the spring of 1912, Jim Europe determined to give New York a public demonstration of the new Negro music. The Clef Club rented Carnegie Hall—sacred home of classical music, of Philharmonic concerts and highbrow song recitals. Conducted by Europe himself, a band of one hundred and twenty-five performers played and sang the strange, syncopated jazz compositions, and a crowded auditorium went wild with enthusiasm. The music required to touch off a dance craze had arrived.

But the dance craze wasn't born of music alone. The cabaret brought it to birth, with the help of professional dancers. Louis Martin was the first to feature, in quick succession, the professionals whose bizarre innovations launched a national mania. Maurice—dark-haired, debonair, colubrine—arrived from Paris already notorious. There he had introduced the *danse des Apaches* to aristocratic patrons of the Café de Paris, and he had been the most admired performer of the tango. Rumor asserted that, in the violence of a dance, he had once broken his woman partner's neck. Once was enough—at least, to excite curiosity in New York. His first performance was a sensation; thereafter, he was known as "the high priest of the decadent dance." All New York flocked to see him, waiting breathlessly for the climactic moment when his pretty blonde partner leaped astride his hips and, clinging to his waist with her bent knees, swung outward and away from his whirling body like a floating sash. Dowagers of the utmost social distinction sent him hundred-dollar bills, pleading that he come to their tables and offer to lead them through the paces of a tango or turkey trot. Frequently they received nothing more for their money than a snub. This provocative rudeness increased his popularity with smart people. Besides, he was elegant, sophisticated, and he spoke, with equal fluency, both the French of the boulevards and the argot of the *apaches*. A romantic figure, certainly. There were so many piquant legends about his early life that nobody guessed the facts. He was not a Parisian *apache* or the illegitimate son of a French aristocrat, but merely a native New Yorker, born and bred in the slums. Yet he had a peculiar importance, for he prefigured a new social type. He paved the way for the gigolo, the costly, pampered, serviceable pet of wealthy women, more showy than a Pomeranian or a Pekingese and perhaps superior as a stimulant to exercise.

However, the celebrity of Maurice was soon eclipsed by that of a pair of dancers who rocketed to worldwide fame. Lanky, blond, humorous Vernon

Castle and his demurely pretty wife, Irene, transformed the dance craze from a transient mania into a permanent element of American civilization. When they teamed up with Jim Europe and began composing their dances to his syncopated music, they initiated a process that eventually made jazz as indispensable to the nation's life as breakfast coffee. And, in somewhat less than three years, they taught the American woman to discard her petticoats, throw away her corset, abbreviate her skirts and bob her hair. The Castles had given up small parts in *The Hen Pecks* to play a comic sketch in a Paris revue. As part of their act they danced Miss Seeley's Texas Tommy, which won them an engagement at the Café de Paris. There they developed a repertory of eccentric new dances which delighted the patrons. On their return to New York they scored an immediate success at Louis Martin's cabaret. Unlike Maurice, they were neither exotic nor "decadent." They were young, married, good-looking, well-mannered, and they danced with an exuberant gaiety that was contagious. The dances they invented were tricky and full of stunts, but puritans could find no taint of indecency in their performance. Socialites who had succumbed to the dance craze but who nevertheless were disturbed by the raging storm of denunciation, hailed the Castles as exponents of grace and decorum. The worst you could say was that some of their inventions showed a touch of absurdity. One night at Martin's, they had as their guest Elsie Janis, a popular star of musical comedy. On the spur of the moment they improvised a new dance, which Miss Janis pronounced "too ridiculous to consider doing again." She was both right and wrong. The "Castle Walk" became a furor. "It sounds silly and it is silly," said the Castles, when the whole nation had taken it up. "That is the explanation of its popularity."

After seeing the Castles, Miss Elisabeth Marbury decided that the dance craze could be rescued from obloquy. She assembled a dozen leaders of New York society, among them Mrs. Stuyvesant Fish, Mrs. T. J. Oakley Rhinelander, and Mrs. Herman Oelrichs. Under their august sponsorship, Castle House, opposite the Ritz-Carlton Hotel, was opened and there the Castles taught the élite. From this institution, word went out to the nation that the modern dances could be made "graceful, artistic, charming and, above all, *refined.*" Who dared question the moral reputability of such dances as the "Innovation," "Lame Duck" or "Half and Half"? One had been introduced at a ball given by Mrs. Stuyvesant Fish; the others were being featured at the dinner dances of equally exalted hostesses. Society was no longer willing to sit through a dinner party politely. Dancing between courses was mandatory, and you never returned to your original place at the table, but ate the next course beside the partner with whom you had just been showing off. "Nowadays we dance morning, noon and night," Mrs. Castle explained in the Castles' best-seller, *Modern Dancing*—and under the patronage of Saint Vitus, all social circumstances were adjusted to the primary obligations of complicated footwork and the free play of every muscle in the body.

The Castles were not only national idols, but national arbiters of etiquette.

You went to study them at their small, smart supper room, Sans Souci, or at Castles in the Air, a cabaret where they danced once every evening. If you were not socially eligible to receive instruction at Castle House, you sought out a teacher to whom they had imparted their method. The cult of joy was a serious matter, and it involved the elderly and middle-aged as well as the young. When the Castles held, in Madison Square Garden, the first of all national competitions for amateurs, newspapers throughout the land reported it as an event of consequence. It was won by a middle-aged couple, Sailing Baruch and his wife, brother and sister-in-law of the wily financier Bernard Baruch, who was making headlines, himself, as adviser to President Wilson. Meanwhile, dainty Irene Castle was setting sartorial fashion. Because Castle dances were mildly acrobatic, she had bobbed her hair, replaced unyielding corsets by an elastic girdle, substituted silk bloomers and a slip for petticoats, adopted short, light, flowing frocks. Imitated on Fifth and Park Avenues, these radical innovations soon produced a nationwide revolution in feminine attire. The final collapse of a whaleboned morality was signalized by "the new lingerie, in which everything is combined in one garment, easily slipped on." And—as the wild younger generation soon discovered—just as easily slipped off.

Prohibition, made absolute and final at midnight on January 16, 1920, ended the cabaret phase of New York's night life. Harried by Federal agents, unable to operate profitably with their immense dance floors and expensive entertainers, the most noted and luxurious establishments eventually closed. Wreckers invaded Louis Martin's, Maxim's, Bustanoby's, Churchill's, Shanley's, Reisenweber's. Even more ironical was the fate which overtook Murray's Roman Gardens, celebrated for its revolving dance floor and exotic décor. Murray's was replaced by Hubert's Museum and Flea Circus, where for thirty cents you could see an assortment of freaks and watch Professor Heckler's talented insects go through their complicated routines. But little talent or training was needed by New Yorkers bent on "making whoopee." During the dry epoch New York was wetter than ever before.

The speakeasy, which pedants insisted should be called the speakeasily, was ubiquitous. Nobody ever knew how many "speaks" there were in the city. Izzy Einstein, one of the great humorists of the period, estimated their number at one hundred thousand. He was "Prohibition agent number one" for the New York area, and the only Federal killjoy who ever achieved high popularity with several million citizens conducting an open rebellion against the Federal Government. You couldn't help liking Izzy; he was a magnificent clown. With his immensely fat, lugubrious partner, Moe Smith, Izzy raided speakeasies right and left—disguised as a waiter, drummer, visiting buyer, grave digger, football player, iceman, musician, automobile cleaner, or Sunday stroller afflicted by thirst. After a long career in amateur theatricals, during which his protean impersonations became famous, Izzy retired to write his memoirs. He dedicated them affectionately to the four thousand, nine hundred and thirty-two citizens he had arrested, and prophesied that "the day

A VILLAGE SPEAKEASY, *by Glenn O. Coleman*

when Prohibition is repealed will not be in our lifetime." Some years after Izzy's switch to literature, another affable public servant put the number of speakeasies at thirty thousand. This was the official estimate of Grover Whalen, who played a two-year stand as Commissioner of Police under New York's favorite comedian, gaudy, giddy Mayor Jimmy Walker. Urbane, handsome, elegant Whalen had a talent for high comedy and was a master of ballyhoo, so his gifts seemed stupidly wasted in the Police Department. He found his true vocation as official metropolitan greeter of celebrities. Equipped with a municipal yacht, marshaling the spouting fireboats, Whalen sailed down the

A SPEAKEASY OF 1927, *by Joseph Webster Golinkin*

harbor to welcome Channel swimmers, Arctic explorers, transatlantic flyers, and that royal, perennial *soubrette,* Queen Marie of Rumania. He then led them up Broadway under a rain of confetti in a deafening parade of touring cars accompanied by platoons of cops. The most spectacular glad hand that New York had ever known, Whalen inculcated a taste for whoopee that could only be fully satisfied by the night clubs.

The speakeasies were as varied in kind as they were numerous. At the bottom of the scale were the "clip joints" or "cab joints" or "steer joints" which preyed on unwary New Yorkers and visiting firemen ignorant of the ways of the metropolis. These places paid taxi-drivers to bring in their victims. Picking a likely customer, the driver would offer to take him to a speak where good booze and hot girls assured a happy evening. The booze was on hand and so were the girls, but the bill was always outrageously high. If the customer showed any disposition to protest, a strong-arm crew appeared. This was usually sufficient to prevent argument. If the customer didn't have enough cash to pay the bill, the proprietor agreed to accept a check. Two or three checks might be written, but the signatures were never sufficiently legible to satisfy the proprietor. He therefore promised to destroy them, and produced an I.O.U. for the customer to sign. On the following morning, a tough guy would turn up at the victim's place of business and demand cash for this document. Inquiry at his bank usually proved that the victim's checks had also been cashed. One of the most reputable speakeasies in Greenwich Village began its business life as a clip joint. The proprietor made a practice of setting up customers to drinks until they were in a condition to buy much more than they had intended. He kept a taxi at the door, ready to take such customers as emerged helplessly drunk down to the waterfront to be robbed. In later years, when he had acquired an eminently respectable clientele, he subjected his liquor to chemical tests before selling it, and sometimes displayed to favored customers a souvenir of the rough earlier days. This was a piece of half-inch steel cable, at one end doubly thick and dipped in lead, and the proprietor retained it "just in case." "Never hit a guy in the head with this," he explained. "You'll split him open like a dropped watermelon. Hit him on the shoulder or the back. It's safer."

The midtown speakeasies were usually domiciled in old brownstone residences. One published list of "night-life don'ts" sternly warned joy-seekers, "Don't ring bells of private houses and insist you are a friend of a friend of the boss's." After nightfall, it was sometimes hard to distinguish a private house from a speak, especially if all the front windows were dark. A conservative dowager who had clung to her old-fashioned home in the West Fifties was exasperated by the persistent ringing of her basement doorbell. Presently, there appeared above both entrances to her home illuminated signs reading, "*This Is* Not *an Illicit Resort.*" Though they were a great help to prospective diners, these signs had constantly to be renewed; wags had a habit of scraping away the underlined third word. In the end, the old lady put her home up for sale and soon afterward it was occupied by a speakeasy.

Most of the better-class brownstone speaks were operated in the guise of clubs, under such titles as The Bombay Bicycle Club, The Town and Country Club, or—more simply—Tony's, Michel's, or Louis'. These resorts issued membership cards if you were introduced and sponsored by a trustworthy customer. Others merely gave you a password which would secure admission. If you were a stranger in town, any policeman was usually willing to direct you to the nearest speak; if he liked your looks, he might even give you its password. You descended the basement steps of a decaying residence and rang the doorbell. You waited patiently until a light came on above the metal-reinforced door. Then a grille snapped open, and the hard eye of the lookout appraised you. If he recognized you from previous visits you were admitted without further ado. If he was a new man, and you seemed "in the know," he sent for the proprietor to pass on you. Once admitted, you might walk through a series of interlocking doors. Eventually you arrived at a bar. The Scotch was poured from bottles seemingly authentic, on which the historic labels had been artfully reproduced. So was the gin. A polite fiction had it that both were imported. In the more expensive speaks, this fiction had some basis in fact. The liquors sold had originally been "imported," but their quantity was tripled by the process known as "cutting"—the addition of alcohol, water and coloring. Beyond the bar, there was a restaurant. The fare, Italian or allegedly French, was likely to be palatable and almost certain to be costly.

It amused many New Yorkers that the city's most notable concentration of speakeasies was not far from the ugly brownstone palace occupied by Mrs. Cornelius Vanderbilt III. West Fifty-second Street, between Fifth and Sixth Avenues, was notorious throughout the country. Almost without exception, every house, on both sides of the street, was a speak, and the after-dark traffic on this single block was always more congested than that on any so-called "residential" cross street in Manhattan. One of its establishments, the Twenty-one Club, known to habitués as Jack and Charlie's, was internationally famous. It represented the ultimate perfection of such institutions, the most luxurious, costly, exclusive and fashionable of all speaks. There you saw, at dinner, stars of the stage and screen, the cream of New York's smart society, all visiting celebrities. Cocktails were priced at one dollar; champagne brought twenty-five dollars a quart; the superlative food was equally expensive. Housed in an ornate mansion, the Twenty-one Club maintained, in addition to its two bars and restaurants, a dance floor with orchestra, lounges for conversation, rooms where you could play ping-pong, backgammon, or mah-jongg. The atmosphere was one of aristocratic elegance, and you would not have surmised that this dignified resort concealed defenses as elaborate as those of a fortress, or electrically controlled devices of such remarkable ingenuity that, in the event of a raid, strategic sections of wall could be made to turn and disappear.

Having dined at a speakeasy and perhaps taken in a Broadway show, you went on to one of the night clubs toward midnight. The night clubs opened and closed and reopened with dizzying rapidity, with bewildering changes of name, management and location. Their protean, ambulant character was largely the result of visits from the successors of Izzy Einstein. The Federal snoopers and ax-men staged frequent raids, sometimes of a spectacular nature. They swamped the courts with "padlock suits"—at one time, more than six hundred were pending. Occasionally they would totally wreck a night club, as in the case of one operated by Helen Morgan, lovely star of *Show Boat*. And invariably they aroused the resentment of patrons prevented from rounding out a gay evening. Did not arrest abrogate that inalienable right to the pursuit of happiness for which, after all, the American Revolution had been fought? No wisecrack by Mayor Walker achieved greater popularity than his definition of a reformer—"a guy who rides through a sewer in a glass-bottomed boat." Not that night clubbers thought of their favorite hot spots as sewers. They merely shared the Mayor's contempt for the Federal killjoys. They rejoiced when Texas Guinan, arrested in one of her series of rendezvous, told her band to play "The Prisoner's Song" as she was led away to the police station, and pungently derided her tormentors after she arrived there.

Miss Guinan presided, in sequence, over New York's most celebrated night clubs. Their celebrity was the result of her presence; she was one of the town's outstanding personages. She claimed that she had turned New York's night life into an essential, basic industry, and nobody ever disputed her title of

"Queen of the Night Clubs." Technically, legally, a "hostess," she brought to this new profession the executive ability of Mrs. Astor, the imagination and wit of Mrs. Fish. Recognizing her important contributions to social history, *The Times* credited her with a "national vogue" and the creation of an entirely new social set. During ten months of her heyday she parlayed a small investment into a fortune of nearly one million dollars. She also brightened the vernacular, introduced many refinements of etiquette, and helped bring prosperity to manufacturers of padlocks. She was the high priestess of hoopla and whoopee.

Nobody ever called her Mary Louise Cecilia, though she was so christened in Waco, Texas, shortly after her birth. She got into public life early, first as a circus bronco rider, later as a chorus girl, vaudeville trouper, the "female Bill Hart" of early Western movies. In 1923, buxom, blonde and middle-aged, she was playing a minor role in a musical at the Winter Garden. One night, friends took her to a speakeasy for after-theater supper. "But it was dull," she recalled later. "Someone suggested that I sing. I didn't need much coaxing, so I sang all I knew—my entire repertoire. First thing you know, we were all doing things. Everybody had a great time." She had discovered her mission; to make the world more amusing, to give everybody a great time. One year later she formed a partnership with Larry Fay, a tall, dark, long-jawed, sinister-looking new tycoon. Fay was a product of Hell's Kitchen, who a few years earlier had been earning twenty-five dollars a week driving a taxi. He got into rum-running. With his profits he bought a fleet of gaudy taxis and by strong-arm methods gained control of the cab stands at the city's two railroad terminals. He then sold out to a large company which also paid him a yearly income to retire permanently from the taxicab business. Though he was to be arrested forty-nine times before he was murdered, Fay had a yearning for respectability. He wanted to associate with people of wealth and social position, to be seen about town dancing with beautiful, jeweled women; he preferred them to be distinguished, but did not disdain them if they were merely notorious. Ownership of a smart night club seemed the easiest way of realizing these ambitions while increasing his wealth. Fay went to Europe to gather ideas. He returned with a knowledge of the fashionable night spots of London and Paris, as well as twelve trunks containing an English wardrobe, to open the swanky El Fey Club with Miss Guinan.

This was the first of Texas' rendezvous; it was to be followed, among others, by the Del Fey, the Three Hundred Club, the Club Intime, and Texas Guinan's. To all of them, she attracted a clientele described by *The Times* as composed of "out-of-town buyers, theatrical celebrities, and a sprinkling of the social and underworld élite." It was the fusion of the last two that constituted her major social innovation. In the old days, at Rector's, the aristocracy of the Gay White Way had tolerated the presence of men like Shang Draper and his pals, had hobnobbed with Abe Hummel. But Miss Guinan blended the Social Register, Broadway stars and showgirls, top-drawer racketeers, and a few intellectuals into a novel, heady mixture. In the end, it produced "café

TEX GUINAN'S PORTABLE NIGHTCLUB, 1928, *by Joseph Webster Golinkin*

society," which proved as dazzling to the American imagination as the sacred Four Hundred.

Like Mrs. Stuyvesant Fish—of whom, probably, she had never heard—Miss Guinan determined to redeem her world from its besetting sin of dullness. She was equally free of illusions, and she had the same remarkable talent for imaginative insult as her illustrious predecessor. Seated in the midst of a nightly bedlam, her diamonds blazing, her gown glittering with sequins, she used a clapper and a police whistle to prod her guests into greater din. She welcomed patrons with a strident, cheerful "Hello, sucker!"—and an amused world, ignoring her jaunty warning that they would be rooked, delighted in the candid, contemptuous greeting. Her inexhaustible high spirits, her flippancy and daffiness were contagious. How could you be offended by her salty, jovial abuse, her cynical ebullience? She laid about her with wisecracks and nifties and made people love it. She wheedled bald, dignified millionaires into playing leap-frog on the dance floor; she ruffled the hair and undid the ties of eminent men, then forced them to perform antics that made them ridiculous; she pelted the bare backs of starchy dowagers with tiny, white celluloid balls. When one of her girls came out to do a turn—at one time she had a mob of seventy-eight, all pretty, who strutted about wearing almost nothing—you couldn't resist her command to "give this little girl a great big hand," especially when, catching your eye, she hurled you a clapper. One night an unknown "live one" came to Miss Guinan's and inspired her second-most-celebrated phrase. He paid the couvert charge for the entire house, distributed fifty-dollar bills to all the girls, and when asked to identify himself refused his name, saying only that he was in the dairy-produce business. Miss Guinan promptly introduced him to the crowd as "the big butter-and-egg man." The phrase soon became part of the American vernacular. Like Sinclair Lewis' Babbitt, it crystallized a national type.

Among the notables present at her night club you might see, at various times, people not likely to congregate elsewhere. Peggy Hopkins Joyce, the ex-Follies girl who traded in millionaire husbands the way husbands traded in last year's car. William Beebe, the scientist who was specializing in queer fish. Stephen Graham, the British author. Aimee Semple McPherson, the Hollywood evangelist. Lady Diana Manners; Lord and Lady Mountbatten. Mae West, appearing in *Sex* and shocking the town. Crazy, ageing Harry Kendall Thaw. Mayor Walker and his dimpled, brunette mistress, Betty Compton. Arnold Rothstein, banker for the racketeers; William J. Fallon, their "great mouthpiece"; "Big Bill" Dwyer, head of the greatest rum-running syndicate; Owney Madden, the reformed gangster who was now in the night-club game and backing Miss West's play. Texas Guinan knew them all, but was impressed by none. Something more than high spirits shaped the retort discourteous that had become her trademark. A moral verdict? Or only a personal distaste—an anachronistic, inconvenient integrity that she could not subdue, that compelled her to include herself among the objects of her derision?

When after-midnight life on Manhattan reached its apogee of gaiety, more than seventy night clubs were running full blast in various parts of the town. Certain features were common to nearly all of them. There were always three beautiful girls who had an institutional status. Failure to respond generously when they visited your table proclaimed you a tightwad. One sold cigarettes at a dollar a package. Another dispensed rag dolls at five dollars each; you were supposed to give your baby a baby-doll. The third beauty was a flower vender; a boutonnière of tiny "real" roses cost five dollars, and a paper gardenia, magnolia or carnation fetched a buck. Naturally, you were not content merely to pay the stated price for these indispensable commodities. As a tribute to beauty, doubling the charge would be appreciated. Some gentlemen carried hip flasks, some ladies brought bottles under their opera cloaks. For these hard-shells the clubs provided set-ups. A pitcher of water from the tap brought two dollars; ginger ale stood you a dollar and a half a glass; a split of charged water parted you from a dollar. Most patrons, however, ordered their liquor in the clubs. Champagne and Scotch whiskey were usually priced at twenty-five dollars a bottle; a pint of rye, if that was all you wished, cost ten dollars. The "couvert charge"—a new invention—ranged from five to twenty dollars per person. A speakeasy proprietor who, for professional reasons, visited Larry Fay's club, told Stanley Walker, city editor of *The Tribune,* that the evening, for a party of four or five, cost thirteen hundred dollars. "It was worth it," he remarked; "I had a hell of a good time." Night clubs were not meant for the niggardly.

Even without the assistance of Federals, some of the clubs occasionally managed to provide unscheduled entertainment for their patrons. The Club Abbey achieved an evening of such extreme exuberance that it was compelled to go out of business. This charming establishment on West Fifty-fourth Street, was a favorite resort of the underworld élite. Among its patrons that night were Larry Fay, Dutch Schultz, Martih Krompier (known to his familiars as "the Crumpet" or "Marty the Wolf"), Charles "Chink" Sherman, a Boston tycoon temporarily in difficulties with the Massachusetts authorities and seeking relaxation in Manhattan, and Detective John J. Walsh of the New York Police Department. Fay, with a party of friends, left for the smart, exclusive Beaux Arts Ball—where, as usual, socialite Mrs. S. Stanwood Menken took the prize for the handsomest costume—long before the Abbey fun began. Detective Walsh later insisted that he departed before it reached its height. Apparently Sherman, who was in a waggish mood, made cracks displeasing to Schultz, who was drunk, and Krompier, his henchman, who was dancing with a girl. The lights were suddenly extinguished. There were bursts of gunfire; tables were upset; crockery, glasses and bottles smashed with an amusing clatter. When the lights came on, Schultz was nursing a bullet wound in his shoulder. But Sherman had been shot, severely clubbed with a chair, and stabbed many times. Miss Mavis King, reputed to be "Broadway's most beautiful cigarette girl"—a title disputed by Texas Guinan's Ethel—rose to the occasion and took Sherman off to a hospital. The boys' genial fun made quite a stir in the press. The Club Abbey soon closed, underwent necessary redecoration, and reopened under another name. The affair had no other serious consequences.

Spontaneous gaiety was likewise carried too far, one summer evening, at the Hotsy Totsy Club, an all-night joint on Broadway popular with the brassier boys and girls of the Roaring Forties. One of its proprietors was Jack "Legs" Diamond, a mobster renowned and feared, but also among the most flamboyant of Broadway playboys. Undersized, frail looking, Diamond was regarded as a mean guy. His talent for inventing novel forms of torture, his taste for needless gunplay and his love of the limelight were soon to make him a problem child to the master minds of the underworld, and his constitutional resistance to bullets did not increase their affection for him. On the night he decided to pep things up at the Hotsy Totsy Club, Diamond and one of his chums, Charles Entratta, were behind the bar. Simon Walker, an ex-convict, and two brothers named Cassidy, notorious tough guys, came to the bar. Conversation regrettably degenerated into an argument. Hyman Cohen, one of Diamond's partners, hastily ordered the band to play as loudly as possible. This precautionary measure indicated that Cohen had an aptitude for mind-reading, unfortunately too limited, since he was later taken for a ride and eliminated. While the band was giving out, Diamond and Entratta used their guns. One Cassidy was badly wounded; the other brother and Walker were killed. Diamond and Entratta considerately left town until several key witnesses had been put in their graves and others had revealed a pronounced state of amnesia. All this was extremely helpful to the Police Department which, when Diamond surrendered some eighteen months later, was able to release him without further inconvenience. In the meanwhile, Entratta had been apprehended, tried and acquitted. The boys had influential political connections, and only a spoil-sport would have punished them for their irrepressible spirits.

These diversions at the Abbey and Hotsy Totsy were exceptional, and were discountenanced by other night clubs—even when the proprietors held high rank in the underworld élite, as many did. Owney Madden was part owner of several clubs, among them, the Cotton Club, a leading Harlem joy spot. His pal, "Big Bill" Duffy, operated the Silver Slipper on West Forty-eighth Street, where the only explosions were caused by the zany comedians Clayton, Jackson and Durante. With Frankie Marlow as partner, Duffy also ran the nearby Club La Vie, which had to be closed when a man was murdered at its door. In partnership with Larry Fay, Marlow opened the smart Ambassadeurs. Fay named the establishment; Marlow, exasperated by his inability to write its name correctly on checks, declared that "what this joint needs is a partner who can spell it." Presumably he went and took lessons in spelling, for he soon opened another club, adjoining the Winter Garden on Broadway, and named it the Rendezvous. For a time, nice people had illusions about the Club Chantee, because admission to it was difficult to manage. Then word went round that the Chantee was run by Richard Whittemore, leader of a gang of desperadoes, thieves and murderers who were employed in the club as waiters or otherwise. But everybody knew that Dutch Schultz was the proprietor of the Embassy Club, in East Fifty-seventh Street, and it remained one of the most fashionable night spots in town, with Helen Morgan, seated atop a piano, making you weep when she sang "Bill" and other equally melancholy songs.

The variety of entertainment offered by the night clubs was remarkable. At the exclusive Sutton Club, on Fifty-seventh Street not far from Sutton Place, you could hear Beatrice Lillie. At the Lido, Libby Holman enchanted you with her blues. At Ciro's, you could see Clifton Webb dance with Mary Hay. At the Trocadero, the featured dancers were Fred Astaire and his sister Adele. At the Mirador, there was—oddly enough—a Russian ballet put on by Michel Fokine. If you wanted a stunning chorus line, you went to The Hollywood, on Broadway. There were nearly naked cuties at Harry Richman's club. At Ziegfeld's Midnight Frolic atop the New Amsterdam Theater *Follies* stars performed, and Paul Whiteman with his band furnished music. Belle Livingstone, a famous chorus girl of the eighteen-nineties whose subsequent career had been colorful as well as active, returned to the scene of her early exploits. She opened a "country club" on East Fifty-eighth Street which, in addition to urban entertainment, offered such Arcadian pastimes as miniature golf and ping-pong. Federal agents, energetically disapproving certain features of her hospitality, caused Miss Livingstone to skip over the adjacent rooftops clad in somewhat too vivid pajamas. Apprehended during this brave revival of ancient chorus routines, she was sent to jail for thirty days; neither art nor business

"SPEAKO DELUXE," *by Joseph Webster Golinkin*

enterprise was sacred to the Federal busybodies. When Miss Livingstone was released from durance, Miss Guinan, to the delight of the whole town, dispatched an armored car to escort her, with appropriate formality, back to joyland.

Joyland, after two o'clock in the morning, soon signified Harlem. Comparatively few white New Yorkers had explored the nocturnal pleasures of the city's Negro community before 1921. But in that year Harlem sent downtown the first of its cultural missions to the "ofays." This took the form of a revue, *Shuffle Along,* written, composed, performed and produced by Negroes. Its success was sensational. The singing of Noble Sissle, the extraordinary jazz piano playing of Eubie Blake, were spectacular novelties. But it was Florence Mills, a diminutive singing-and-dancing comedienne, who took the town by storm. Immediately hailed as a great artist, Miss Mills was soon starred, at Broadway's Plantation Club, in an elaborate Negro production made by Lew Leslie. Subsequently, Leslie took Miss Mills and her company to London and Paris, where she evoked enormous enthusiasm. Her fame enhanced by European acclaim, Miss Mills later brought to the New York stage *Dixie to Broadway* and *Blackbirds.* Meanwhile, Negro revues had become the rage on Broadway, and the downtown audience was introduced to the art of such eminent Harlem stars as Ethel Waters, the magnificent blues singer, and Bill "Bojangles" Robinson, whose stunt of tap-dancing up and down a staircase brought him fame as great as that of any Russian ballet dancer. Moreover, year after year, Negro artists were winning acclaim in serious plays and operas. There was Charles Gilpin in Eugene O'Neill's *The Emperor Jones;* Paul Robeson in O'Neill's *All God's Chillun Got Wings;* Rose McClendon in *Deep River;* Jules Bledsoe in *In Abraham's Bosom,* and later singing "Old Man River" in *Show Boat.* There was the remarkable cast of the Theater Guild's production of *Porgy.* At the end of the decade there was Richard B. Harrison in *The Green Pastures,* at the head of a large company so brilliant that nearly all of them received individual praise from the critics. All this made it natural for white New Yorkers of various types to explore Harlem.

The swarming, prosperous crowds bent on nocturnal diversion found Harlem exotic and colorful. To them it seemed a citadel of jazz and laughter where gaiety began after midnight. From then onward, you saw throngs on Lenox and Seventh Avenues, ceaselessly moving from one pleasure resort to another. Long after the cascading lights of Times Square had flickered out, these boulevards were ablaze. Lines of taxis and private cars kept driving up to the glaring entrances of the night clubs. Until nearly dawn the subway kiosks poured crowds onto the sidewalks. The legend of Harlem by night—exhilarating and sensuous, throbbing to the beating of drums and the wailing of saxophones, cosmopolitan in its peculiar sophistications—crossed the continent and the ocean.

Several of the larger night clubs were nationally famous, and their names were well known in Montmartre itself. For Harlem had sent to Montmartre its highest paid chorus girl, beautiful Josephine Baker, whose name became a household word in Europe; Florence Jones, a singer who opened a celebrated Parisian cabaret; Ada Smith du Congé, a singer whose orange-colored hair made her known as "Bricktop," and whose night club was one of the sights of Paris. But there were equally remarkable talents to be found at the Cotton Club, on Lenox Avenue; at Connie's Inn and Small's Paradise, on Seventh Avenue; at The Nest, in Jungle Alley. These clubs maintained permanent companies of performers for their floor shows, which were miniature revues. They also featured the finest jazz orchestras, whose principals were themselves celebrities: Duke Ellington; Fletcher Henderson; the "scat-singer" Cab Calloway; the great hot player Louis Armstrong, known as "Satchmo"; the drummer Sid Catlett. The Cotton Club was the most fashionable of these establishments, attracting a clientele of wealthy whites—theatrical folk, professional people, and socialites. It was therefore the goal of every Negro entertainer, whether singer, tap-dancer, or band leader. But, as guests, Negroes were denied admission. Occasionally, at the Cotton Club, you found the show headed by a great star. Johnny Hudgins, perhaps, or statuesque Ethel Waters singing "Dinah," "The St. Louis Blues," her raucous number, "Shake That Thing," or "Stormy Weather." And at the three other clubs you found fast shows and star performers also. Connie's Inn, a huge subterranean place, often featured "Snake Hips" Earl Tucker. At Small's Paradise, the waiters sometimes broke into a Charleston while carrying heavily laden trays, and the place was noted for its Monday-morning breakfasts which began before dawn and lasted until noon.

These celebrated clubs were quite as expensive as the downtown resorts, so in them you saw many more whites than Negroes. If you wanted to see middle-class Harlem on pleasure bent, you went up earlier in the evening, to the Savoy, on Lenox Avenue. The Savoy was Harlem's ballroom de luxe. Its dance floor was immense, its jazz was always superb. Viewed from the entrance to the hall, the effect was astounding. A jostling, laughing, swaying throng filled the aisles between the tables, and the vast floor seethed with couples performing steps of an incredible complexity. It was here that you saw, long before they were translated to the night clubs or theaters, the dances which all America would later be practicing—the Charleston, the Black Bottom, the Lindy Hop, the Shuffle.

From the Savoy, which closed at two o'clock, you might go on to one of the places in Jungle Alley. This was Harlem's name for One Hundred and Thirty-third Street between Lenox and Seventh Avenues, a single block that contained several dozen restaurants, cabarets and night clubs. At the Clam House, a long, narrow, crowded room, you could hear Gladys Bentley. She was a fat, jovial singer who, accompanying herself at the piano, gave out with songs that were far too torrid to please respectable folk; but this specialty made her a favorite with downtown sophisticates. Next door to the Clam House was Tillie's Inn, a dim, low-ceilinged cabaret where the prices were low, the fried chicken with yams was renowned, and the entertainment was devised, not for the tourist trade, but for the pleasure of Harlem patrons. Tillie's was an informal rendezvous for Negro writers, musicians, theatrical people; a true cabaret, where some of the guests often performed to please their friends. There were artists already acclaimed as great by Harlem, but still virtually unknown to white New Yorkers, and occasionally you heard them at Tillie's. You might hear them, also, if you went to Harlem's two leading theaters: the Lincoln and the Lafayette, where Sunday-night performances were notable events. It was only later that white New Yorkers would "discover" the jazz pianists James P. Johnson and Thomas "Fats" Waller, inventors of fabulous "hot licks." And, although their phonograph recordings eventually made them famous, the blues singer Bessie Smith and her rival, Clara Smith, who was billed in Negro theaters as "the world's greatest moaner," were never, in New York, heard outside the theaters of Harlem.

But in order to see and hear the most celebrated Negro entertainers at the top of their form, you had to be taken by one of them to the Vaudeville Comedy Club. This was their rendezvous when they had finished their night's work, their private club, closed to the public, where they came to enjoy themselves. It was a large subterranean room in the same building as the Savoy, and the fun there seldom began before four or five o'clock in the morning. After performing in the night clubs where they earned their livelihood, some of the members of the Vaudeville Comedy Club invariably entertained their colleagues. The audience of critical professionals put them on their mettle; in sheer exuberance they gave their best. As a result, their singing, dancing and music were usually far more exciting than any they ever offered the general public. The impromptu show at the Vaudeville Comedy Club hit its stride toward seven in the morning, and if you were fortunate enough to be taken there you were likely to remain, in a state of exhilaration, until nine or ten, when the crowd began to think of calling it a night and going home.

Like white New York, Harlem had an underworld into which explorers from downtown were sometimes able to penetrate. For a few years, in various halls, there were frequent "drags"—quasi-public balls featuring fashion parades, with prizes, for homosexuals dressed in women's attire. Many of the contestants wore spectacular, elaborate costumes and were so expert in their female impersonation that only the most careful scrutiny enabled onlookers to identify them as males. There were little cafés that catered especially to homosexuals and Lesbians; there were others to which noted "sporting men" brought their stables of women. There were flats where gambling could be enjoyed in almost any form. Other flats were conducted as resorts for "junkers" or drug-addicts. The narcotics ring operating in New York was able to flood Harlem with a full line of its commodities, apparently without police interference. Some kinds of dope could be bought from peddlers within a stone's throw of the Tree of Hope, which by day and night was one of the chief centers of Harlem street life. This tree stood on Seventh Avenue and One Hundred and Thirty-first Street, in front of Connie's Inn, and superstitious people believed it to have magical powers. Leaning against it was said to bring you luck, so there was usually a crowd gathered about it. The dope peddlers found many of their clients there; an imperceptible signal advised a purchaser to tail the peddler to some nearby hallway where the transaction could be completed. Marijuana, heroin, cocaine, morphine were the lifeblood of the hophead flats, costly luxuries never identified by name but alluded to as "tea," "muggles," "sticks," "snow," "happy dust" and other designations even more recondite. Another feature of Harlem life often exploited by the underworld was the "rent party." These affairs went on almost every evening. Some were legitimate efforts of unfortunate tenants to raise money to pay their landlords. But most of them were raffish, and many were dangerous. You went to somebody's flat, bringing your liquor; you paid an admission fee, usually one dollar, and joined the crowd. Whatever might happen later was nobody's business.

The great crowds that nightly surged up to Harlem from downtown in pursuit of pleasure seldom saw any more of the Negro metropolis than its night clubs and hot spots. There were other aspects of its life that were more interesting and more significant. Harlem's population ranged over an economic scale from dire poverty to substantial wealth. Among its residents there were six or seven millionaires, and many families of moderate wealth. Some of these wealthy people lived in the rows of handsome houses designed, thirty years earlier, by Stanford White, and now locally known as "Strivers' Row" because they were so expensive to keep up. Others lived on "Sugar Hill." This was the area extending from One Hundred and Fortieth to One Hundred and Forty-fifth Streets, between Edgecombe Avenue on the east and Convent Avenue on the west, which contained many modern apartment houses. The vast majority of Harlem's population were ordinary, hard-working people who found that fewer jobs were open to them than to any similar white groups, who existed in perpetual economic insecurity, and never saw the inside of a night club unless they were employed in one. There was, in addition, a large, prosperous middle class of business and professional people whose education, tastes and recreations were in no way unlike those of white New Yorkers of the same economic status. As James Weldon Johnson reported, Harlem had "strictly social sets that go in for bridge parties, breakfast parties, cocktail parties, for high-powered cars, week-ends and exclusive dances." It likewise had "sophisticated, fast sets, initiates in all the wisdom of worldliness."

In elegance and luxury the parties given by Mrs. A'Leilia Walker, for example, were comparable to those offered by fashionable hostesses on Park Avenue and Sutton Place. Mrs. Walker was Harlem's wealthiest woman, and its outstanding "sophisticate." Her principal residence was "Villa Lewaro," a magnificent estate in Irvington-on-Hudson which she had inherited from her mother, but she also maintained a mansion on One Hundred and Thirty-sixth Street. She was the daughter of Mrs. C. J. Walker—the famous "Madame" Walker who, having begun life in extremely humble circumstances, made vast wealth from a treatment which removed the "kink" from hair, building up a business which spanned the United States and also covered the West Indies. Mrs. A'Leilia Walker had been educated in Europe, had traveled widely; she was, essentially, a worldly cosmopolitan. A woman of lively mind and commanding spirit, she used her social leadership to forge a group unique in New York. The reception rooms of her home were spacious and handsomely furnished; besides these there was, on the top floor, a suite known to her friends as "The Dark Tower" because, for their pleasure, she had turned it into a club. It was there that she gave many of her most memorable parties, at which you met not only Harlem's social aristocracy, but its intellectual and artistic élite also, as well as those members of the white intelligentsia who had made an enthusiastic discovery of the recent rich flowering of Negro talent. Though Mrs. Walker's hospitality had obvious affinities with that of Park Avenue and Sutton Place, its tenor was very different. In effect, her parties resembled the Sunday gatherings which, so many years earlier, Miss de Wolfe and Miss Marbury had assembled in their home on Irving Place.

That white writers, artists, musicians were brought socially in contact with their Negro colleagues was mainly due to the novelist Carl Van Vechten. He was the first to herald, in articles written for *Vanity Fair* and other publications, what came to be called the Negro Renaissance. His novel, *Nigger Heaven* —its title had a note of tragic irony—portrayed the life of educated, sophisticated Harlem, a civilization unknown to white readers, exotic and fascinating. Van Vechten had a wide acquaintance in Harlem, and no expression of Negro talent in the arts and literature failed to gain his enthusiastic interest. He was a leading figure in the New York literary world, social by temperament and a genial host; with his wife, the actress Fania Marinoff, he had long made his home on West Fifty-fifth Street the rallying point of a brilliant, varied circle. After his discovery of Harlem, Van Vechten began bringing together, in his home, Negro and white writers, musicians, singers, painters and composers. These gatherings, at first a notable social innovation, soon became an established custom. From them, there developed an expanding, interracial coterie which, having interests in common, found it natural to meet frequently. At Van Vechten's, at Mrs. Walker's, at various other homes in Harlem, midtown Manhattan and Greenwich Village, you had an opportunity to become acquainted with the most distinguished Negroes of the time. There was James Weldon Johnson, former diplomat, author, poet, publicist and the outstanding intellectual leader of his people. There were the singers Roland Hayes, Paul Robeson and Taylor Gordon, whose recitals of spirituals were bringing this genre of Negro folk music before a national audience. There was Hall Johnson, leader of a choir famous throughout the country. There was the composer William Grant Still, the painter Aaron Douglas. There were the literary group: the poets, Countee Cullen and Langston Hughes; Claude McKay and Jean Toomer, who wrote both verse and fiction; the novelists Jessie Fauset, Walter White, Zora Neale Hurston and Nella Larsen; Eric Walrond, Rudolph Fisher, Wallace Thurman. There was George S. Schuyler, a vigorous journalist. There were the actors and actresses, the singers and dancers who were known to Broadway, and others connected with the Lafayette Theater and the little-theater groups that successively were launched in Harlem. These were the people who were making Harlem the center of a vigorous cultural life.

In 1930, Harlem was a community of more than two hundred thousand people—a city within the greater city. Negro Harlem began at Cathedral Parkway, the northern boundary of Central Park. It was bounded on the east by Lexington Avenue and the Harlem River, on the west, irregularly, by Morningside, St. Nicholas, Convent and Edgecombe Avenues. It stretched northward as far as the Polo Grounds, just above One Hundred and Fifty-fifth Street. Twenty years earlier, the Negro population of Manhattan had been only some sixty thousand, and fewer than six Negroes were owners of real estate. But by 1930, Negroes owned and controlled Harlem property valued at between fifty and sixty million dollars. So swiftly had this transformation occurred that few white New Yorkers were aware how Harlem—once a citadel of middle-class white domesticity—had been converted into a Negro metropolis which was not only New York's nocturnal playground but also the intellectual and artistic capital of the Negro world.

25

Some Liked It Cold

To the nation, but especially to the city which he professed to love, Mayor James J. Walker typified New York. He wanted to please everybody all the time, and from this grandly universal total he saw no reason to exclude himself. Nearing fifty, he could have passed for thirty-five. He was short and very thin; he carried himself with a jaunty, cocky air; he dressed like a sharpie. Notwithstanding his perennial adolescence, his unfailing bounce, he had the look of an ageing Broadway juvenile. Once he told some reporters that he had read no more than fifteen books from cover to cover. "What little I know," he explained, "I have learned by ear." This is an actor's method, and Walker was an accomplished comedian. You couldn't say that he tried to impersonate civic virtue; he was aware that the role had become obsolete. Installed in City Hall when the festive era was at its height, he cast himself in a part that accorded with the times. For the metropolis of nearly seven million inhabitants, he enacted a civic playboy. At this job, he worked hard.

Invariably, at the dinners, rallies and parades he attended—and sometimes at the night clubs, also—a band struck up "Will You Love Me in December as You Do in May?" It was a hit tune of 1908, for which he had supplied the lyric, the fruit of a youthful flirtation with Tin Pan Alley. But, tactfully, no band ever played, in his presence, another of his songs, dating from the same period and prophetically entitled "After They Gather the Hay." Among his friends, Walker was fond of showing off his talent for playing the piano. As a pianist, he wasn't too good, and sometimes he remarked deprecatingly that his left hand didn't know what his right hand was doing. He had a habit of humming while he played; usually, he was slightly off-key. He liked the society of theatrical folk and millionaires. They reciprocated his affection, often touchingly. After his first election, in 1925, a prominent Philadelphia magnate, Jules Mastbaum, renovated Mayor Walker's childhood home on St. Luke's Place, in Greenwich Village, as a gift. When Mastbaum died, a year later, the newspaper publisher Paul Block succeeded him as benefactor. Block's generosity was apparently unbounded. He paid the Mayor's hotel bills, tailor bills and contributed to his other personal expenses. Walker loved New York, but he also enjoyed getting away from it all; during his first two years of office, nearly one-quarter of his time was spent in junkets to other places, and for these Block often provided a private railroad car, or other expensive amenities of travel. As a further expression of his regard, Block also opened a joint brokerage account with the Mayor, in which Walker invested no money, but from which he eventually received nearly a quarter of a million dollars in cash.

Jimmy—as the whole town affectionately called him—was also extremely popular with the editors, star newspaper reporters and columnists who foregathered at Billy La Hiff's Tavern on West Forty-eighth Street. He often joined them there, at a table in a "corner" booth that was locally almost as famous as the Algonquin's Round Table. New York rang with rumors about Jimmy, but none of them got into the press. The handsome lamps which the city traditionally affixed to the entrance of the Mayor's home burned brightly all night on St. Luke's Place. But Jimmy's residence was occupied only by Mrs. Walker, the wife of his youth who, as a vaudeville singer, had popularized his songs. Jimmy himself lived uptown, first at the Ritz-Carlton Hotel and subsequently at the fashionable Mayfair Hotel on Park Avenue. He was seldom ready to leave his quarters before noon. There were many days when he didn't show up at City Hall, though he usually managed to give the biweekly public meetings of the Board of Estimate a tone of hilarious vaudeville. His notorious unpunctuality evoked from Governor Alfred E. Smith the quip that, "If you make a date with Jim in December, he will keep it next May." When Jimmy found time to attend to public business, his keen mind, his ability to grasp a complex situation quickly evoked the admiration of experts. But the leisure available for his official duties diminished. However, Jimmy and Betty Compton, the musical-comedy actress with whom he was constantly seen around town, had plenty of time to supervise a fancy bit of private enterprise. This was the conversion of the old Casino, overlooking the Mall in Central Park, into an ornate, costly, exclusive restaurant and night club. Jimmy had secured the lease of this city property for one of his friends, Sidney Solomon. With the architectural and decorative counsel of the Mayor and Miss Compton, Solomon managed to spend nearly four hundred thousand dollars in making it an appropriate place for Jimmy to display his private life to the public. Many of Jimmy's political conferences were held in an upstairs salon of this luxurious establishment. The atmosphere of the Casino was more gratifying than that of City Hall.

While the Mayor, clad in snappy evening clothes, was seen gadding about town, gossip of widespread corruption in his administration began to circulate. But His Honor seemed immune to the kind of criticism which, in earlier times, had damaged the careers of men in public life. Jimmy had a talent for silencing fault-finders with a flippant wisecrack. He was glib, saucy, a master of the fast comeback. His wit kept the town laughing; his keen sense of fun was infectious. Occasionally he would make an earnest speech, extolling the great metropolis, denouncing those who, from base motives, sought to tarnish its fair name. Occasionally, at City Hall, he would make some swift, adroit move that pleased "the people" and won him praise as the guardian of their interests. Wasn't Jimmy the quintessence of New York? Didn't he represent its holiday mood, its vivacity and splendor, its pre-eminence among American cities as the pleasure capital of the hemisphere? Americans of the festive era found Jimmy a symbol of the kind of life to which they aspired. New Yorkers adored him. Even to them, he made the city seem romantic; he gave them new reasons for loving it, being proud of it. And, besides, he was good for business. He was the best advertisement New York had ever had, its ambassador to the entire world. In these circumstances, it was easy to ignore gossip, to condone possible derelictions about which nobody except embittered "reformers" cared to be informed.

According to Gene Fowler, his friend and biographer, the Honorable Jimmy, with Miss Compton, was enjoying the evening of Sunday, November 4, 1928, at Woodmansten Inn, a suburban night club in Westchester. At a nearby ringside table "several men allied with underworld activities were sitting with women companions." One of these estimable characters went to the Mayor's table and whispered something in his ear. Jimmy seemed disturbed, called for his check, prepared to depart immediately. The band leader, Vincent Lopez, a close pal of the Mayor's, left his orchestra and accompanied Miss Compton and Jimmy to the door. To Lopez, the Mayor explained his perturbation. Arnold Rothstein had just been shot; that meant plenty of trouble. As things turned out, it did. The murder of Rothstein was the first of a long chain of incidents which led to official investigations and sensational exposures and, more than a decade later, culminated in a series of trials, prosecuted by the district attorneys Thomas E. Dewey and William O'Dwyer, that shocked the nation.

Though Jimmy Walker was elected to a second term as Mayor, his extraordinary luck did not hold. Odd, spectacular events followed one another a little too quickly. "How much longer," demanded the eminent clergyman, Dr. John Haynes Holmes, "shall we be amused by this little man?" Public amusement notably diminished with the onset of the Great Depression. At the direction of Governor Franklin D. Roosevelt, the Appellate Division of the state judiciary undertook an investigation of the Magistrates' Courts of New York City, designating the noted jurist Samuel Seabury to conduct it. The resulting disclosures caused the New York Legislature to appoint a committee, with Seabury as counsel, charged with investigating the government of New York City. At the conclusion of a long, relentless inquiry, Seabury recom-

TAMMANY HALL, 14th Street, *by John Sloan*

mended to Governor Roosevelt that Mayor Walker be removed from office.
The Governor held removal hearings from which Walker emerged with scant
credit, and before Roosevelt could announce his decision, Walker suddenly

resigned from office and sailed for Europe. His failure to keep his left and right hands simultaneously informed, his propensity for being slightly off-key, were not merely musical disabilities. In the end, they brought him to temporary disgrace.

Behind the sparkling front of Manhattan's gay night life, resonant with jazz and running with liquor, a network of corruption spread over New York. Its citizens were in open rebellion against Prohibition. They wanted liquor; they condoned the illegal practices which assured a wet metropolis. The effect was to make crime profitable on a scale never before conceived. To an ambitious but not squeamish young man, the vocational education acquired in a reformatory was more useful than an Ivy League diploma. Crime was "big business" and the new magnates who dominated it were men whose widely diversified enterprises touched the life of the community at many salient points. Like their illustrious predecessors, the great industrialists and financiers of the late nineteenth century, these new robber barons found that the law often obstructed their projects. So they resorted to the practice which their predecessors had adopted—they bought politicians whose power procured them a high degree of immunity. Such eminent Tammany leaders as Thomas F. Foley, James J. Hines, Thomas M. Farley, Albert Marinelli and others entered into profitable alliances with them. Through these political allies, they were able to subvert, for their own ends, the civil government of New York. Indirectly, they controlled the police, the public prosecutors, many magistrates and judges in the higher courts, a large number of administrative officials. They were thus the real overlords of the largest, wealthiest city in the United States.

The magnitude of their operations, their power, wealth and extraordinary business acumen made many of these new tycoons outstanding. No mere small-scale enterpriser, with limited vision and weak nerve, could rise to head one of the great rum-running syndicates. It was a business that yielded tremendous profits, but it required an enormous investment of capital and the taking of great risks. Furthermore, operating a syndicate was an extremely complex enterprise. Fleets of speedboats and trucks manned by tough hoodlums had to be dispatched with precise accuracy. Drops, or warehouses, had to be provided. These were usually large garages, with concealed sub-basements to which access was gained by elevators. The elevator doors, when closed, appeared to be solid walls. The elevators had to be capable of receiving a loaded ten-ton truck and quickly dropping it from view. A syndicate also had to own, or control, a printing plant that turned out fake labels and counterfeit revenue stamps, and a bottle factory able to duplicate the bottles used by foreign distillers. It had to run a cutting plant. It had to employ sales and bookkeeping staffs. It had to have trustworthy pay-off men, able to bribe members of the Coast Guard and rural as well as New York police. It had to have lawyers and bondsmen available at all times, in the event of unforeseen arrests; their prompt appearance was likely to prevent an arrested man from talking indiscreetly. You might have thought that co-ordinating the manifold operations of a great rum-running syndicate was a full-time job.

But several of the tycoons who made fortunes in these enterprises were men with a genius for business organization, and they became active in other fields likewise. In 1920, Big Bill Dwyer was a longshoreman. Three years later, he rated as a magnate, maintaining suites of offices in two buildings on Times Square, occupying a handsome suburban residence on Long Island and owing the Federal Government nearly one million dollars in income taxes. In addition to his rum-running syndicate, Dwyer was a partner in several night clubs, an owner of race tracks, the proprietor of a professional hockey team, and a large investor in spectator sports. The interests of Irving Wexler—better known as Waxey Gordon—were no less diversified. Gordon had begun his career as a pickpocket on the lower East Side. After several terms in reformatories, he moved up in the professional scale, reappearing as a slugger for a gang. In this capacity he was tried for murder and discharged, but a simple case of assault and robbery brought him a term in Sing Sing. However, by the mid-nineteen-twenties, Gordon was installed in a fine suite of offices on Forty-second Street and Broadway. He had made millions out of syndicate operations, and was investing his wealth in other enterprises. He was the proprietor of two skyscraping hotels in the Roaring Forties, west of Times Square. He owned a brewery in New Jersey, and had an interest in a large distillery in upstate New York. He maintained an ornate apartment on Central Park West, a luxurious summer home on the New Jersey shore, a fleet of expensive cars. As a man of wealth, he recognized an obligation to the arts and discharged it by backing two Broadway musicals, one of which turned out to be a smash hit.

Francesco Castiglia, another great syndicate tycoon, was less flamboyant than Gordon but, in the end, far more successful. Castiglia was more widely celebrated under the name of Frank Costello. Born in Italy, he was raised in the slums of East Harlem and, with sound practical judgment, he abandoned formal education at the age of eleven. Thirteen years later, having meanwhile won a local reputation as a gunman, he was sentenced to a term in the penitentiary for illegal possession of a weapon. Subsequent ventures, some of which were in conventional lines of business, prospered notably. Costello made judicious investments in real estate; these paid off well. So he was reputed to be a wealthy man before he organized the highly profitable rum-running syndicate which he conducted from offices on Lexington Avenue, near Grand Central Station. In this line, he was a big-shot from the outset, a close friend of Jimmy Hines, the Tammany potentate, and of Arnold Rothstein. One of Rothstein's protégés, Philip Kastel, a dapper individual known as "Dandy Phil," became Costello's partner. Kastel had operated a night club in Montreal and a bucket shop in New York; partnership with Costello lifted him into the big time. It was probably Costello, the man of imagination and vision, who first saw the possibilities in another business which eventually made him a great power in New York politics and a nationally known figure. This was the operation of slot machines, pungently described by the columnist Westbrook Pegler as "one-armed bandits." The partners organized a syndicate to place more than five thousand of these devices in speakeasies, stationery stores, candy shops and similar establishments throughout New York. Ostensibly candy-vending machines, a simple alteration of the mechanism converted them into gambling devices which, if certain combinations were hit by players, returned coins instead of candy. Except in speakeasies, most of them responded to the dropping of a nickel in the slot, and they became so popular with children that ladders were often supplied to enable tiny tots to reach them. The gross return on the five thousand slot machines placed in New York was said to run as high as one hundred thousand dollars daily. Not all of this golden harvest was reaped by the partners; there were heavy business expenses to be met. Among them was the maintenance of an efficient private police force to "recover" machines stolen by neighborhood gangs and presumably punish the thieves.

Naturally, tycoons like Dwyer and Gordon and Costello, men of large affairs, living in costly homes, moving in the highest political circles, bitterly resented the imputation that they were racketeers. All of them insisted that they were "legitimate businessmen." This was also the contention of Larry Fay, who ran his enterprises from handsome offices in an uptown skyscraper. "I'm a businessman," Fay always protested, "just a regular businessman like any broker or merchant." You could sympathize with his annoyance, for he too was a man of vision. He revived the economic theory so notably imposed on American big business by the elder J. P. Morgan—the doctrine that "wasteful competition" among enterprisers must give way to the recognition of a "community of interest." Fay chose the milk industry, dominated in New York by two great corporations, but also served by independent producers among whom a disastrous competition prevailed. Using the persuasive talents of a corps of mobsters, Fay organized the independents into a "trade association," for which he established a code of "fair practice." In return for his services, he received a royalty of five cents on every forty-quart can of milk which the "members" shipped into the city. Fay's concept was elaborated in spectacular fashion by a pair of breezy, rough-diamond magnates who saw that, by creating a so-called trade association, dominating a labor union and making ruthless use of a goon squad, many industries could be given a streamlined efficiency at a high profit—with the cost of their expert services passed on to the public in the form of increased prices. Louis "Lepke" Buchalter and Jacob "Gurrah" Shapiro applied this system to the garment trades and the fur industry; to the baking industry—into which they muscled by way of the flour-trucking business; to the operation of movie theaters. A combination of terrorism and economic inventiveness paid off magnificently for Lepke and Gurrah Jake. Their squad of goons, reputed to number more than two hundred and fifty, were specialists in suave methods of persuasion: extortion, bomb-throwing, miscellaneous violence and, if necessary, murder. Moreover, Lepke and Gurrah Jake always kept their minds on the main chance. So they made the services of their mob available to Tammany politicians in primaries and elections. The arrangement was mutually advantageous.

It was certainly unfortunate that the new tycoons became chiefly notorious because of the indiscreet behavior of their cohorts and the violence inseparable from their enterprises. Economic competition often made murder imperative, and occasionally the boys showed a taste for the macabre in their choice of methods. Frankie Marlow was taken for a ride and assassinated; madcap young Vincent Coll was lured into a telephone booth in a drug store near his hotel on West Twenty-third Street and machine-gunned to death; Jack Diamond—who became known as "the clay pigeon" because he was ambushed and thoroughly shot up several times on the streets of New York, and once in his hotel bedroom, but always recovered—was finally dispatched by gunfire in an Albany lodging house: all of these were normal, or conventional, slayings. But more picturesque methods were not unknown. Some victims were beaten into a daze, then ingeniously roped so they would strangle themselves when they recovered consciousness. Others were encased in cement and tossed over the side of a boat, or, securely bound and weighted, dropped into the East River from a pier, or merely burned alive in their own cars.

The activities of their gunmen produced a distorted impression of the new plutocracy in the minds of most New Yorkers. Since sudden death was an inevitable hazard of big business as they were developing it, what wonder that they elevated obsequies to a ceremonial splendor which earlier millionaires had reserved for nuptials and balls? The great public funeral of Frankie Yale, a noted Brooklyn magnate, cost fifty-two thousand dollars. Thirty-eight cars heaped with stupendous floral offerings followed the hearse. Ten thousand mourners either attended the requiem mass, or assembled at the cemetery; the streets through which the cortege passed were jammed with people. The funeral of Danny Iamascia, bodyguard and factotum of Dutch Schultz, was equally impressive. Thirty-five automobiles were required to transport the horticultural tributes, and no less than one hundred and twenty-five were used to convey the deceased's grief-stricken friends to his grave. The splendor of these funerals led the general public to conclude that the new plutocrats regarded death as their major opportunity for extravagant expenditure.

From the aftermath of Rothstein's murder, it became clear that he had been the Morgan of the new plutocracy, its banker and master of economic strategy. His fortune was estimated at from two to ten million dollars. He owned valuable real estate, maintained large accounts in excellent banks, lived in an expensive Fifth Avenue apartment. It was his opinion, as he often said, that the majority of the human race were dubs and dumbbells, and he was always ready to turn to profit the fact that they had rotten judgment and no brains. Nothing irked Rothstein more than that people thought him crooked. Only because he had learned how to do things and how to size people up and dope out methods for himself! Never, he protested, had he been connected with a crooked deal.

The mystery of Rothstein's murder was never solved. He lived for two days after being shot in a hotel suite where a card game was in progress. But, like many another of the new tycoons, he went to his grave faithful to the common code: he refused to name his assailant. The scope of his activities, the leading role that he played in making crime big business, were quickly established. His profession of never having been connected with a crooked deal turned out to be the most memorable example of his wit. After Rothstein's death, his private files were seized by the authorities, and it appeared that some of their contents had already been removed. Most of the information which they yielded was permanently suppressed. Perhaps his papers implicated too many people of consequence in New York—politicians, public officials and others. But it was subsequently alleged that his most significant function was in acting as intermediary between the underworld and the great financial institutions that, unwittingly, furnished the capital which made possible illicit operations of tremendous magnitude. Rothstein had large investments in real estate and prime securities. These could always be pledged with financial institutions for loans. It was Rothstein's practice to take out insurance on the lives of the underworld clients to whom he advanced money which he had borrowed on his personal collateral. If they got killed in the course of their operations, he was indemnified. If they attempted to default on their loans, the insurance policies set a profitable price on their heads that Rothstein was capable of collecting— he had trigger-men on his payroll who knew how to dispose of welchers. And if his clients pulled off their coups, Rothstein not only made more than a banker's normal interest on his loans, but also received a large share of the profits. His ruling passion was money, and his attorney, William J. Fallon, gave a curious description of him. Rothstein, Fallon said, was "a man who dwells in doorways . . . a mouse standing in a doorway, waiting for his cheese." But, since no man is a hero to his lawyer, it is possible that Fallon diminished Rothstein's real stature. A taste for profits is common to bankers, yet you wouldn't have compared the elder J. P. Morgan to a mouse.

Fallon exemplified the kind of legal talent which the new tycoons required in their operations. As counsel for the major figures of the underworld, he was called "the great mouthpiece." He had an amazing ability to secure jury disagreements which freed his clients—the vote so frequently stood at eleven to one in favor of conviction that Fallon was also known as "the jail robber." Auburn-haired, handsome in a flamboyant way, Fallon was an eloquent pleader whose theatrical sense was so acute that David Belasco had once tried to persuade him to desert the law for the stage. He was among the most notorious of Broadway playboys, a familiar figure in all the best night clubs, a charter member of the odd society invented by Miss Guinan. Under his spectacular front, disguised by his extraordinary audacity, there lurked a brilliant mind. Fallon's mastery of criminal law, his command of technicalities, his knowledge of medicine and psychiatry won him the reluctant admiration of eminent jurists and honorable members of the bar who despised his character. Like Rothstein, he came of good stock. He had received an excellent education; the influence of religion pervaded his youth. Yet the moral climate of the festive era was registered by Fallon's peculiar ethics. He regarded the bribing of jurors as a proper professional expedient. He could hardly help doing so.

With full knowledge of the terms and the consequences of his bargain, quite freely and only for money, he had sold his services to a crime machine.

That Fallon's ethics, however peculiar, were far from unique became increasingly clear to New Yorkers during the years following Rothstein's murder. An aura of *Alice in Wonderland* seemed to envelop the administration of municipal affairs. It was charged that one magistrate had paid ten thousand dollars for his appointment; that another had received, from a corporation, a fee of one hundred and ninety thousand dollars for procuring an advantageous lease of city property. And there was the diverting case of a banquet in honor of Magistrate Albert H. Vitale held in a Bronx restaurant. Among the guests who joined in paying tribute to this eminent dispenser of justice were a leading underworld tycoon and six well-known gangsters. Also present were a police detective and two court attendants, all of whom were armed. In these circumstances, it seemed remarkable that the banquet was held up by seven gunmen, who disarmed the police detective and court attendants, and then proceeded to rob the assembled guests of their jewelry and cash. However, within three hours after this fantastic exploit, by methods never explained, Magistrate Vitale managed to retrieve the pistol of which the police detective had been relieved. But, as later became evident, Magistrate Vitale was in many ways a remarkable man. On an official salary of twelve thousand dollars a year, he had managed to deposit in his bank more than one hundred thousand dollars in a period of five years.

Conditions in the Police Department were scarcely better than those which obtained in the Magistrates' Courts. During the course of Samuel Seabury's investigation, the public learned that the Police Department's famous "vice squad"—a group of patrolmen who operated in plain clothes—had been "framing" the arrests of thousands of women by employing stool-pigeons. The accusations of these informers, never identified in court, had been used to jail many innocent victims. One of the stoolies, a character named Chile Mapocha Acuna, revealed this pleasant practice of the police. One of the allegedly innocent victims, Mrs. Vivian Gordon, testified about her arrest by a member of the vice squad. She was expected to supply additional, and probably more damaging evidence, but was unable to do so. Her body was found in Van Cortlandt Park; she had been strangled. It was notable, however, that shortly after these revelations were made, one of the more powerful underworld plutocrats, Charles "Lucky" Luciano, succeeded in setting up a racket in prostitution, forming a "combination" which covered a majority of the call flats, as well as the "bookers" who routed their stables of girls through these institutions.

Meanwhile, crime was rampant in New York. A rash of sensational murders and other deeds of violence had broken out after the slaying of Rothstein. There was increasing complaint against elderly District Attorney Thomas C. T. Crain for failure to prosecute hundreds of cases. The new plutocracy was falling into disrepute. The District Attorney did nothing about it, but the tycoons took measures to reduce any further undesirable publicity. Many of the murders and other crimes which were arousing wrath against the racketeers resulted from unrestricted competition among them. Should they not recognize their community of interest and eliminate wasteful competition? If the highest echelon agreed to adopt a principle of co-operation, the number of murders could be drastically reduced. In fact, murder and the uglier forms of violence, which were bad for business, might be made contingent upon absolute necessity, and permissible only when authorized by the very top bosses. A convention of these bosses—it became known as "the peace conference of 1929"—was held in Atlantic City, and there Frank Costello was said to have urged the adoption of this program, proposing that the rackets be organized into cartels on a nationwide basis. Costello's program reflected the historic tendency of all American business to reach some form of monopolistic agreement that would smooth away the rougher excrescences of competition. It won him the honorific title of "Prime Minister of the Underworld" —a title which, two decades later, the American people would learn was abundantly justified. Apparently Costello convinced his colleagues. They appointed a chairman to serve as impartial arbiter for their industry, to function in the same capacity as Will H. Hays in the movie industry, and Judge Kenesaw Mountain Landis, the czar of baseball. The tycoon whom they elevated to this distinguished but difficult office was Henry Goldberg. Known as "Dutch" Goldberg and "Uncle" Goldberg, he was unique in having won the universal confidence and affection of his colleagues. But more than a decade was to pass before the American public would discover the ultimate refinement and efficiency of which this new system was capable. These were exposed, in the early nineteen-forties, by William O'Dwyer, then District Attorney in Brooklyn, who uncovered the operations of an organization that came to be called "Murder, Inc."—and which, in the Brooklyn area, served as an industrial judicial tribunal, holding kangaroo courts, passing sentences of death, and decreeing executions that were promptly carried out by skilled, official deputies.

During the interval, however, there came to power in New York the most spectacular monopolist of the era: Dutch Schultz, a native of the Bronx whose real name was Arthur Flegenheimer. His greatest business exploit was suggested by his attorney, J. Richard Davis. "Dixie" Davis, a tailor's son, rose from metaphorical rags to factual riches without the painful struggle that legend makes indispensable to this saga of American success. As a young lawyer, Davis practiced in the magistrates' courts of Harlem, the political bailiwick of Tammany leader James J. Hines. Among its preponderantly Negro population the illicit form of gambling known as "numbers" or the "policy" game—exploited by Al Adams during the reign of Boss Croker— was highly popular. Davis, in his law practice, specialized in defending the operators of this game at cut rates. He was a suave, impressive figure, given to wearing well-tailored, dark-hued suits and white starched collars; in appearance, a model of conventional respectability. Long experience had convinced him that the policy game was being conducted with conspicuous economic waste. There were too many operators, or "bankers," in the field. Too much money was being spent on "ice"—political protection. What the policy industry needed was monopoly; streamlined organization under an impartial czar who would impose, and enforce, a code of fair practice. Davis took this program of economic reorganization to Dutch Schultz. Schultz took action. Under his brilliant administration, the policy game soon yielded an annual return estimated at one hundred million dollars.

Schultz was a small man, deceptively mild looking. He was often overcome by sudden rages. These were dangerous to people who happened to be around when they occurred; Schultz was a celebrated expert with the "typewriter," or sub-machine gun, reputedly likely to shoot and kill on the slightest provocation. When he died, at the age of thirty-three, he had been arrested thirteen times, in several instances on charges of homicide, and it was known that he had been guilty of a number of murders. But he served only one sentence in prison, for a robbery committed during his adolescence, when he was merely an unpromising Bronx hoodlum. Though he died in Newark, New Jersey, a fugitive from justice in New York, he had been forced to "go on the lam" only because he was under indictment for evasion of income taxes—a situation into which any major capitalist might have been betrayed, as he was, by the stupidity of his legal staff. Yet Schultz had not been without public honor in the community. At one time, he served as a deputy sheriff of Bronx County, appointed to this post by Edward J. Flynn, Democratic boss of that area, who stood in the topmost rank in the hierarchy of Tammany Hall. Schultz's appointment was subsequently canceled and his badge of office withdrawn. But he could always reflect that the honor had come to him before the days of his power and glory; that it represented an early recognition of his extraordinary promise. For, nominally at least, he had served as an officer of the law while also employed as trigger-man by two notorious underworld enterprisers, Legs Diamond and Owney Madden.

Like the elder John D. Rockefeller, whom in many ways he resembled as an economic innovator, Schultz might have been described as having the soul of a bookkeeper. He was abstemious, money-loving, frugal, hard-working. He cared nothing for gambling, or golf, or the nocturnal diversions of playboys. He abhorred the self-indulgence and luxury to which his millionaire colleagues were addicted. Except for his talent for the coining of vivid underworld slang, Schultz's personality was rather colorless. Among his more lurid contemporaries, he stood out as a humdrum figure—a model of industry who possessed a remarkable aptitude for business organization. It was entirely characteristic that death found him hard at work. He was shot up, late one night, in a Newark tavern, while conferring with his lieutenants, the fabulous figures of his enterprises spread out on a table before him. During the lingering hours in a hospital when he strove unsuccessfully to fight off death, it seemed that he was chiefly exasperated by the shooting affray because it was an unwelcome, needless interruption of business.

Some years after Schultz's death, James J. Hines of Tammany Hall was arrested and indicted on charges relating to his connection with the Dutchman and with Dixie Davis. To deliver the vote in his district, Hines required money and an army. Schultz had possessed both, and he needed the use of such political power as, in New York, Hines alone exercised. Already Hines had tested Schultz's political usefulness. His mob had proved an excellent resource in elections, and only an innocent could question the value of his money in future campaigns, as well as in the day-to-day activities of an efficient district leader. Hines was no innocent. He was the man who, although only a private citizen holding no elective office, theoretically lacking any power legally conferred by the people, nevertheless held in his grasp the police, the courts and the public prosecutors of the world's second largest city —the man who, for all practical purposes, determined the law and controlled its application. When, ultimately, District Attorney Thomas E. Dewey proved that Hines had been the paid hireling of a thug known as Dutch Schultz; when it became clear that, during his long and honorable career Hines had freely associated with, and gladly served, a large roster of racketeers—many New Yorkers were disposed to condone his lapse from grace. He was the product of a political system for which, as citizens presumably discharging their civic duties, New Yorkers were themselves responsible. So for Jimmy Hines, as for Jimmy Walker, a sneaking affection lingered on in the city. They were victims of a change in mood on the part of the public; in a way, casualties of the Great Depression that, blotting out the festive era, once again turned the minds of the people to rectitude and morality, to clean politics and reform, and that brought about the election of Fiorello H. LaGuardia as Mayor of New York.

THE BOWERY, *by Reginald Marsh*

EPILOGUE

AND EVEN NOW

Today New York is the New World's greatest metropolis. More than seven million, eight hundred thousand Americans live in the city proper. Its population is twice as large as that of Chicago, three times as large as that of either Philadelphia or Los Angeles. But New York signifies something more than the city proper. It is the vital center of an immense metropolitan area. This embraces northeastern New Jersey, part of Putnam County and all of Westchester County in New York State, much of southern Connecticut and nearly all of Long Island. The combined populations of the city and these tributary regions come close to fifteen million. You can think of "greater New York" as having more inhabitants than the whole of New England—than either California or Pennsylvania.

It is this fact which determines the most conspicuous feature of New York life. This is the tidal wave of humanity that perpetually sweeps over Manhattan. For a century New Yorkers have been obsessed by the vision of "rapid transit." It still remains a beguiling mirage. In the past twenty years transportation has been radically altered. The subway system has been greatly extended. Except for the Third Avenue line, the elevated railroads have been demolished. Street-cars have given way to motor buses. Like wild geese, thirteen thousand taxicabs continuously honk in the canyons of Manhattan. But, at any hour of the day, midtown traffic is a surrealist nightmare, complete with sound effects. The morning and evening rush hours merely intensify it. One of the curiosities of New York is the underground city of subways, where you will find restaurants, delicatessens, candy shops, haberdashers, florists, bookstores and dealers in many other kinds of goods. Venture into it between the hours of five and six-thirty in the afternoon, and watch some four million citizens swarming homeward. They seem barely to be moving. They are being propelled by the pressure of the masses behind them. The illusion of inertia persists above the subterranean city. From river to river, most of the avenues show lines of vehicles, tightly jammed end to end, in what appears to be an unbroken stall, their drivers raising a deafening din. During the evening rush hour Manhattan looks as if it were frozen into immobility. Nevertheless, the vast tide is really inching up. It is one of the major miracles of the city that New Yorkers actually reach their homes.

Every day the human tide is swelled by three or four million people from out of town. The city's two railroad terminals, planned to meet the traffic needs of half a century ago, have long since become inadequate. An extraordinary bus terminal, occupying an entire city block west of Times Square, provides additional facilities. La Guardia Airport in Queens, largest in the world, was outgrown even before its completion. Another huge airport is being developed at Idlewild, on the shore of Jamaica Bay, and there are auxiliary airports at Newark and Teterboro in New Jersey. In the past twenty years, additional magnificent bridges have been opened over Manhattan's rivers. Most notable of these are the George Washington across the Hudson, the Henry Hudson across the Harlem, the Triborough across the East River, linking Queens with upper Manhattan and the Bronx. Two vehicular tunnels have been built under the Hudson; one under the East River; one under New York harbor from the Battery to Brooklyn. Traffic ceaselessly flows over the bridges and through the tunnels. Traffic moves swiftly up and down two riverside "throughways"—the elevated West Side Highway along the Hudson, and the beautiful Franklin D. Roosevelt Drive along the East River. Day and night, New York is millions of people in transit.

Gaze down on Manhattan Island from the air, and you will see the world's most extravagant architectural fantasy. It won't look the same next week. Some New Yorkers are sentimental about old buildings, rich in historical associations or reminiscent of departed glories. Others rejoice when these monuments are torn down and replaced by something genuinely up to date. Today, as for a century past, the face of Manhattan is always in process of change. On Washington Square North, a lovely uniform row of Georgian mansions survived for more than a century. Half of the row has made way for a towering apartment house. Business is invading Park Avenue as far north as Fifty-ninth Street, with huge office buildings replacing yesterday's apartment houses. The Ritz-Carlton Hotel, a showcase for elegance during the festive era, is demolished because a business structure will yield higher profits. Even contemporary monuments are not immutable. The Empire State Building soars higher than ever, its useless mooring mast for dirigibles now topped by a remunerative, slender shaft for television broadcasting. Rockefeller Center remains a midtown marvel that draws all sightseers. But one of its elaborate, luxurious theaters has been converted into a television studio.

Meanwhile, spectacular changes are resulting from New York's long-range program of slum clearance. From Brooklyn Bridge to Twenty-third Street, along the East River; in Chelsea, the midtown West Side, Harlem and Queens you will find parked communities of tall apartments—public and semi-public housing developments erected for families in both the low- and moderate-income brackets. The developments that have been financed exclusively by public funds commemorate certain eminent civic leaders: Governor Alfred E. Smith, Lillian Wald and Jacob Riis on the lower East Side; John Lovejoy

Elliott in Chelsea; James Weldon Johnson in Harlem. Robert Moses, City Construction Co-ordinator, recently predicted that, "in less than ten years one person out of every thirteen in New York City will look to the City Housing Authority as his landlord." The chronic shortage of housing also affects the very wealthy, and their plight is not being neglected. Symbolic of the efforts of private enterprise to rescue them from homelessness is Carlton House on Madison Avenue where, according to *The New Yorker,* rents start at thirty-six hundred dollars a year for the smallest one-and-a-half-room apartment, and ascend to undisclosed fabulous heights. "Most of the tenants won't be there more than a month or so a year. For those who *are* there, Carlton House plans to change the bed linen twice a week." Probably the most debated of recent architectural additions to New York is the capitol of the United Nations overlooking the East River, now rising on six square blocks of Manhattan Island that have ceased to be American territory. The Secretariat Building—thirty-nine stories of green glass and aluminum grid with blank marble side-walls—is described by its architect, Wallace Harrison, as "a machine for living, a world's workshop." But Frank Lloyd Wright, dean of America's modern architects, has condemned it as "a glorification of negation, a dead-pan box."

Curious stories about New York real estate sometimes come to light. The descendants of Peter Stuyvesant recently sold a corner plot on Third Avenue and Twelfth Street. It was originally part of the Dutch governor's farm, acquired in 1650 and held by his family for three hundred years. In the West Bronx, a tract of two blocks lately passed into new ownership for the second time in two hundred and seventy-five years. It had never been improved with buildings. Part of the Morrisania estate granted to Colonel Lewis Morris in 1676, it was bought by John Jacob Astor III in 1880, and always remained as it had been in Colonial days. In 1853, foresighted Charles E. Appleby purchased from the city a grant of land then mainly under the waters of the Hudson between Thirty-ninth and Fortieth Streets. According to the terms of his grant, Appleby was required to fill in streets and build wharves and bulkheads. This work was left undone by Appleby and his heirs. Eventually, the city filled in the area, built streets, constructed piers. As a result, in 1928 Appleby's descendants sued the city for trespass, and ultimately received more than three million dollars in awards, interest and damages. They still own the property, which today—largely because of the city's trespass—is valued at more than one hundred and fifty times what it cost their ancestor.

Nothing surprises New Yorkers more than finding that their paradise of towering cliffs is subject to the whims of Nature. In 1950, a prolonged drought reduced the city's water supply to a trickle. The municipal authorities, abreast of scientific developments, hired a rain-maker to seed clouds above the upstate watershed. They also drastically curtailed the use of water. Cars went unwashed; air-conditioning machinery ceased to function; citizens were urged to decrease their bathing, shaving, dishwashing. Ice and water carafes disappeared from restaurant tables. In various parts of the city laundries and other industrial users of water arranged to have wells drilled on their premises. A large Park Avenue hotel resorted to more primitive methods. Years earlier, the site had been occupied by a brewery, reputed to have a spring-fed well. Since nobody remembered its location, the hotel imported a dowser from rural New England. He located the forgotten well with his diving-rod, and the hotel was able to restore the comfort of air-conditioning to patrons whose baths continued to be rationed.

In spring and summer, New Yorkers treasure the green islands that dot their town. They make pilgrimages to the larger parks. They visit the flower dis-

"NIGHT HAS A THOUSAND EYES," *by Berenice Abbott*

plays on the promenade of Rockefeller Center, and its twelve landscaped sky-gardens. In the midtown East Side, you will see families dining outdoors, in the shade of ancient, scraggly ailanthus trees that have defied long years of smog, soot and noxious fumes. All over town, on cliffside terraces, masses of trees burst into leaf. Citizens who dwell between the basement and the penthouse grow shrubs and kitchen herbs in window-boxes. Even the very poor buy flowers and plants from the horse-drawn wagons of itinerant vendors, who today are among the sole remaining chanters of street cries.

Though you might not believe it, an enthusiastic affection for animals is one of the most obvious traits of New Yorkers. During lunch hour, on mild days, the struggle to secure a front-row seat on the open-air terrace of the Central Park Zoo cafeteria, directly overlooking the sea lions' pool, is just as intense as the after-theater rush to obtain a table at El Morocco. In one of the great apartment buildings on fashionable Sutton Place South there lives a once famous Metropolitan Opera soprano, now very old and ailing. She adores circus animals, and when the Ringling Circus came to town a year ago arrangements were made to have the elephants detour, on their march from the railroad yards to Madison Square Garden, in order to pass beneath her windows. Unfortunately, her physician decided that the excitement would be too much for her. However hurried, New Yorkers never pass a pet-shop window without stopping to cluck over scrambling puppies or supercilious kittens. On any middle-class residential street, in the early morning and late at night, you will see ladies wearing fur wraps over their pajamas, airing their dogs. The pedigreed canines that inhabit the most expensive quarters lead lives almost as complex as those of their mistresses. They are served by their own beauty parlors, caterers, schools of etiquette, hired walking companions —and they even have a psychiatrist to deal with the neuroses sometimes produced by their pampered existence. One of New York's wealthiest hostesses used to keep a panther in her apartment, to the discomfort of nervous guests, and nowadays you will occasionally meet on Fifth Avenue a young woman leading a miniature deer on a leash. On tenement roofs throughout the city, as twilight falls, pigeon-fanciers release their coveys to execute magnificent spiral flights against the darkening sky. And sometimes wild animals—apparently cognizant of the city's zoöphilia—invade New York. During last year's football season a reddish-gray fox turned up in the Yankee Stadium and led a happy life under the bleachers for nearly two months.

By its detractors, New York is often described as a godless city. But its places of worship represent every form of religious faith that flourishes anywhere in the world. On Washington Heights is the shrine of the only American citizen who has been elevated to the Roman Catholic canon of saints. Mother Francesca Saverio Cabrini founded the Missionary Sisters of the Sacred Heart of Jesus in her native Italy. A tiny, frail nun, she came to New York in 1889 with six members of her order. Before her death in 1917, she established schools, orphanages, hospitals and other institutions throughout the United States. She was canonized as Saint Frances Xavier Cabrini in 1946, and her tomb is under the altar of the chapel of Mother Cabrini High School. At the Russian Orthodox Church of Christ the Savior, facing Mt. Morris Park, you can witness the solemn, picturesque midnight ritual formerly attended by the Czars of Russia in celebration of Easter. In a building on West Ninety-fourth Street the Buddhists of the city hold their services. Perhaps the most unusual congregation in New York is that of the Commandment Keepers, five thousand colored Jews whose synagogue is in the heart of Negro Harlem. They are descendants of the Falashas who, according to legend, fled from Palestine more than twenty-five hundred years ago and found refuge in the highlands of Ethiopia. The members of this congregation are strictly orthodox in their faith and rituals, but have little contact with their white co-religionists. They do not acknowledge themselves to be Negroes, but they assert that "all genuine Jews are black men." Their services are presided over by a chief rabbi, Reverend Wentworth Arthur Matthew. On the streets of Harlem he is a notable figure because he wears the traditional skullcap and also because, unlike most other residents of the community, he dresses only in severe black.

New Yorkers live surrounded by oddities which seldom impress them. Nobody thinks it strange that the Sutton Place quarter, which contains some of the city's costliest dwellings, also has three social settlements and one of the largest municipal public baths. In so commonplace a matter as bathing, you can be as individualistic as you please. For years, a distinguished Arctic explorer preached the Eskimo philosophy of taking no baths whatever. On the other hand, if you have exotic tastes in bathing you can indulge them without great effort. In both Brooklyn and uptown Manhattan there are establishments where, sitting on tiers of stone slabs in a painfully hot steam room, the patrons flagellate themselves with twigs. This is bathing in the Finnish style. You can also resort to Turkish baths of a luxury such as no Turk ever imagined, and in the salons of Fifth Avenue beauticians women enjoy hygienic ministrations so complex that bathing scarcely describes them.

Should you choose to do so, you may depute your domestic responsibilities and your social life to the management of specialists. There are services which will send maids to do your housework—probably a different one every day, but you need never see them. There are services which will deliver your dinner, piping hot, at an appointed hour. There are establishments which will give your parties for you, providing everything except the guests. If you do not know anybody to invite, you will find in many buses the advertisement of a lady whose profession it is to introduce shy, lonely people to congenial members of the opposite sex. Should this scheme embarrass you, certain newspapers carry the announcements of "friendship clubs" which hold frequent meetings featuring lectures and dancing. These organizations offer to enrich the mind while extending the acquaintance, but if your desire is for matrimony without tedious preliminaries, this can be gratified also. More than a dozen marriage brokers are listed in the classified telephone directory. One of them, if you are too busy to visit her office, will call at your home. Another offers the hopeful inducement, "All couples with own licenses married immediately." The formal amenities of marriage can be entrusted to a specialist who, on short notice, will provide a "hotel wedding" complete with bridal gown, flowers, refreshments and other requisites. If this seems too pretentious, furs, jewelry and a gown for the bride, as well as formal attire for the groom, may be rented. Frugal-minded folk can likewise rent, for the joyous occasion, an array of wedding presents and an ornate but inedible cake. Even the marital future need occasion no anxiety to either party. If difficulties develop, they can be passed on to another category of specialist—the marriage counselors.

Gastronomically, New Yorkers may, if they wish, tour the world without ever leaving Manhattan. Chinese, Italian and kosher restaurants are to be found throughout the city; the best are located in Chinatown, downtown Little Italy and the lower East Side. The national cuisines of Belgium, Holland, Germany, Austria, Switzerland, the Scandinavian countries, Finland, Russia, Spain, Greece, India, Japan, Mexico and Brazil are all represented in midtown. The Armenian quarter on lower Lexington Avenue, the Syrian quarter on Washington Street, the Czechoslovak and Hungarian colonies on upper Second Avenue offer restaurants where both cookery and atmosphere are authentically foreign. In the *barrio* of East Harlem you can sample favorite dishes of Puerto Rico; in West Harlem there are eating places frequented by natives of the French West Indies and Haiti. There are a half-dozen internationally famous French restaurants where the prices are astronomical, the menus and wine lists are unsurpassed. These establishments enjoy the favor of New York's three exclusive societies of gourmets, and are much patronized by celebrities whose professional careers do not compel them to believe that the good life is best nourished by blackstrap molasses, wheat germ and vitamins.

Certain restaurants are as renowned for their clientele as their cuisine. Café society lunches and dines at the Colony and Twenty-One and reassembles after theater in the Cub Room of the Stork Club, and El Morocco. The élite of Times Square—a region described by Billy Rose as "a triangle full of squares running around in circles"—foregather at the older of Lindy's two establishments on Broadway. The aristocracy of professional sport and visiting delegations from Hollywood, frequent Toots Shor's. The favorite rendezvous of the theatrical profession is Sardi's, and none of the stars who shine there enjoys a greater prestige than Miss Renée Carroll, reputedly America's richest hat-check girl, an authority on the drama who takes a mildly skeptical view of its foremost exponents. Society, in the old beatified sense promulgated by Mrs. Astor and Ward McAllister, has no accredited rendezvous and its very existence is problematical. The *Social Register,* directory of the hypothetically élite, runs to nearly one thousand printed pages and lists approximately thirty thousand names. This inflationary aggregate is equivalent to collective anonymity. It cannot be coped with even by Miss Elsa Maxwell, professional gloom-dispeller to both the socially disgruntled and augustly bored. Always seen "with the best people at the proper seasons," Miss Maxwell is probably the world's champion party-giver. Yet she no longer organizes fêtes like the scavenger hunt which, nearly twenty years ago, had all New York in a dither. On that occasion a large group of socially eminent citizens were required to race about the city and return, at an appointed time, "with all manner of curious trophies, such as a hair from a distinguished politician's mustache, live animals and Marilyn Miller's underpanties."

With a larger playgoing public than ever before in its history, New York today has fewer legitimate theaters than it had twenty years ago. Most of the remaining old theaters are now movie grind-houses, and many comparatively new ones have been converted into radio and television studios. But the first nights of leading producers are civic events which crowd the sidewalk with spectators, autograph collectors and photographers who are supervised by squads of police. The sidewalk throngs come to gape at celebrities, who arrive tardily in the hope of being remarked by other celebrities. After the audience has staged a preliminary show, it settles down to see the play. Orchestra seats for opening nights are an index of current prestige, since it is the conviction of all producers that this portion of the theater must be filled mainly by distinguished people. Inclusion among the privileged is not secured by way of the box office, but through enrollment on the eligible lists of individual producers. Among the most envied people in New York, therefore, are Mr. and Mrs. Ira Katzenberg, who receive aisle seats in the first row of the orchestra for all opening nights, an honor shared by nobody else since the days of Diamond Jim Brady.

The same celebrities whose presence attracts crowds by night cause no commotion whatever when they appear on the streets of the city by day. Eminent Americans of all kinds walk about Manhattan almost unrecognized. Few strollers on Park Avenue are aware of having passed ex-President Hoover, or John D. Rockefeller, Jr., who are frequently to be seen there. Ten thousand eager fans have jammed Madison Square Garden at a reception in honor of radio commentator Mary Margaret McBride, but her arrivals and departures cause no suspension of traffic around Rockefeller Center. The shopping expeditions of Katharine Cornell, Greta Garbo, or Margaret Truman are accomplished without evidence of public interest. It is practically a convention among New Yorkers that celebrities are to be stared at only when they are on parade. Respect for individual privacy is essential in a city whose inhabitants spend most of their lives immersed in crowds.

As a result, New York is, among other things, a place where eccentrics are seldom molested, even if their idiosyncrasies provoke speculation. For many years Mrs. Consuelo Bailey Kear wandered about the city on summer days, wearing an enormous, floppy picture hat and a heavy fur coat, carrying a second fur coat on her arm, and towing on a string a carton containing all her possessions. She chose to disappear, and it was only after five years that the bank which handled her considerable fortune instituted a search for her. Equally unnoticed was the existence of Mrs. Matthew Astor Wilks who, living as a recluse in a Fifth Avenue apartment, recently died at the age of eighty leaving an estate valued at some eighty million dollars. Mrs. Wilks was the daughter of Hetty Green, a financial wizard of the turn of the century celebrated for her miserliness, and she had claimed public attention only when her mother had finally permitted her to marry as a spinster of forty. Even more typical of New York's attitude toward eccentricity was the case of the Collyer brothers. Elderly, wealthy, owners of valuable real estate, Homer and Langley Collyer barricaded themselves in their ramshackle family mansion in Harlem. The neighbors knew that Homer Collyer was paralyzed and blind. They saw Langley Collyer, wearing a cap, a celluloid collar and shabby old clothes held together by pins, making furtive excursions to procure the buns, peanut butter and oranges which were the brothers' principal diet. One day the police received a telephone call informing them that there was a dead body in the Collyer home. The police broke into the house and found the body of Homer. Three weeks later, and ten feet away in the same room, they found the body of Langley, caught in one of the many booby traps which he had built to catch possible thieves. During the interval, the police had removed from the Collyer home one hundred and twenty tons of hoarded junk which filled most of its rooms from floor to ceiling. Among the possessions cherished by the hermit brothers with indiscriminate affection were fourteen grand pianos, five violins, an organ, thousands of empty bottles and cans, immense stacks of old newspapers, and the accumulated heritage of objects with which their parents had originally furnished the mansion.

One significant change in New York life has occurred during the last decade, and its social consequences are already becoming apparent. Until the Second World War the average New Yorker—whether he occupied a tower apartment, a private house, or a cold-water flat—was free to move whenever he chose, and he usually moved with appalling frequency. The housing shortage has cost him this freedom, and he is not likely to regain it in the foreseeable future. Formerly the most rootless of all Americans, he is today nearly as fixed as any villager. Yet instead of contracting his experience, the change has expanded it. He leads a double life; his existence is both cosmopolitan and parochial. He is a citizen of the largest, most densely populated, most fantastically varied human hive on earth. But he is also a resident of a particular neighborhood—and, more and more, New York is becoming a metropolis of small communities each of which has its distinctive local atmosphere. Though you may not have even a bowing acquaintance with the family that, for ten years, has lived in the apartment across the hall, your neighborhood attachments are numerous, and warmer than might be supposed. The man who runs the corner newsstand, the greengrocer, the tailor who presses your clothes not only value your custom but will adopt you as a friend. To them, you are not merely an anonymous source of livelihood, but an individual, a personality. Readily enough, you will discover that they, too, are individuals and personalities who lead lives as little humdrum as your own, whose activities, when you hear about them, introduce you to strange and novel aspects of the town.

The new sense of having acquired permanent roots intensifies the love which, traditionally, most New Yorkers have always felt for their city. Home is no longer a transient residence, but a neighborhood. Beyond the small town which you inhabit—an affair of a few square blocks—lies Cosmopolis with its inexhaustible wonders. You know that you will never know the whole of New York; no matter how long you may live, there will always remain an unexplored margin, an undiscovered realm. But the splendor, the unique beauty are forever present as you go your ways. The city foaming up in light at nightfall. The clustered towers of lower Manhattan glittering in the sunlight of early morning. The long sweep of Park Avenue on a frosty December night, with its marshaled Christmas trees ablaze. South Street in mid-afternoon, with its ancient warehouses and rattling trucks, its swooping, crying seagulls, its odor of the Atlantic. The Plaza in a blue midsummer dusk, with young couples strolling hand in hand toward the enveloping silence of Central Park.

And New York is more than a physical city. It is a way of life. "New York gives the directest proof yet of successful Democracy, and of the solution of that paradox, the eligibility of the free and fully developed individual with the paramount aggregate." So wrote Walt Whitman, most devoted of the city's lovers, a century ago. It still remains true.

Index